MASAHIRO HIKOKUBO

Congrats on our second volume! Congrats
on running the series for over a year! We're
gonna keep it up, step on the gas and
ramp up our story "sense"! We're counting
on you guys for the support "sense"!

MASASHI SATO

When the first volume went on sale, my
friends celebrated with me. I'm a very
lucky guy. Have fun watching Yusei
rip up the track at the D1 Grand Prix!!

Volume 2
SHONEN JUMP Manga Edition

Story by **MASAHIRO HIKOKUBO**
Art by **MASASHI SATO**
Production Assistance **STUDIO DICE**

Translation & English Adaptation **TAYLOR ENGEL AND IAN REID, HC LANGUAGE SOLUTIONS**
Touch-up Art & Lettering **JOHN HUNT**
Designer **FAWN LAU**
Editor **MIKE MONTESA**

YU-GI-OH! 5D's © 2009 by Masahiro Hikokubo, Masashi Sato
All rights reserved.
First published in Japan in 2009 by SHUEISHA Inc., Tokyo.
English translation rights arranged by SHUEISHA Inc.

Based on Animation TV series YU-GI-OH! 5D's
© 1996 Kazuki Takahashi
© 2008 NAS • TV TOKYO

Printed in the U.S.A.

Published by VIZ Media, LLC
P.O. Box 77010
San Francisco, CA 94107

10 9 8 7 6 5 4 3 2 1
First printing, February 2012

www.viz.com

www.shonenjump.com

Yu-Gi-Oh! 5D's™

VOLUME 2

THE D1 GRAND PRIX BEGINS!!

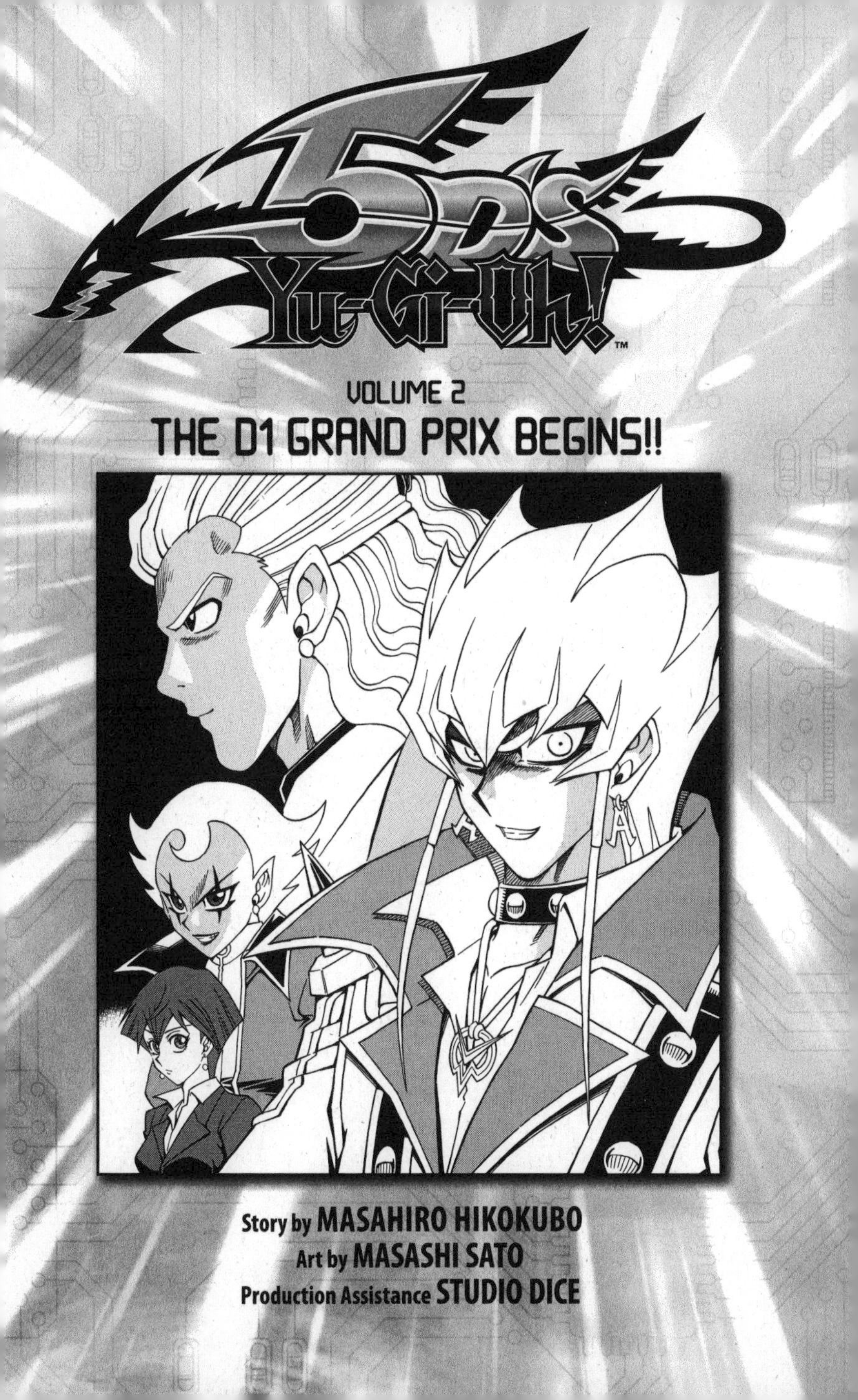

Story by MASAHIRO HIKOKUBO
Art by MASASHI SATO
Production Assistance STUDIO DICE

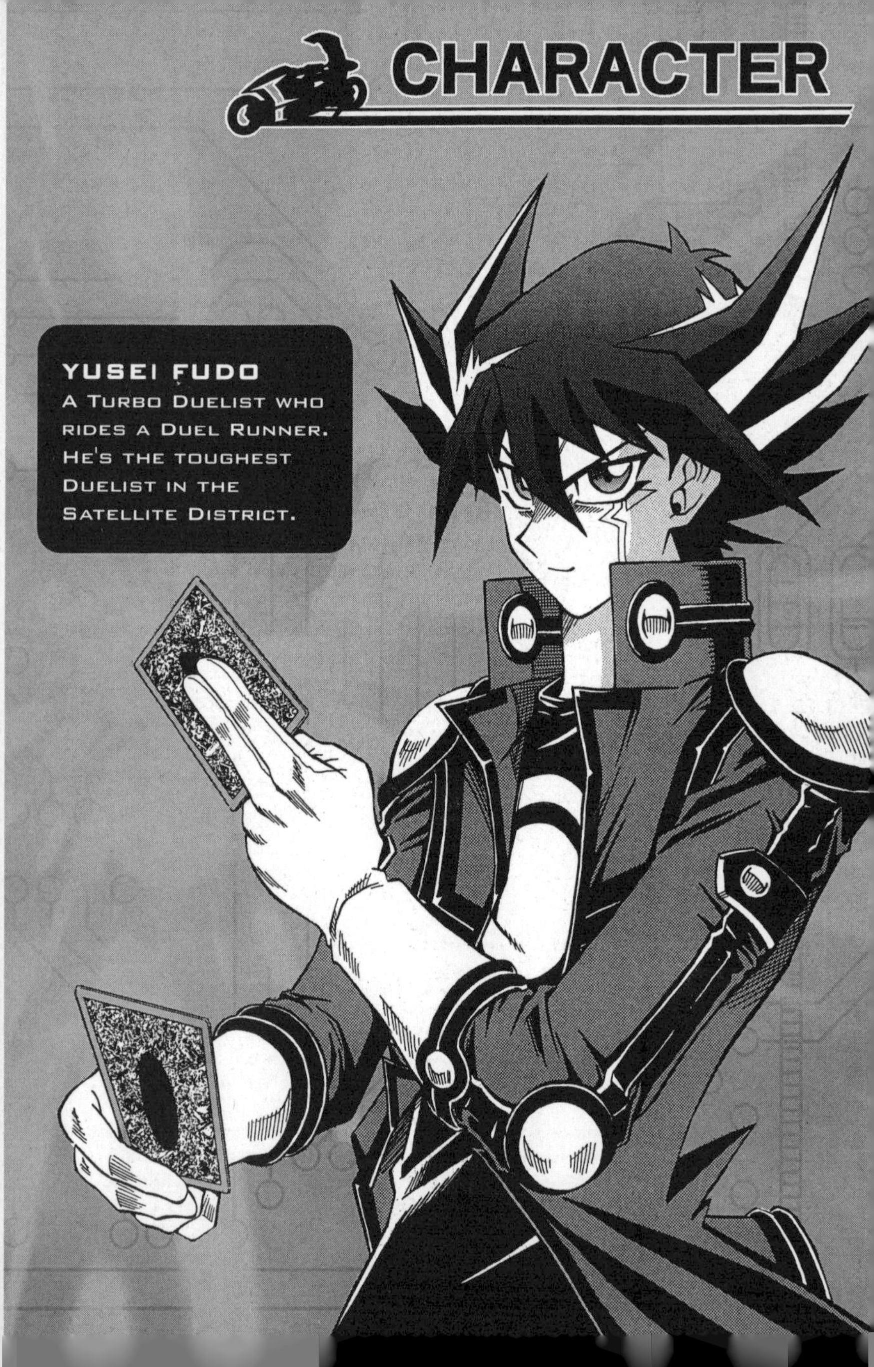
CHARACTER
YUSEI FUDO
A TURBO DUELIST WHO RIDES A DUEL RUNNER. HE'S THE TOUGHEST DUELIST IN THE SATELLITE DISTRICT.

JACK ATLAS
A Turbo Duelist known as "the King," and feared by all around him.

AKIZA IZINSKI
A turbo duelist who holds the title "Queen of Queens."

SECT
He's like a kid brother to Yusei. His goal is to beat Yusei in a Turbo Duel.

STORY

New Domino City, in the year 20XX, Turbo Duels, fought from the seats of motorcycle-shaped Duel Disks called "Duel Runners," are the hottest game in town.

After Sect is knocked unconscious, Yusei duels the Skeleton Knight to save his friend. Then while taking Sect to the hospital, Jack Atlas suddenly attacked and forced Yusei to duel. Yusei crashed out and lost, and swore to duel Jack again. Now Yusei has entered the D1 Grand Prix, the battle to determine the toughest Duelist in the world!!

Yu-Gi-Oh! 5D's

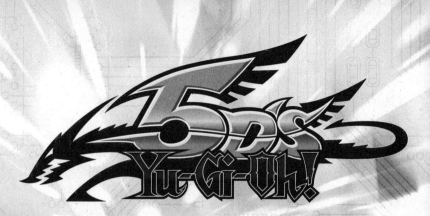

VOLUME 2

THE D1 GRAND PRIX BEGINS!!

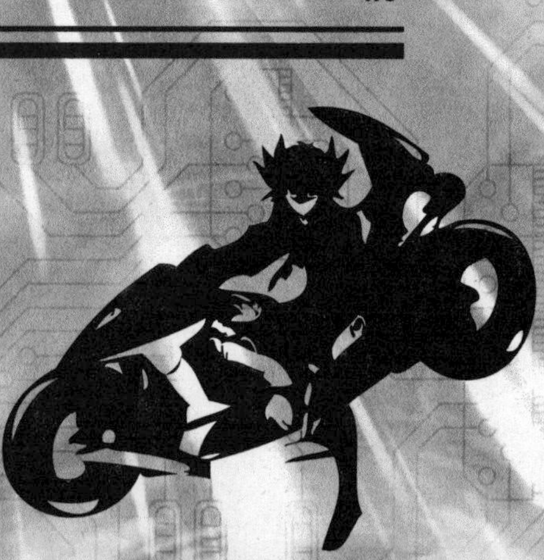

RIDE-09

THE D1 GRAND PRIX BEGINS!!

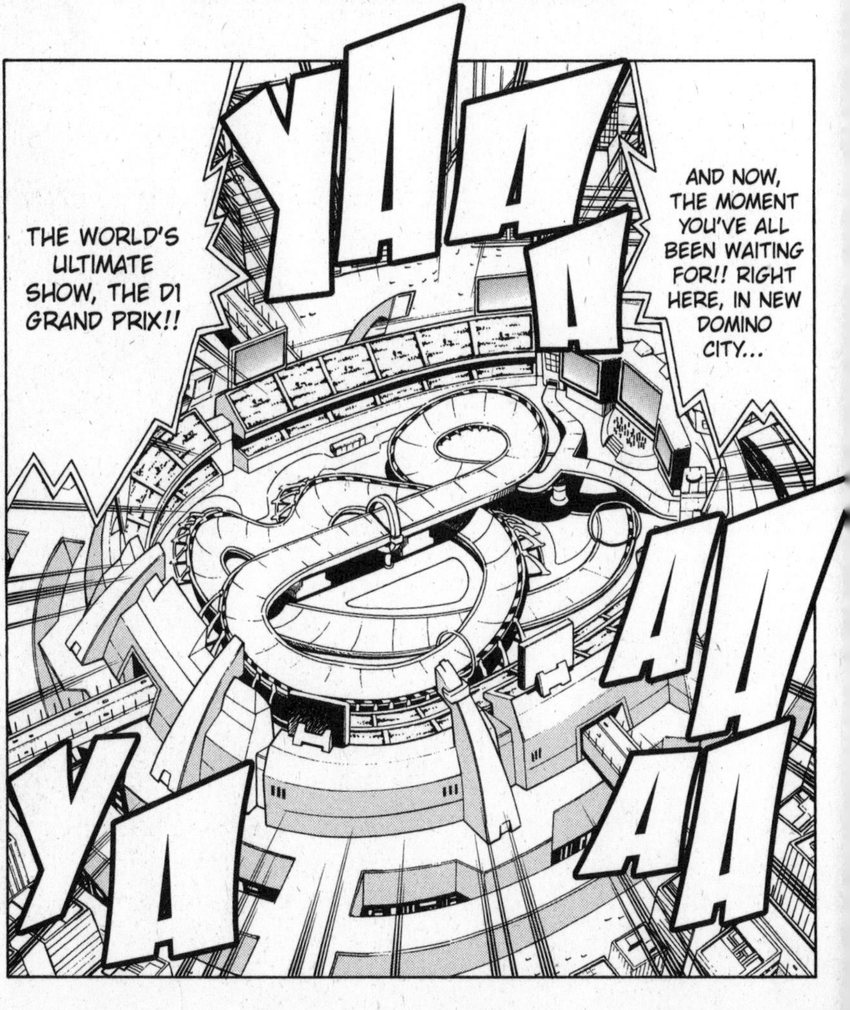
AND NOW, THE MOMENT YOU'VE ALL BEEN WAITING FOR!! RIGHT HERE, IN NEW DOMINO CITY...
THE WORLD'S ULTIMATE SHOW, THE D1 GRAND PRIX!!
YAAA
AA
AA
YA

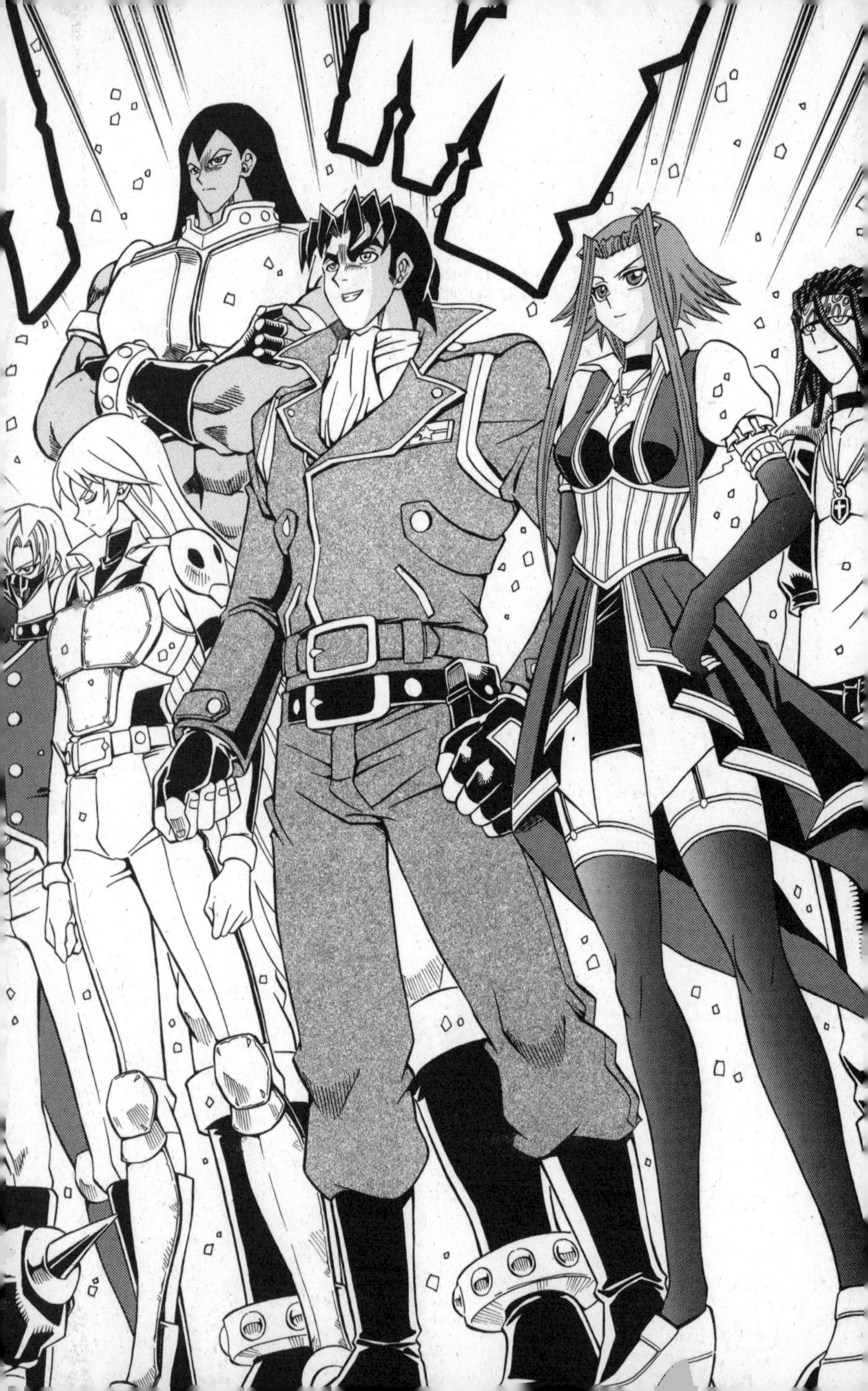

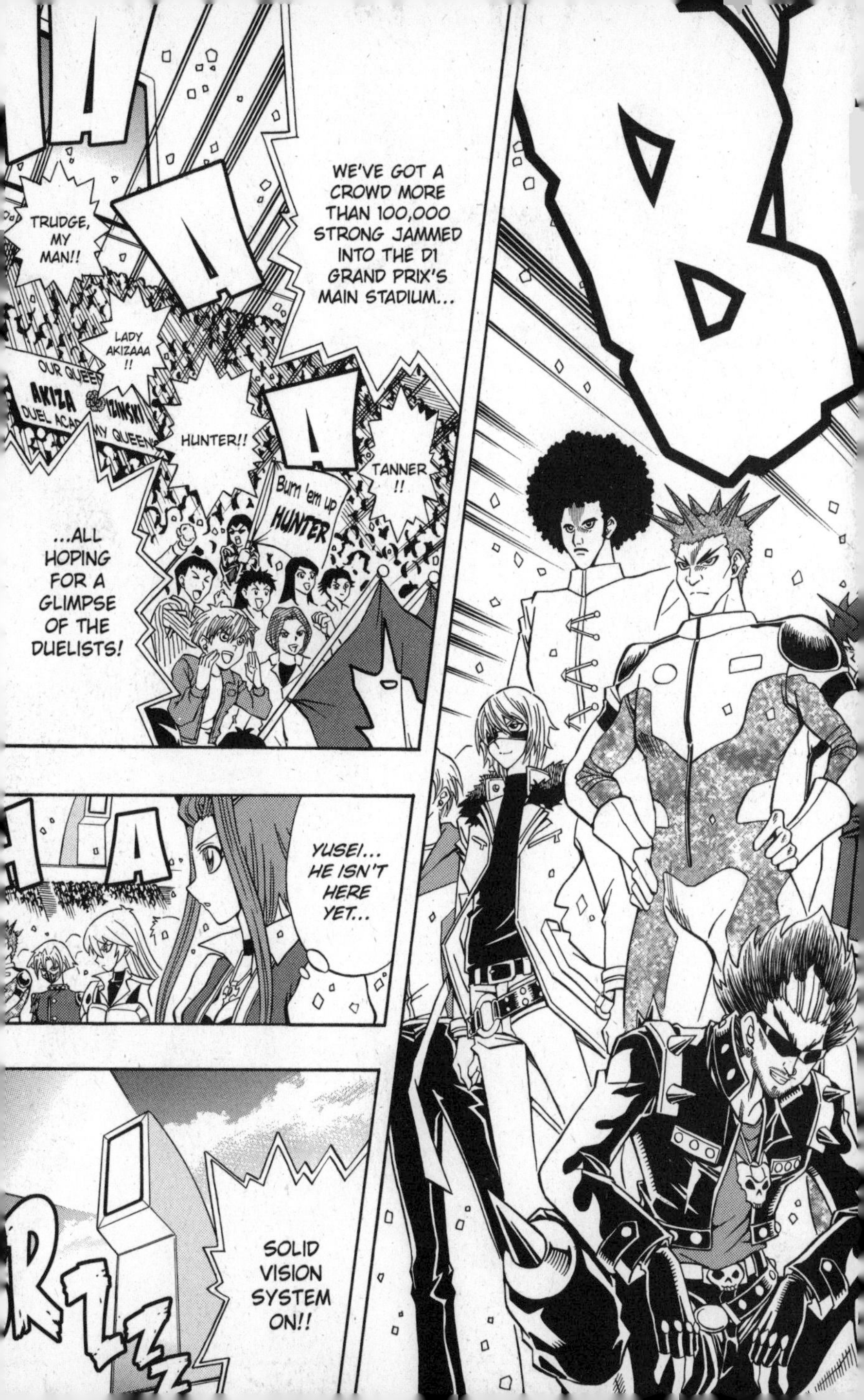

WE'VE GOT A CROWD MORE THAN 100,000 STRONG JAMMED INTO THE D1 GRAND PRIX'S MAIN STADIUM...
TANNER!!
HUNTER!!
Burn 'em up HUNTER
LADY AKIZAAA!!
TRUDGE, MY MAN!!
OUR QUEEN AKIZA DUEL ACAD
IZINSKI MY QUEEN
...ALL HOPING FOR A GLIMPSE OF THE DUELISTS!
YUSEI... HE ISN'T HERE YET...
SOLID VISION SYSTEM ON!!

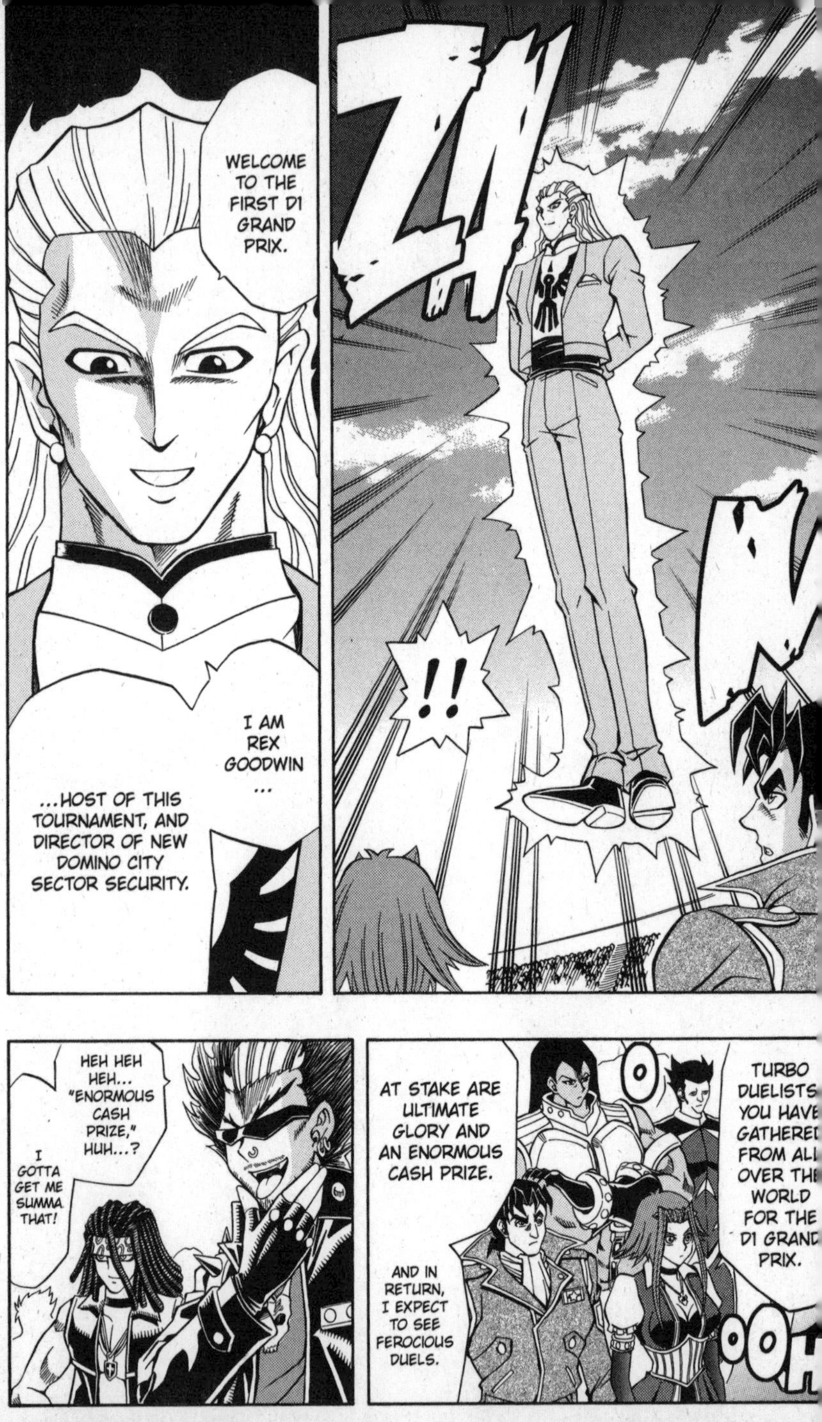
ZA
!!
WELCOME TO THE FIRST D1 GRAND PRIX.
I AM REX GOODWIN...
...HOST OF THIS TOURNAMENT, AND DIRECTOR OF NEW DOMINO CITY SECTOR SECURITY.
TURBO DUELISTS, YOU HAVE GATHERED FROM ALL OVER THE WORLD FOR THE D1 GRAND PRIX.
AT STAKE ARE ULTIMATE GLORY AND AN ENORMOUS CASH PRIZE.
AND IN RETURN, I EXPECT TO SEE FEROCIOUS DUELS.
OOH
HEH HEH HEH... "ENORMOUS CASH PRIZE," HUH...?
I GOTTA GET ME SUMMA THAT!

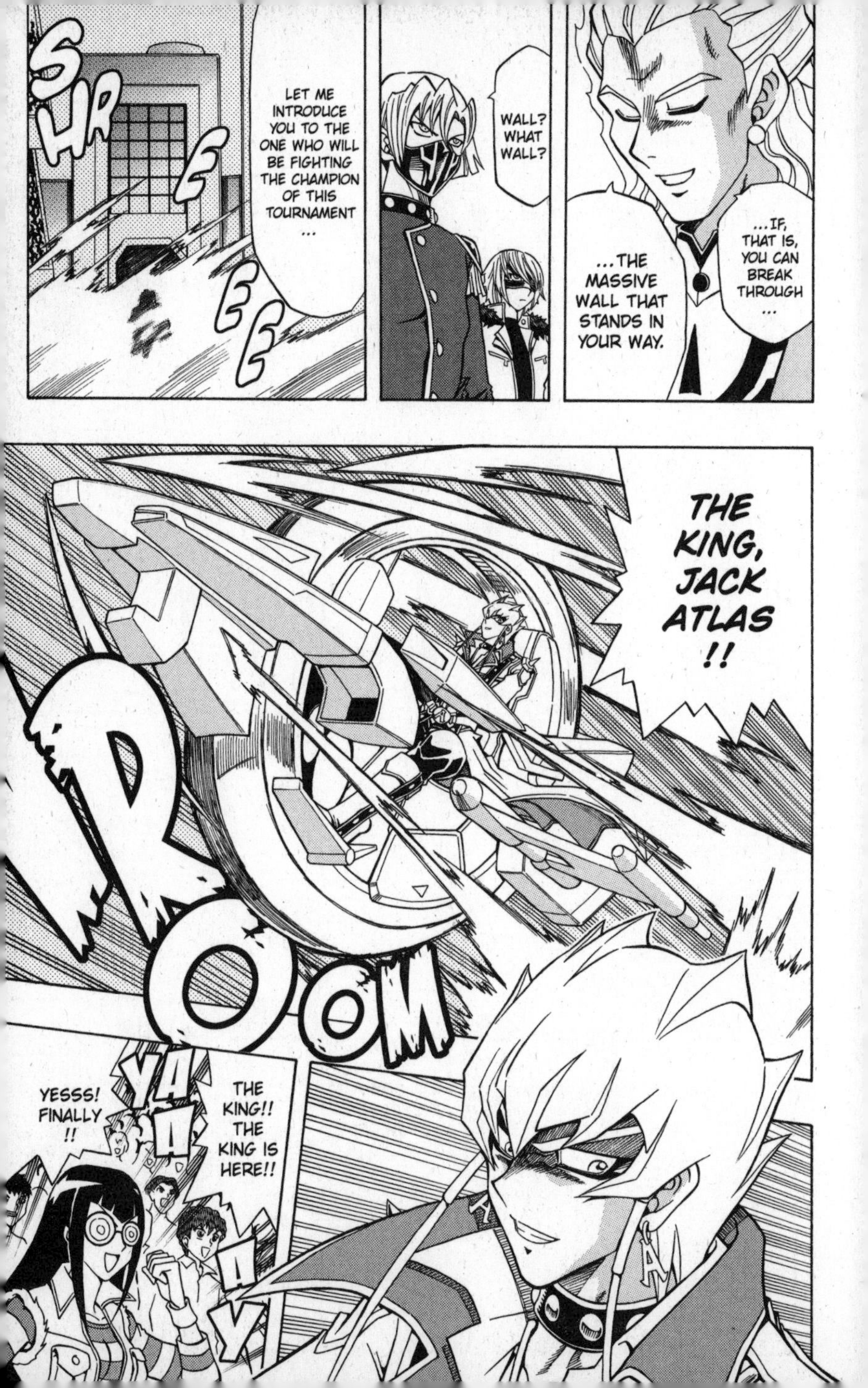
...THE MASSIVE WALL THAT STANDS IN YOUR WAY.
...IF, THAT IS, YOU CAN BREAK THROUGH...
WALL? WHAT WALL?
LET ME INTRODUCE YOU TO THE ONE WHO WILL BE FIGHTING THE CHAMPION OF THIS TOURNAMENT...
SHREEEE
THE KING, JACK ATLAS!!
VROOOM
THE KING!! THE KING IS HERE!!
YESSS! FINALLY!!
YAAAY

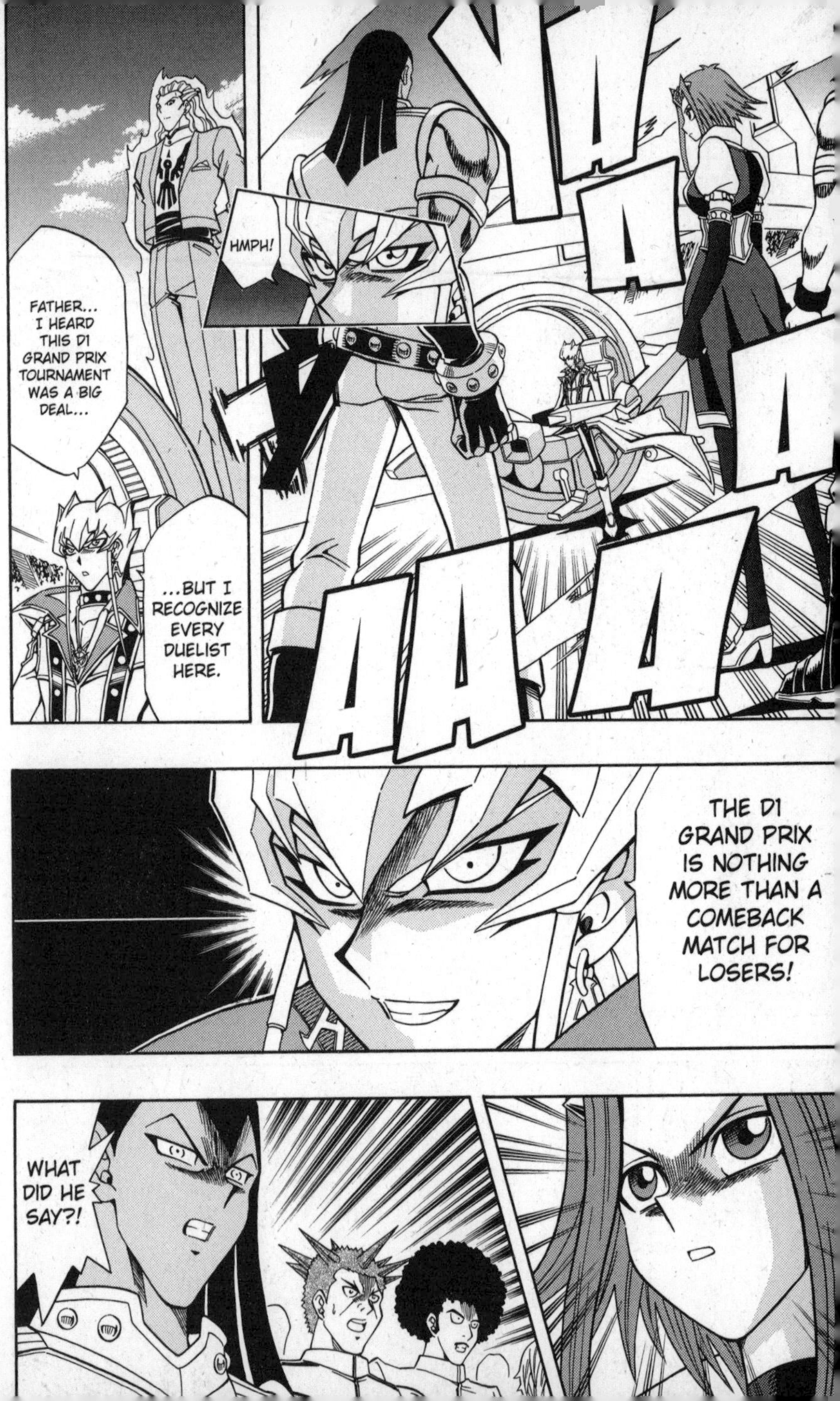
YAAAAAA
HMPH!
FATHER... I HEARD THIS D1 GRAND PRIX TOURNAMENT WAS A BIG DEAL...
...BUT I RECOGNIZE EVERY DUELIST HERE.
THE D1 GRAND PRIX IS NOTHING MORE THAN A COMEBACK MATCH FOR LOSERS!
WHAT DID HE SAY?!

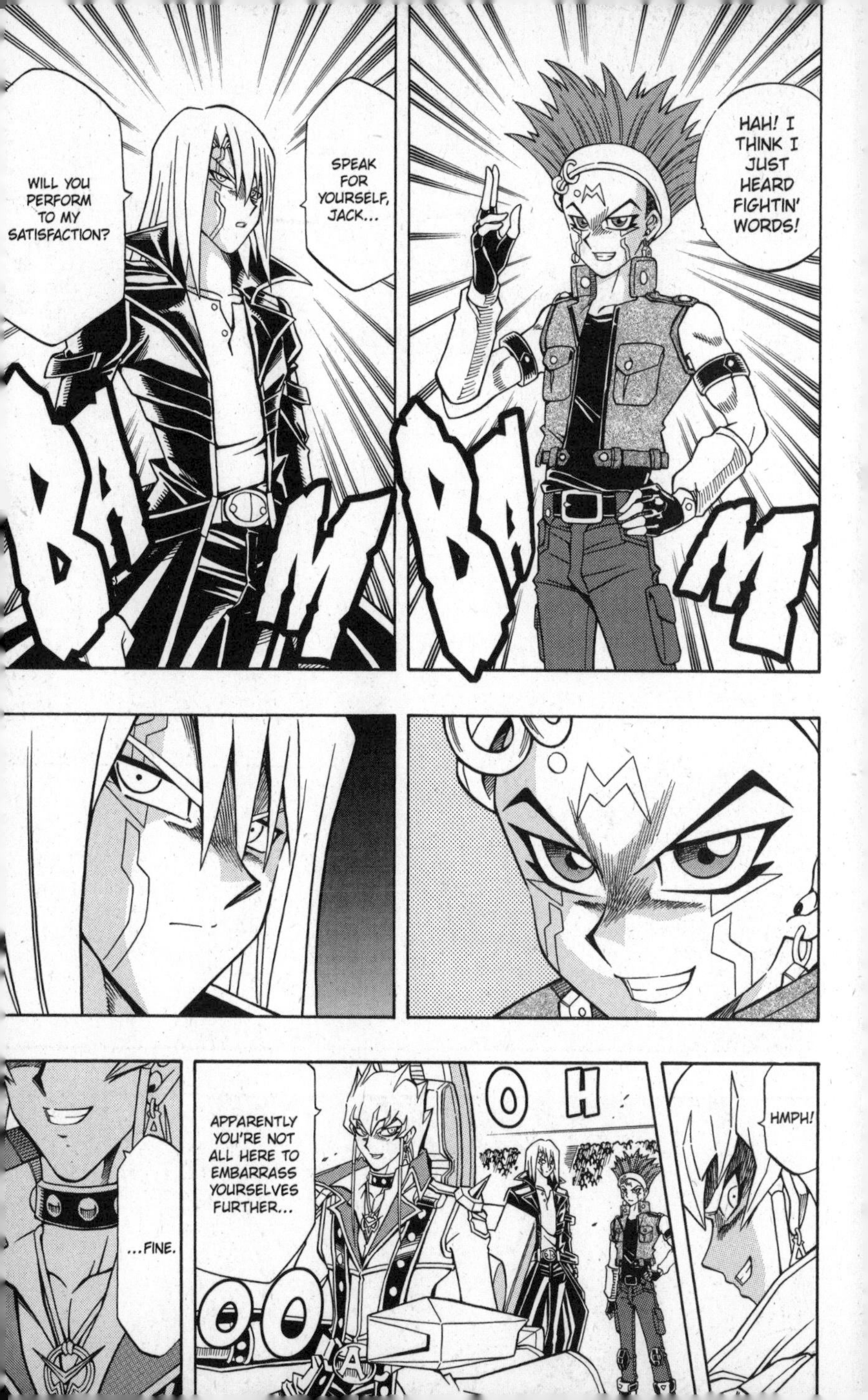
HAH! I THINK I JUST HEARD FIGHTIN' WORDS!
BAM
SPEAK FOR YOURSELF, JACK...
WILL YOU PERFORM TO MY SATISFACTION?
BAM
HMPH!
OH
APPARENTLY YOU'RE NOT ALL HERE TO EMBARRASS YOURSELVES FURTHER...
OO
...FINE.

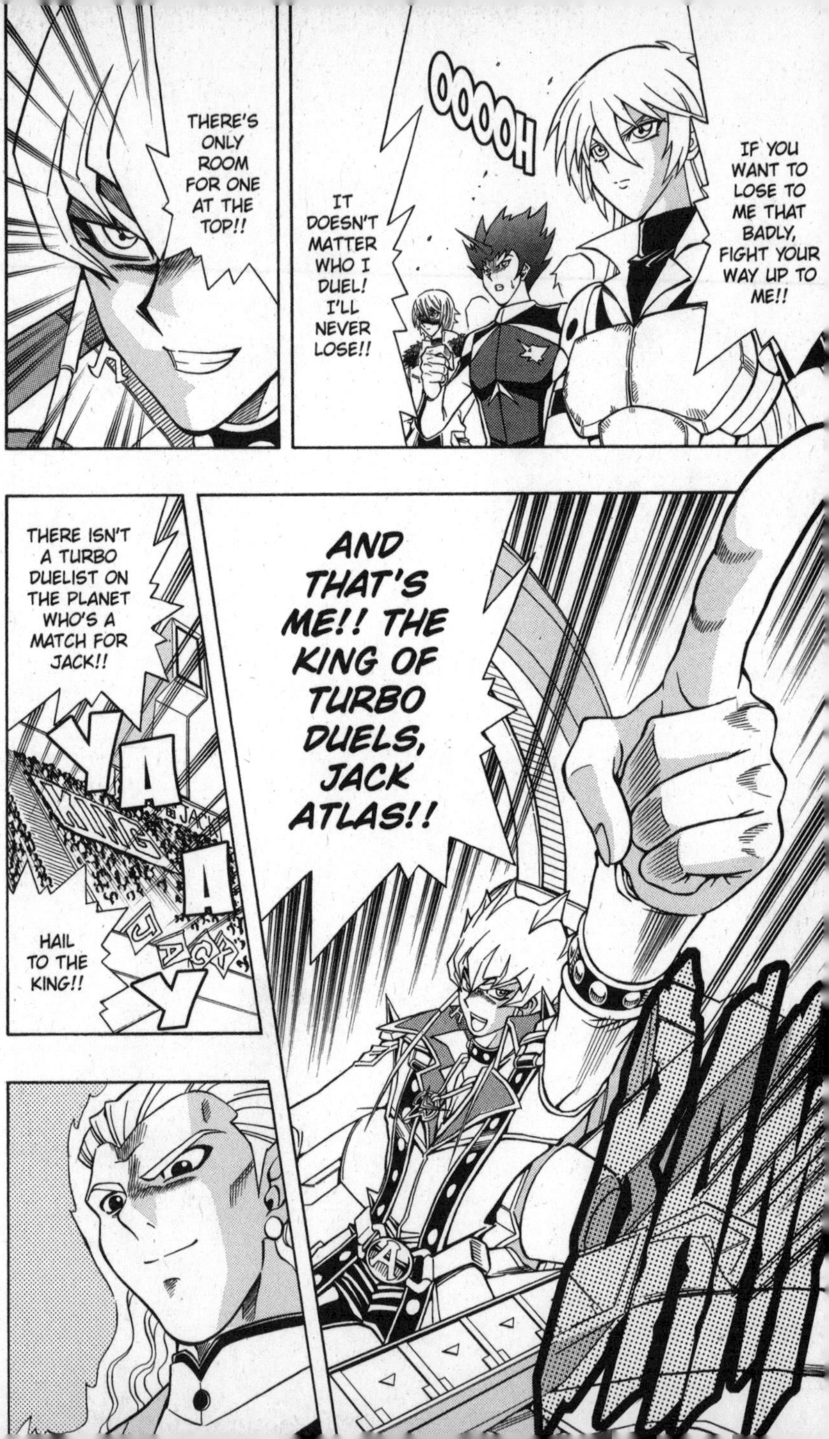
IF YOU WANT TO LOSE TO ME THAT BADLY, FIGHT YOUR WAY UP TO ME!!
OOOOH
IT DOESN'T MATTER WHO I DUEL! I'LL NEVER LOSE!!
THERE'S ONLY ROOM FOR ONE AT THE TOP!!
AND THAT'S ME!! THE KING OF TURBO DUELS, JACK ATLAS!!
THERE ISN'T A TURBO DUELIST ON THE PLANET WHO'S A MATCH FOR JACK!!
YAAY
KING
HAIL TO THE KING!!

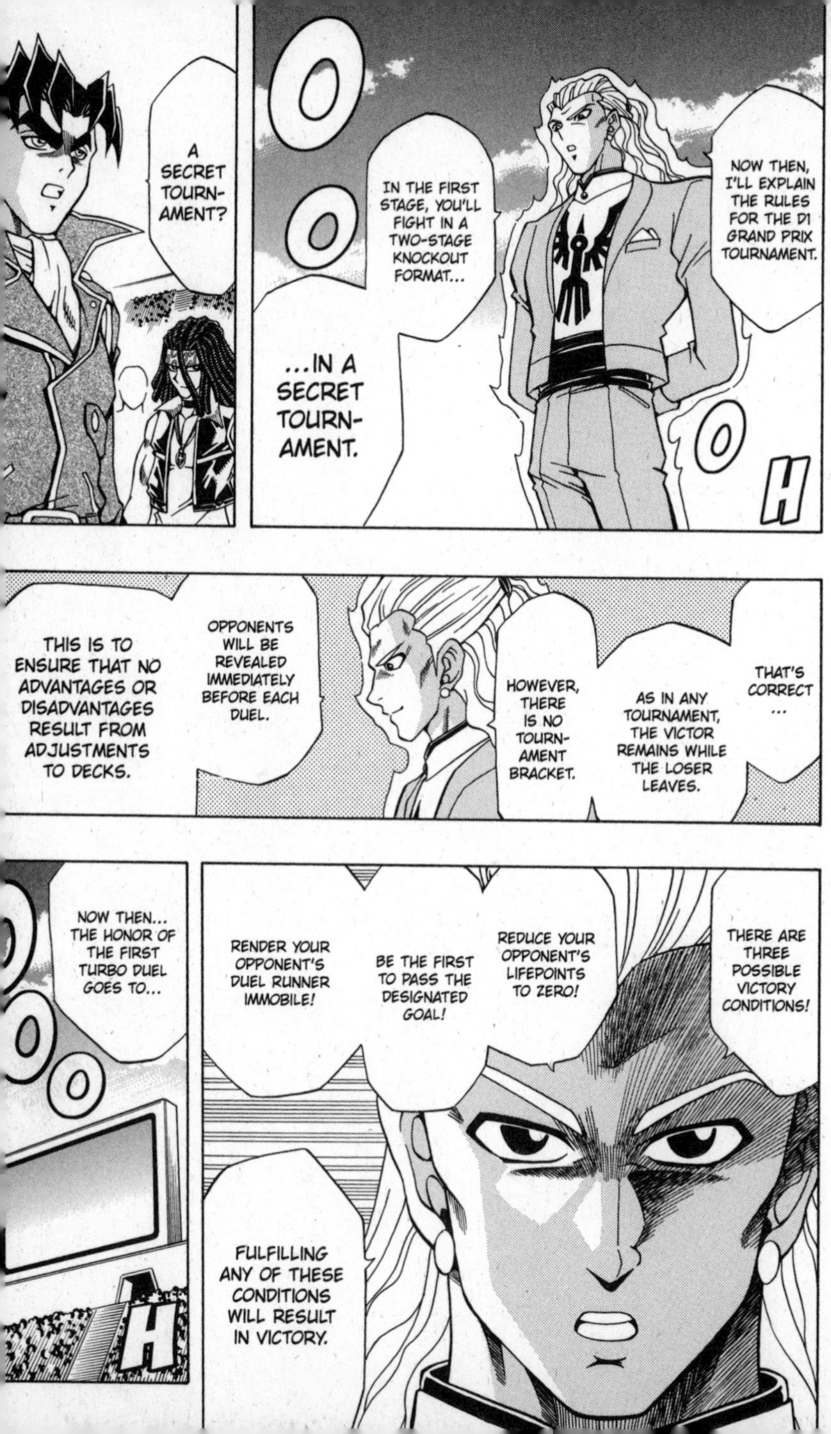
NOW THEN, I'LL EXPLAIN THE RULES FOR THE D1 GRAND PRIX TOURNAMENT.
IN THE FIRST STAGE, YOU'LL FIGHT IN A TWO-STAGE KNOCKOUT FORMAT...
...IN A SECRET TOURN-AMENT.
OOOOH
A SECRET TOURN-AMENT?
THAT'S CORRECT ...
AS IN ANY TOURNAMENT, THE VICTOR REMAINS WHILE THE LOSER LEAVES.
HOWEVER, THERE IS NO TOURN-AMENT BRACKET.
OPPONENTS WILL BE REVEALED IMMEDIATELY BEFORE EACH DUEL.
THIS IS TO ENSURE THAT NO ADVANTAGES OR DISADVANTAGES RESULT FROM ADJUSTMENTS TO DECKS.
THERE ARE THREE POSSIBLE VICTORY CONDITIONS!
REDUCE YOUR OPPONENT'S LIFEPOINTS TO ZERO!
BE THE FIRST TO PASS THE DESIGNATED GOAL!
RENDER YOUR OPPONENT'S DUEL RUNNER IMMOBILE!
FULFILLING ANY OF THESE CONDITIONS WILL RESULT IN VICTORY.
NOW THEN... THE HONOR OF THE FIRST TURBO DUEL GOES TO...
OOOOH

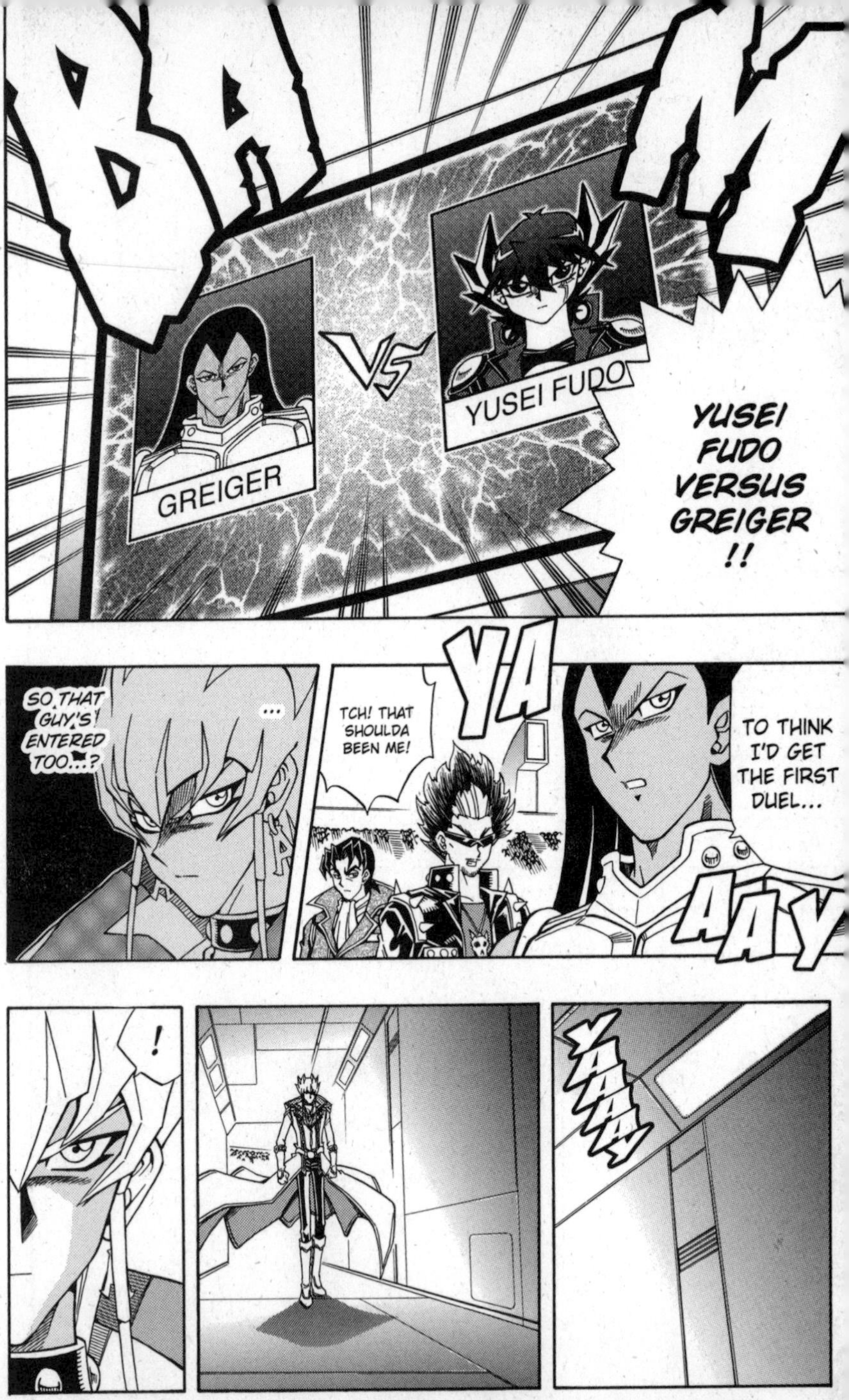
BAM
YUSEI FUDO
VS
GREIGER
YUSEI FUDO VERSUS GREIGER !!
YA
TO THINK I'D GET THE FIRST DUEL...
AAY
TCH! THAT SHOULDA BEEN ME!
...
SO THAT GUY'S ENTERED TOO...?
YAAAAY
!

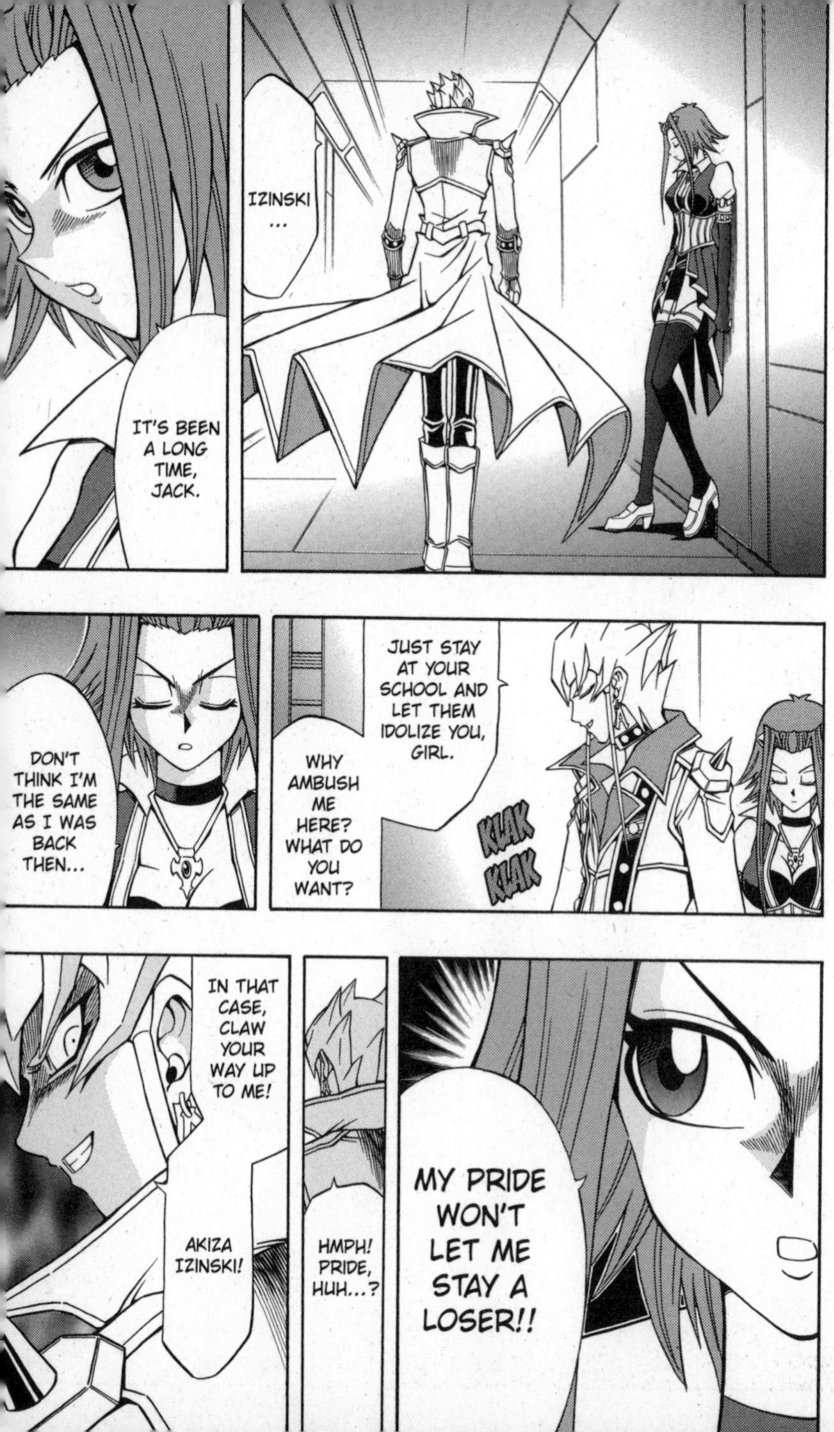
IZINSKI ...
IT'S BEEN A LONG TIME, JACK.
JUST STAY AT YOUR SCHOOL AND LET THEM IDOLIZE YOU, GIRL.
KLAK KLAK
WHY AMBUSH ME HERE? WHAT DO YOU WANT?
DON'T THINK I'M THE SAME AS I WAS BACK THEN...
MY PRIDE WON'T LET ME STAY A LOSER!!
HMPH! PRIDE, HUH...?
IN THAT CASE, CLAW YOUR WAY UP TO ME!
AKIZA IZINSKI!

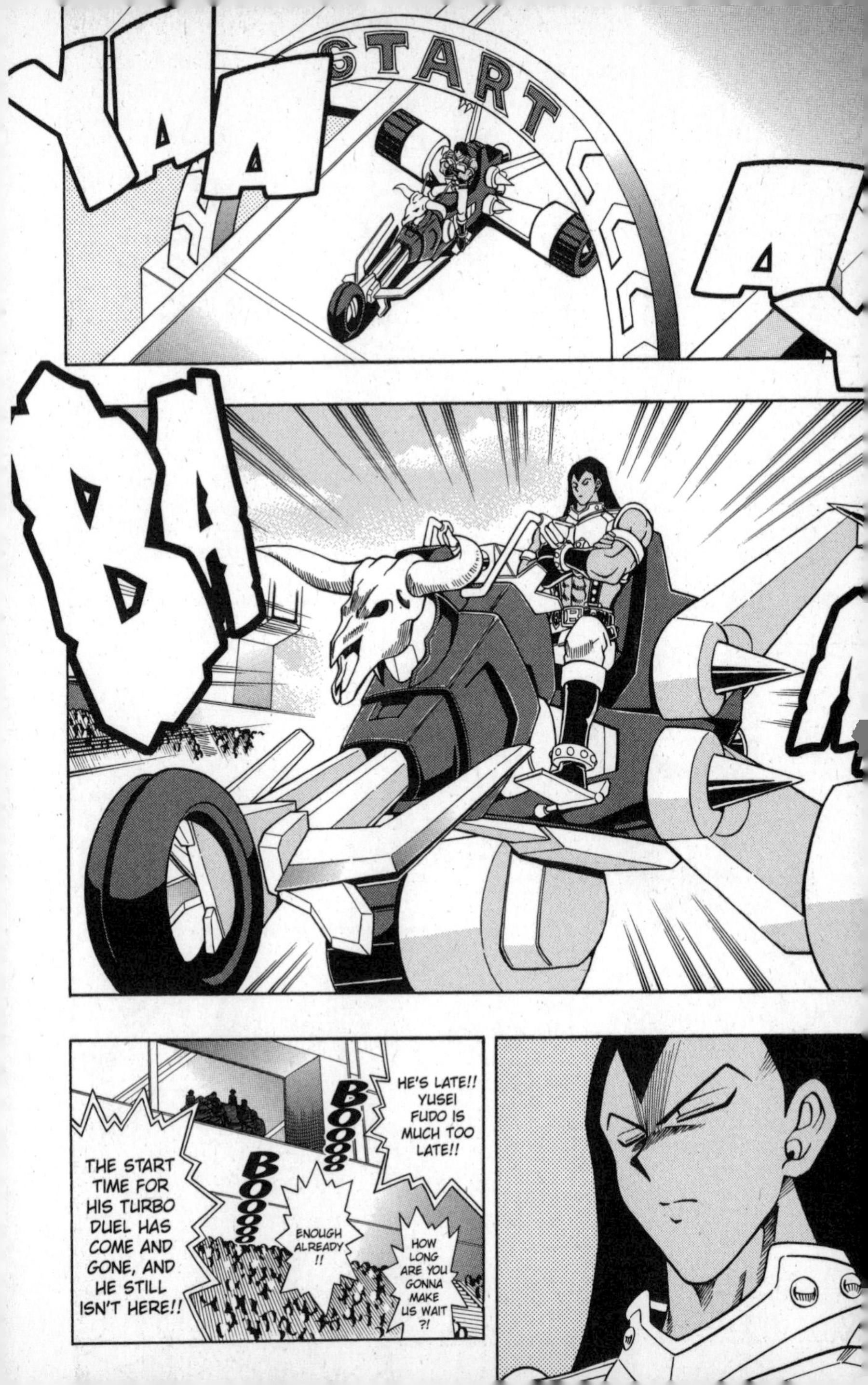
START
YAA
A
BA
HE'S LATE!! YUSEI FUDO IS MUCH TOO LATE!!
BOOOOO
THE START TIME FOR HIS TURBO DUEL HAS COME AND GONE, AND HE STILL ISN'T HERE!!
BOOOOOO
ENOUGH ALREADY!!
HOW LONG ARE YOU GONNA MAKE US WAIT?!

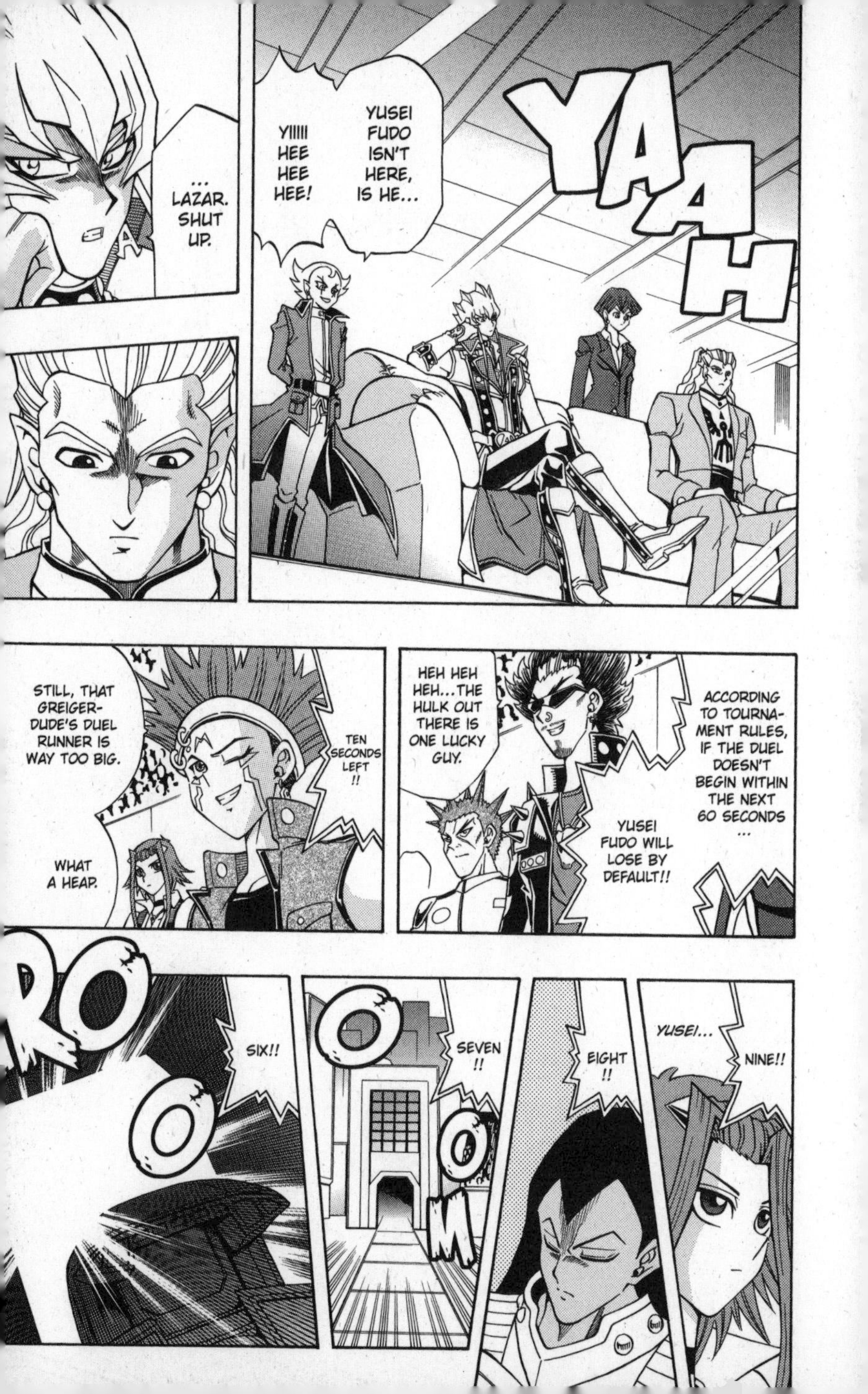
YAAH
YUSEI FUDO ISN'T HERE, IS HE...
YIIIII HEE HEE HEE!
...LAZAR. SHUT UP.
ACCORDING TO TOURNAMENT RULES, IF THE DUEL DOESN'T BEGIN WITHIN THE NEXT 60 SECONDS...
HEH HEH HEH...THE HULK OUT THERE IS ONE LUCKY GUY.
YUSEI FUDO WILL LOSE BY DEFAULT!!
TEN SECONDS LEFT!!
STILL, THAT GREIGER-DUDE'S DUEL RUNNER IS WAY TOO BIG.
WHAT A HEAP.
YUSEI...
NINE!!
EIGHT!!
SEVEN!!
SIX!!
ROOOOM

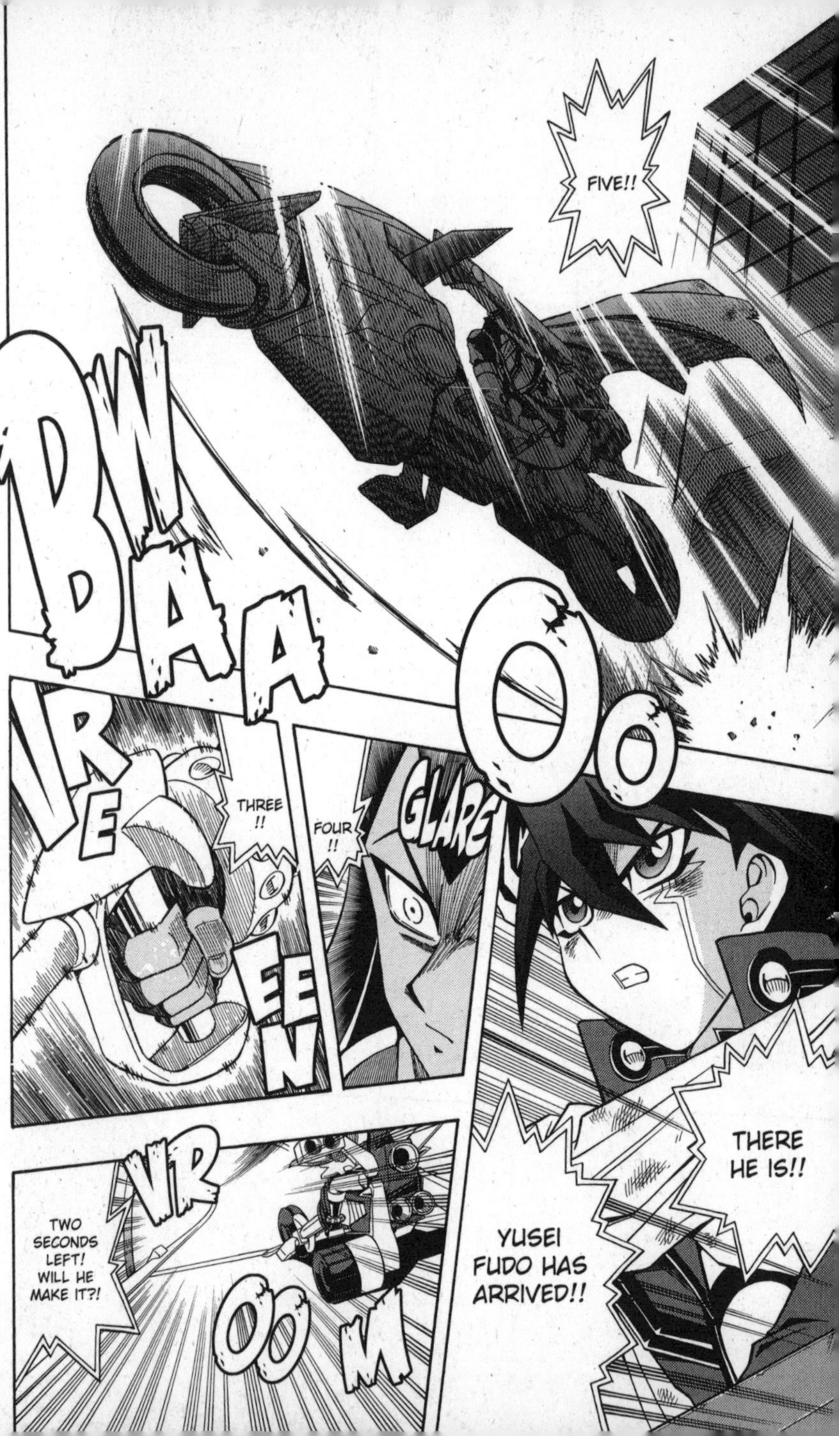
FIVE!!
BWAAOOO
GLARE
THERE HE IS!!
YUSEI FUDO HAS ARRIVED!!
FOUR!!
THREE!!
VREEEN
VR
TWO SECONDS LEFT! WILL HE MAKE IT?!
OOM

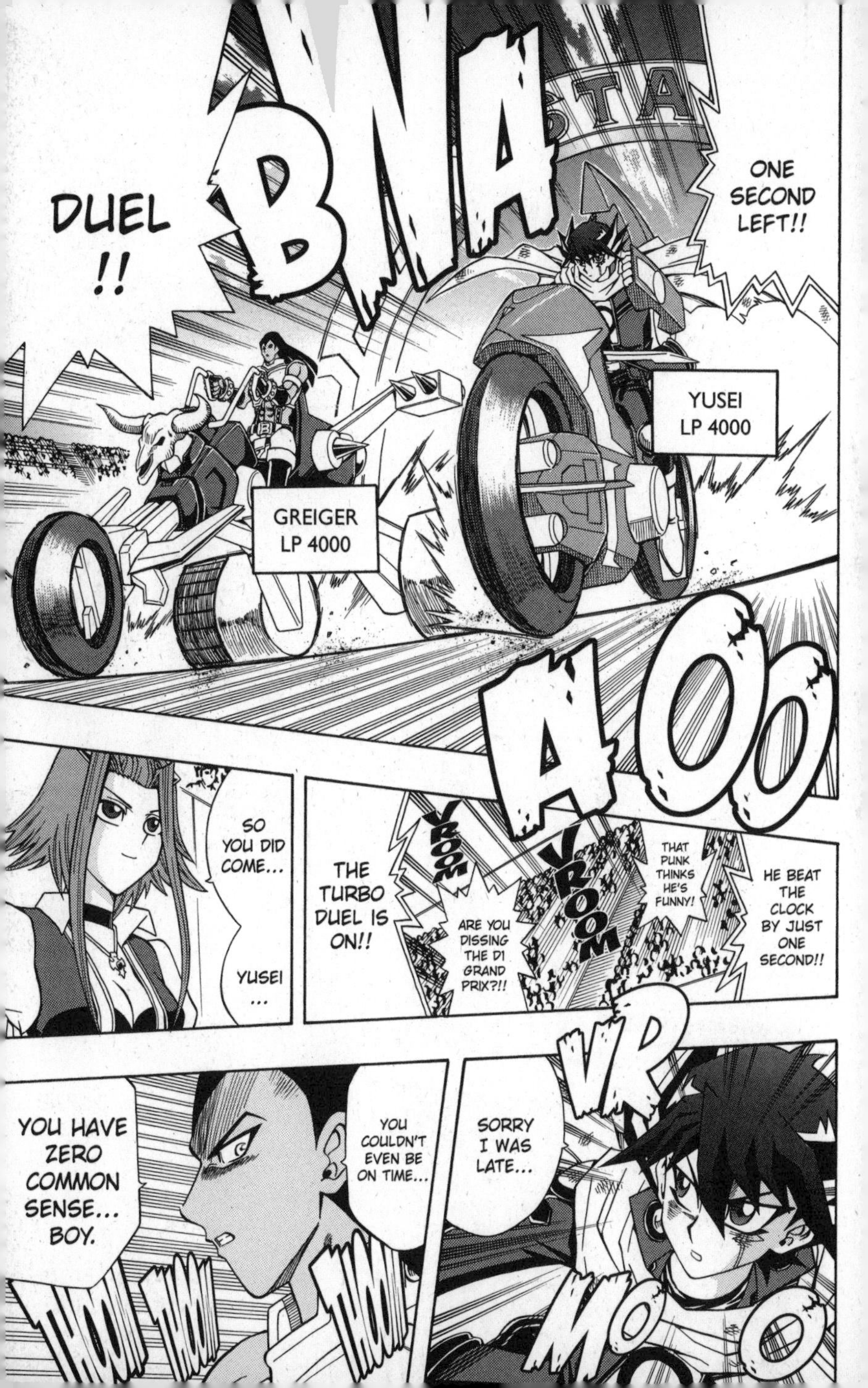
ONE SECOND LEFT!!
YUSEI LP 4000
DUEL !!
GREIGER LP 4000
HE BEAT THE CLOCK BY JUST ONE SECOND!!
THAT PUNK THINKS HE'S FUNNY!
VROOM
VROOM
ARE YOU DISSING THE D1 GRAND PRIX?!!
THE TURBO DUEL IS ON!!
SO YOU DID COME...
YUSEI ...
SORRY I WAS LATE...
YOU COULDN'T EVEN BE ON TIME...
YOU HAVE ZERO COMMON SENSE... BOY.

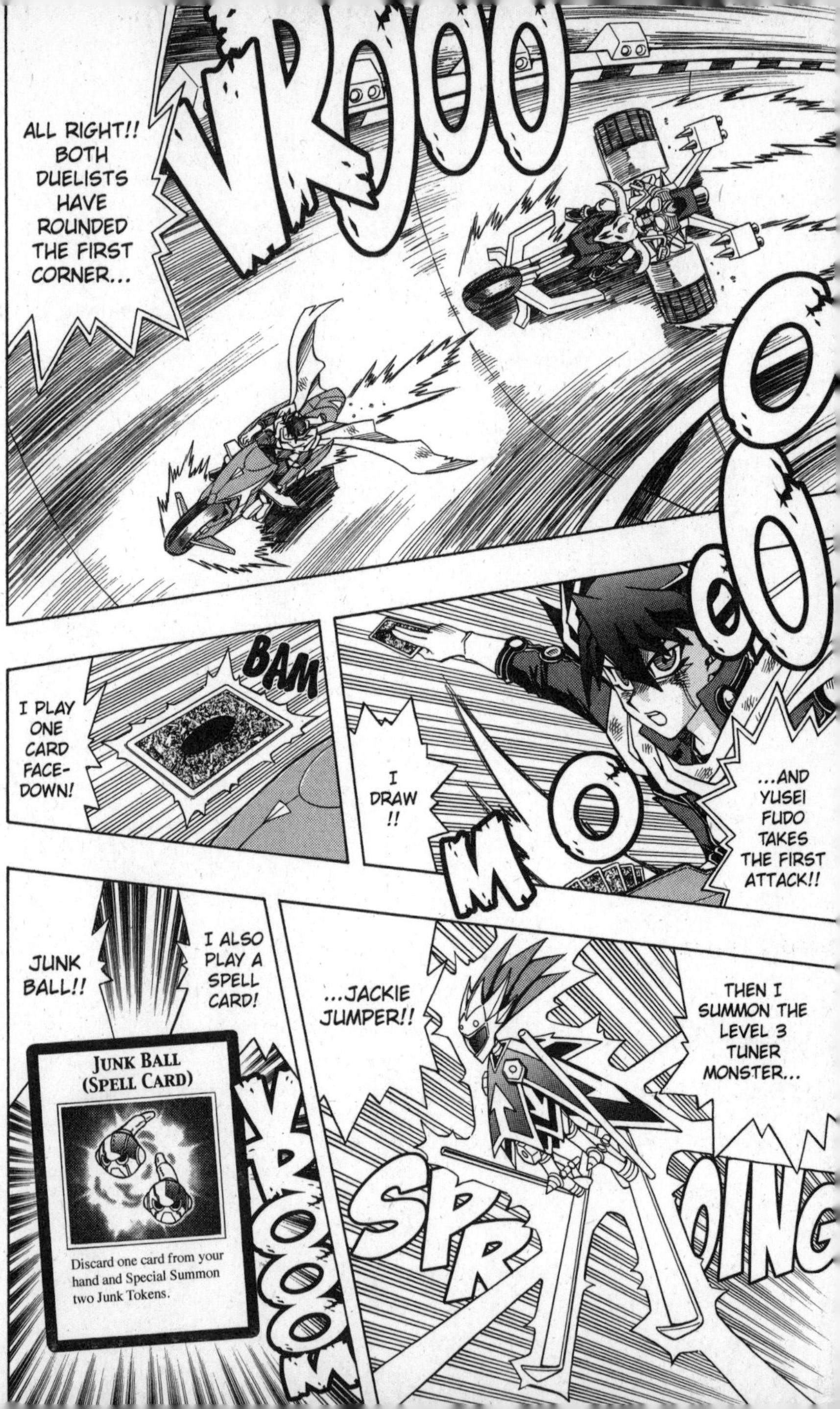
VROOO
ALL RIGHT!! BOTH DUELISTS HAVE ROUNDED THE FIRST CORNER...
OOOOOM
...AND YUSEI FUDO TAKES THE FIRST ATTACK!!
I DRAW!!
BAM
I PLAY ONE CARD FACE-DOWN!
THEN I SUMMON THE LEVEL 3 TUNER MONSTER...
...JACKIE JUMPER!!
SPROING
I ALSO PLAY A SPELL CARD!
JUNK BALL!!
JUNK BALL (SPELL CARD)
Discard one card from your hand and Special Summon two Junk Tokens.
VROOOOM

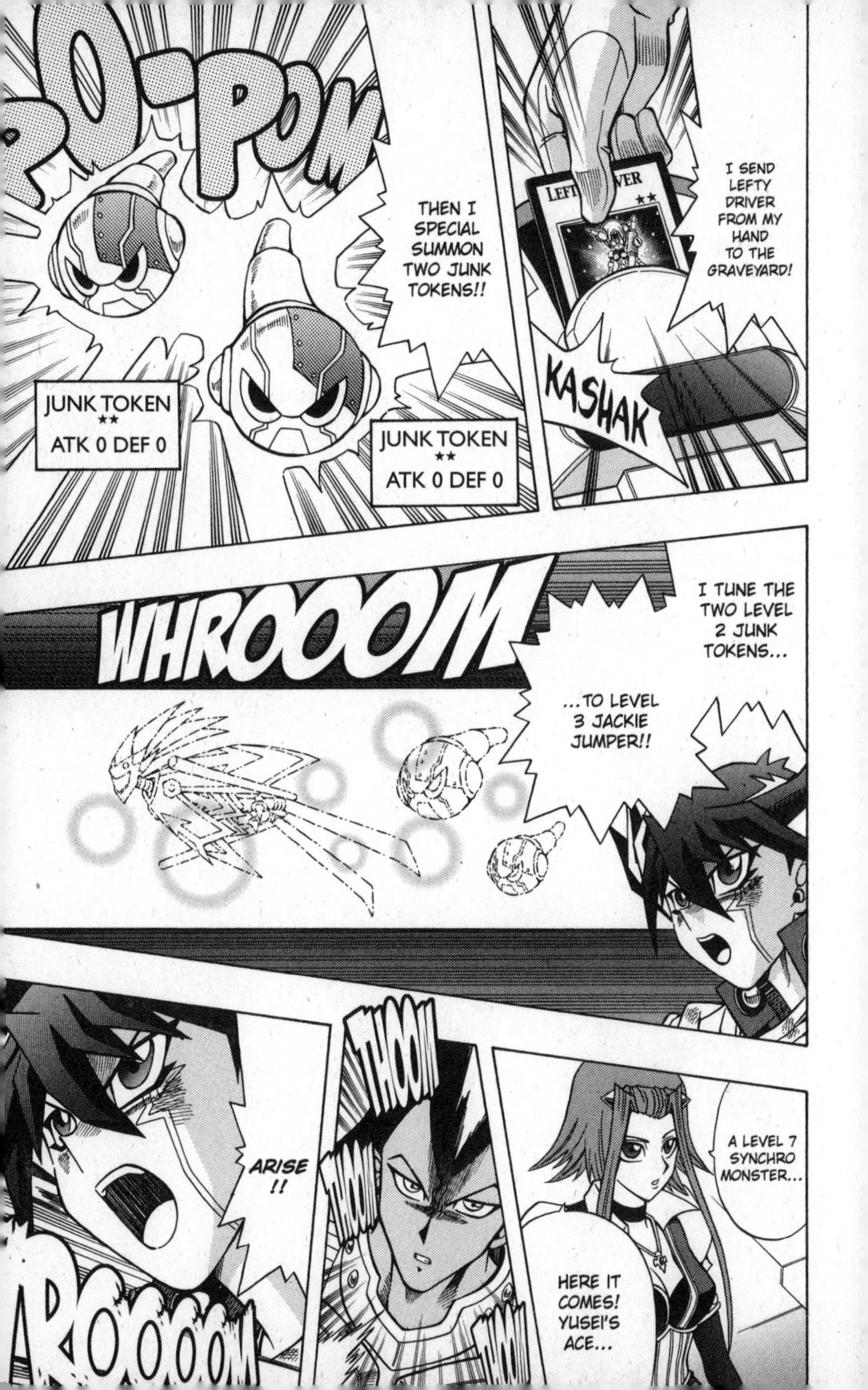

I SEND LEFTY DRIVER FROM MY HAND TO THE GRAVEYARD!
KASHAK
THEN I SPECIAL SUMMON TWO JUNK TOKENS!!
JUNK TOKEN ★★ ATK 0 DEF 0
JUNK TOKEN ★★ ATK 0 DEF 0
I TUNE THE TWO LEVEL 2 JUNK TOKENS...
...TO LEVEL 3 JACKIE JUMPER!!
WHROOOM
A LEVEL 7 SYNCHRO MONSTER...
HERE IT COMES! YUSEI'S ACE...
THOOM
ARISE !!
AROOOOM

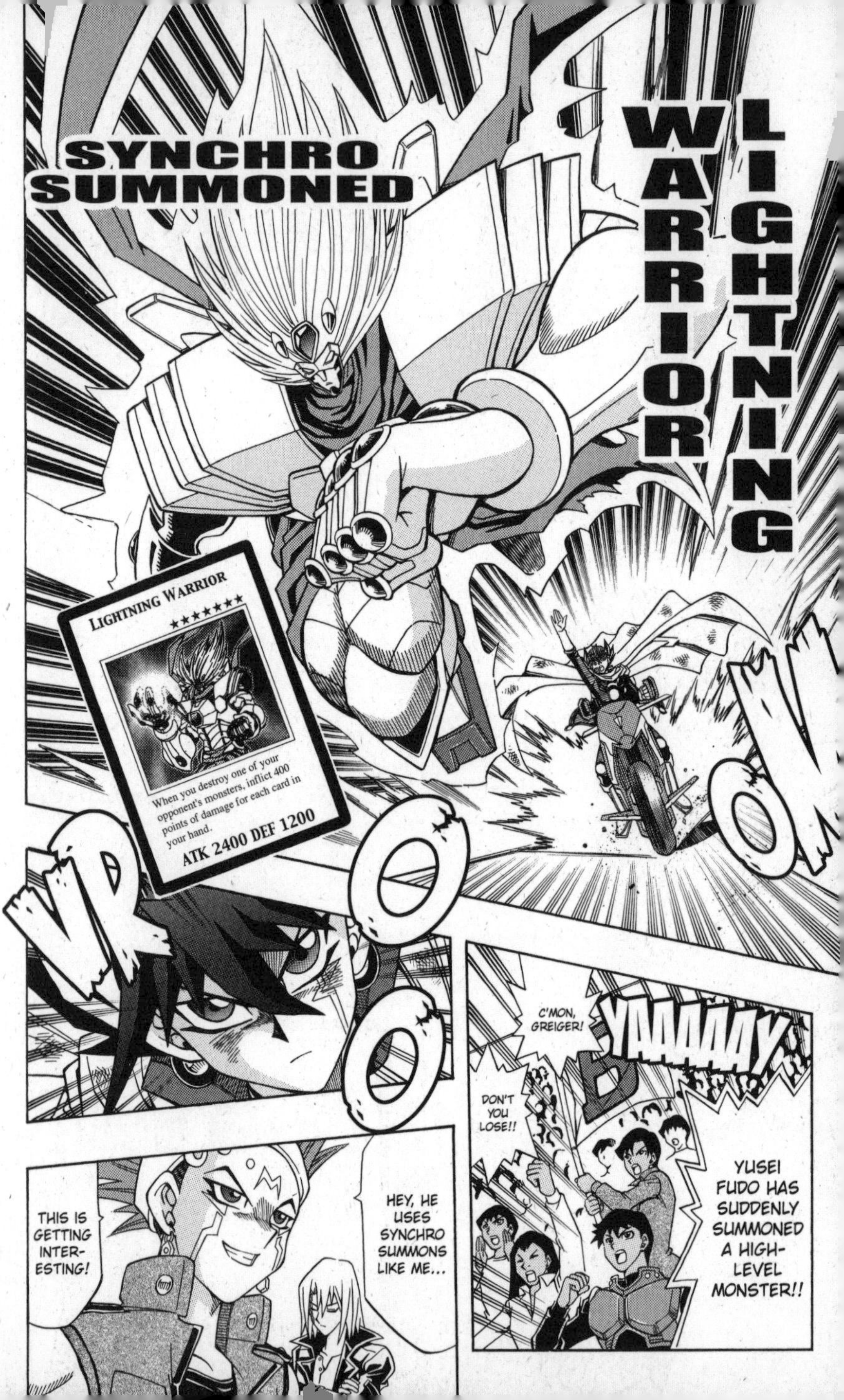
LIGHTNING WARRIOR
SYNCHRO SUMMONED
LIGHTNING WARRIOR
★★★★★★★
When you destroy one of your opponent's monsters, inflict 400 points of damage for each card in your hand.
ATK 2400 DEF 1200
C'MON, GREIGER!
YAAAAAY
DON'T YOU LOSE!!
YUSEI FUDO HAS SUDDENLY SUMMONED A HIGH-LEVEL MONSTER!!
HEY, HE USES SYNCHRO SUMMONS LIKE ME...
THIS IS GETTING INTER-ESTING!

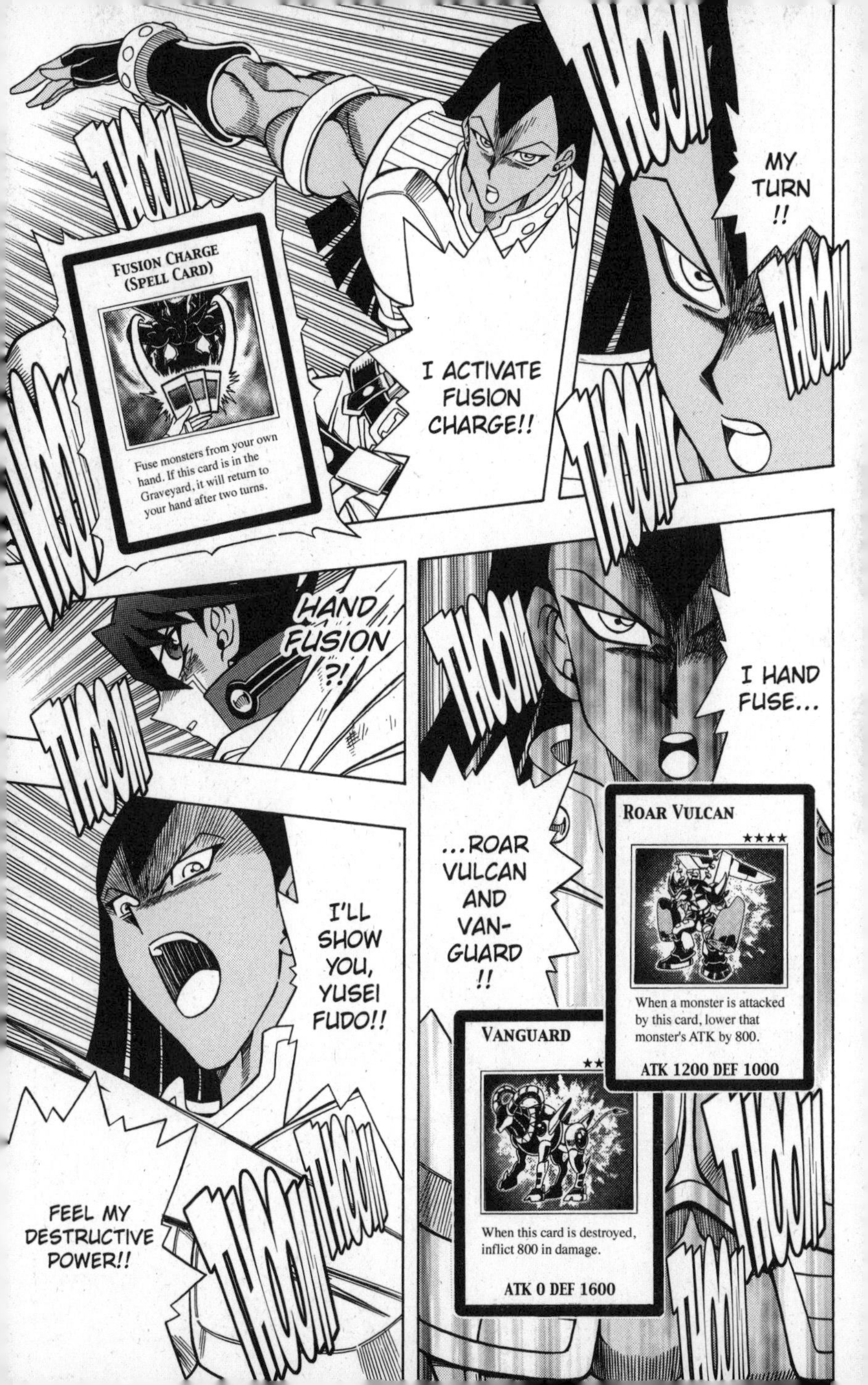
THOOM
MY TURN!!
THOOM
THOOM
THOOM
I ACTIVATE FUSION CHARGE!!
THOOM
THOOM
FUSION CHARGE (SPELL CARD)
Fuse monsters from your own hand. If this card is in the Graveyard, it will return to your hand after two turns.
I HAND FUSE...
THOOM
...ROAR VULCAN AND VANGUARD!!
ROAR VULCAN
When a monster is attacked by this card, lower that monster's ATK by 800.
ATK 1200 DEF 1000
VANGUARD
When this card is destroyed, inflict 800 in damage.
ATK 0 DEF 1600
THOOM
THOOM
HAND FUSION?!
THOOM
I'LL SHOW YOU, YUSEI FUDO!!
THOOM
THOOM
FEEL MY DESTRUCTIVE POWER!!

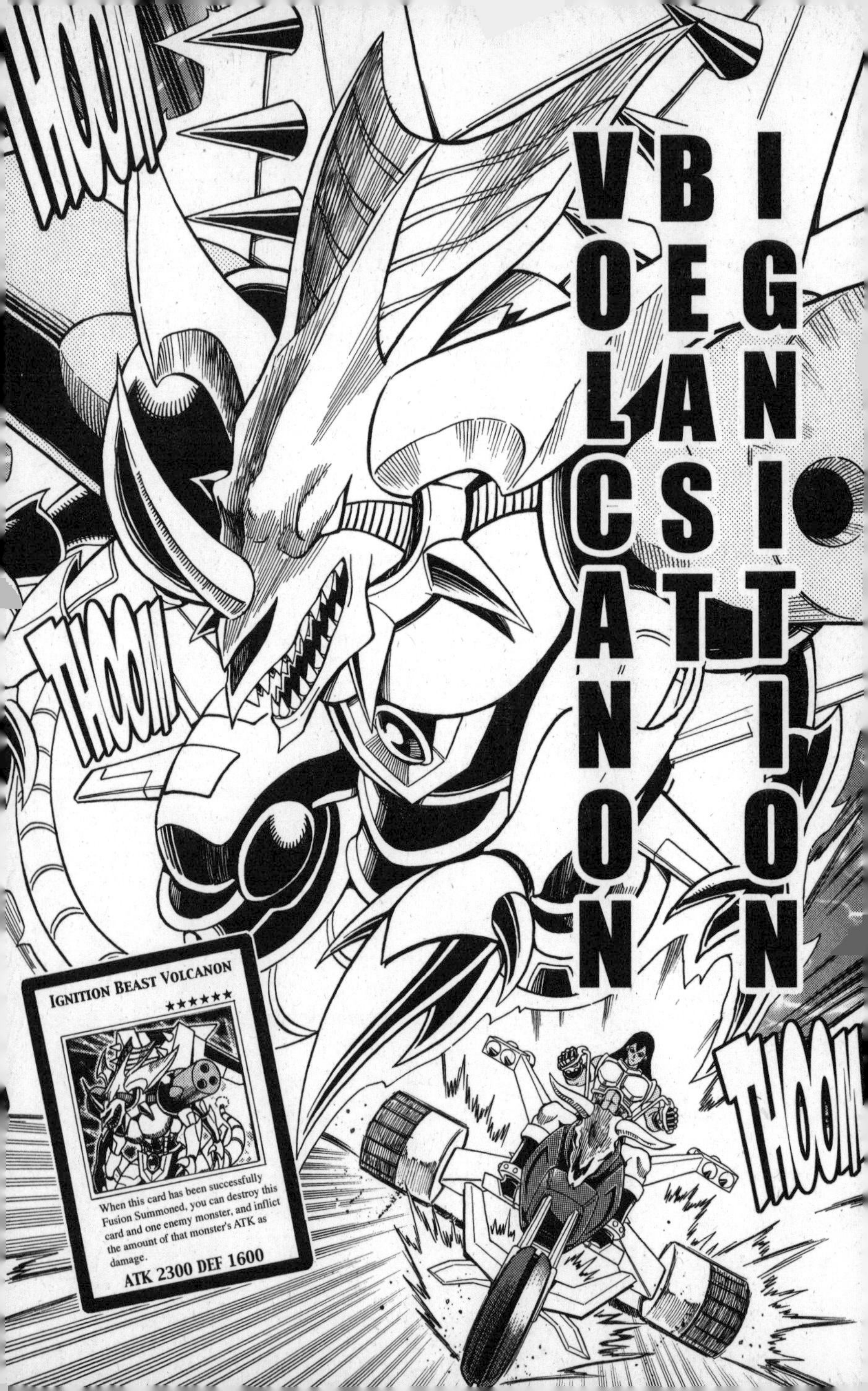
IGNITION BEAST VOLCANON
THOOM
THOOM
IGNITION BEAST VOLCANON
★★★★★★
When this card has been successfully Fusion Summoned, you can destroy this card and one enemy monster, and inflict the amount of that monster's ATK as damage.
ATK 2300 DEF 1600
THOOM

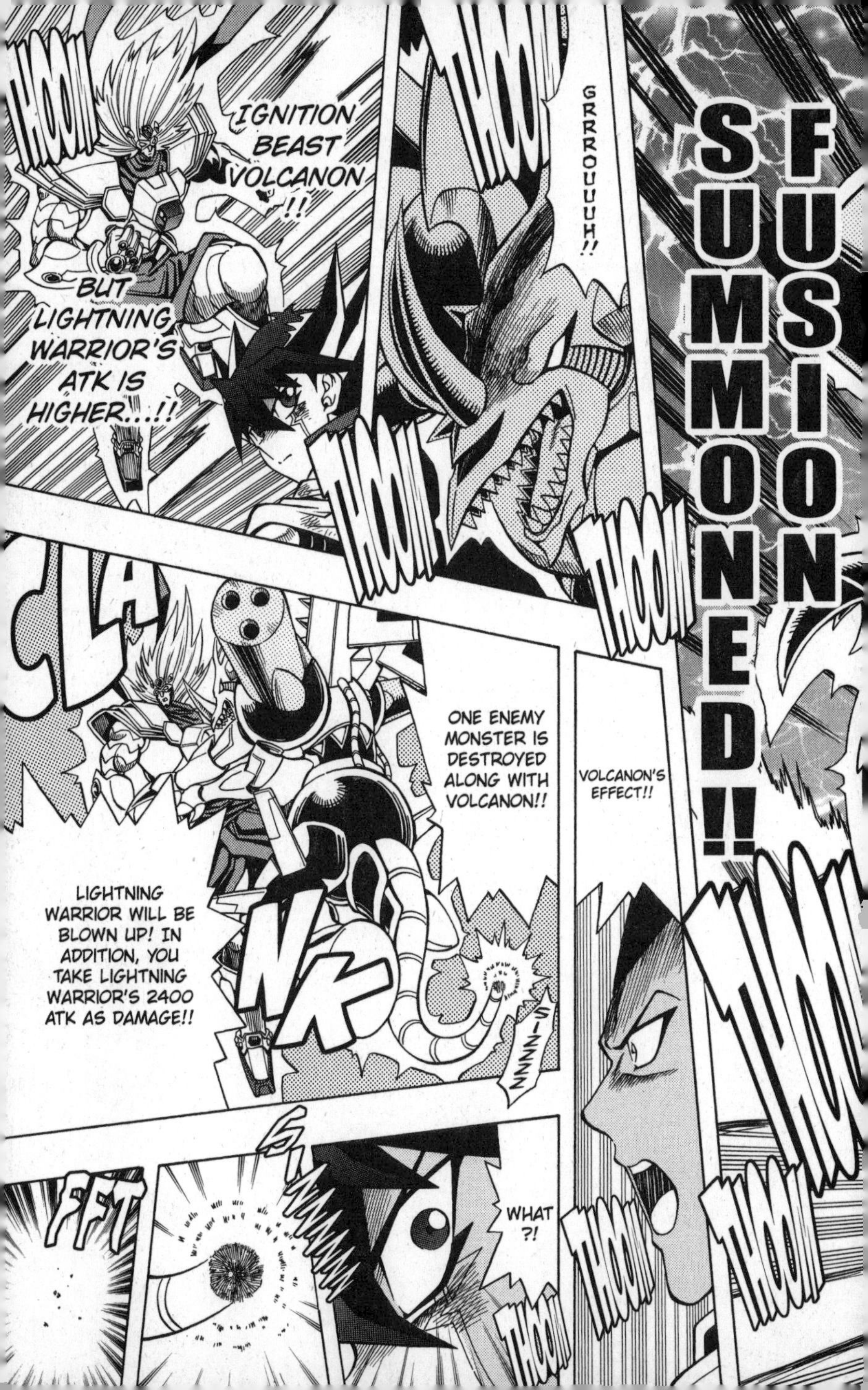
FUSION SUMMONED!!
GRRROUUUH!!
THOOM
THOOM
THOOM
THOOM
IGNITION BEAST VOLCANON!!
BUT LIGHTNING WARRIOR'S ATK IS HIGHER...!!
THOOM
THOOM
VOLCANON'S EFFECT!!
ONE ENEMY MONSTER IS DESTROYED ALONG WITH VOLCANON!!
LIGHTNING WARRIOR WILL BE BLOWN UP! IN ADDITION, YOU TAKE LIGHTNING WARRIOR'S 2400 ATK AS DAMAGE!!
NK
SIZZZZ
THOOM
THOOM
THOOM
WHAT?!
FFT

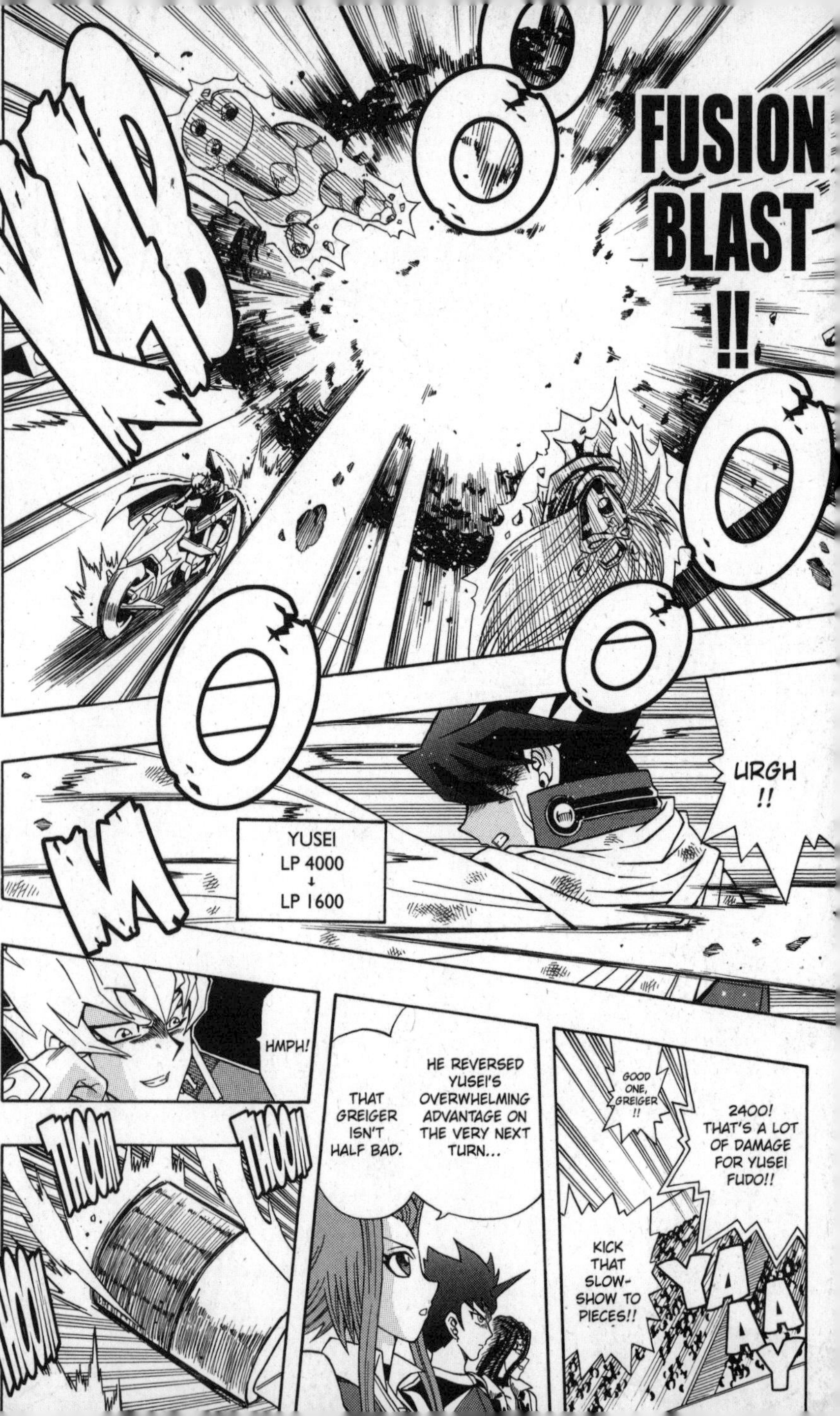
FUSION BLAST!!
URGH!!
YUSEI
LP 4000
↓
LP 1600
GOOD ONE, GREIGER!!
2400! THAT'S A LOT OF DAMAGE FOR YUSEI FUDO!!
KICK THAT SLOW-SHOW TO PIECES!!
YAAAY
HE REVERSED YUSEI'S OVERWHELMING ADVANTAGE ON THE VERY NEXT TURN...
THAT GREIGER ISN'T HALF BAD.
HMPH!
THOOM
THOOM
THOOM

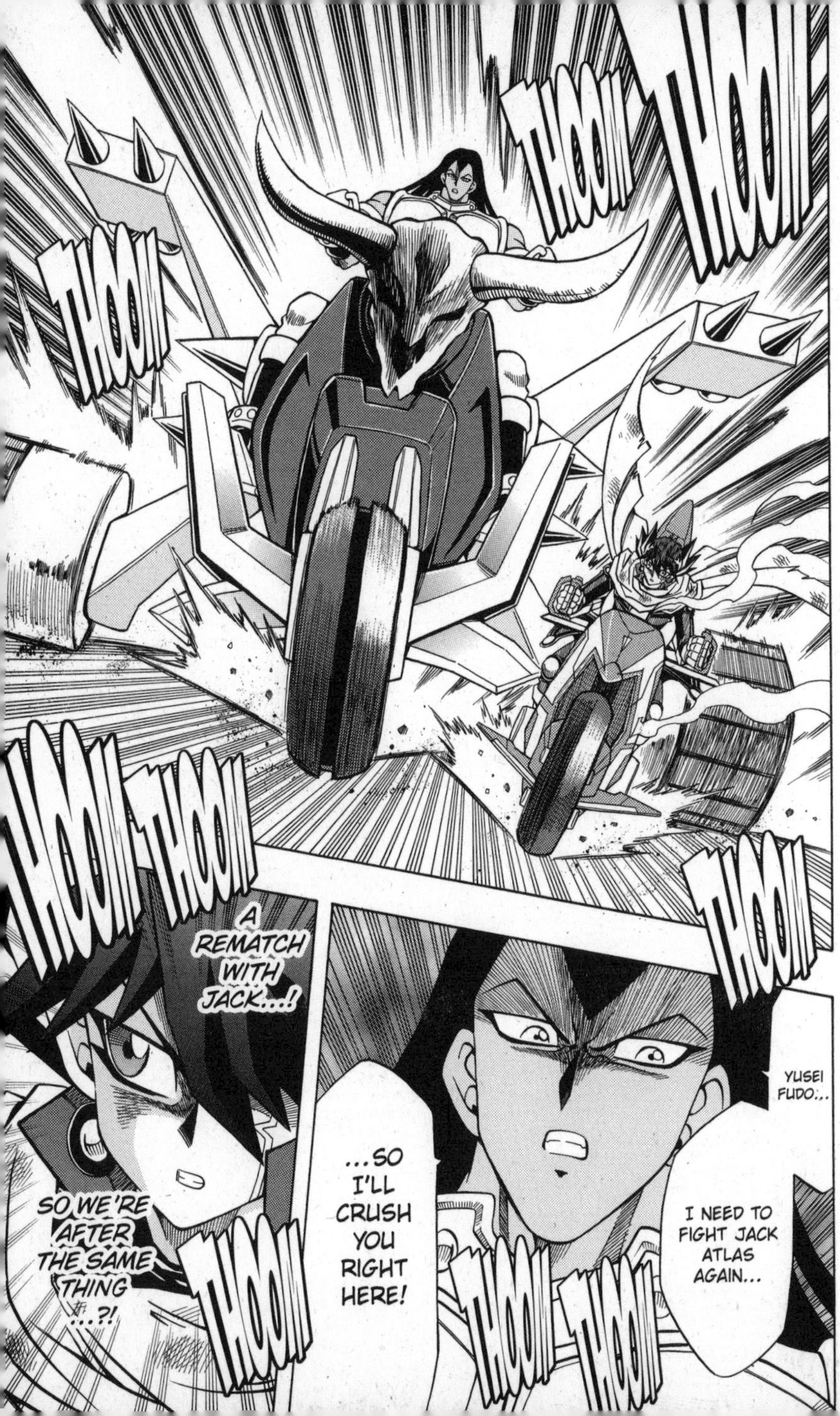
THOOM
THOOM
THOOM
THOOM
THOOM
THOOM
YUSEI FUDO...
I NEED TO FIGHT JACK ATLAS AGAIN...
...SO I'LL CRUSH YOU RIGHT HERE!
THOOM
THOOM
A REMATCH WITH JACK...!
SO WE'RE AFTER THE SAME THING...?!
THOOM

5D's TRACKS

THE 9TH

BY SATOMASA

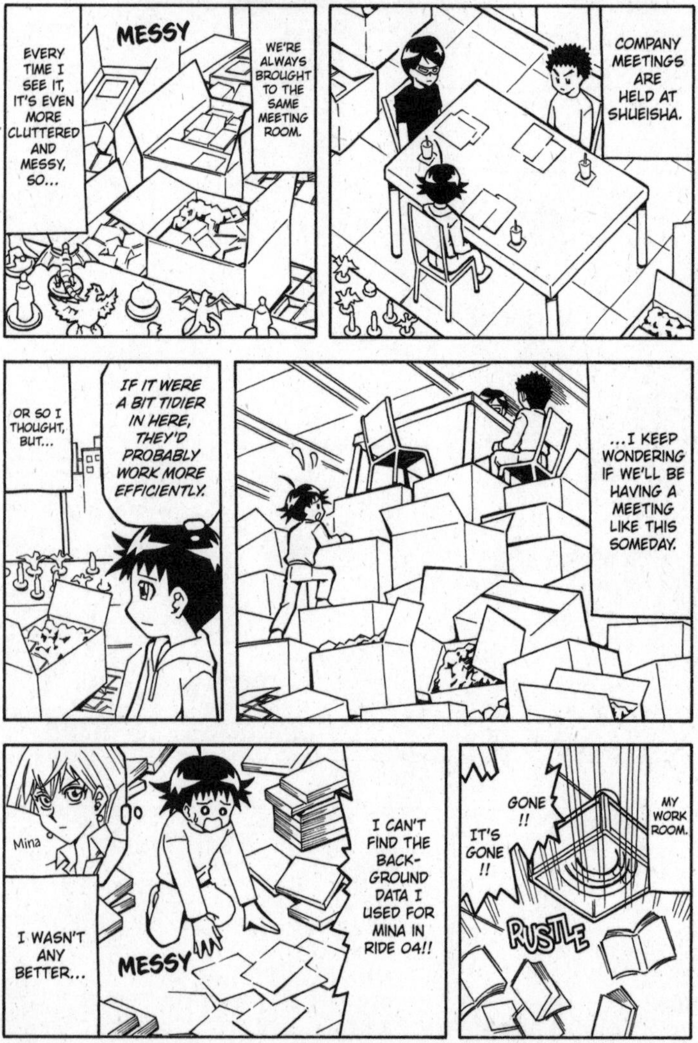
COMPANY MEETINGS ARE HELD AT SHUEISHA.
WE'RE ALWAYS BROUGHT TO THE SAME MEETING ROOM.
MESSY
EVERY TIME I SEE IT, IT'S EVEN MORE CLUTTERED AND MESSY, SO...
...I KEEP WONDERING IF WE'LL BE HAVING A MEETING LIKE THIS SOMEDAY.
IF IT WERE A BIT TIDIER IN HERE, THEY'D PROBABLY WORK MORE EFFICIENTLY.
OR SO I THOUGHT, BUT...
MY WORK ROOM.
GONE!!
IT'S GONE!!
RUSTLE
I CAN'T FIND THE BACK-GROUND DATA I USED FOR MINA IN RIDE 04!!
Mina
MESSY
I WASN'T ANY BETTER...

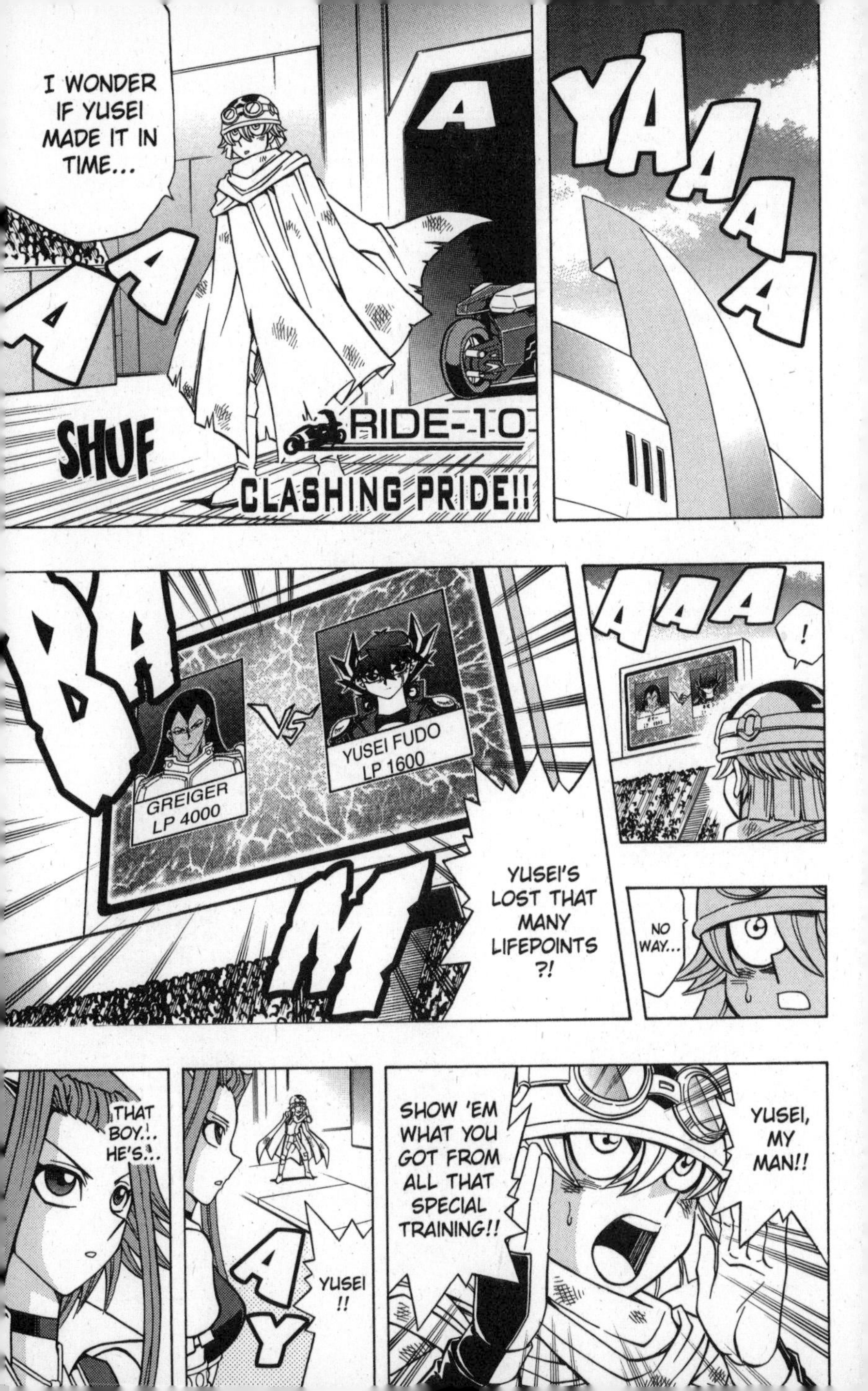

YAAAAAA
I WONDER IF YUSEI MADE IT IN TIME...
A
AA
A
SHUF
RIDE-10
CLASHING PRIDE!!
AAA
!
NO WAY...
BAM
GREIGER LP 4000
VS
YUSEI FUDO LP 1600
YUSEI'S LOST THAT MANY LIFEPOINTS ?!
YUSEI, MY MAN!!
SHOW 'EM WHAT YOU GOT FROM ALL THAT SPECIAL TRAINING!!
AY
YUSEI !!
THAT BOY... HE'S...

RIDE-10

CLASHING PRIDE!!

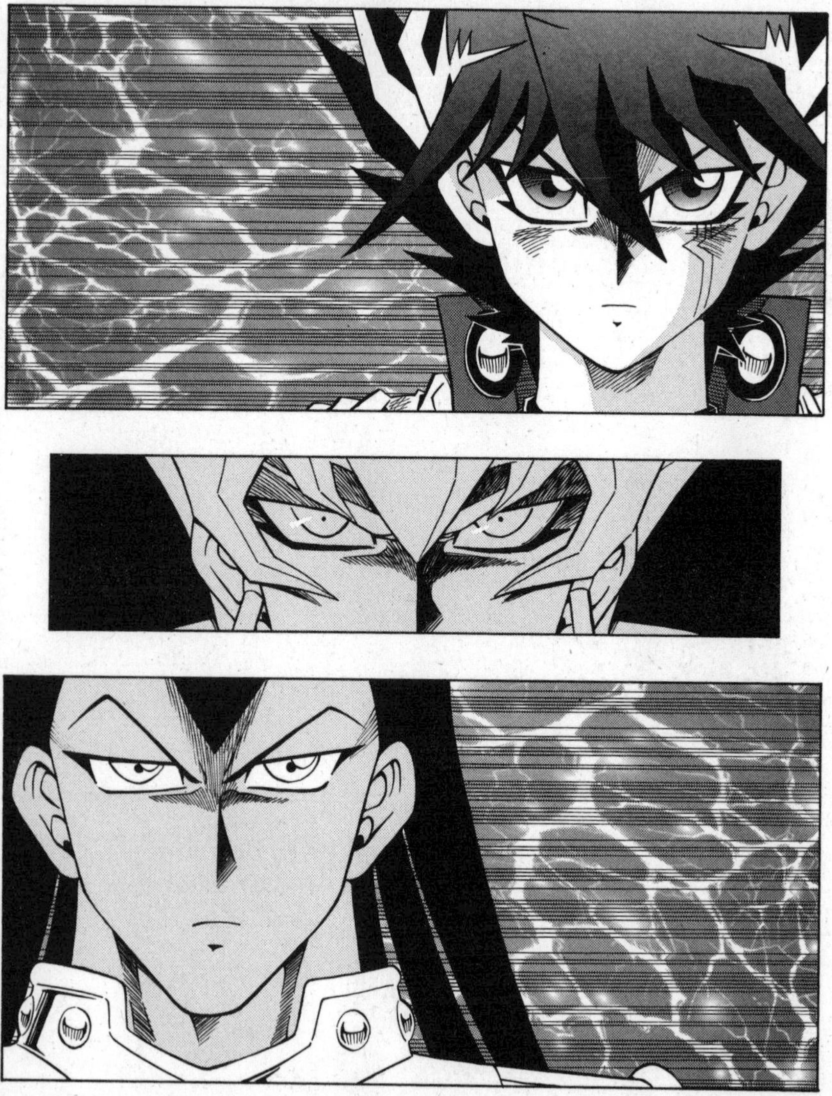

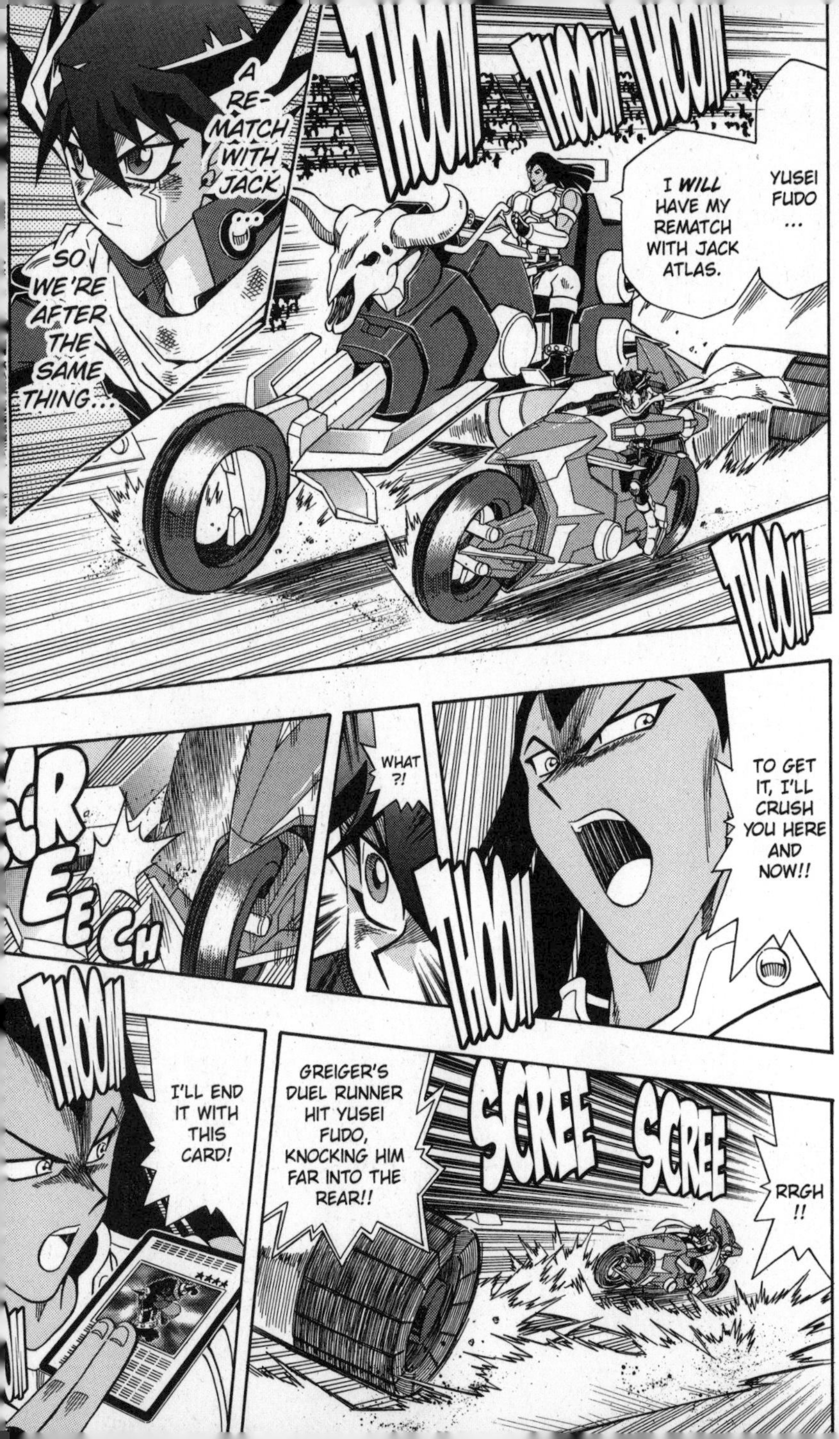
THOOM
THOOM THOOM
YUSEI FUDO ...
I WILL HAVE MY REMATCH WITH JACK ATLAS.
THOOM
A RE-MATCH WITH JACK
SO WE'RE AFTER THE SAME THING...
TO GET IT, I'LL CRUSH YOU HERE AND NOW!!
THOOM
WHAT ?!
SCREEECH
SCREE SCREE
RRGH !!
GREIGER'S DUEL RUNNER HIT YUSEI FUDO, KNOCKING HIM FAR INTO THE REAR!!
THOOM
I'LL END IT WITH THIS CARD!

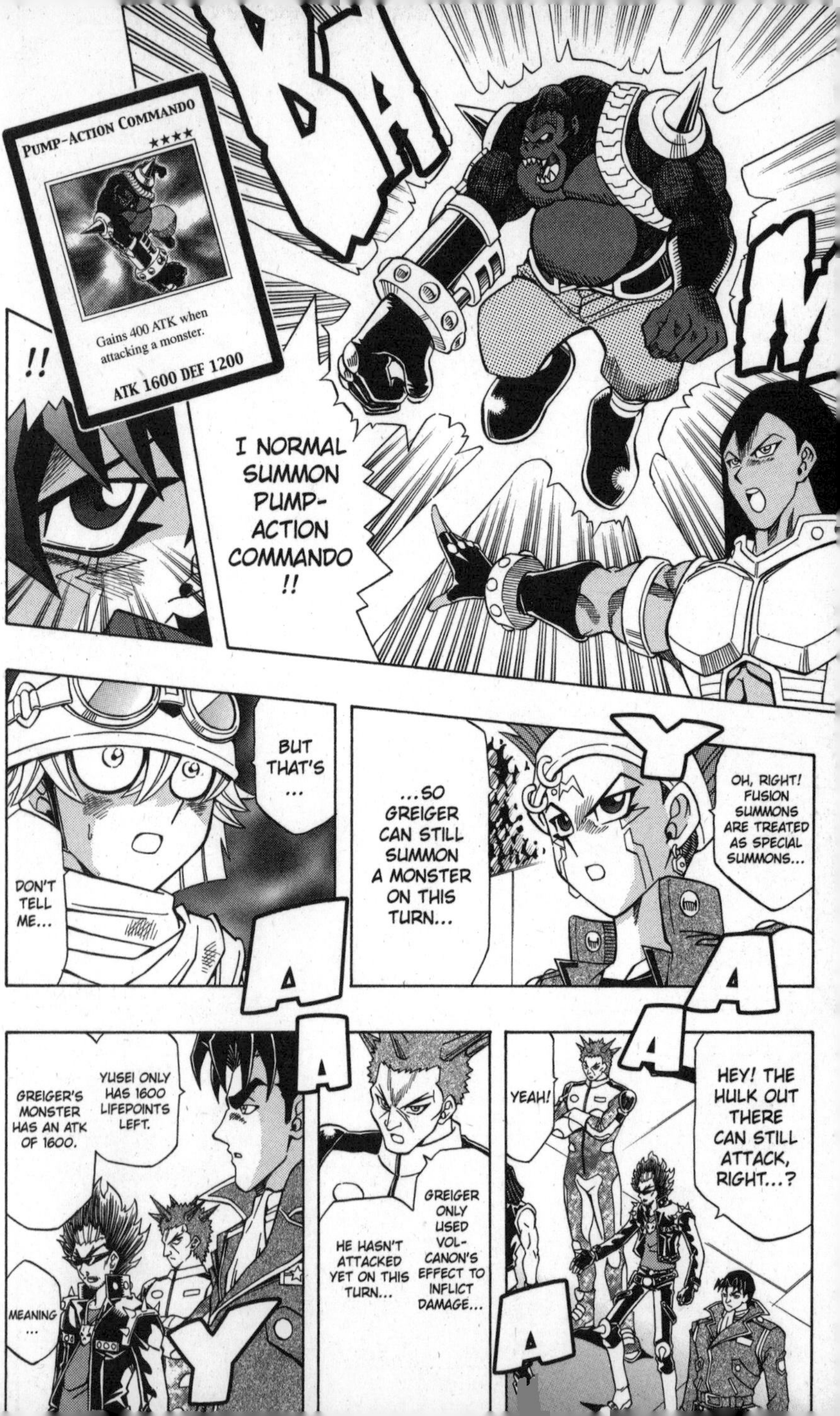

I NORMAL SUMMON PUMP-ACTION COMMANDO !!
PUMP-ACTION COMMANDO ★★★★
Gains 400 ATK when attacking a monster.
ATK 1600 DEF 1200
!!
OH, RIGHT! FUSION SUMMONS ARE TREATED AS SPECIAL SUMMONS...
...SO GREIGER CAN STILL SUMMON A MONSTER ON THIS TURN...
BUT THAT'S ...
DON'T TELL ME...
HEY! THE HULK OUT THERE CAN STILL ATTACK, RIGHT...?
YEAH!
GREIGER ONLY USED VOL-CANON'S EFFECT TO INFLICT DAMAGE...
HE HASN'T ATTACKED YET ON THIS TURN...
YUSEI ONLY HAS 1600 LIFEPOINTS LEFT.
GREIGER'S MONSTER HAS AN ATK OF 1600.
MEANING ...

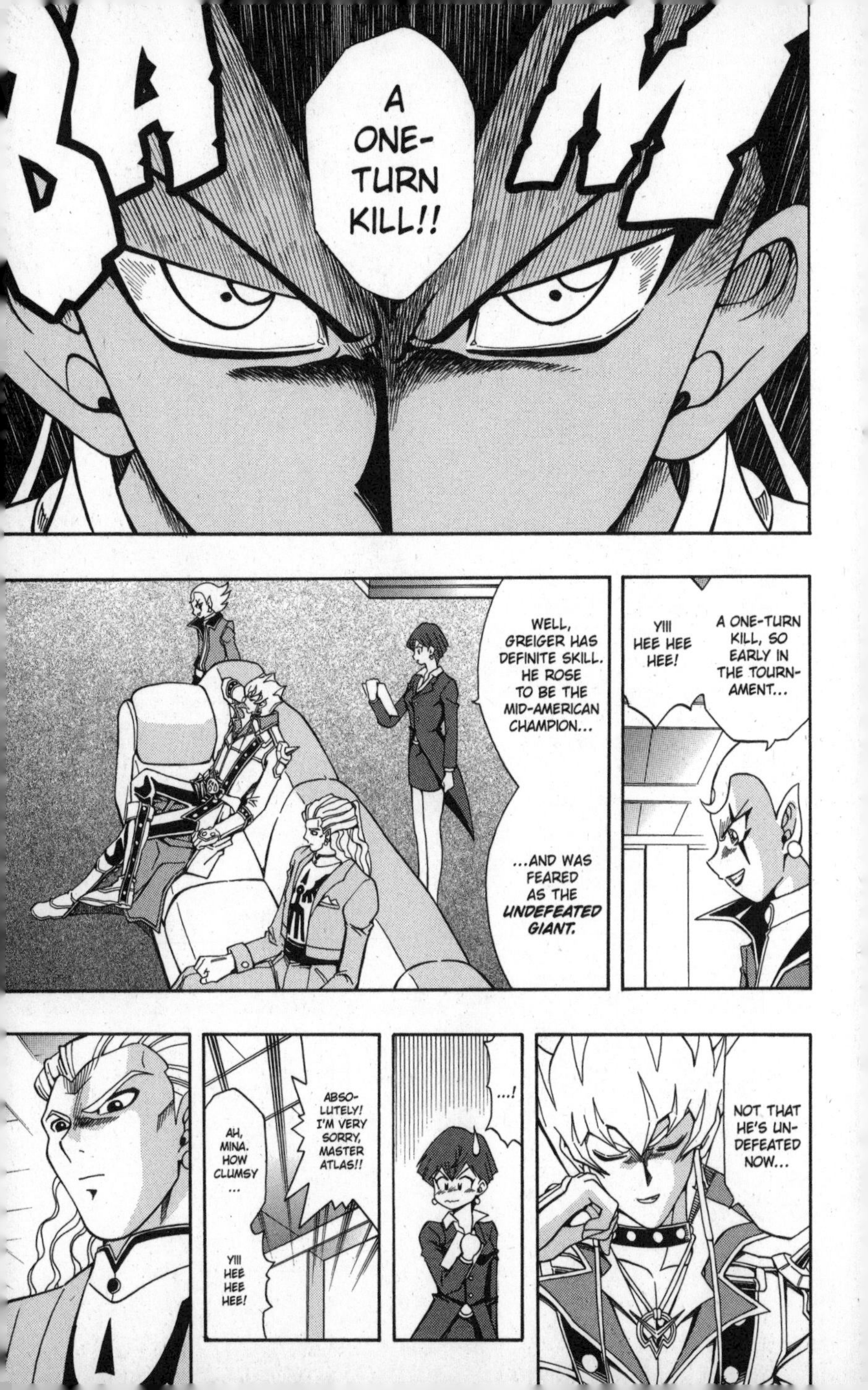
A ONE-TURN KILL!!
A ONE-TURN KILL, SO EARLY IN THE TOURNAMENT...
YIII HEE HEE HEE!
WELL, GREIGER HAS DEFINITE SKILL. HE ROSE TO BE THE MID-AMERICAN CHAMPION...
...AND WAS FEARED AS THE *UNDEFEATED GIANT.*
NOT THAT HE'S UN-DEFEATED NOW...
...!
ABSO-LUTELY! I'M VERY SORRY, MASTER ATLAS!!
AH, MINA. HOW CLUMSY...
YIII HEE HEE HEE!

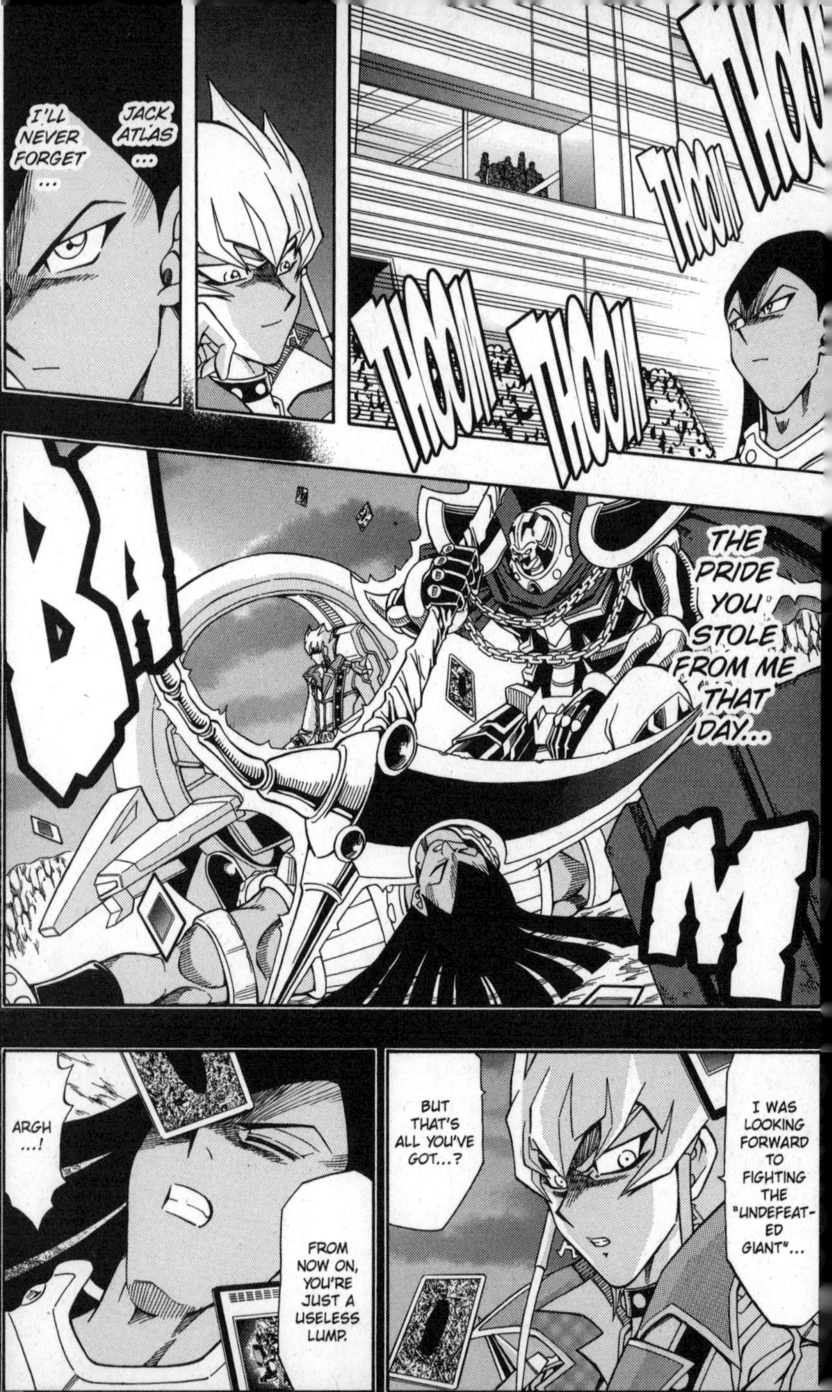
THOOM THOOM
THOOM
THOOM
JACK ATLAS...
I'LL NEVER FORGET...
THE PRIDE YOU STOLE FROM ME THAT DAY...
BAM
I WAS LOOKING FORWARD TO FIGHTING THE "UNDEFEAT-ED GIANT"...
BUT THAT'S ALL YOU'VE GOT...?
FROM NOW ON, YOU'RE JUST A USELESS LUMP.
ARGH...!

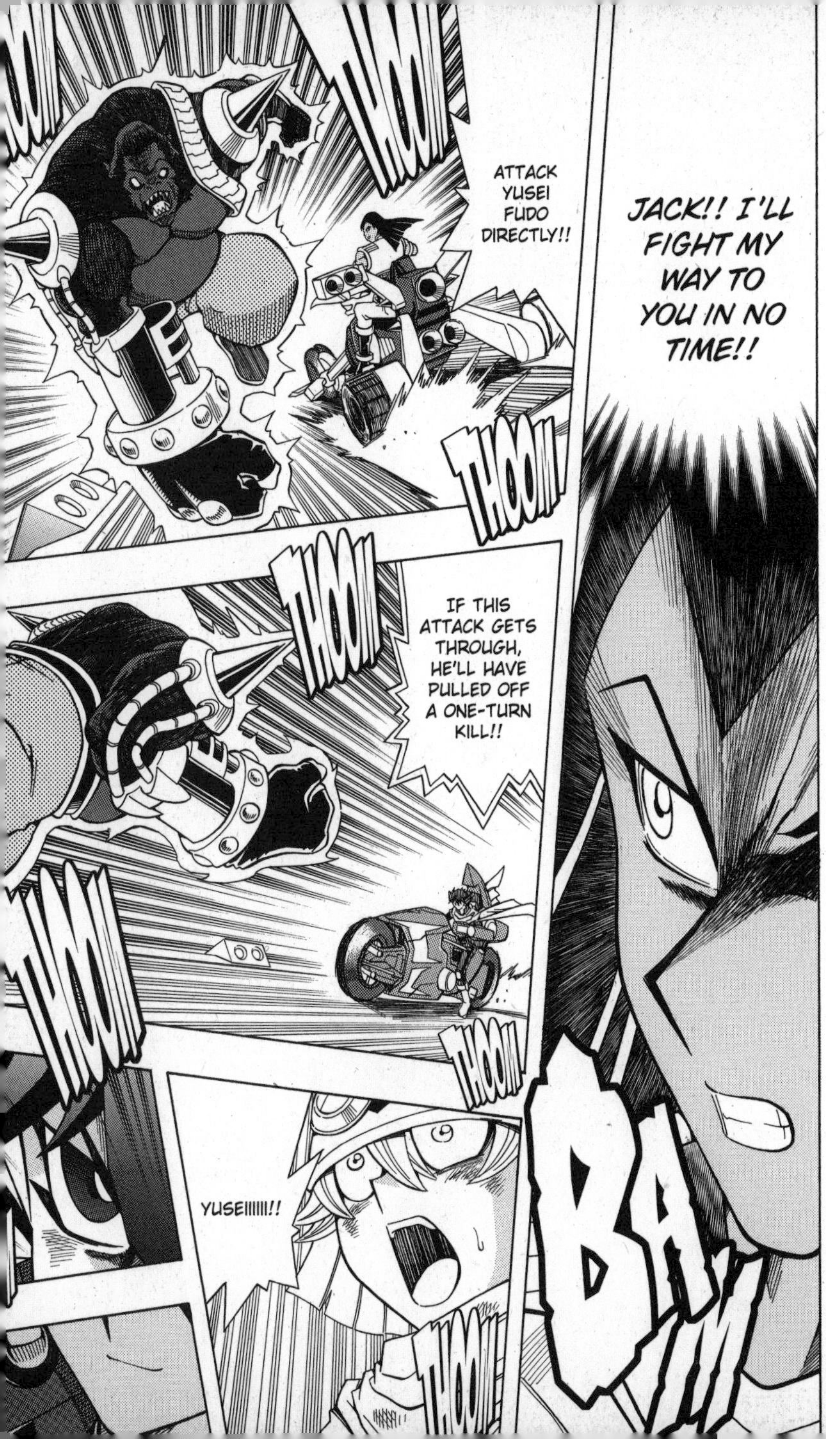
JACK!! I'LL FIGHT MY WAY TO YOU IN NO TIME!!
BAM
THOOM
THOOM
ATTACK YUSEI FUDO DIRECTLY!!
THOOM
THOOM
IF THIS ATTACK GETS THROUGH, HE'LL HAVE PULLED OFF A ONE-TURN KILL!!
THOOM
THOOM
YUSEIIIIII!!

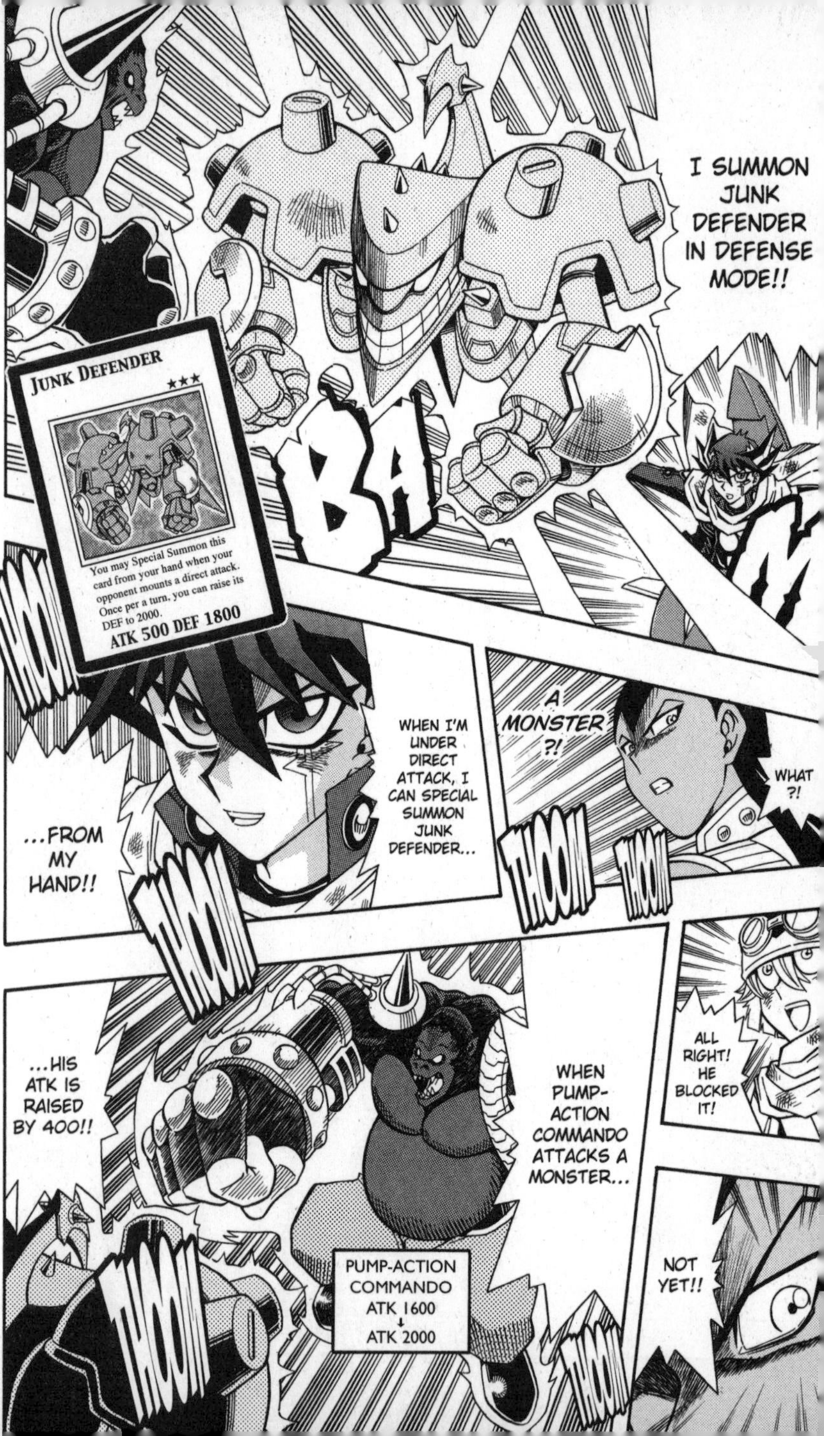
I SUMMON JUNK DEFENDER IN DEFENSE MODE!!
BA
JUNK DEFENDER
★★★
You may Special Summon this card from your hand when your opponent mounts a direct attack. Once per a turn, you can raise its DEF to 2000.
ATK 500 DEF 1800
THOOM
A MONSTER ?!
WHAT ?!
THOOM
THOOM
WHEN I'M UNDER DIRECT ATTACK, I CAN SPECIAL SUMMON JUNK DEFENDER...
...FROM MY HAND!!
THOOM
ALL RIGHT! HE BLOCKED IT!
NOT YET!!
WHEN PUMP-ACTION COMMANDO ATTACKS A MONSTER...
...HIS ATK IS RAISED BY 400!!
PUMP-ACTION COMMANDO ATK 1600 ↓ ATK 2000
THOOM
THOOM

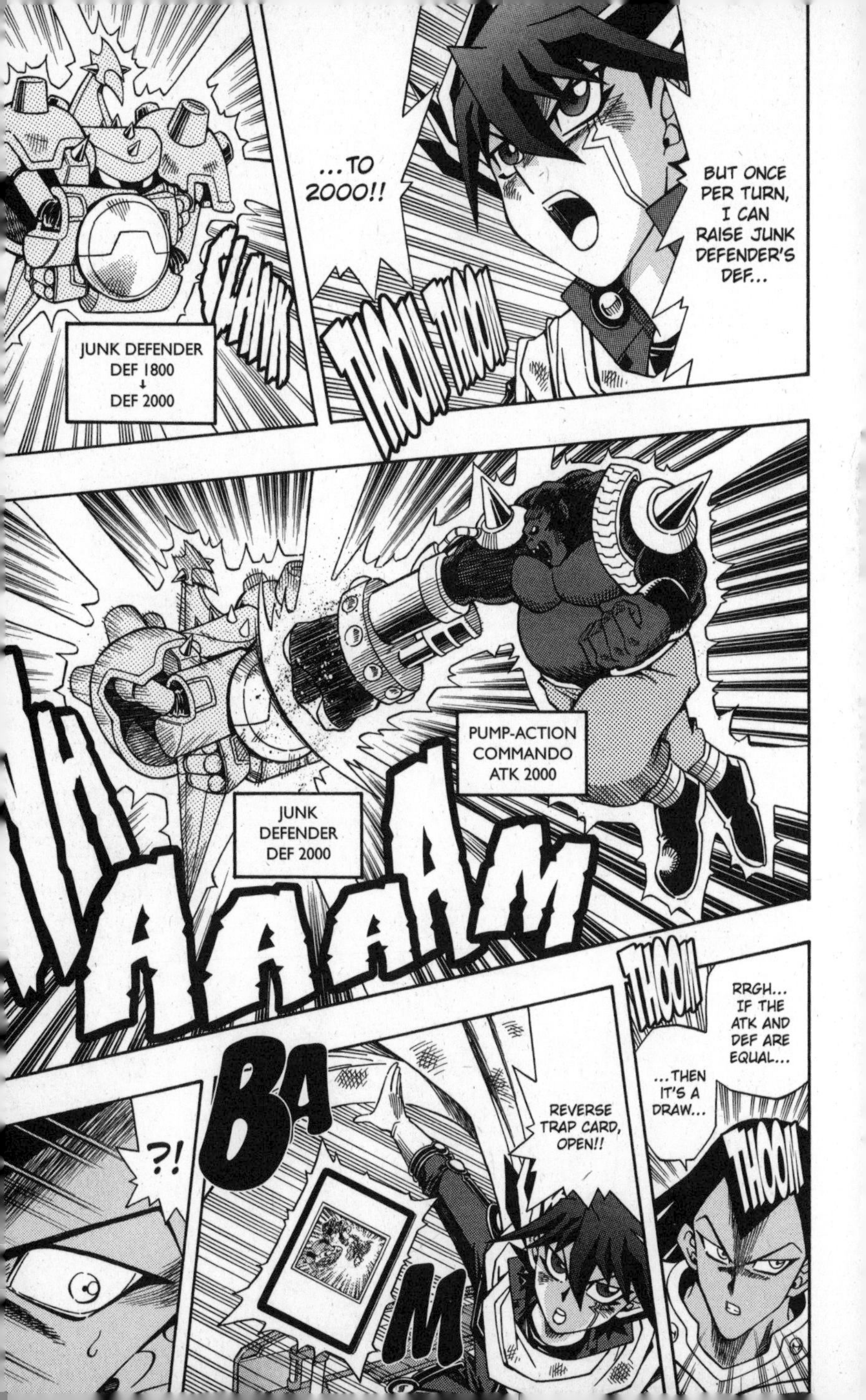
BUT ONCE PER TURN, I CAN RAISE JUNK DEFENDER'S DEF...
...TO 2000!!
THOOM THOOM
CLANK
JUNK DEFENDER
DEF 1800
↓
DEF 2000
PUMP-ACTION COMMANDO ATK 2000
JUNK DEFENDER DEF 2000
AAAM
THOOM
RRGH... IF THE ATK AND DEF ARE EQUAL...
...THEN IT'S A DRAW...
THOOM
REVERSE TRAP CARD, OPEN!!
BAM
?!

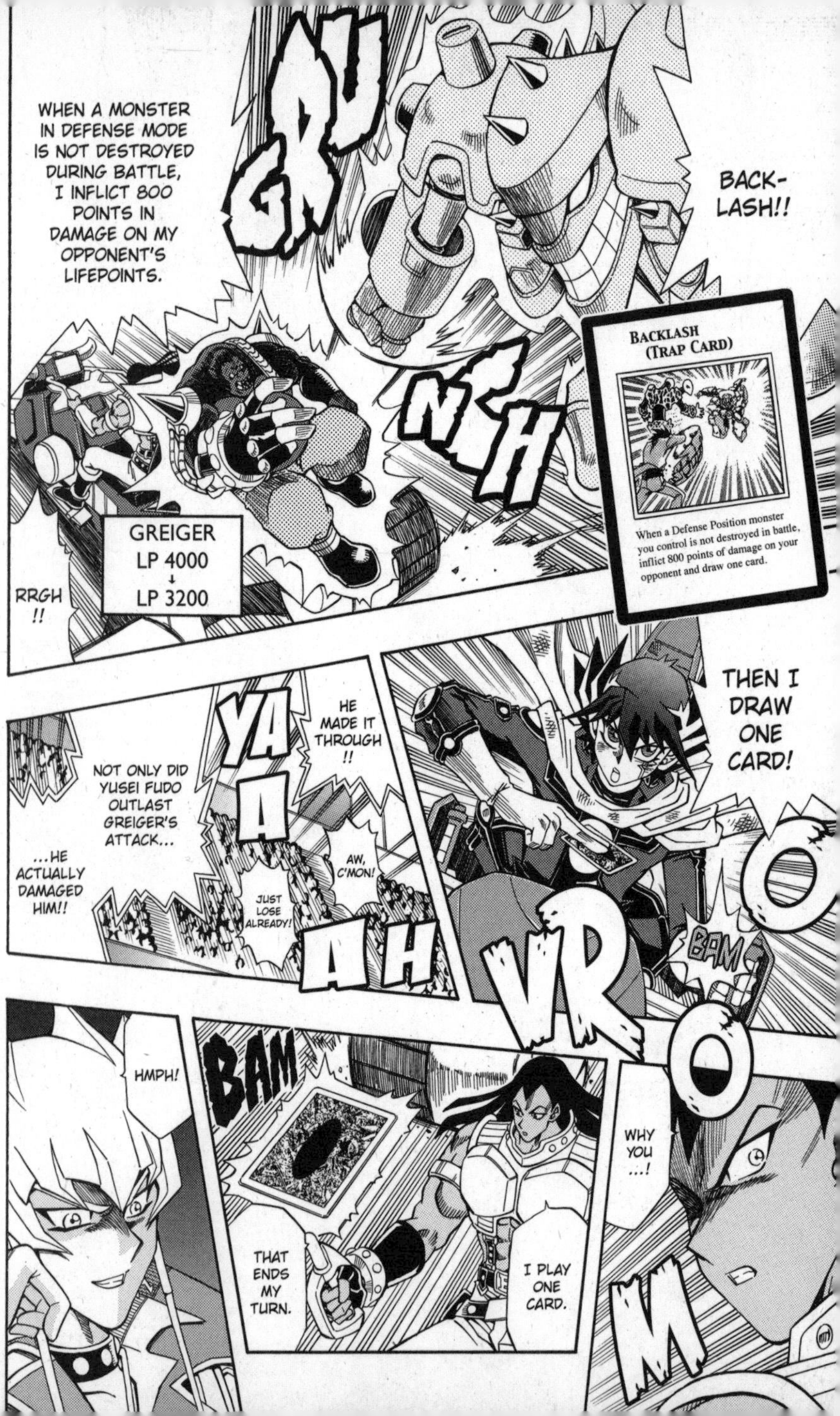

BACK-LASH!!
BACKLASH (TRAP CARD)
When a Defense Position monster you control is not destroyed in battle, inflict 800 points of damage on your opponent and draw one card.
N'H
GRU GR
WHEN A MONSTER IN DEFENSE MODE IS NOT DESTROYED DURING BATTLE, I INFLICT 800 POINTS IN DAMAGE ON MY OPPONENT'S LIFEPOINTS.
GREIGER LP 4000 ↓ LP 3200
RRGH !!
THEN I DRAW ONE CARD!
VROOM
BAM
HE MADE IT THROUGH !!
YAAAH
NOT ONLY DID YUSEI FUDO OUTLAST GREIGER'S ATTACK...
AW, C'MON!
JUST LOSE ALREADY!
...HE ACTUALLY DAMAGED HIM!!
WHY YOU ...!
M
BAM
I PLAY ONE CARD.
THAT ENDS MY TURN.
HMPH!

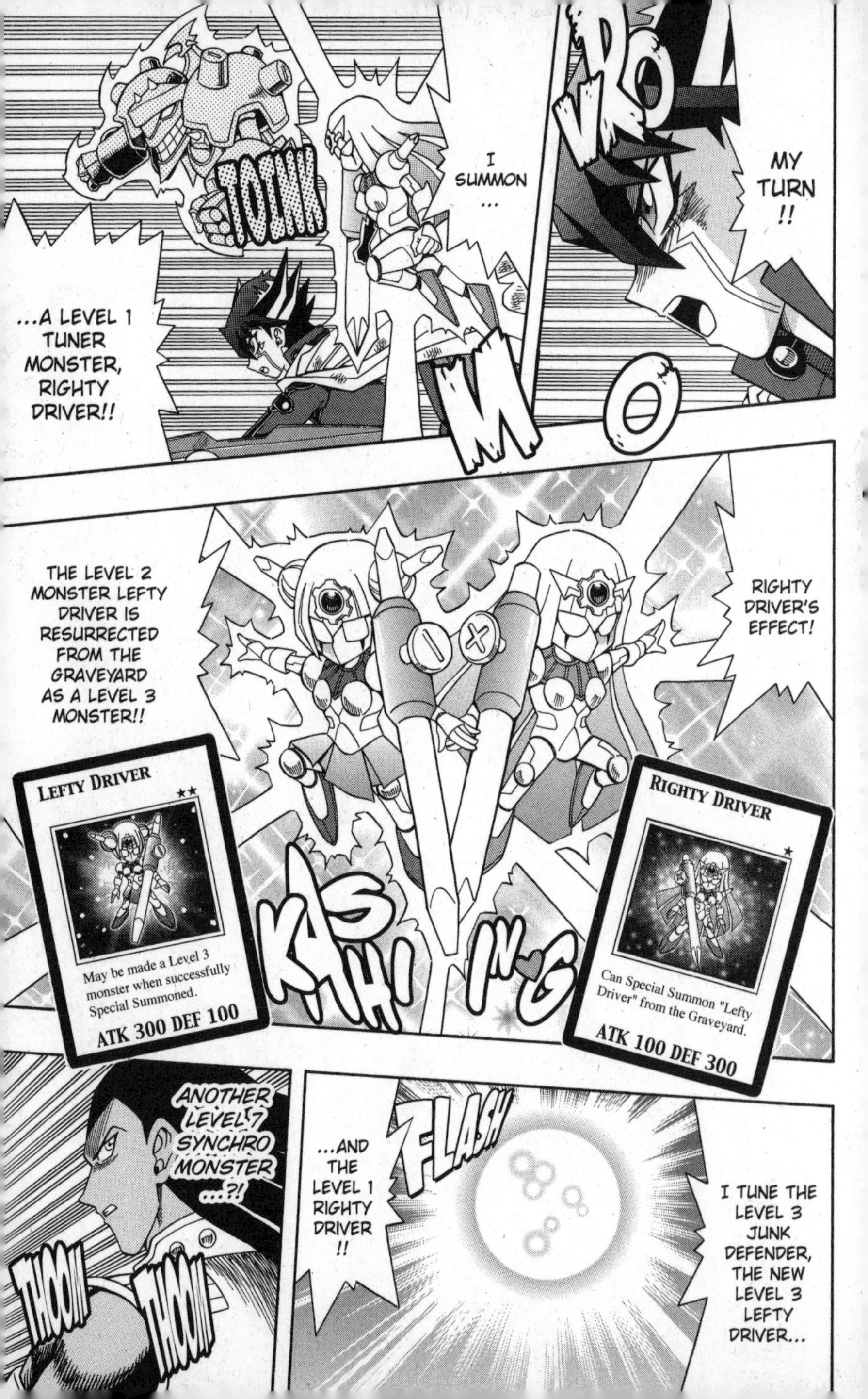
MY TURN !!
I SUMMON ...
TOINK
...A LEVEL 1 TUNER MONSTER, RIGHTY DRIVER!!
RIGHTY DRIVER'S EFFECT!
THE LEVEL 2 MONSTER LEFTY DRIVER IS RESURRECTED FROM THE GRAVEYARD AS A LEVEL 3 MONSTER!!
RIGHTY DRIVER
Can Special Summon "Lefty Driver" from the Graveyard.
ATK 100 DEF 300
LEFTY DRIVER
May be made a Level 3 monster when successfully Special Summoned.
ATK 300 DEF 100
I TUNE THE LEVEL 3 JUNK DEFENDER, THE NEW LEVEL 3 LEFTY DRIVER...
FLASH
...AND THE LEVEL 1 RIGHTY DRIVER !!
ANOTHER LEVEL 7 SYNCHRO MONSTER ...?!
THOOM
THOOM

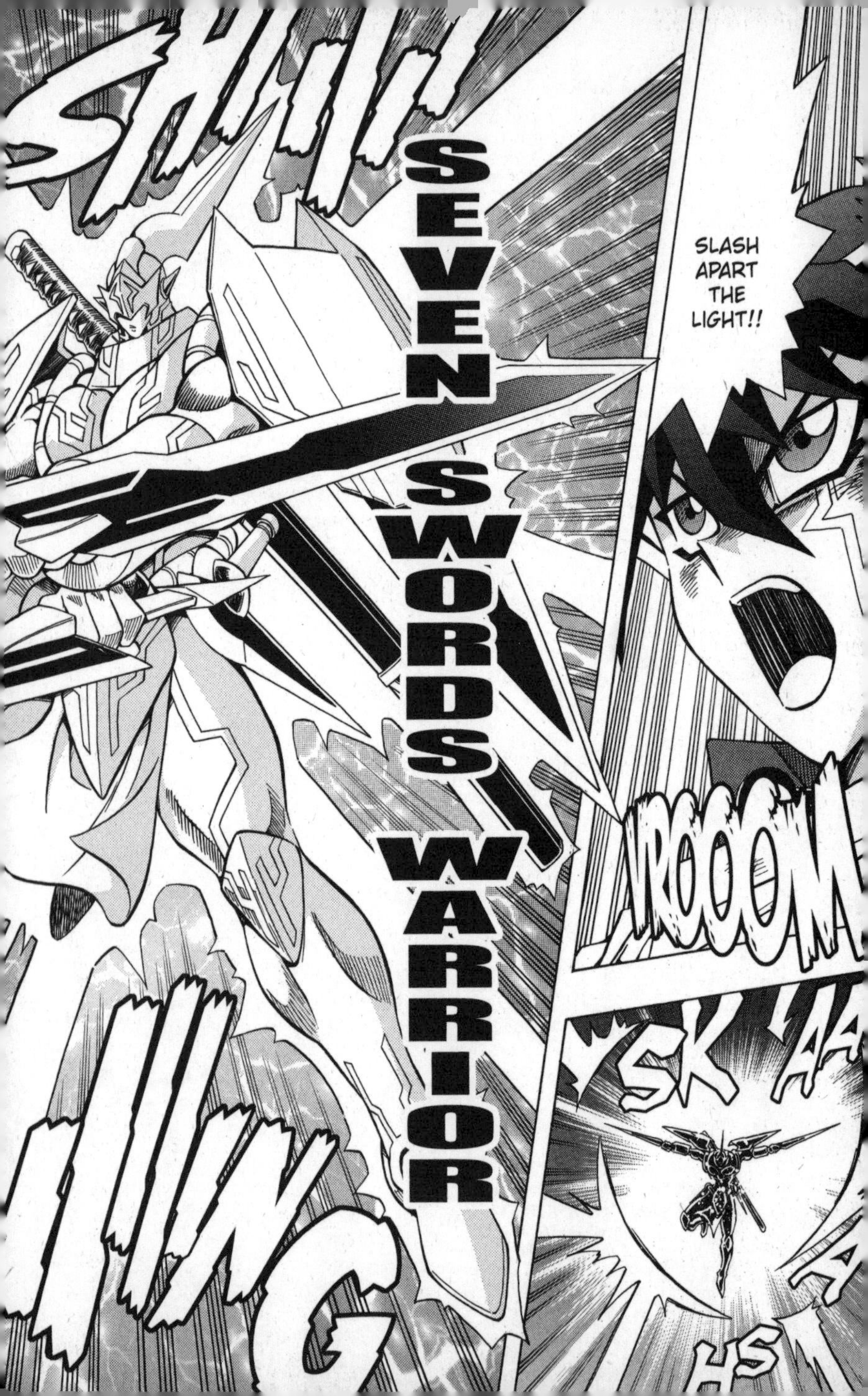
SLASH APART THE LIGHT!!
VROOOM
SK
HS
SEVEN SWORDS WARRIOR

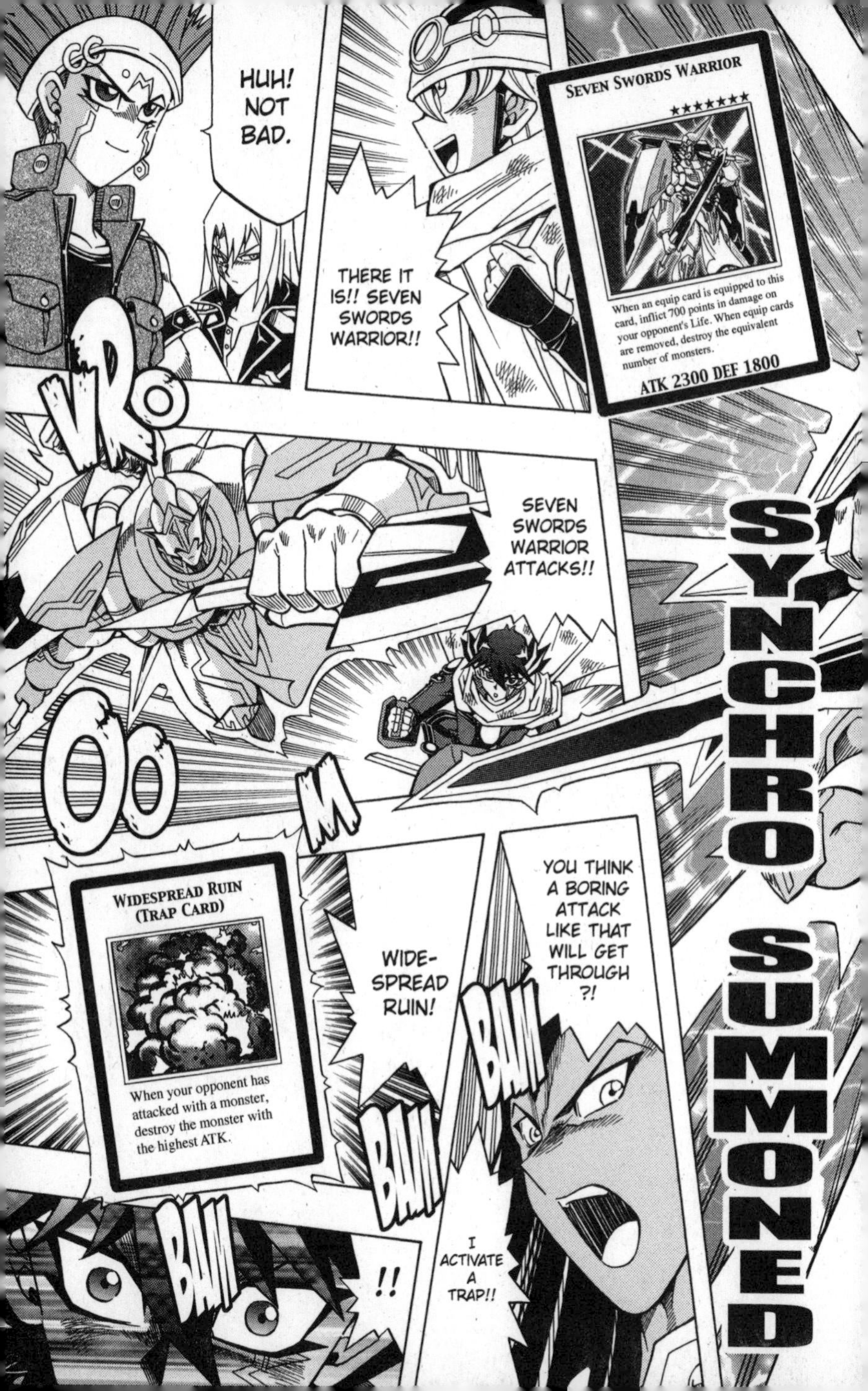
SYNCHRO SUMMONED
THERE IT IS!! SEVEN SWORDS WARRIOR!!
SEVEN SWORDS WARRIOR
★★★★★★★
When an equip card is equipped to this card, inflict 700 points in damage on your opponent's Life. When equip cards are removed, destroy the equivalent number of monsters.
ATK 2300 DEF 1800
HUH! NOT BAD.
SEVEN SWORDS WARRIOR ATTACKS!!
VROOOM
YOU THINK A BORING ATTACK LIKE THAT WILL GET THROUGH ?!
BAM
I ACTIVATE A TRAP!!
BAM
WIDE-SPREAD RUIN!
WIDESPREAD RUIN (TRAP CARD)
When your opponent has attacked with a monster, destroy the monster with the highest ATK.
BAM
!!

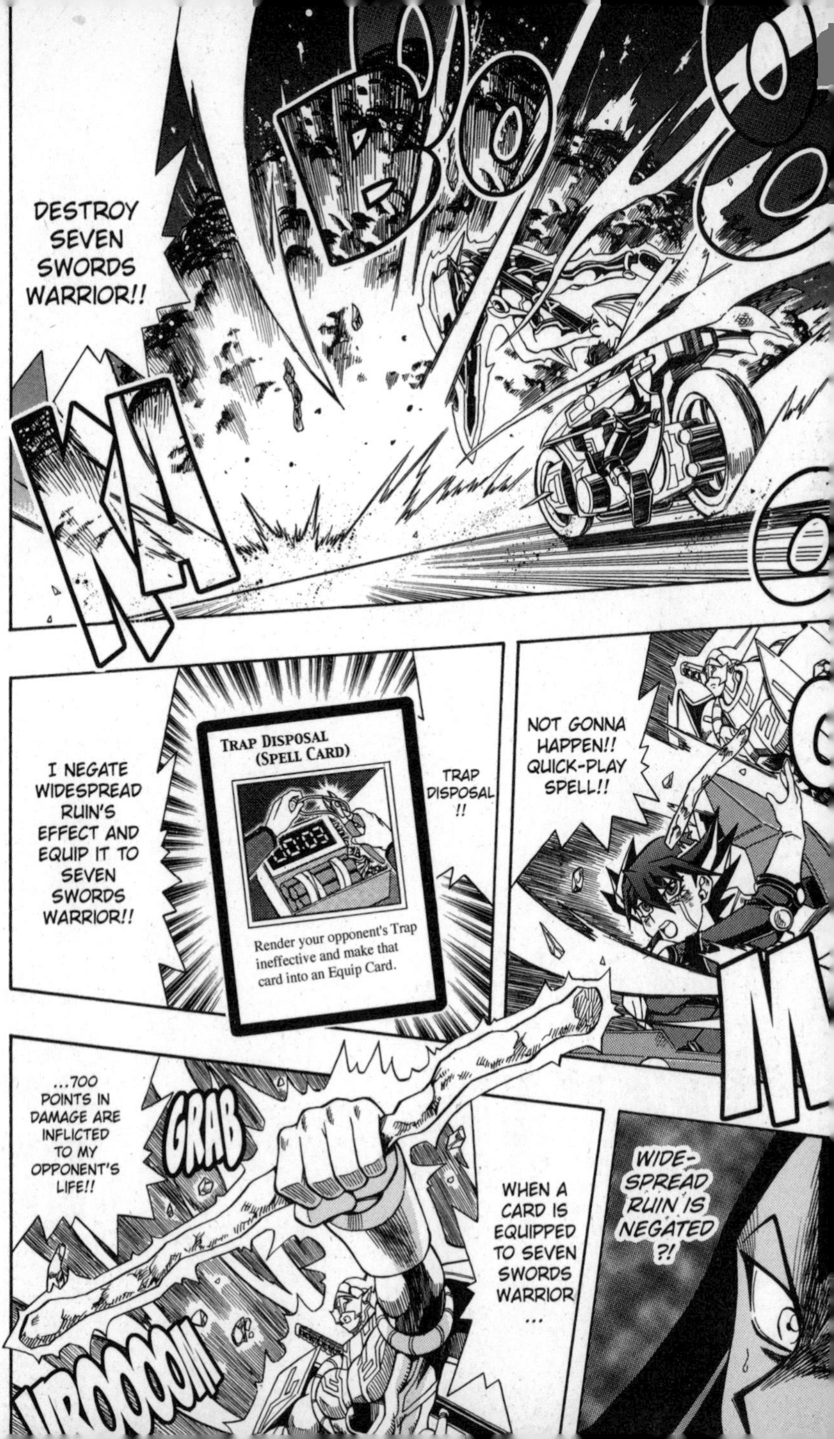
DESTROY SEVEN SWORDS WARRIOR!!
NOT GONNA HAPPEN!! QUICK-PLAY SPELL!!
TRAP DISPOSAL!!
TRAP DISPOSAL (SPELL CARD)
Render your opponent's Trap ineffective and make that card into an Equip Card.
I NEGATE WIDESPREAD RUIN'S EFFECT AND EQUIP IT TO SEVEN SWORDS WARRIOR!!
WIDE-SPREAD RUIN IS NEGATED?!
WHEN A CARD IS EQUIPPED TO SEVEN SWORDS WARRIOR...
GRAB
...700 POINTS IN DAMAGE ARE INFLICTED TO MY OPPONENT'S LIFE!!

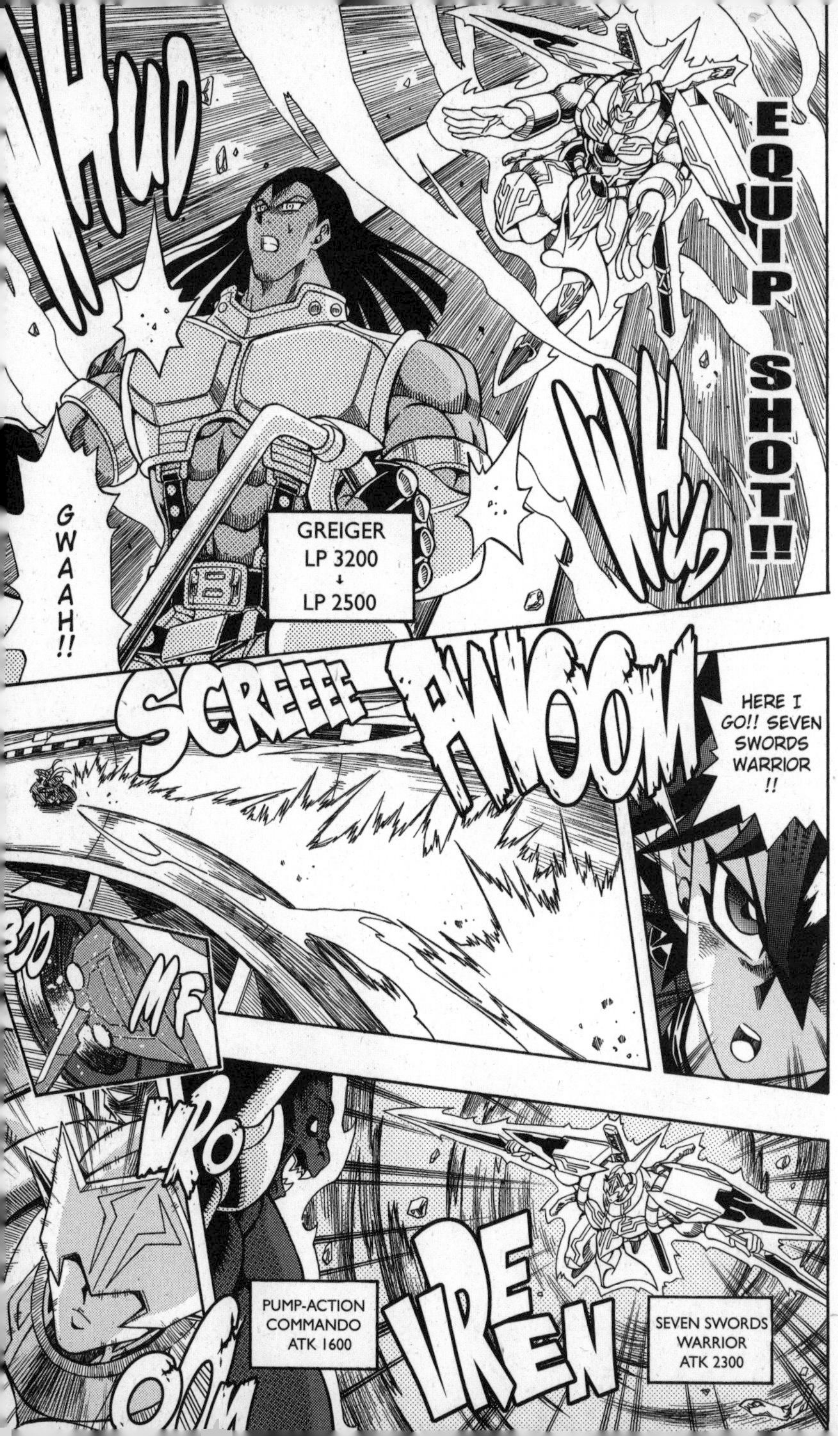
EQUIP SHOT!!
WHUD
WHUD
GREIGER
LP 3200
↓
LP 2500
GWAAAH!!
HERE I GO!! SEVEN SWORDS WARRIOR !!
AWOOM
SCREEEE
SEVEN SWORDS WARRIOR
ATK 2300
VREEN
PUMP-ACTION COMMANDO
ATK 1600

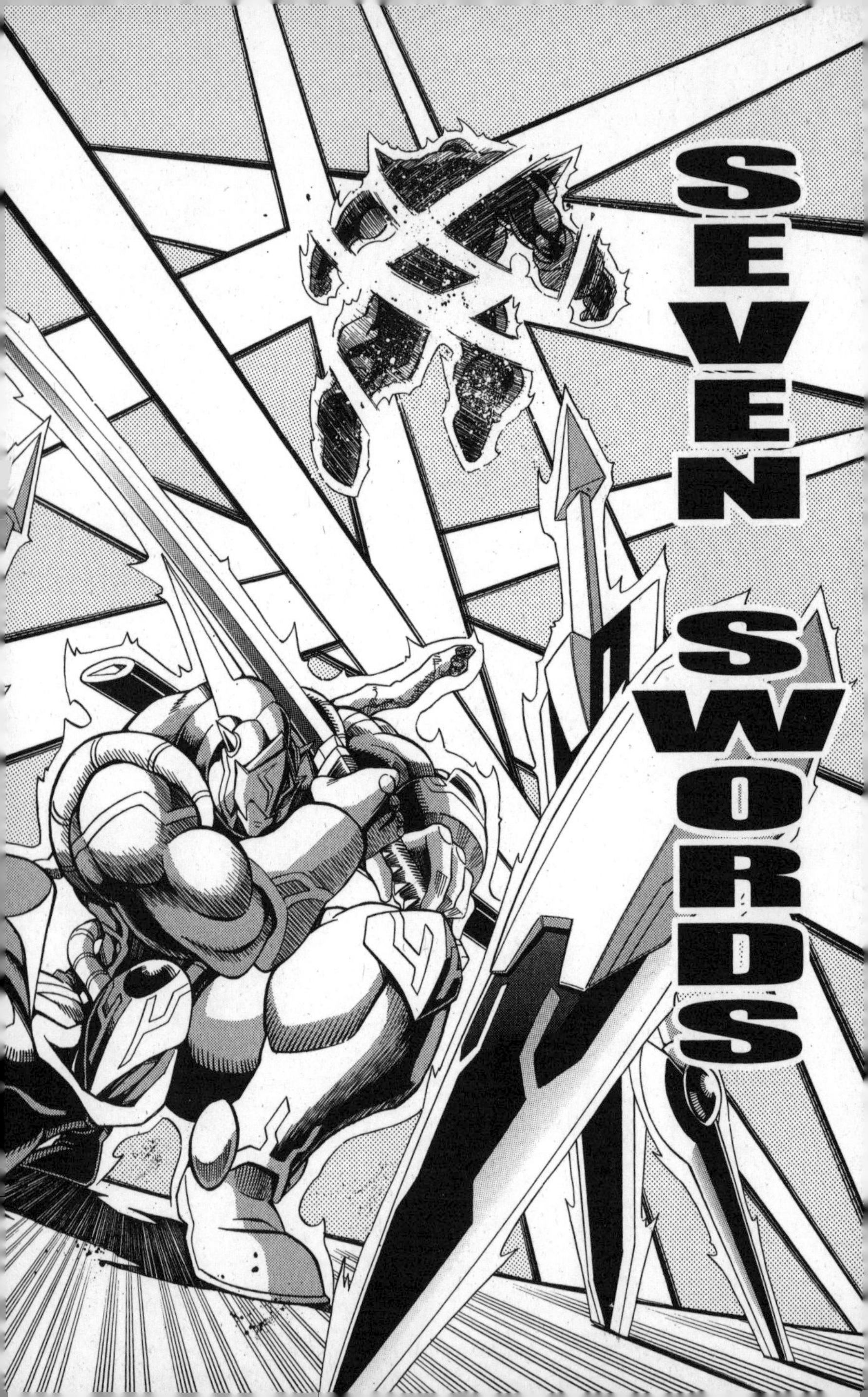
SEVEN SWORDS

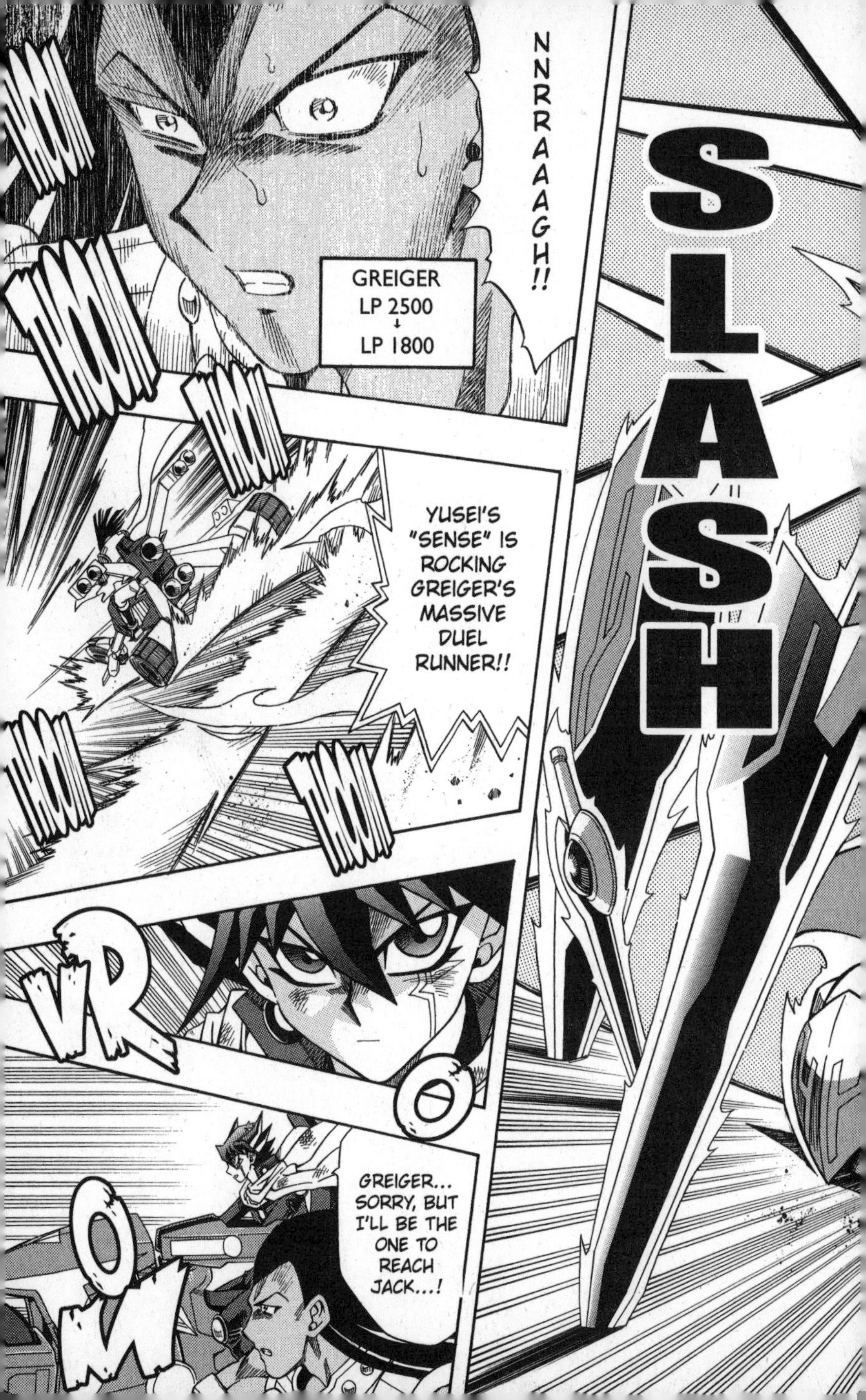
SLASH
NNRRAAAAGH!!
GREIGER
LP 2500
↓
LP 1800
THOOM
THOOM
THOOM
YUSEI'S "SENSE" IS ROCKING GREIGER'S MASSIVE DUEL RUNNER!!
THOOM
THOOM
VR
O
O
M
GREIGER... SORRY, BUT I'LL BE THE ONE TO REACH JACK...!

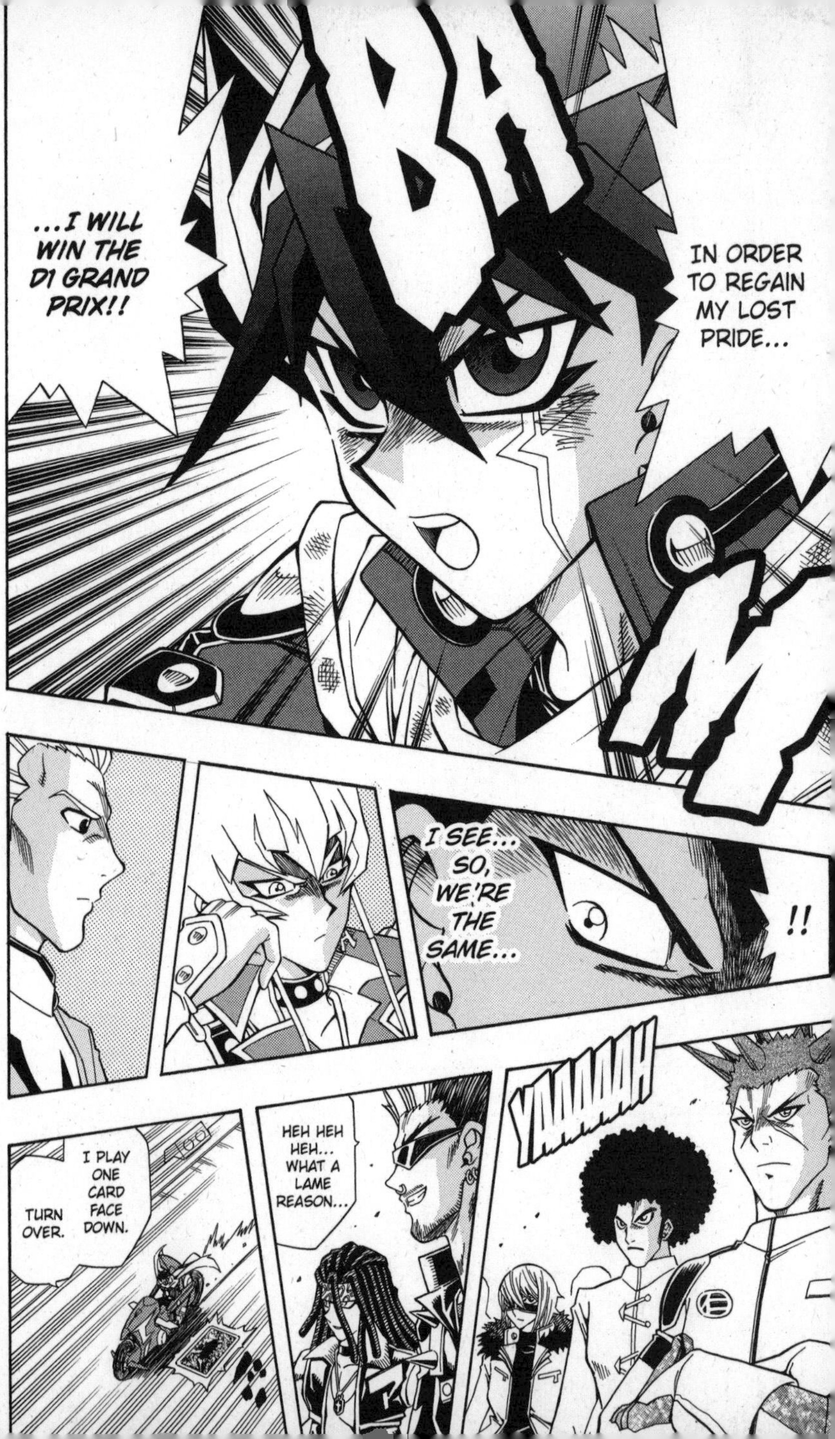
BAM
IN ORDER TO REGAIN MY LOST PRIDE...
...I WILL WIN THE D1 GRAND PRIX!!
!!
I SEE... SO, WE'RE THE SAME...
YAAAAAH
HEH HEH HEH... WHAT A LAME REASON...
I PLAY ONE CARD FACE DOWN.
TURN OVER.

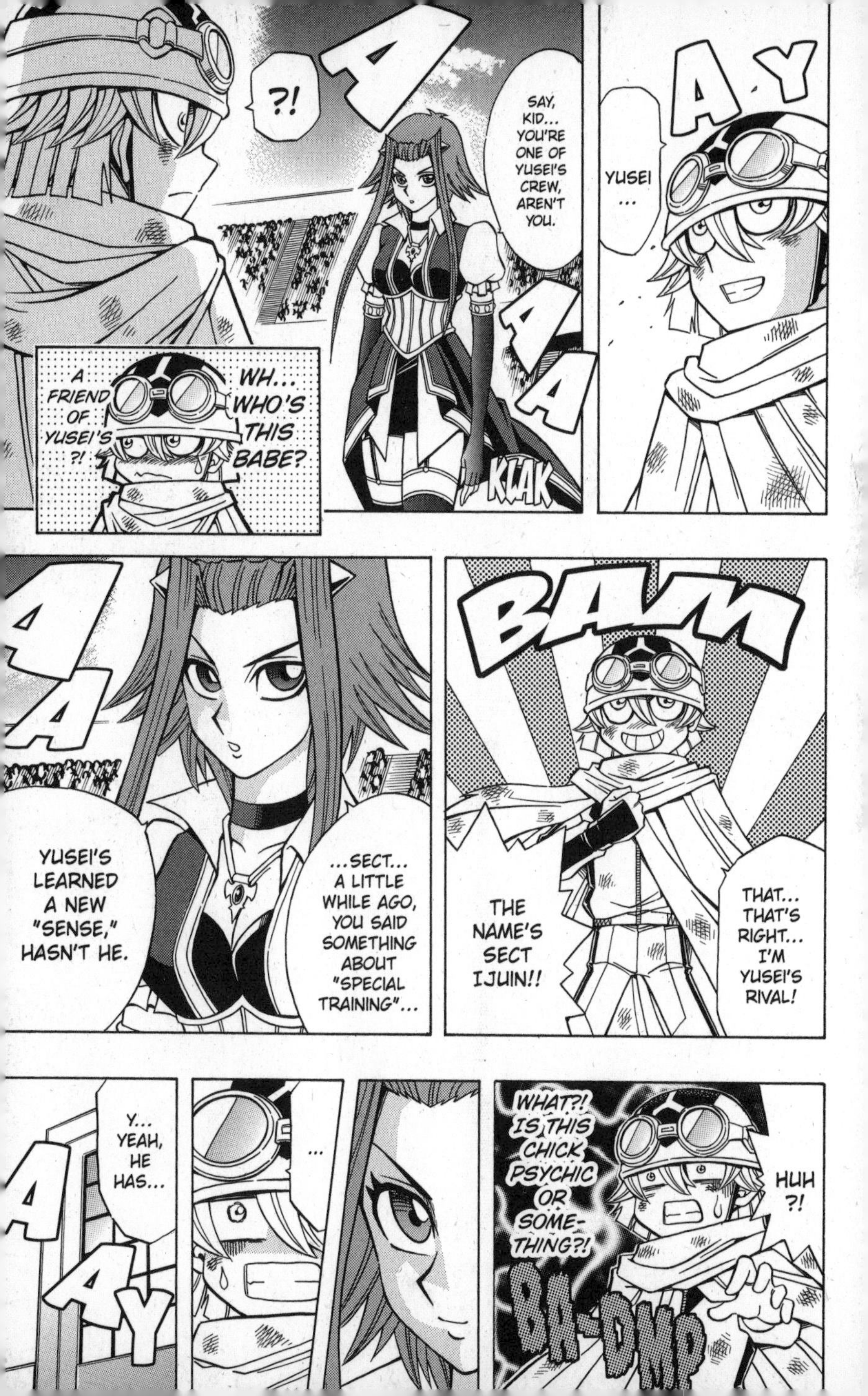
A Y
YUSEI ...
SAY, KID... YOU'RE ONE OF YUSEI'S CREW, AREN'T YOU.
A
A
KLAK
A
?!
WH... WHO'S THIS BABE?
A FRIEND OF YUSEI'S ?!
BAM
THAT... THAT'S RIGHT... I'M YUSEI'S RIVAL!
THE NAME'S SECT IJUIN!!
A
A
...SECT... A LITTLE WHILE AGO, YOU SAID SOMETHING ABOUT "SPECIAL TRAINING"...
YUSEI'S LEARNED A NEW "SENSE," HASN'T HE.
HUH ?!
WHAT?! IS THIS CHICK PSYCHIC OR SOMETHING?!
BA-DMP
...
Y... YEAH, HE HAS...
A
A
Y

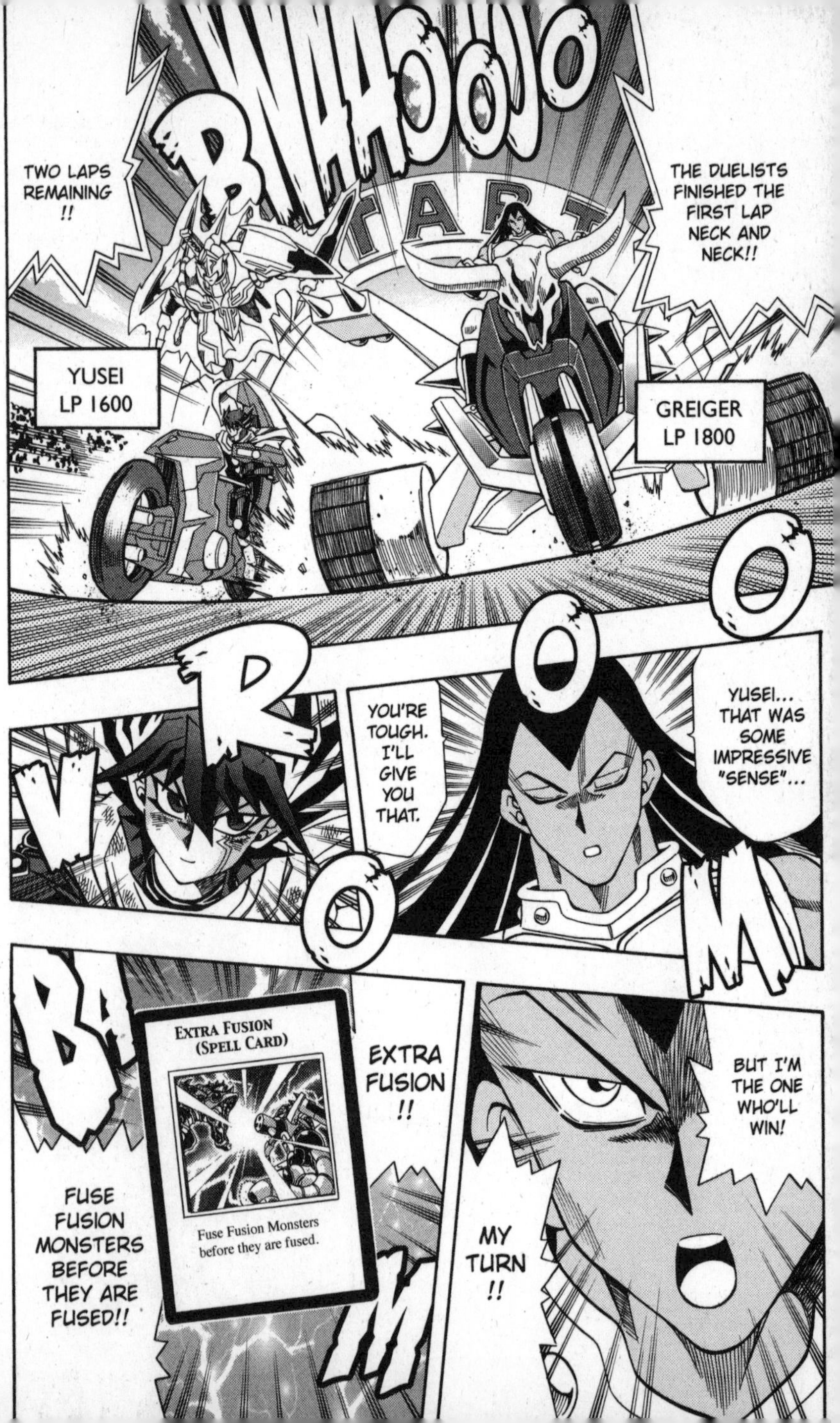
THE DUELISTS FINISHED THE FIRST LAP NECK AND NECK!!
TWO LAPS REMAINING!!
GREIGER LP 1800
YUSEI LP 1600
YUSEI... THAT WAS SOME IMPRESSIVE "SENSE"...
YOU'RE TOUGH. I'LL GIVE YOU THAT.
VROOOM
BUT I'M THE ONE WHO'LL WIN!
MY TURN!!
EXTRA FUSION!!
EXTRA FUSION (SPELL CARD)
Fuse Fusion Monsters before they are fused.
FUSE FUSION MONSTERS BEFORE THEY ARE FUSED!!
BAM

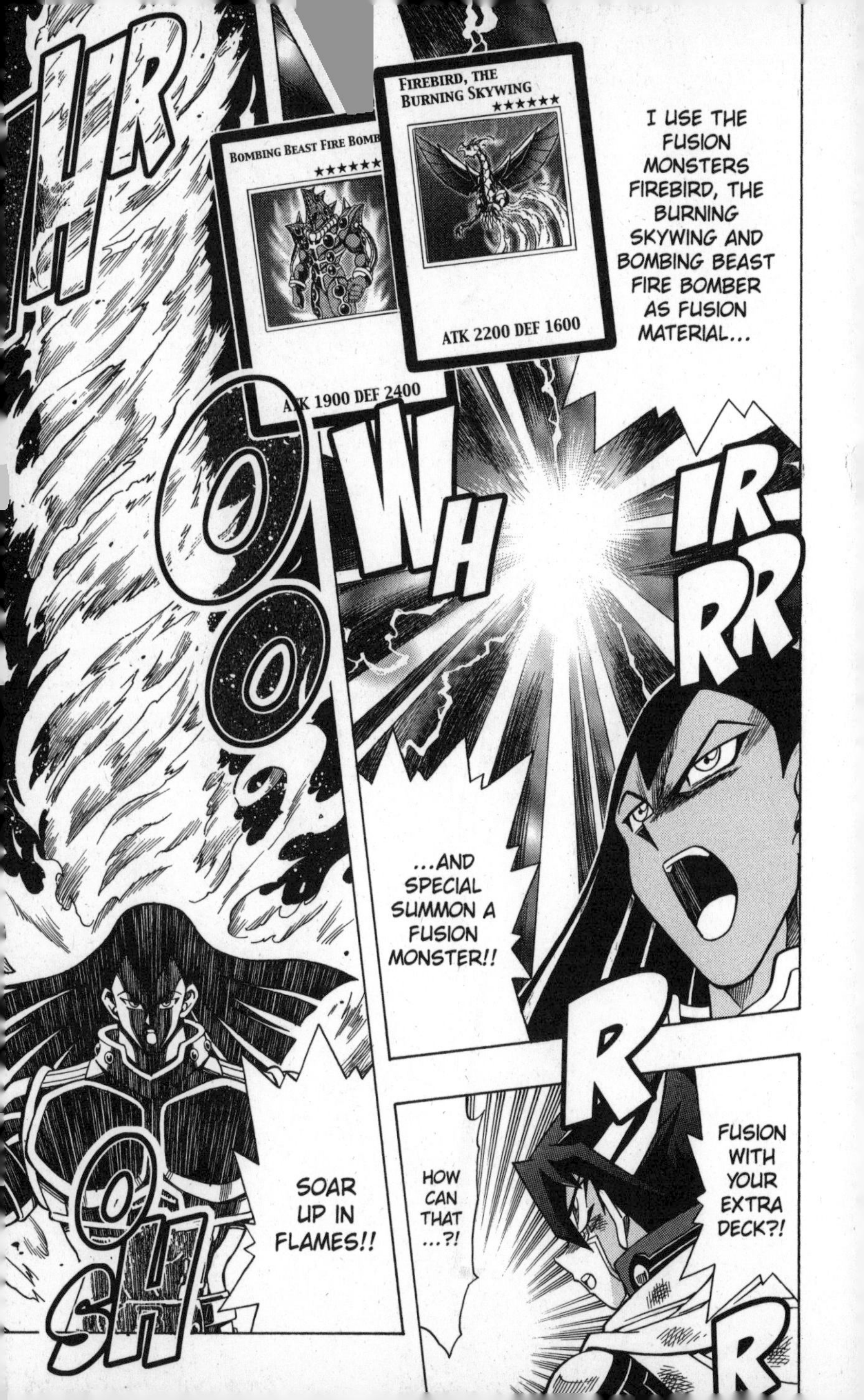
I USE THE FUSION MONSTERS FIREBIRD, THE BURNING SKYWING AND BOMBING BEAST FIRE BOMBER AS FUSION MATERIAL...
FIREBIRD, THE BURNING SKYWING
ATK 2200 DEF 1600
BOMBING BEAST FIRE BOMB
ATK 1900 DEF 2400
WHOOO
IR-RRR
...AND SPECIAL SUMMON A FUSION MONSTER!!
R
FUSION WITH YOUR EXTRA DECK?!
HOW CAN THAT ...?!
SOAR UP IN FLAMES!!
OSH
R

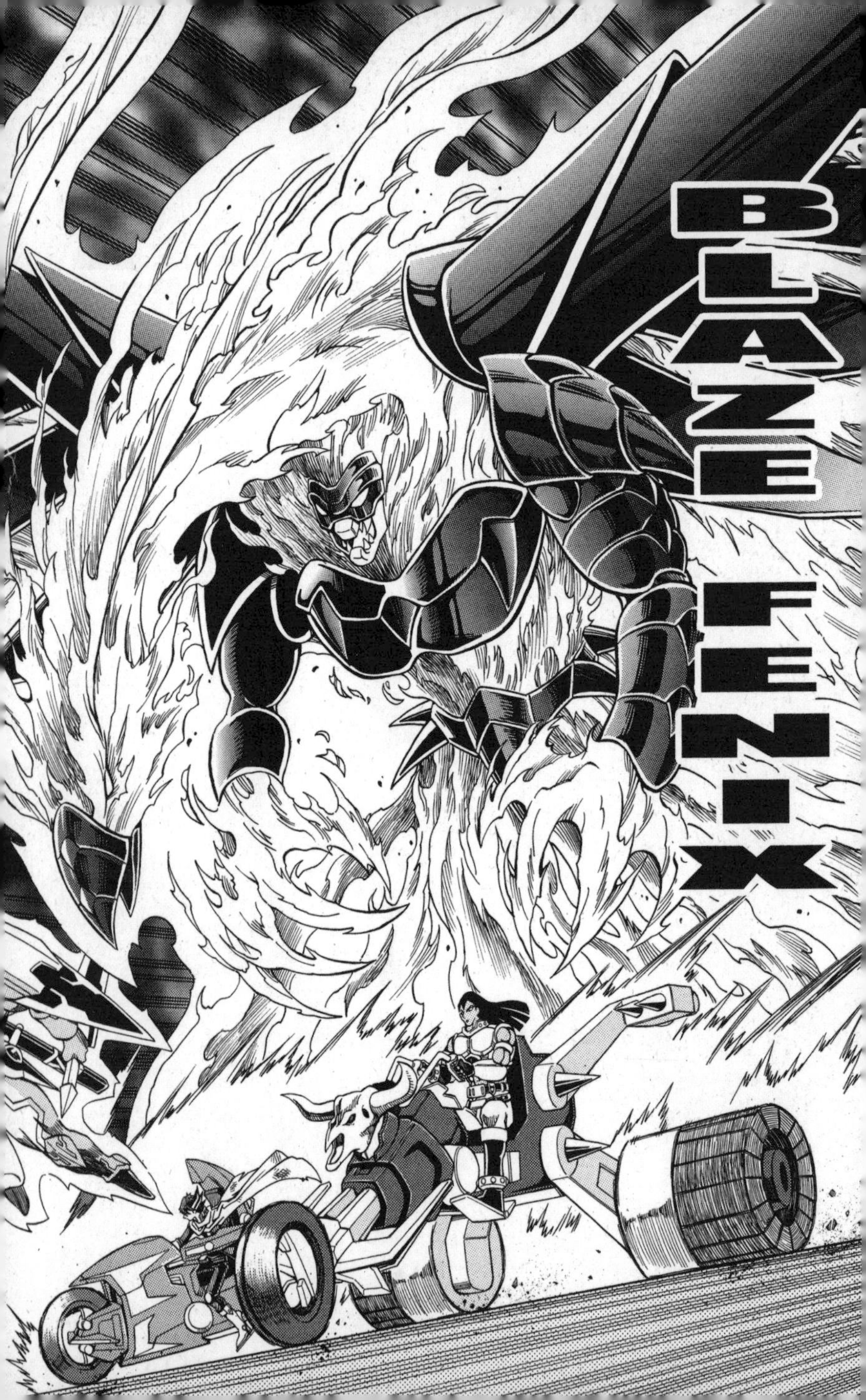
BLAZE FENIX

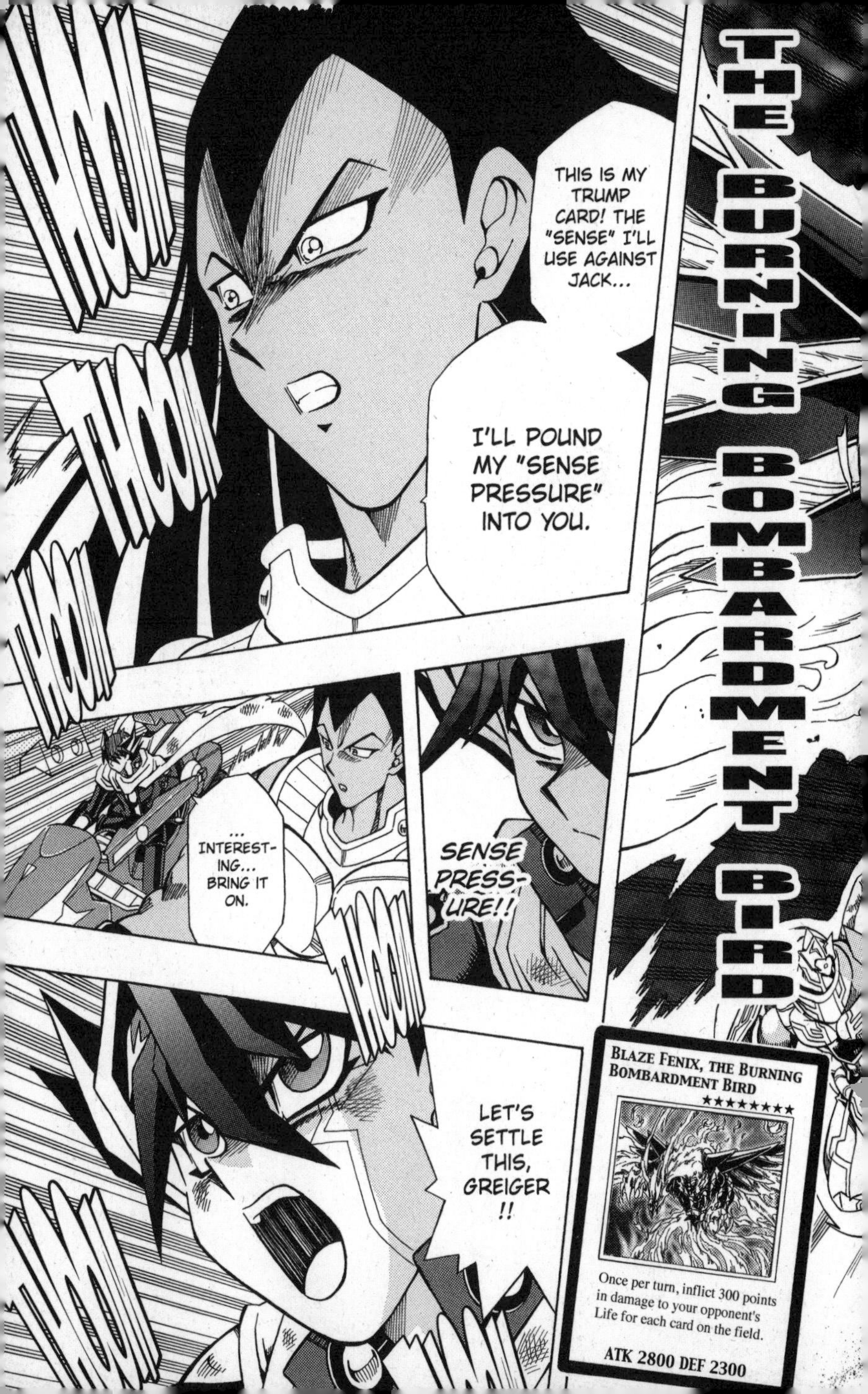
THE BURNING BOMBARDMENT BIRD
BLAZE FENIX, THE BURNING BOMBARDMENT BIRD
★★★★★★★★
Once per turn, inflict 300 points in damage to your opponent's Life for each card on the field.
ATK 2800 DEF 2300
THOOM
THOOM
THOOM
THIS IS MY TRUMP CARD! THE "SENSE" I'LL USE AGAINST JACK...
I'LL POUND MY "SENSE PRESSURE" INTO YOU.
SENSE PRESS-URE!!
... INTEREST-ING... BRING IT ON.
THOOM
LET'S SETTLE THIS, GREIGER!!
THOOM

5D's TRACKS BY SATOMASA

THE 10TH

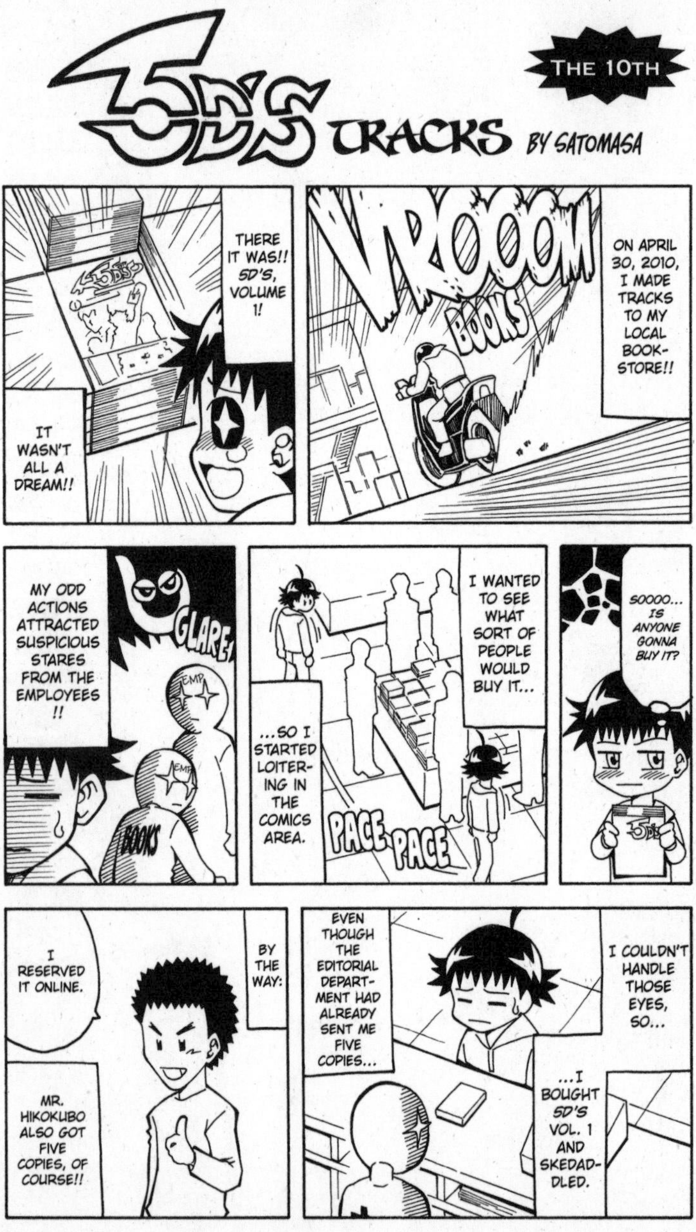
ON APRIL 30, 2010, I MADE TRACKS TO MY LOCAL BOOK-STORE!!
VROOOM
BOOKS
THERE IT WAS!! *5D'S*, VOLUME 1!
IT WASN'T ALL A DREAM!!
SOOOO... IS ANYONE GONNA BUY IT?
I WANTED TO SEE WHAT SORT OF PEOPLE WOULD BUY IT...
...SO I STARTED LOITER-ING IN THE COMICS AREA.
PACE PACE
MY ODD ACTIONS ATTRACTED SUSPICIOUS STARES FROM THE EMPLOYEES!!
GLARE
BOOKS
I COULDN'T HANDLE THOSE EYES, SO...
EVEN THOUGH THE EDITORIAL DEPART-MENT HAD ALREADY SENT ME FIVE COPIES...
...I BOUGHT *5D'S* VOL. 1 AND SKEDAD-DLED.
BY THE WAY:
I RESERVED IT ONLINE.
MR. HIKOKUBO ALSO GOT FIVE COPIES, OF COURSE!!

RIDE-11
SENSE VS. SENSE!!

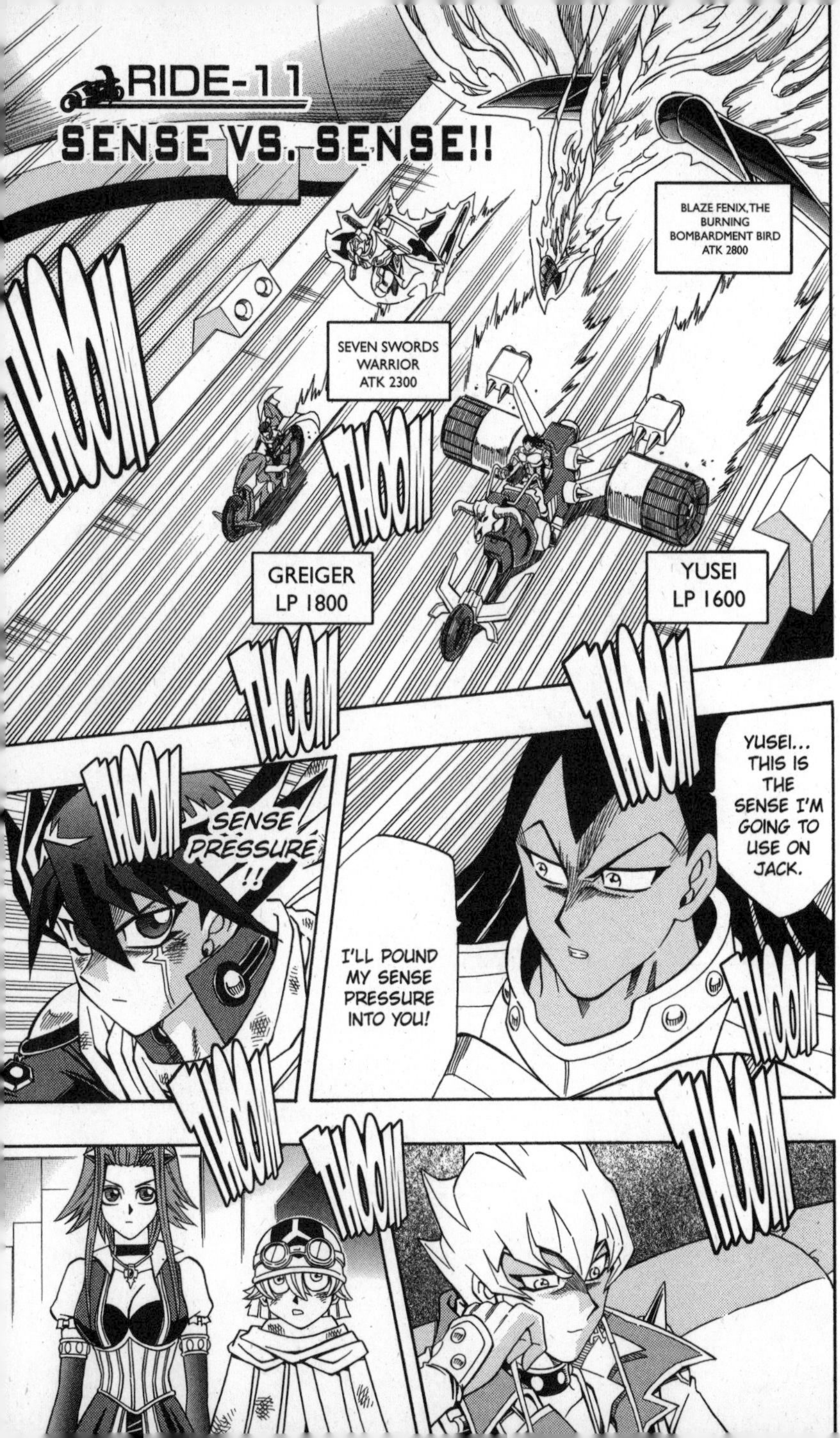
BLAZE FENIX, THE BURNING BOMBARDMENT BIRD ATK 2800
SEVEN SWORDS WARRIOR ATK 2300
THOOM
THOOM
YUSEI LP 1600
GREIGER LP 1800
THOOM
THOOM
YUSEI... THIS IS THE SENSE I'M GOING TO USE ON JACK.
I'LL POUND MY SENSE PRESSURE INTO YOU!
THOOM
THOOM
SENSE PRESSURE!!
THOOM
THOOM
THOOM

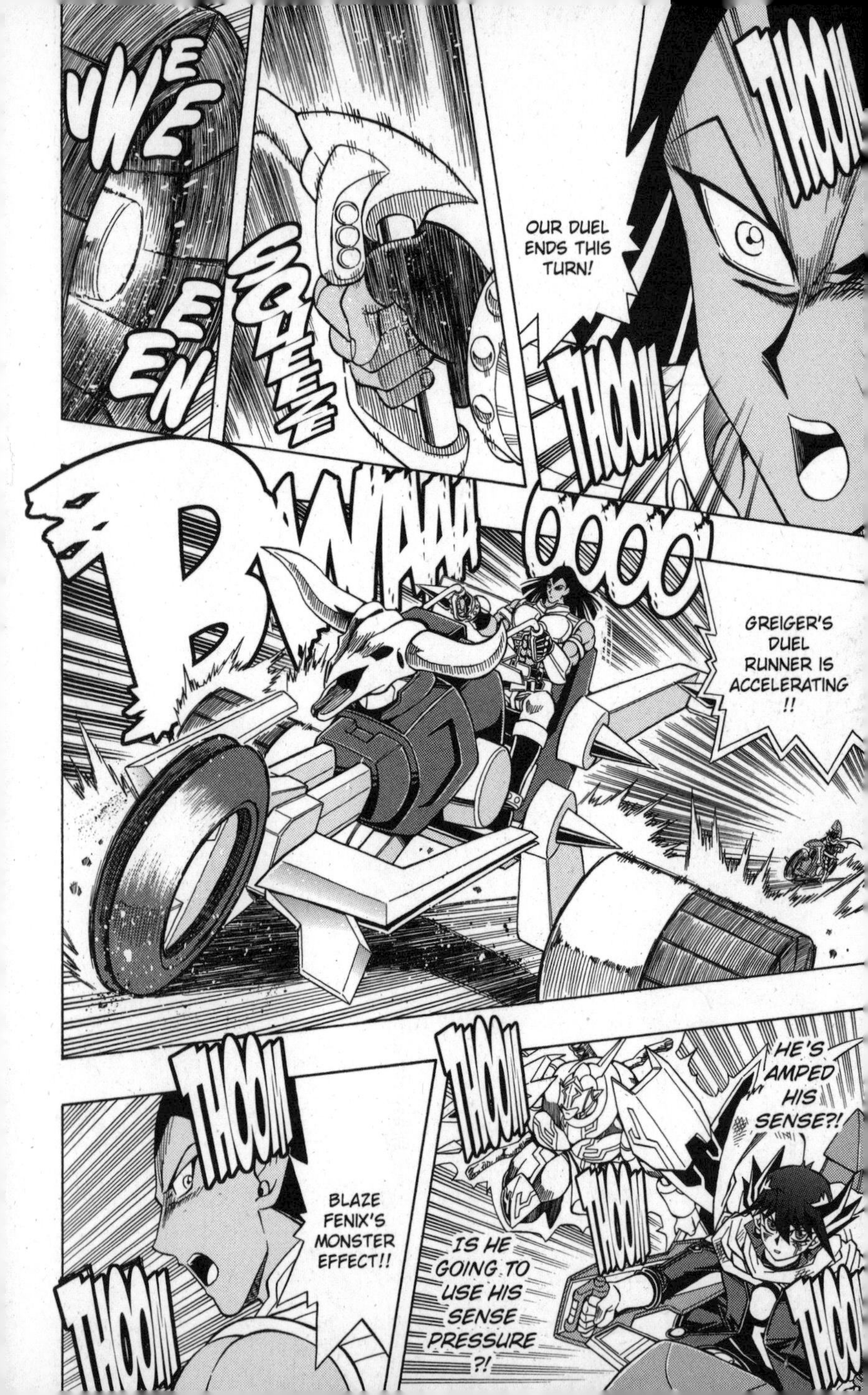
THOOM
OUR DUEL ENDS THIS TURN!
THOOM
SQUEEEZE
VWEEEEN
BWAAAOOOO
GREIGER'S DUEL RUNNER IS ACCELERATING!!
THOOM
HE'S AMPED HIS SENSE?!
THOOM
IS HE GOING TO USE HIS SENSE PRESSURE?!
THOOM
THOOM
BLAZE FENIX'S MONSTER EFFECT!!
THOOM

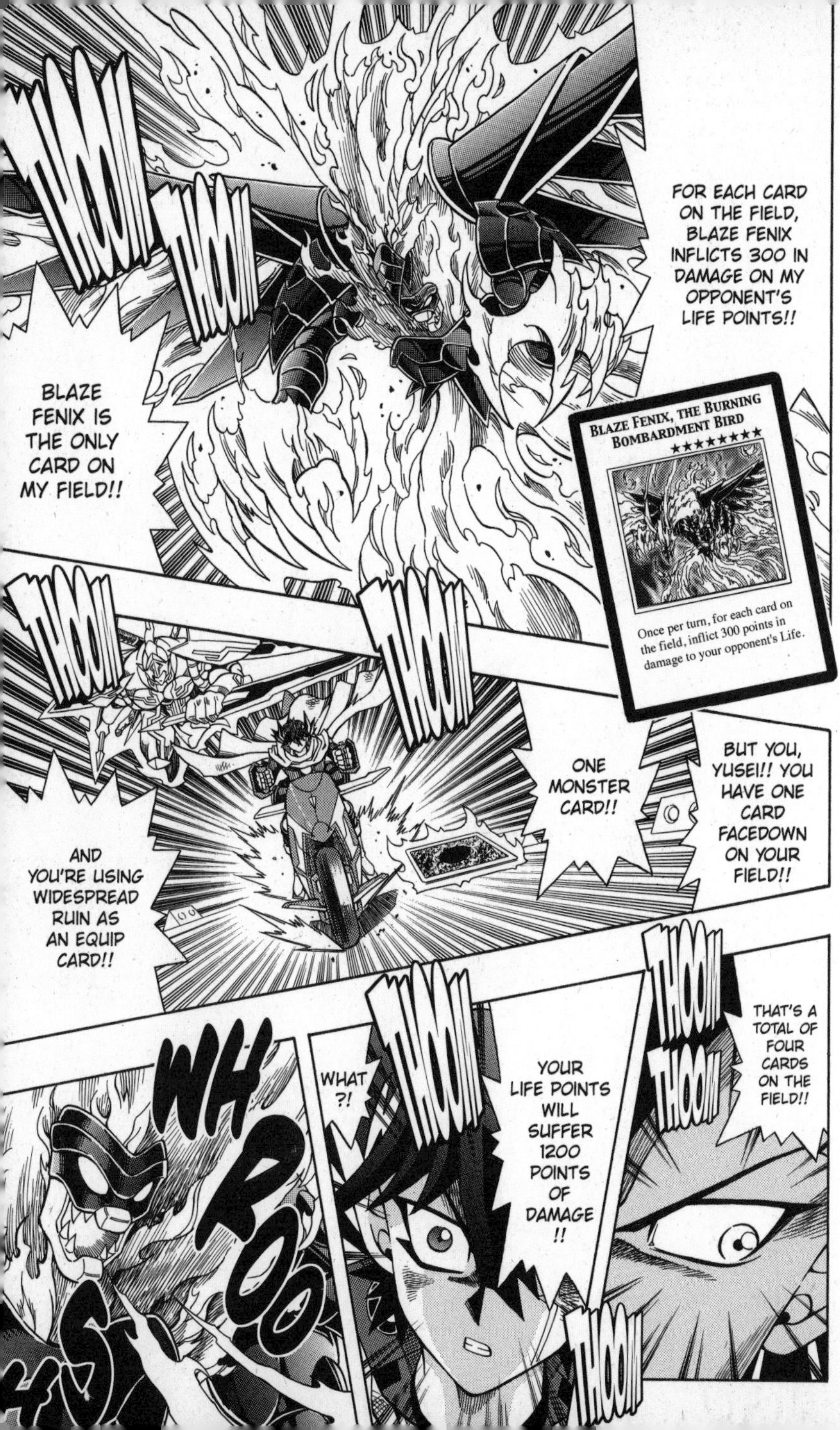
FOR EACH CARD ON THE FIELD, BLAZE FENIX INFLICTS 300 IN DAMAGE ON MY OPPONENT'S LIFE POINTS!!
THOOM
THOOM
BLAZE FENIX IS THE ONLY CARD ON MY FIELD!!
BLAZE FENIX, THE BURNING BOMBARDMENT BIRD
★★★★★★★★
Once per turn, for each card on the field, inflict 300 points in damage to your opponent's Life.
THOOM
THOOM
BUT YOU, YUSEI!! YOU HAVE ONE CARD FACEDOWN ON YOUR FIELD!!
ONE MONSTER CARD!!
AND YOU'RE USING WIDESPREAD RUIN AS AN EQUIP CARD!!
THAT'S A TOTAL OF FOUR CARDS ON THE FIELD!!
THOOM THOOM
YOUR LIFE POINTS WILL SUFFER 1200 POINTS OF DAMAGE!!
THOOM
THOOM
WHAT?!
WHROOSH

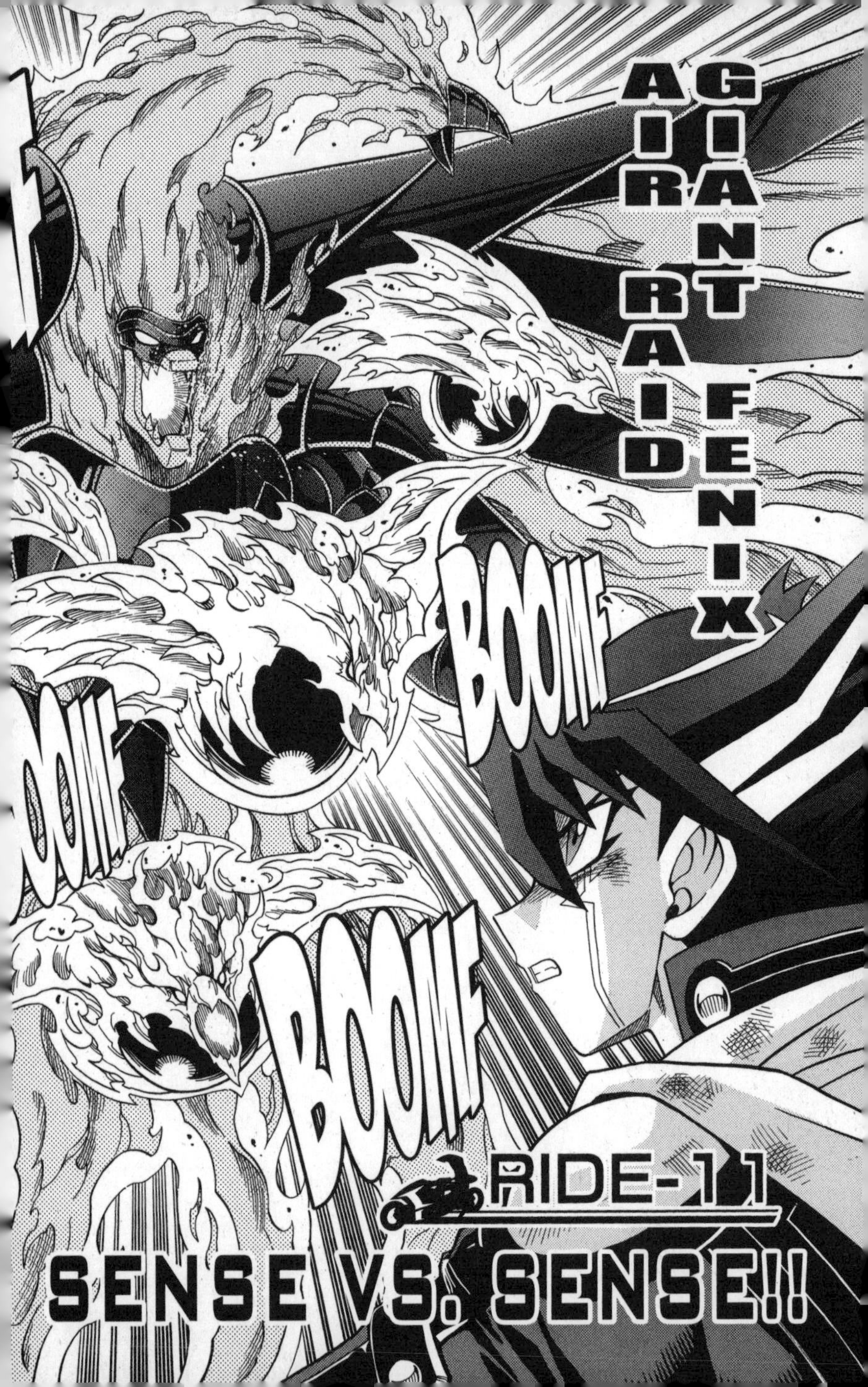
GIANT FENIX
AIR RAID
BOOMF
OOMF
BOOMF
RIDE-11
SENSE VS. SENSE!!

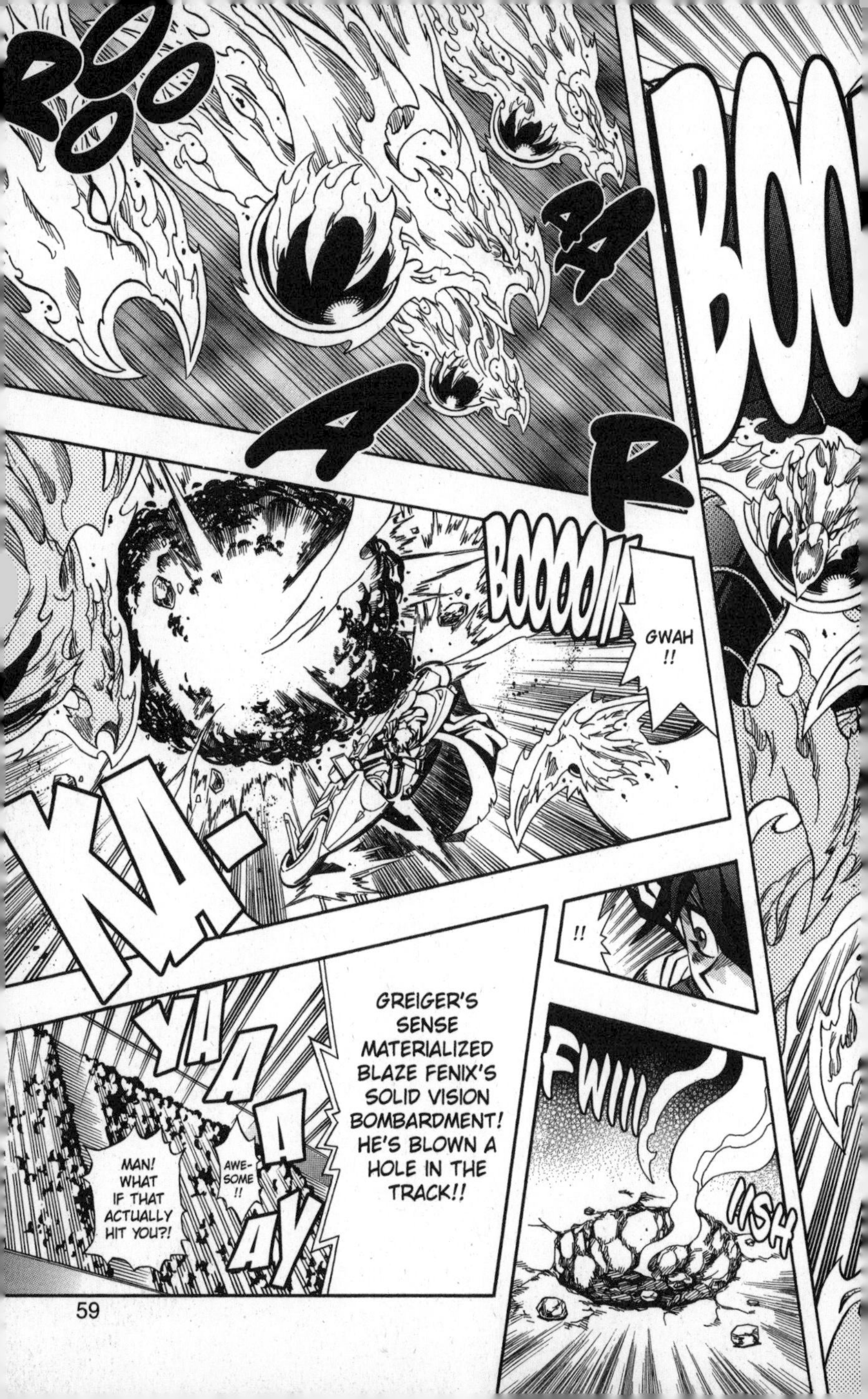
BOO
BOOO
AA
A
R
BOOOOM!!
GWAH!!
KA-
!!
FWIIIISH
GREIGER'S SENSE MATERIALIZED BLAZE FENIX'S SOLID VISION BOMBARDMENT! HE'S BLOWN A HOLE IN THE TRACK!!
AWE-SOME!!
MAN! WHAT IF THAT ACTUALLY HIT YOU?!
YAAAAY

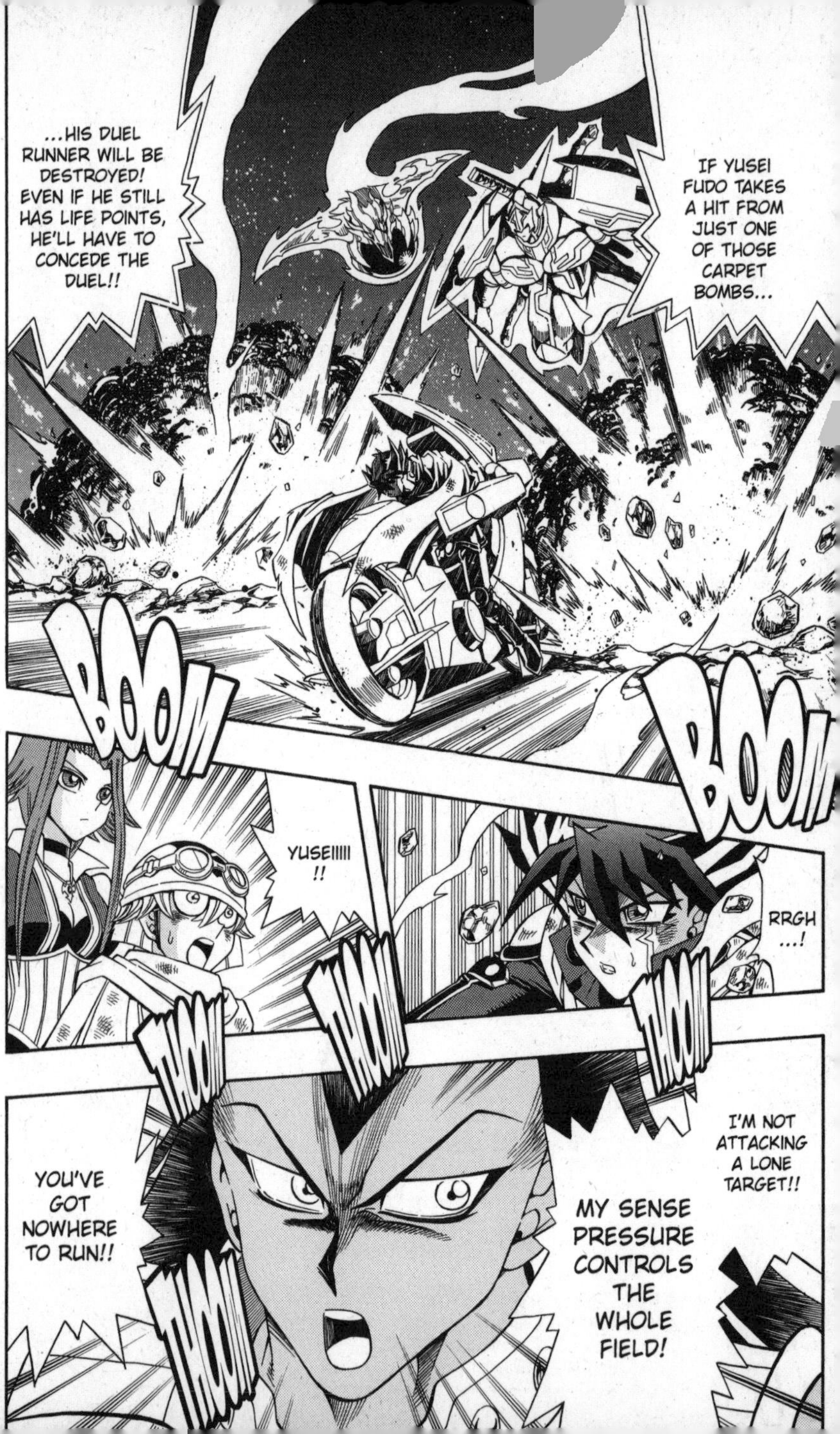
IF YUSEI FUDO TAKES A HIT FROM JUST ONE OF THOSE CARPET BOMBS...
...HIS DUEL RUNNER WILL BE DESTROYED! EVEN IF HE STILL HAS LIFE POINTS, HE'LL HAVE TO CONCEDE THE DUEL!!
BOOM
BOOM
RRGH ...!
THOOM
YUSEIIIII !!
THOOM
THOOM
I'M NOT ATTACKING A LONE TARGET!!
MY SENSE PRESSURE CONTROLS THE WHOLE FIELD!
YOU'VE GOT NOWHERE TO RUN!!
THOOM

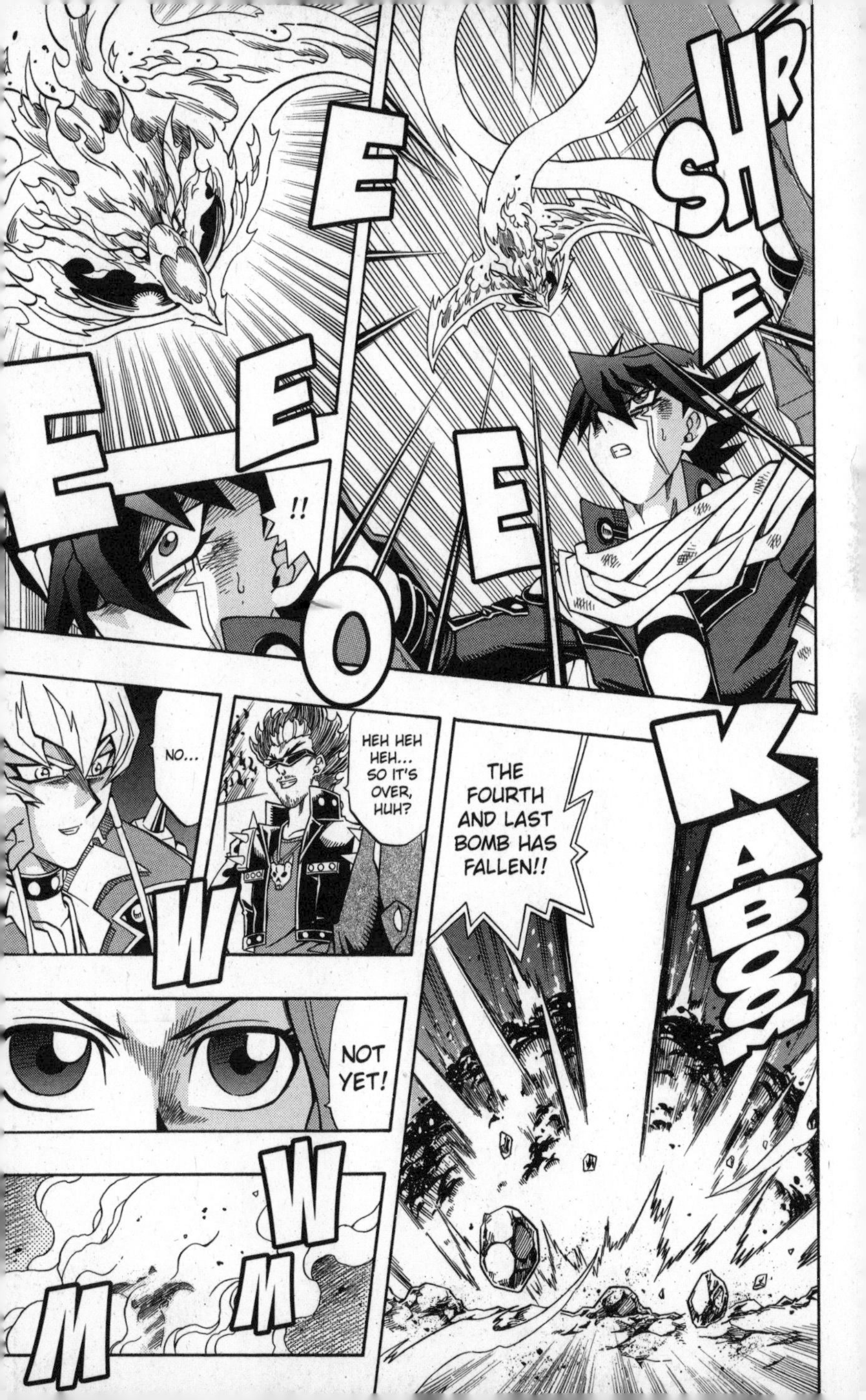

SHR
EEEEEE
!!
KABOOM
THE FOURTH AND LAST BOMB HAS FALLEN!!
HEH HEH HEH... SO IT'S OVER, HUH?
NO...
W
NOT YET!
W
M
M

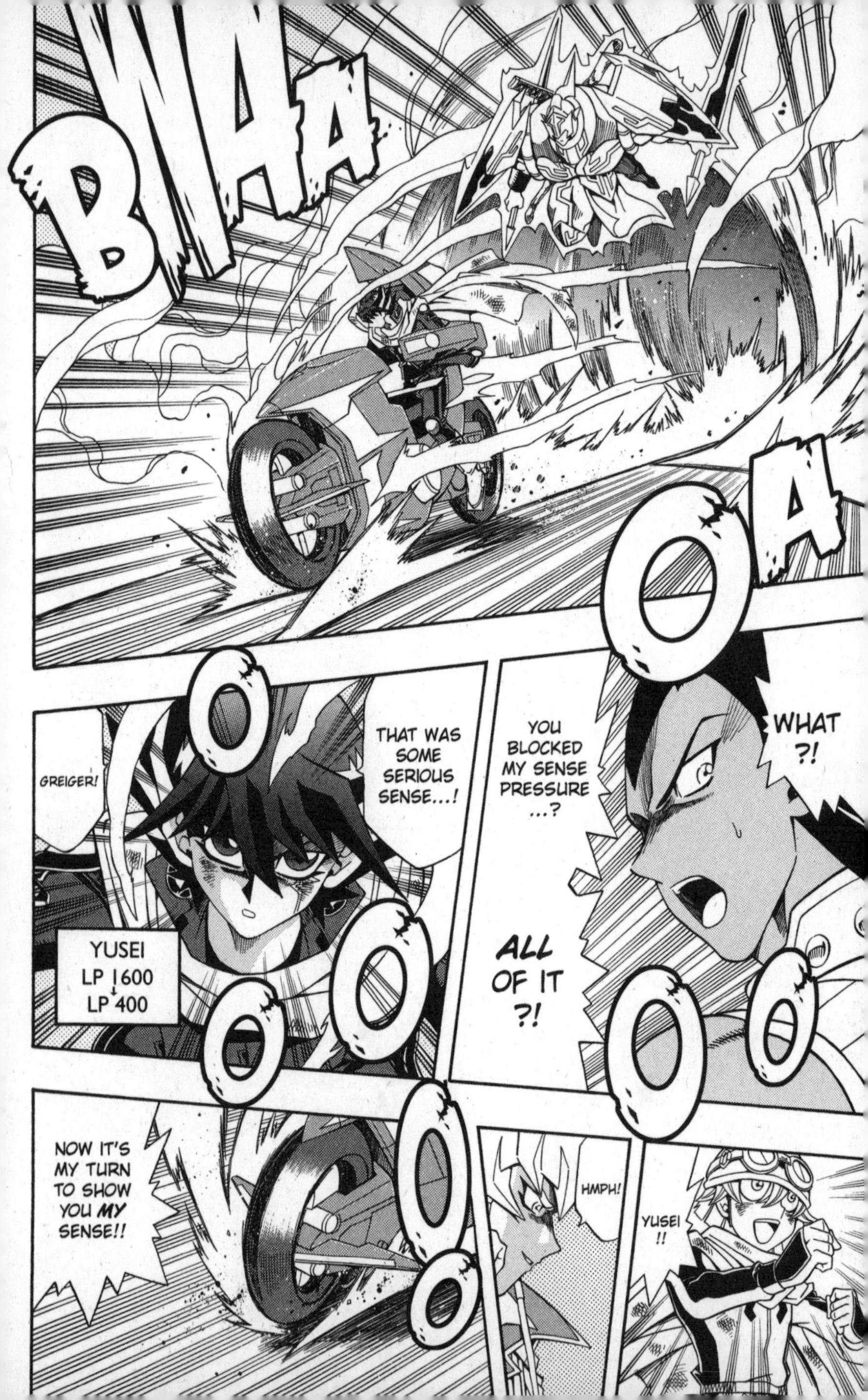
WHAT ?!
YOU BLOCKED MY SENSE PRESSURE ...?
ALL OF IT ?!
THAT WAS SOME SERIOUS SENSE...!
GREIGER!
YUSEI LP 1600 ↓ LP 400
YUSEI !!
HMPH!
NOW IT'S MY TURN TO SHOW YOU *MY* SENSE!!

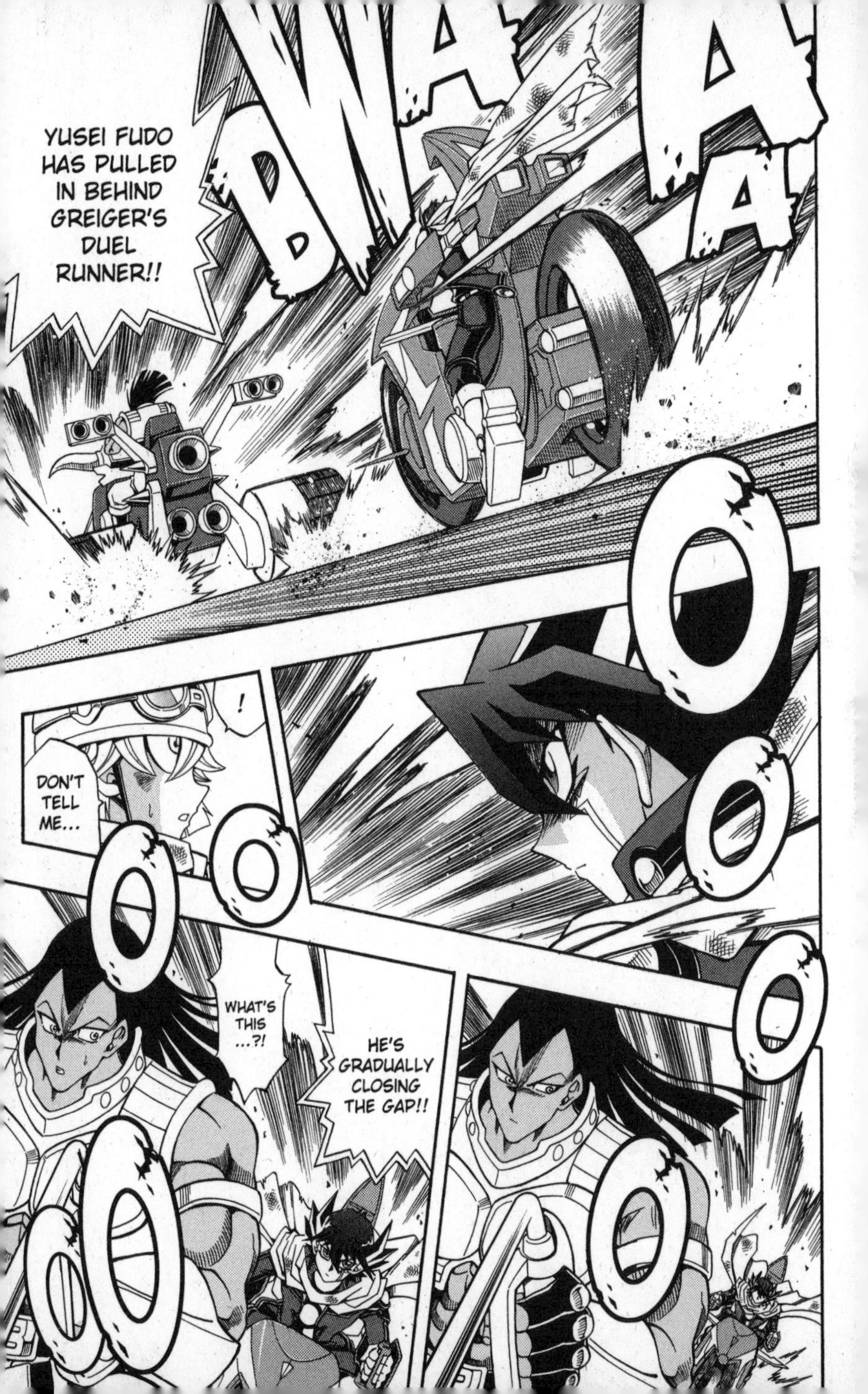
YUSEI FUDO HAS PULLED IN BEHIND GREIGER'S DUEL RUNNER!!
!
DON'T TELL ME...
HE'S GRADUALLY CLOSING THE GAP!!
WHAT'S THIS ...?!

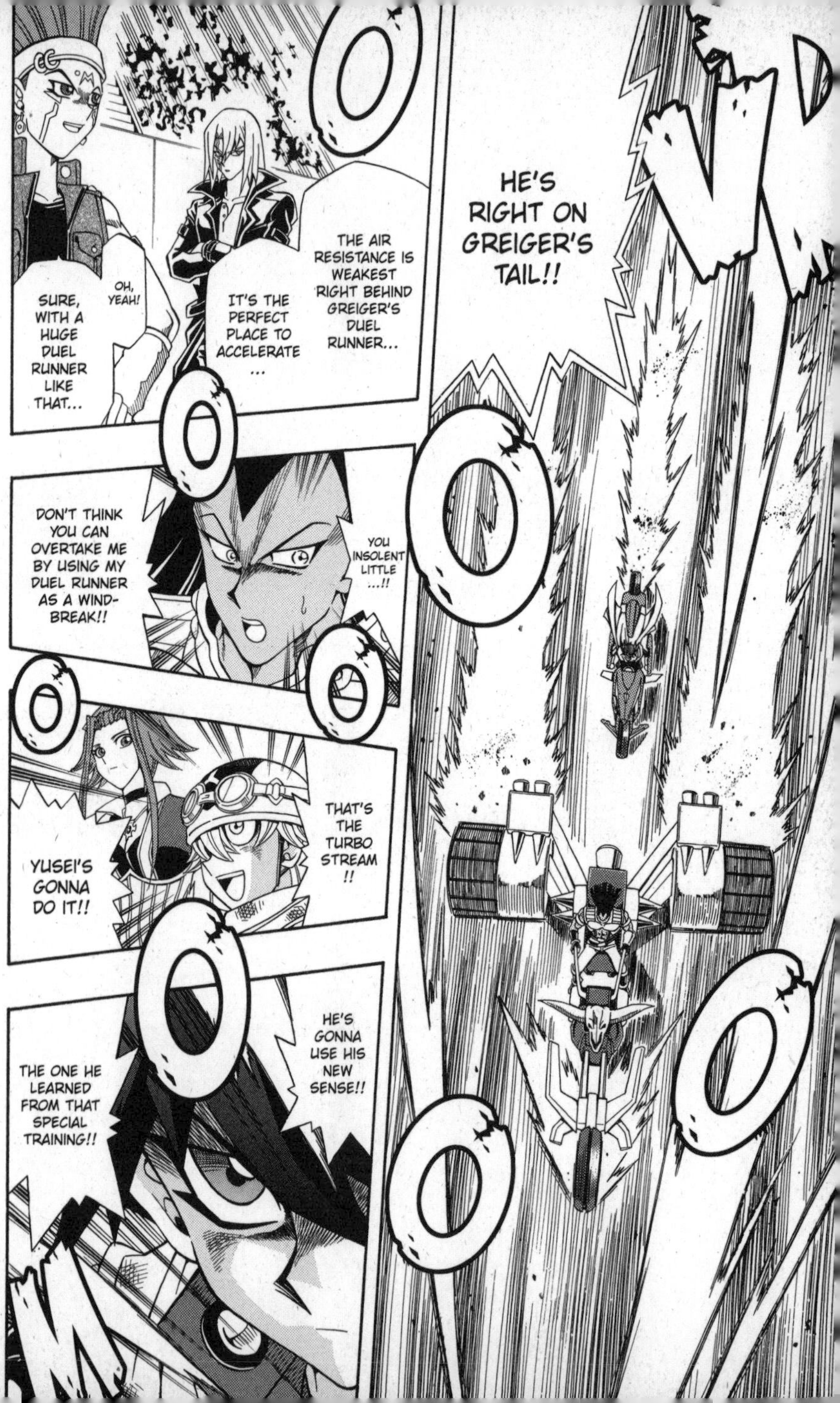
HE'S RIGHT ON GREIGER'S TAIL!!
THE AIR RESISTANCE IS WEAKEST RIGHT BEHIND GREIGER'S DUEL RUNNER...
IT'S THE PERFECT PLACE TO ACCELERATE ...
OH, YEAH!
SURE, WITH A HUGE DUEL RUNNER LIKE THAT...
YOU INSOLENT LITTLE ...!!
DON'T THINK YOU CAN OVERTAKE ME BY USING MY DUEL RUNNER AS A WIND-BREAK!!
THAT'S THE TURBO STREAM !!
YUSEI'S GONNA DO IT!!
HE'S GONNA USE HIS NEW SENSE!!
THE ONE HE LEARNED FROM THAT SPECIAL TRAINING!!

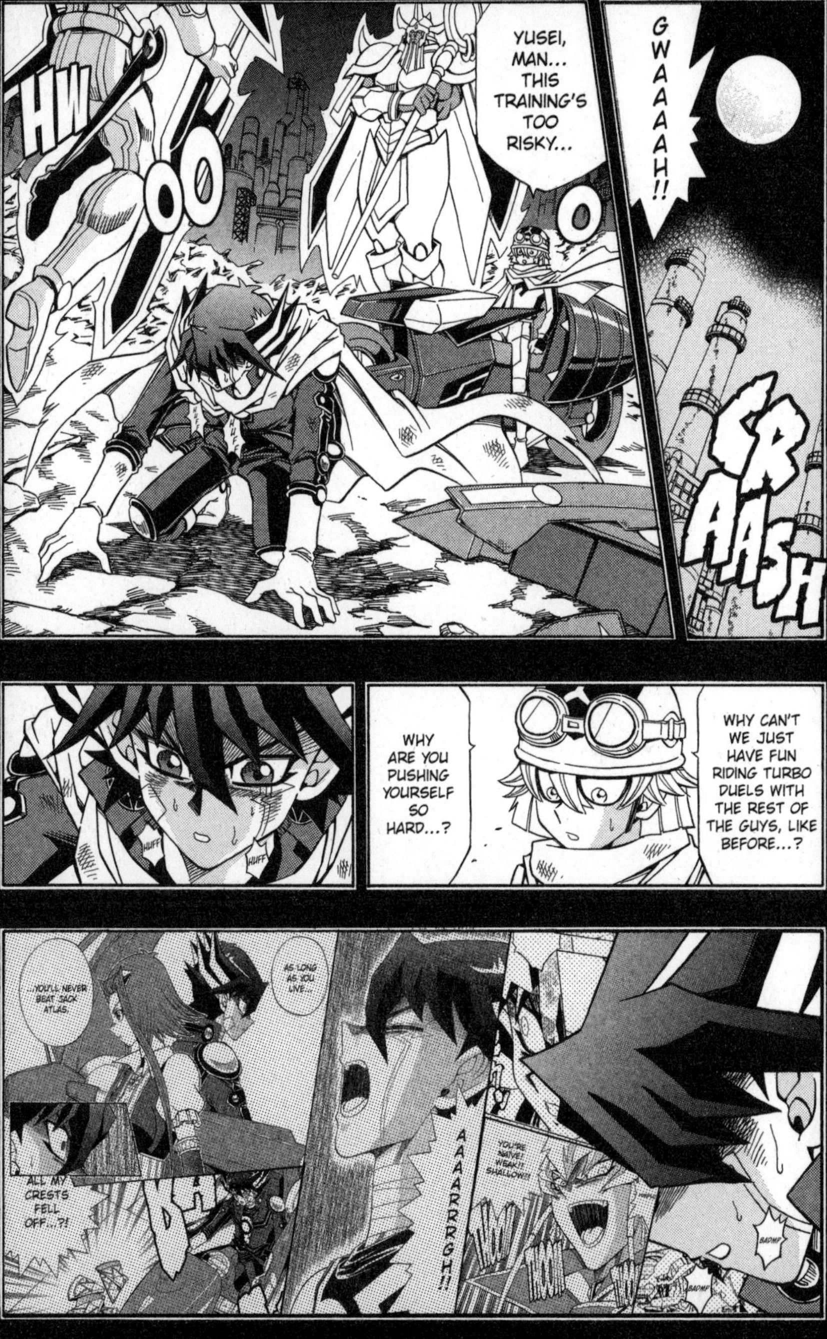
GWAAAAAAH!!
CRAASH
YUSEI, MAN... THIS TRAINING'S TOO RISKY...
HUFF
HUFF
WHY CAN'T WE JUST HAVE FUN RIDING TURBO DUELS WITH THE REST OF THE GUYS, LIKE BEFORE...?
WHY ARE YOU PUSHING YOURSELF SO HARD...?
HUFF
HUFF
BADMP
BADMP
YOU'RE NAIVE! WEAK!! SHALLOW!!!
AAAARRRGH!!
AS LONG AS YOU LIVE...
...YOU'LL NEVER BEAT JACK ATLAS.
ALL MY CRESTS FELL OFF...?!

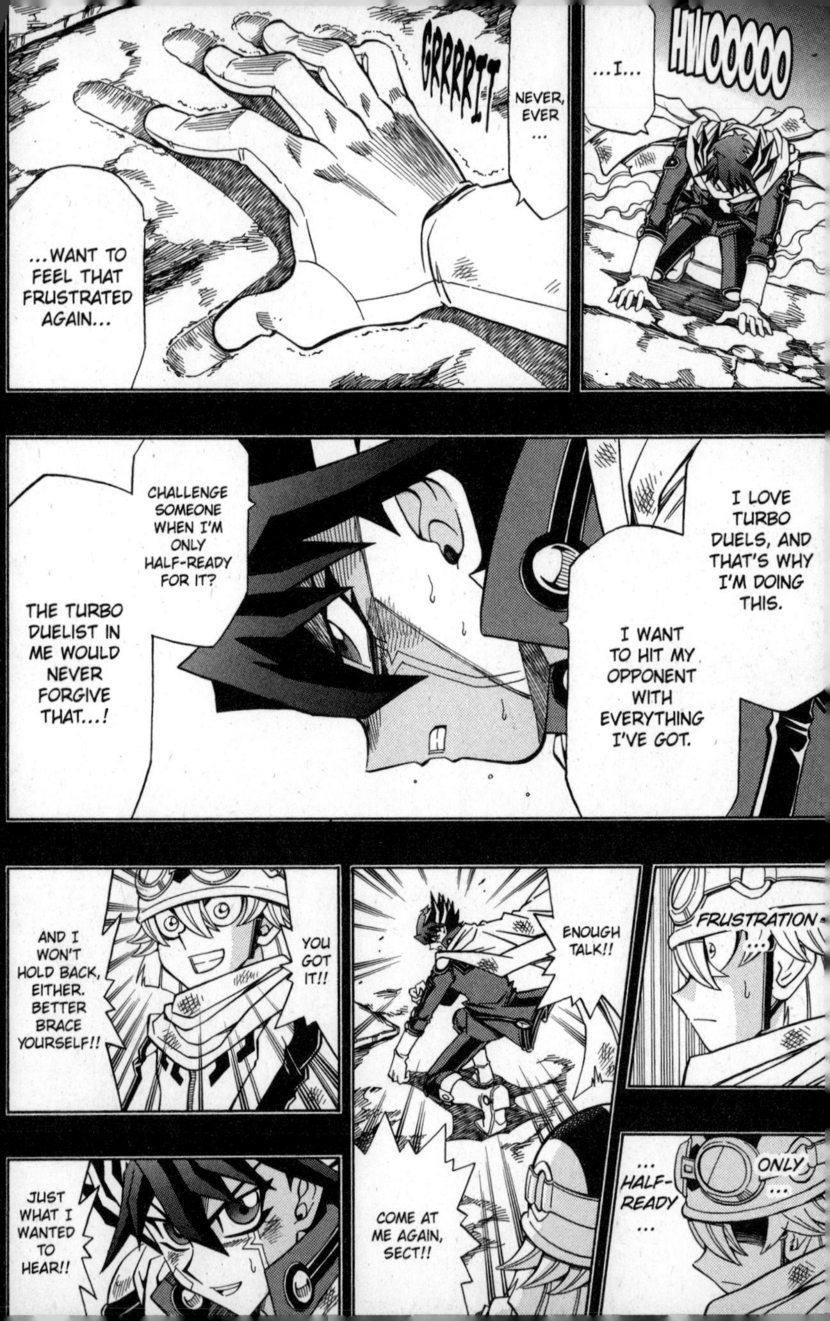
HWOOOOO
...I...
NEVER, EVER ...
GRRRRIT
...WANT TO FEEL THAT FRUSTRATED AGAIN...
I LOVE TURBO DUELS, AND THAT'S WHY I'M DOING THIS.
I WANT TO HIT MY OPPONENT WITH EVERYTHING I'VE GOT.
CHALLENGE SOMEONE WHEN I'M ONLY HALF-READY FOR IT?
THE TURBO DUELIST IN ME WOULD NEVER FORGIVE THAT...!
FRUSTRATION ...
ONLY ...
... HALF-READY ...
ENOUGH TALK!!
COME AT ME AGAIN, SECT!!
YOU GOT IT!!
AND I WON'T HOLD BACK, EITHER. BETTER BRACE YOURSELF!!
JUST WHAT I WANTED TO HEAR!!

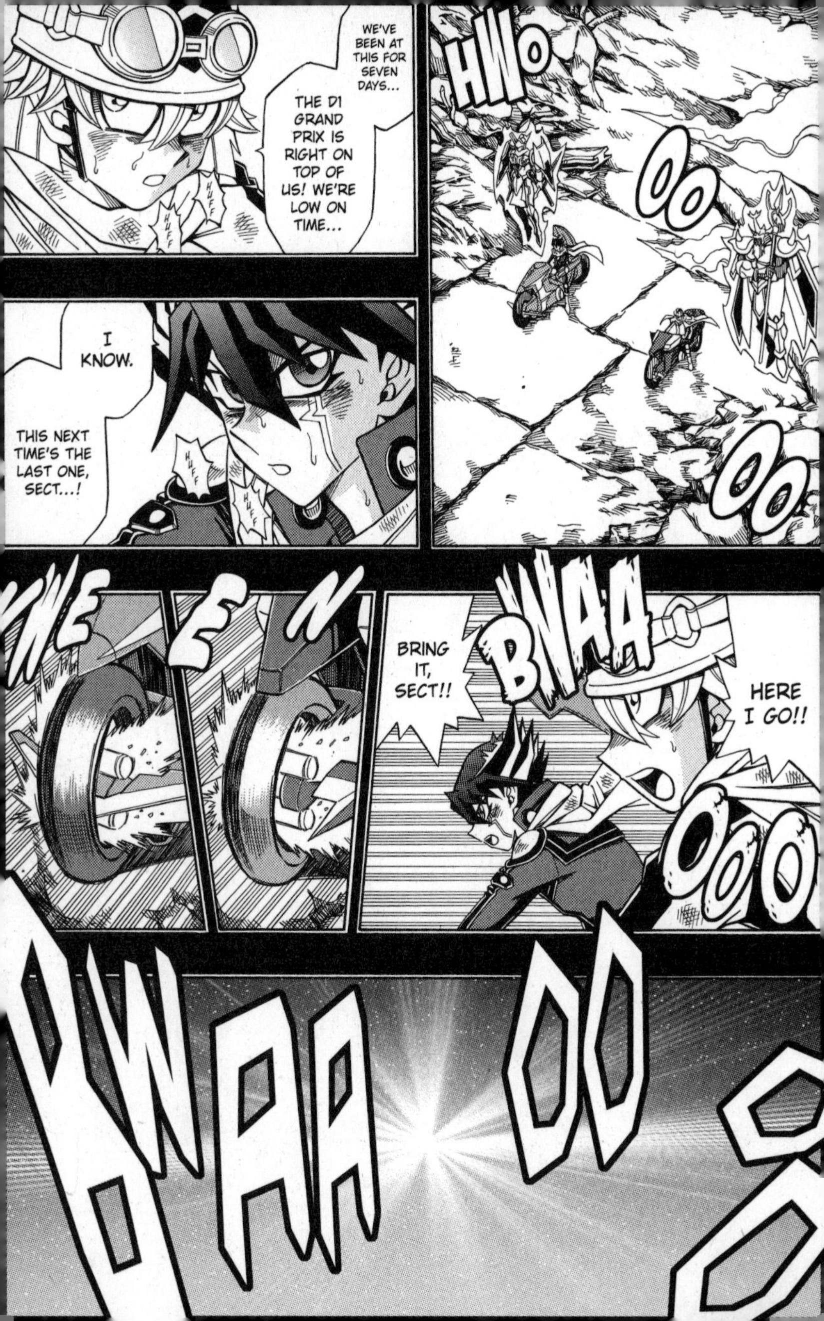

HWO
OO
OO
WE'VE BEEN AT THIS FOR SEVEN DAYS...
THE D1 GRAND PRIX IS RIGHT ON TOP OF US! WE'RE LOW ON TIME...
HUFF
HUFF
I KNOW.
THIS NEXT TIME'S THE LAST ONE, SECT...!
HUFF
HUFF
BWAA
HERE I GO!!
BRING IT, SECT!!
OOO
N
E
WHE
HWAA
DO

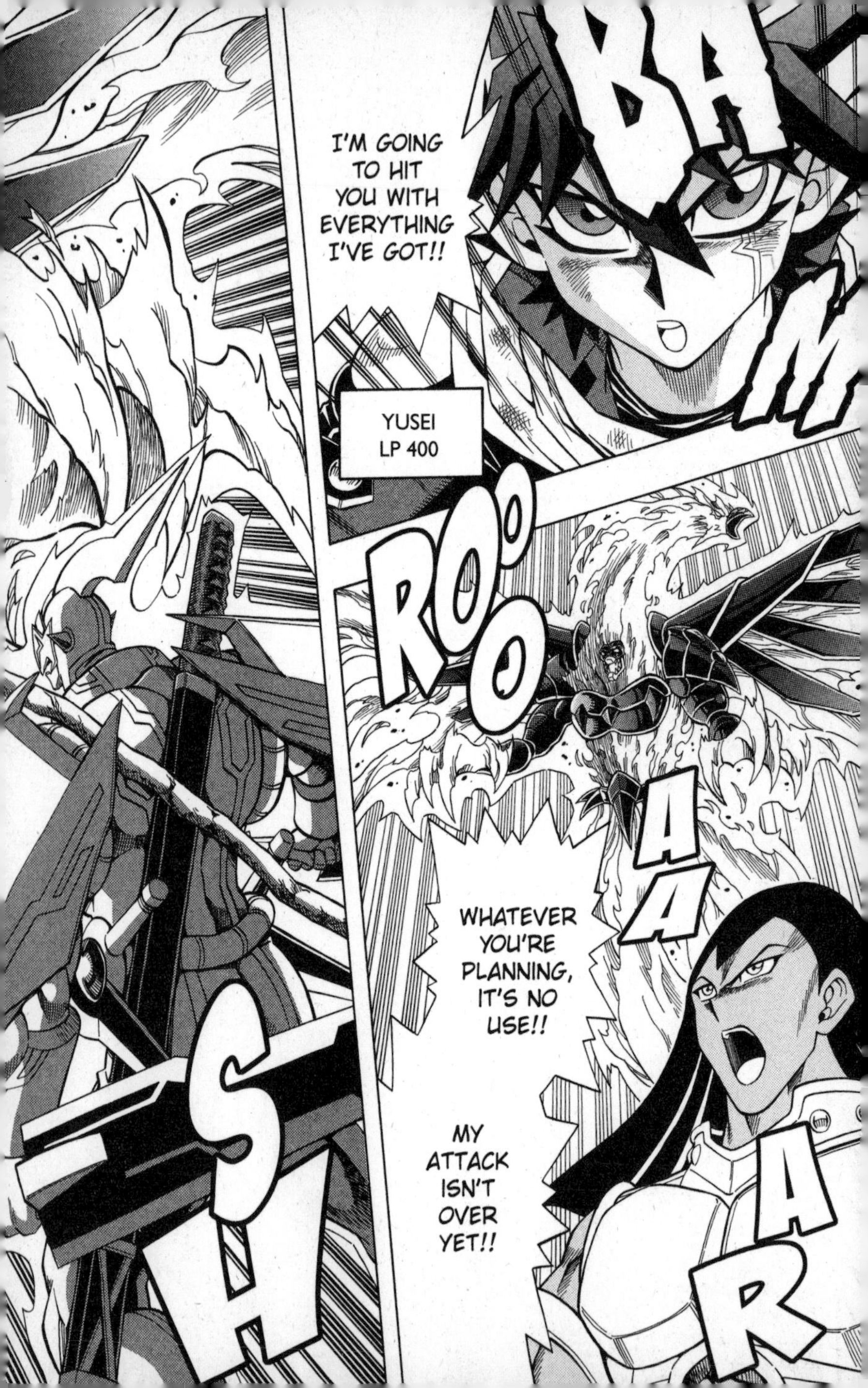
BA
M
I'M GOING TO HIT YOU WITH EVERYTHING I'VE GOT!!
YUSEI
LP 400
ROOOO
AA
WHATEVER YOU'RE PLANNING, IT'S NO USE!!
MY ATTACK ISN'T OVER YET!!
AR
SH

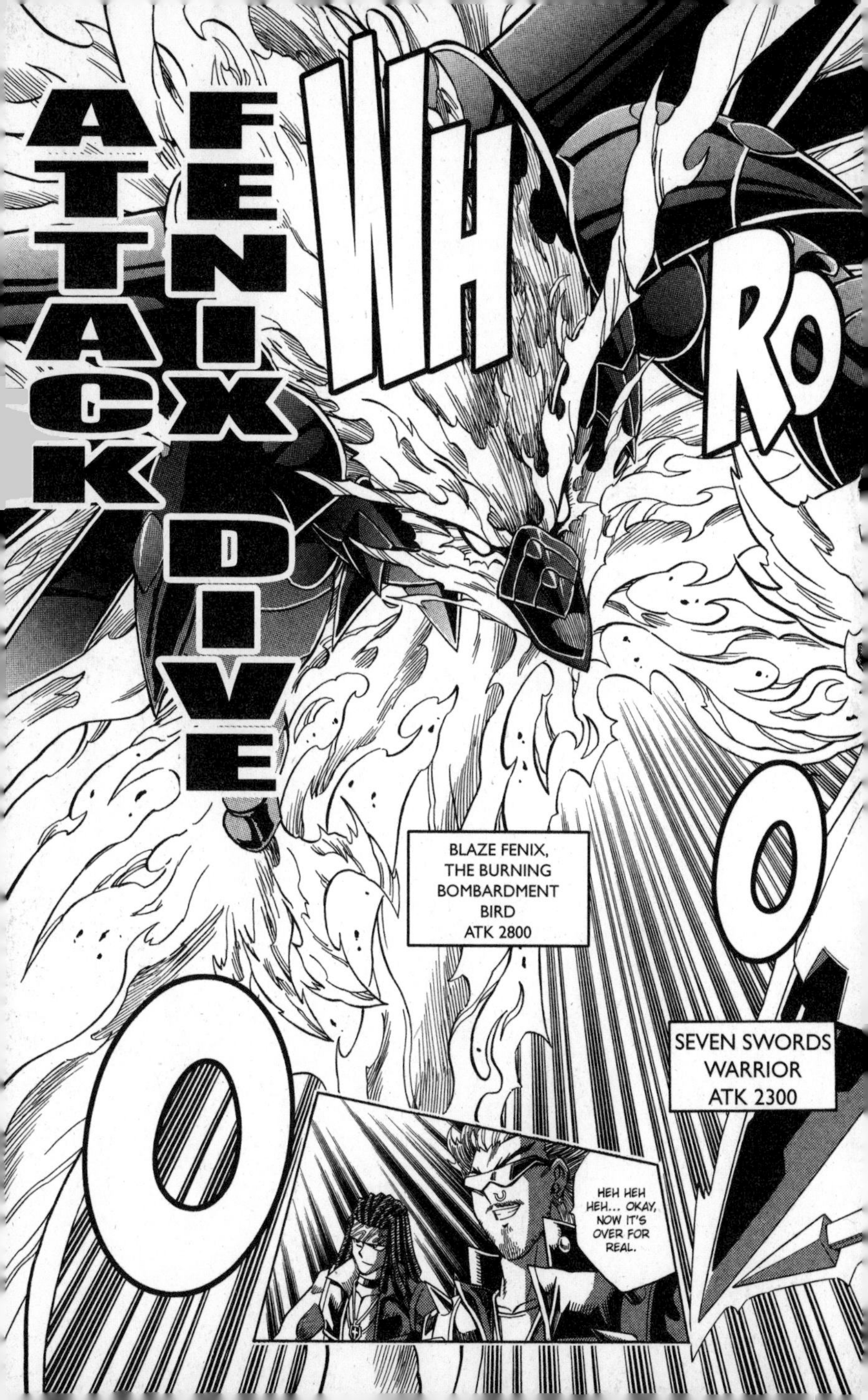
FENIX DIVE
ATTACK
WH
RO
BLAZE FENIX, THE BURNING BOMBARDMENT BIRD ATK 2800
O
SEVEN SWORDS WARRIOR ATK 2300
O
HEH HEH HEH... OKAY, NOW IT'S OVER FOR REAL.

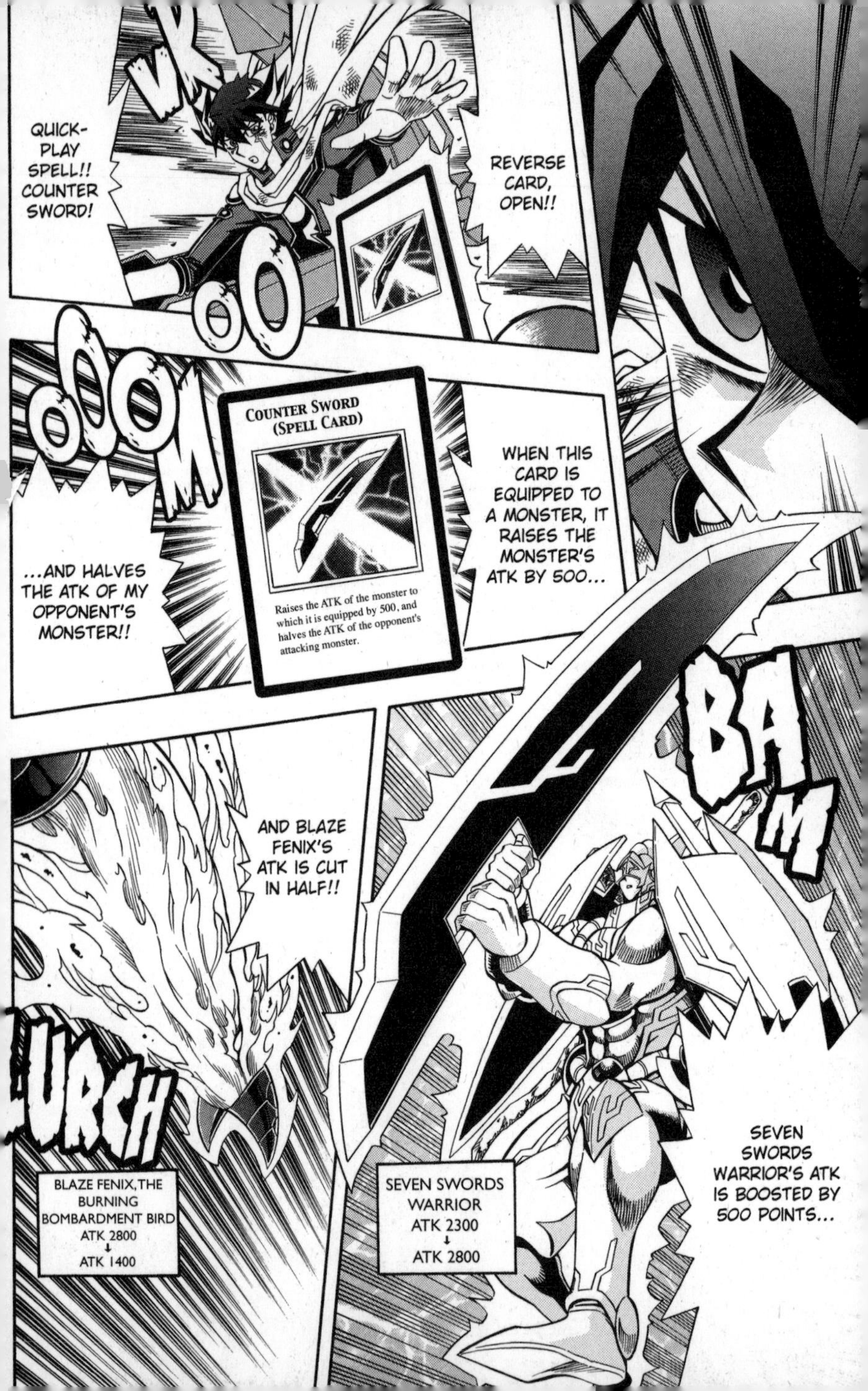
REVERSE CARD, OPEN!!
QUICK-PLAY SPELL!! COUNTER SWORD!
WHEN THIS CARD IS EQUIPPED TO A MONSTER, IT RAISES THE MONSTER'S ATK BY 500...
COUNTER SWORD (SPELL CARD)
Raises the ATK of the monster to which it is equipped by 500, and halves the ATK of the opponent's attacking monster.
...AND HALVES THE ATK OF MY OPPONENT'S MONSTER!!
BAM
SEVEN SWORDS WARRIOR'S ATK IS BOOSTED BY 500 POINTS...
SEVEN SWORDS WARRIOR ATK 2300 ↓ ATK 2800
AND BLAZE FENIX'S ATK IS CUT IN HALF!!
BLAZE FENIX, THE BURNING BOMBARDMENT BIRD ATK 2800 ↓ ATK 1400

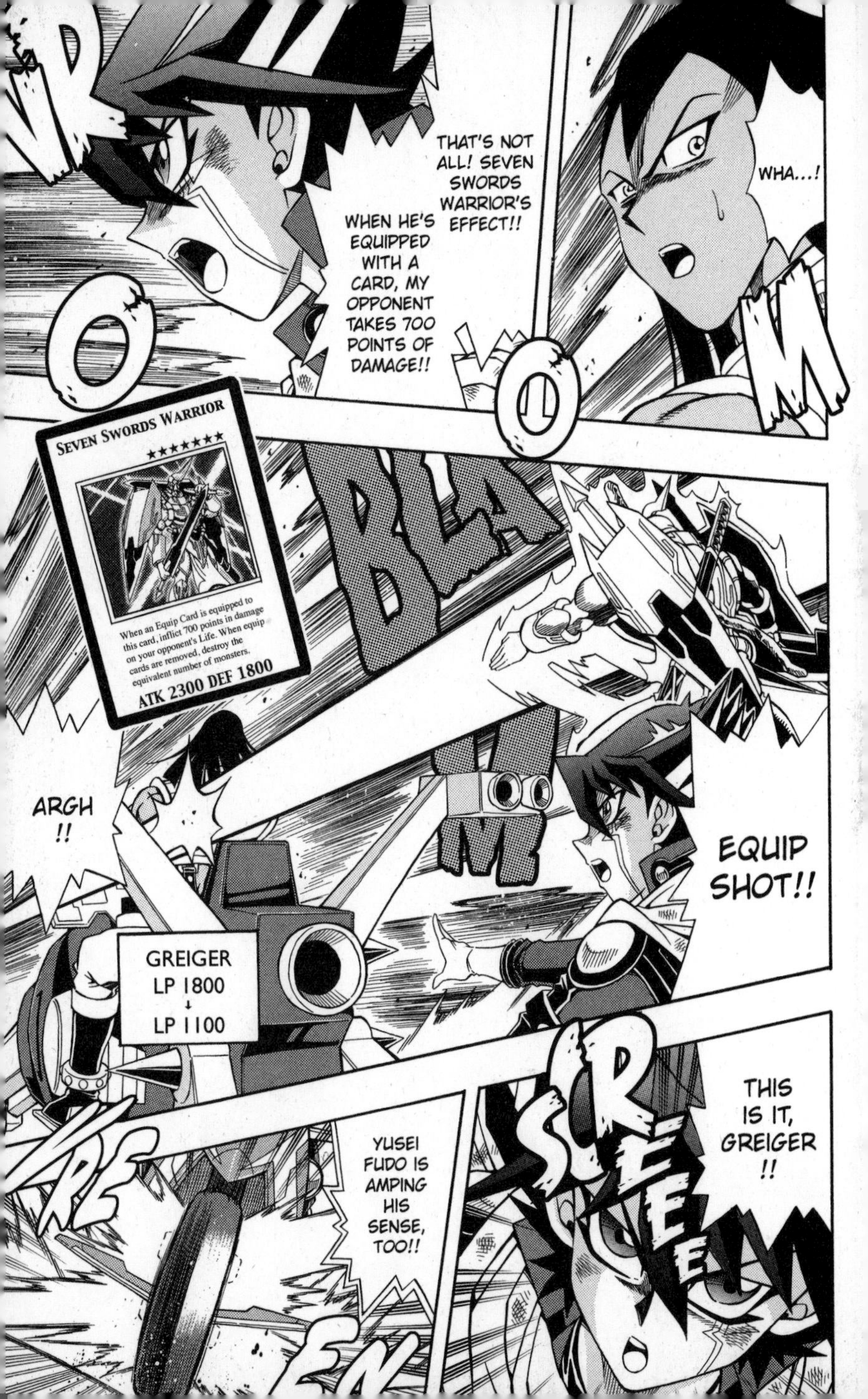
WHA...!
THAT'S NOT ALL! SEVEN SWORDS WARRIOR'S EFFECT!!
WHEN HE'S EQUIPPED WITH A CARD, MY OPPONENT TAKES 700 POINTS OF DAMAGE!!
SEVEN SWORDS WARRIOR
When an Equip Card is equipped to this card, inflict 700 points in damage on your opponent's Life. When equip cards are removed, destroy the equivalent number of monsters.
ATK 2300 DEF 1800
EQUIP SHOT!!
ARGH!!
GREIGER LP 1800 ↓ LP 1100
THIS IS IT, GREIGER!!
YUSEI FUDO IS AMPING HIS SENSE, TOO!!

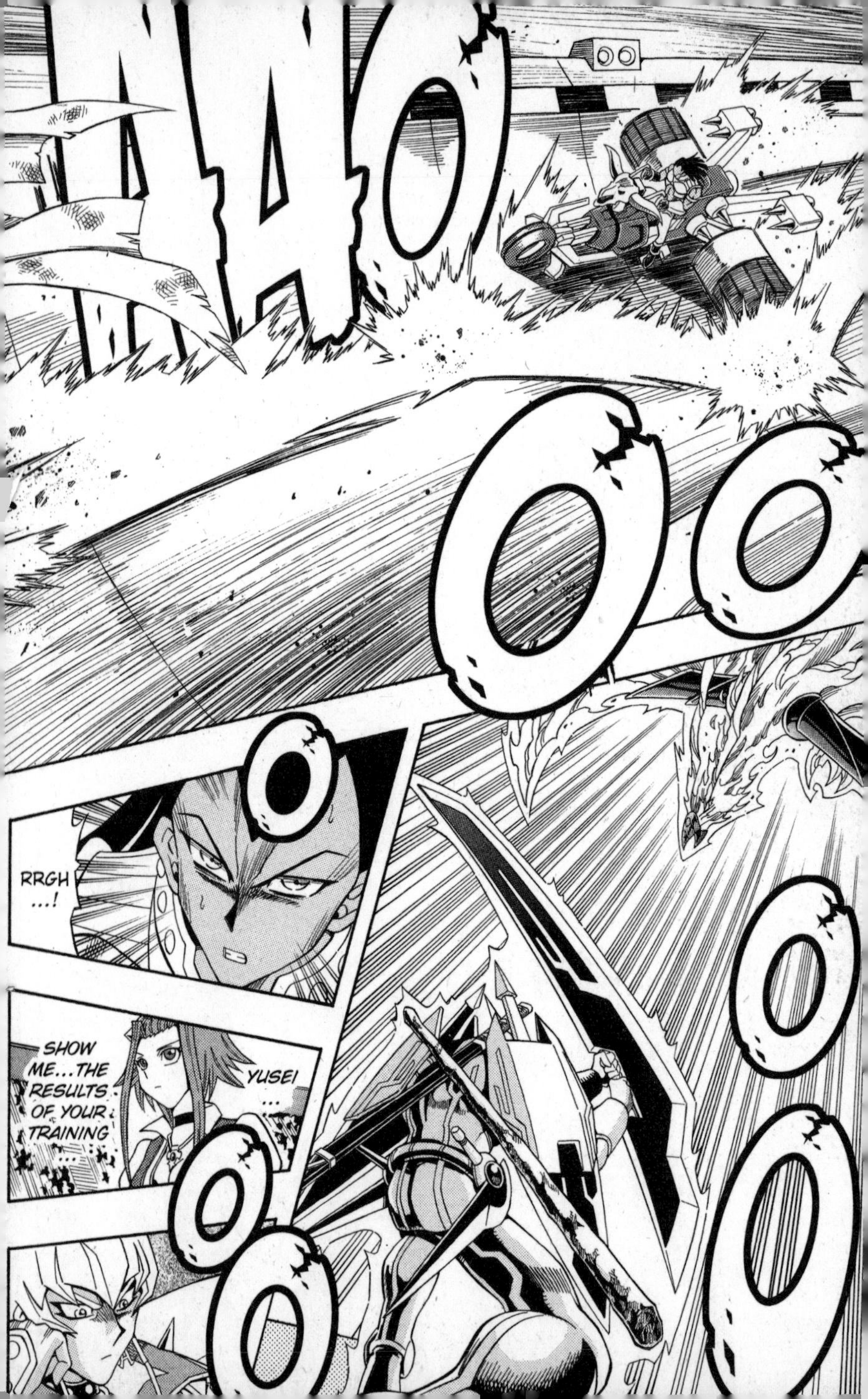
RRGH ...!
YUSEI ...
SHOW ME...THE RESULTS OF YOUR TRAINING ...

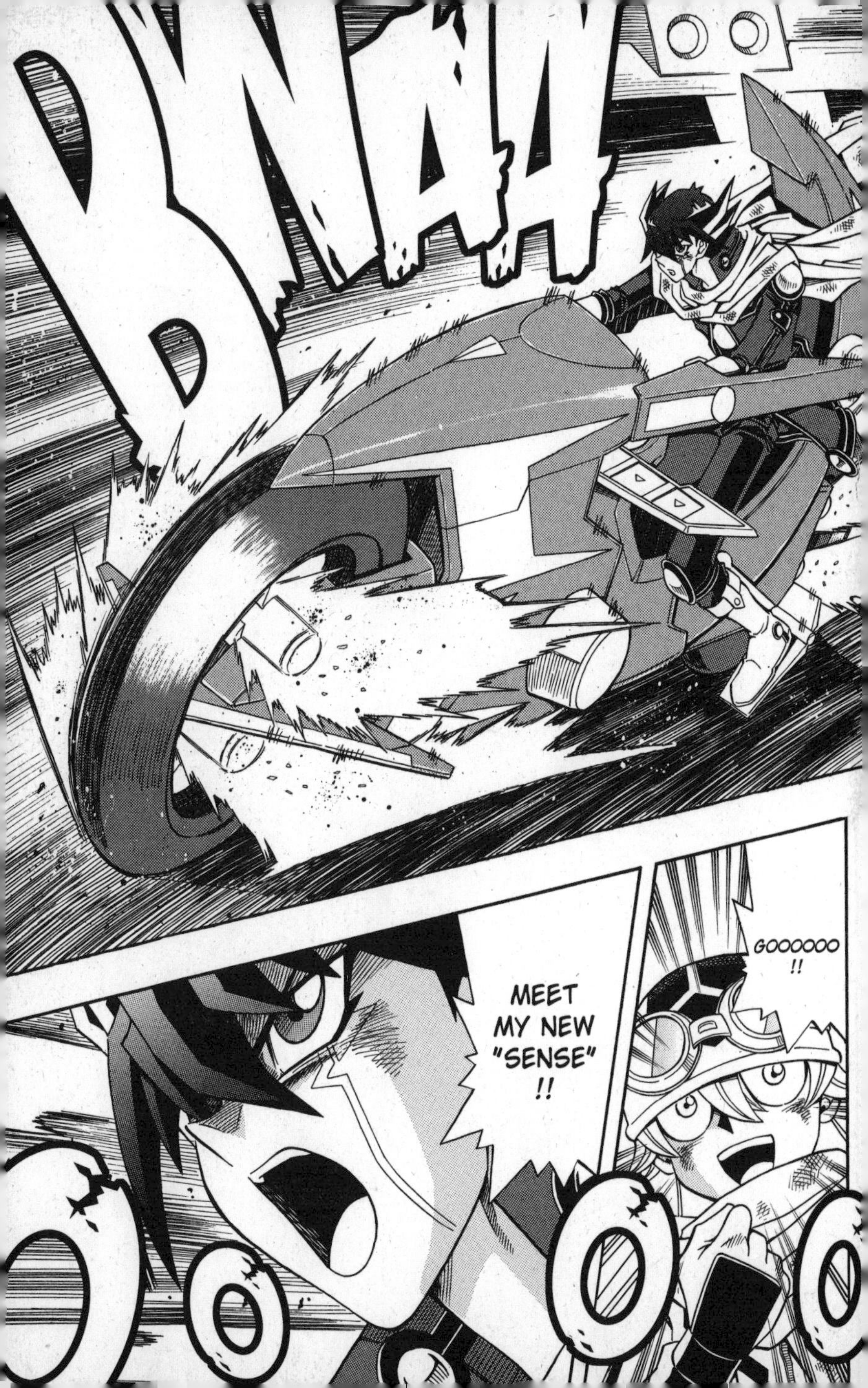
GOOOOOO!!
MEET MY NEW "SENSE"!!

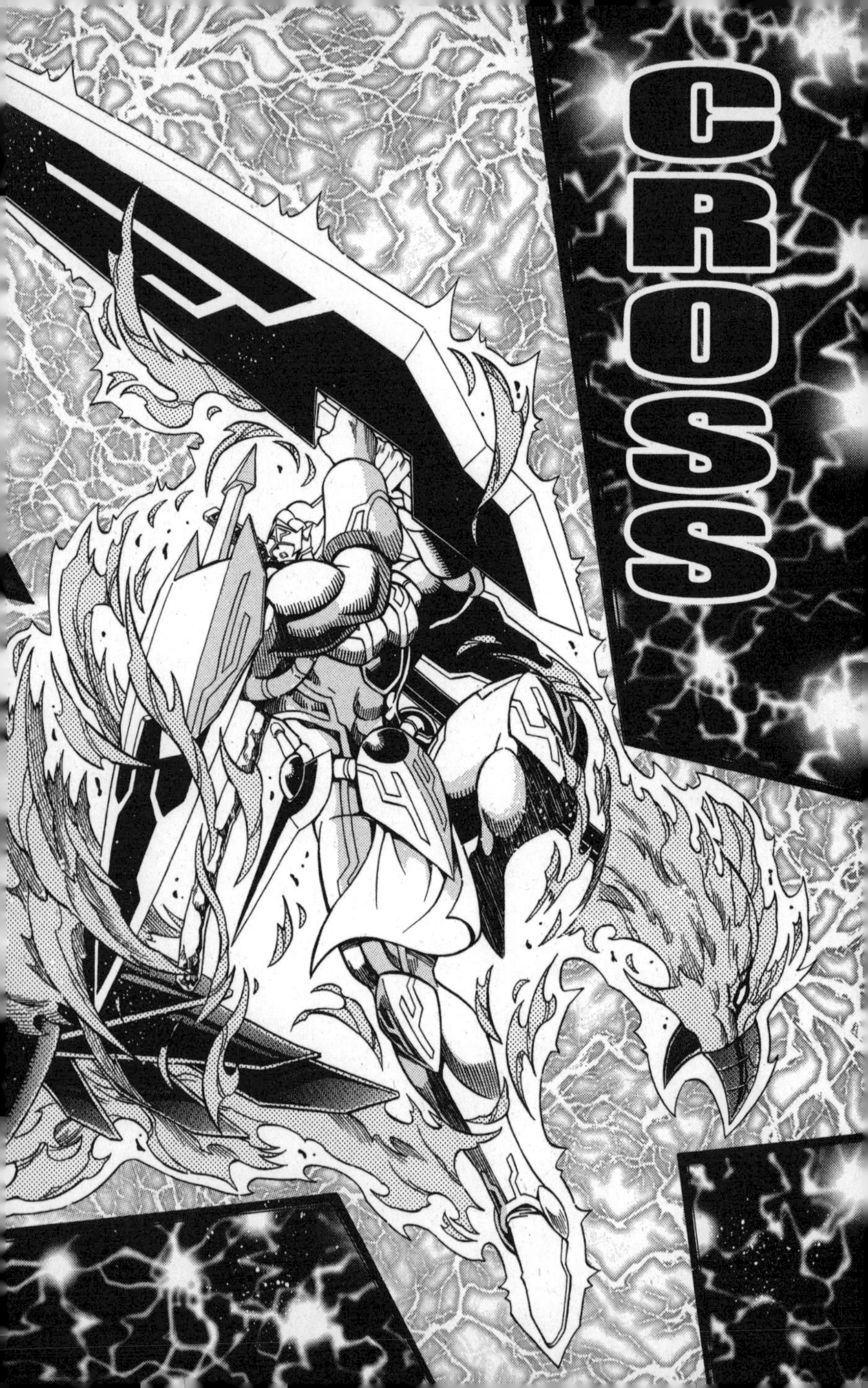
CROSS

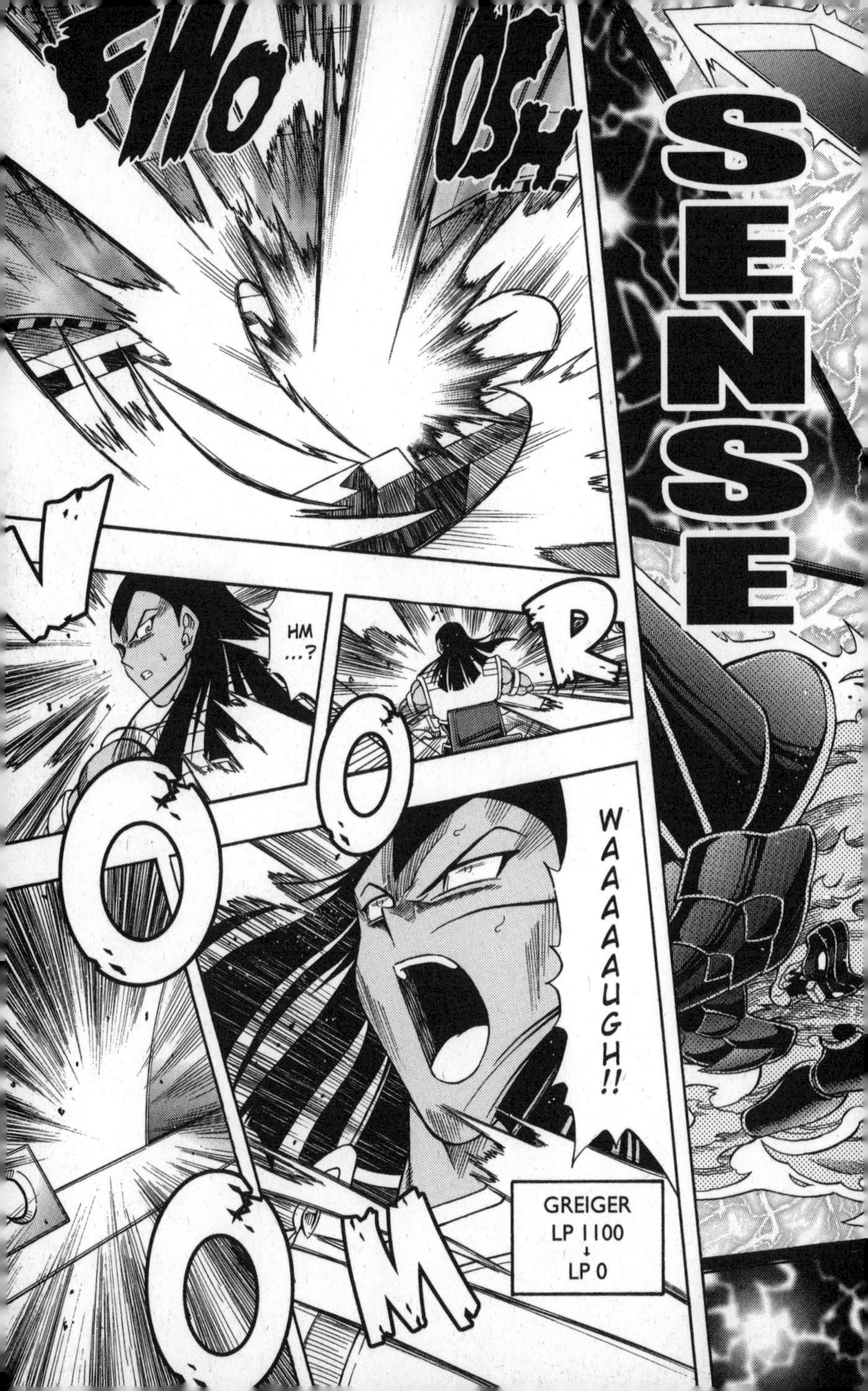
SENSE
FWOOSH
R
HM ...?
V
WAAAAAUGH!!
GREIGER
LP 1100
↓
LP 0
OOOM

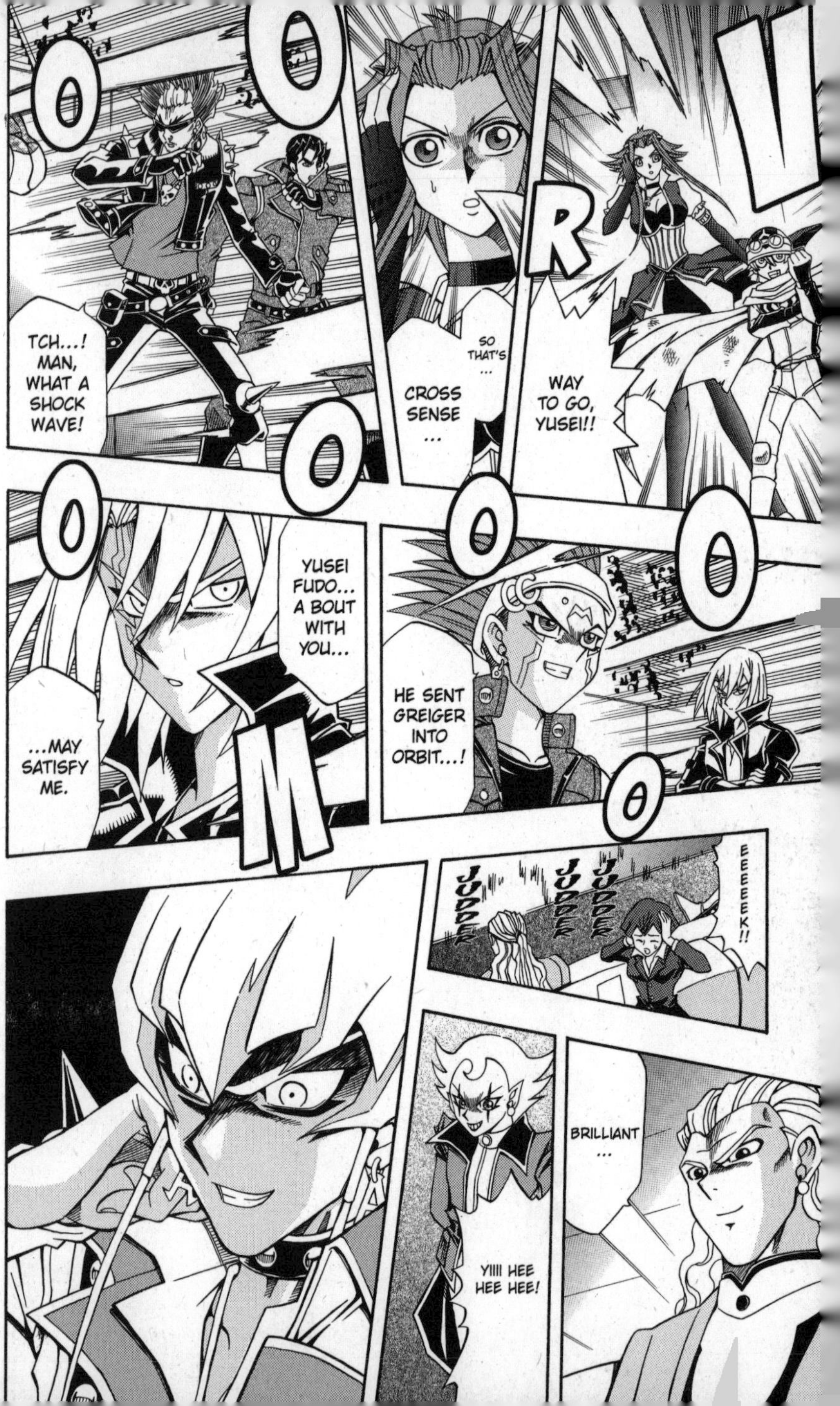
VROOOOOOOM
WAY TO GO, YUSEI!!
SO THAT'S...
CROSS SENSE...
TCH...! MAN, WHAT A SHOCK WAVE!
HE SENT GREIGER INTO ORBIT...!
YUSEI FUDO... A BOUT WITH YOU...
...MAY SATISFY ME.
EEEEEK!!
JUDDER
JUDDER
JUDDER
BRILLIANT...
YIIII HEE HEE HEE!

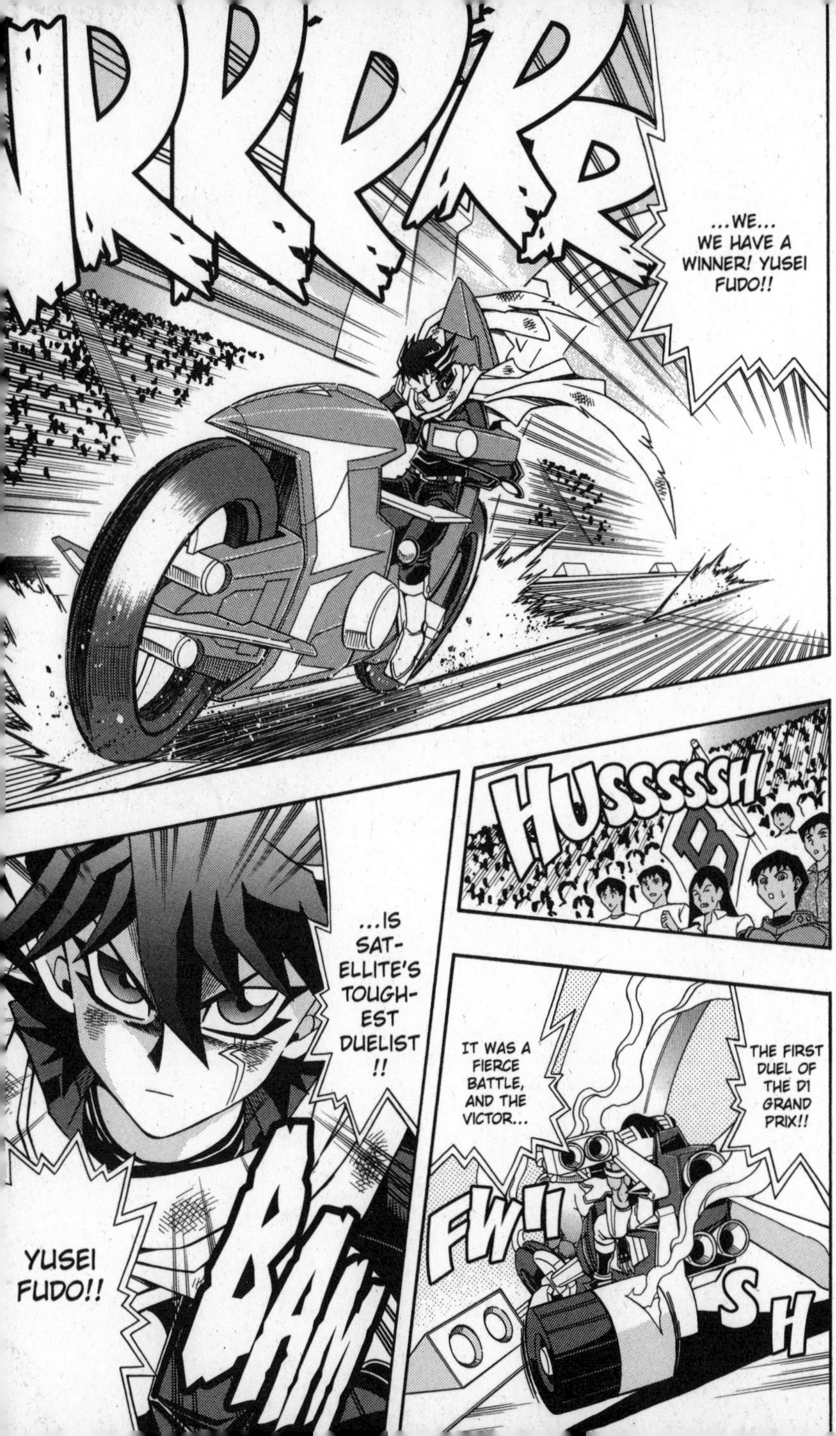
...WE... WE HAVE A WINNER! YUSEI FUDO!!
HUSSSSH
THE FIRST DUEL OF THE D1 GRAND PRIX!!
IT WAS A FIERCE BATTLE, AND THE VICTOR...
FW!!SH
...IS SAT-ELLITE'S TOUGH-EST DUELIST!!
YUSEI FUDO!!
BAM

5D's TRACKS

THE 11TH

BY SATOMASA

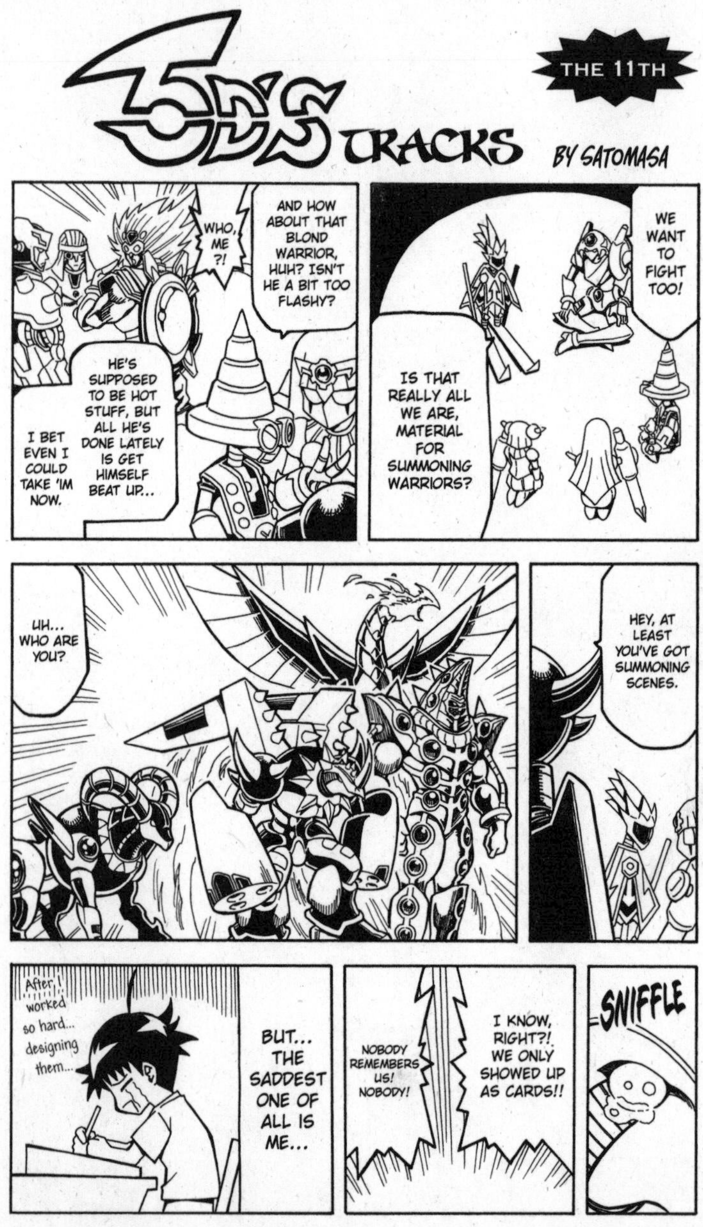

WE WANT TO FIGHT TOO!
IS THAT REALLY ALL WE ARE, MATERIAL FOR SUMMONING WARRIORS?
AND HOW ABOUT THAT BLOND WARRIOR, HUH? ISN'T HE A BIT TOO FLASHY?
WHO, ME ?!
HE'S SUPPOSED TO BE HOT STUFF, BUT ALL HE'S DONE LATELY IS GET HIMSELF BEAT UP...
I BET EVEN I COULD TAKE 'IM NOW.
HEY, AT LEAST YOU'VE GOT SUMMONING SCENES.
UH... WHO ARE YOU?
SNIFFLE
I KNOW, RIGHT?! WE ONLY SHOWED UP AS CARDS!!
NOBODY REMEMBERS US! NOBODY!
BUT... THE SADDEST ONE OF ALL IS ME...
After I worked so hard... designing them...

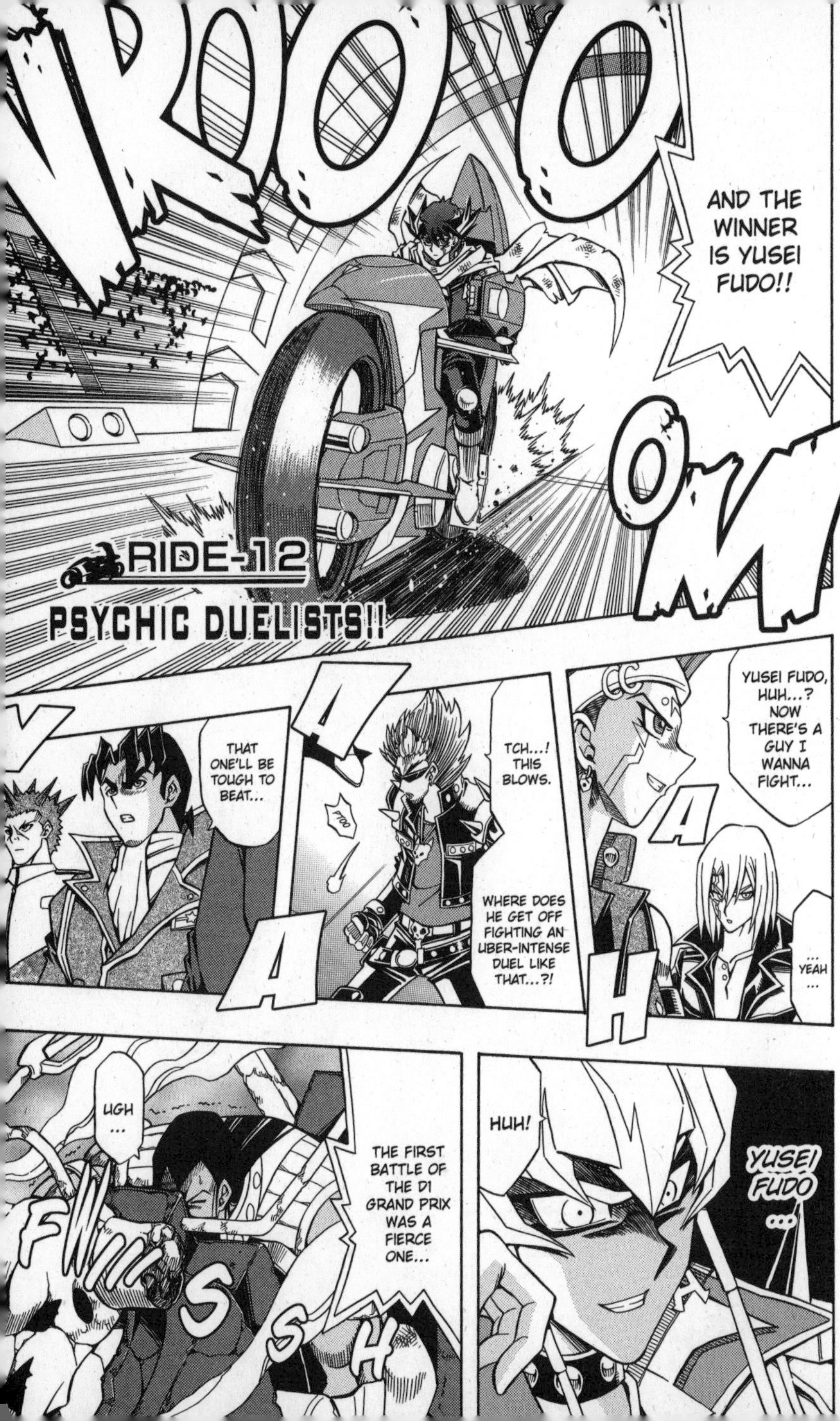
AND THE WINNER IS YUSEI FUDO!!
RIDE-12
PSYCHIC DUELISTS!!
YUSEI FUDO, HUH...? NOW THERE'S A GUY I WANNA FIGHT...
... YEAH ...
TCH...! THIS BLOWS.
PTOO
WHERE DOES HE GET OFF FIGHTING AN UBER-INTENSE DUEL LIKE THAT...?!
THAT ONE'LL BE TOUGH TO BEAT...
YUSEI FUDO ...
HUH!
THE FIRST BATTLE OF THE D1 GRAND PRIX WAS A FIERCE ONE...
UGH ...

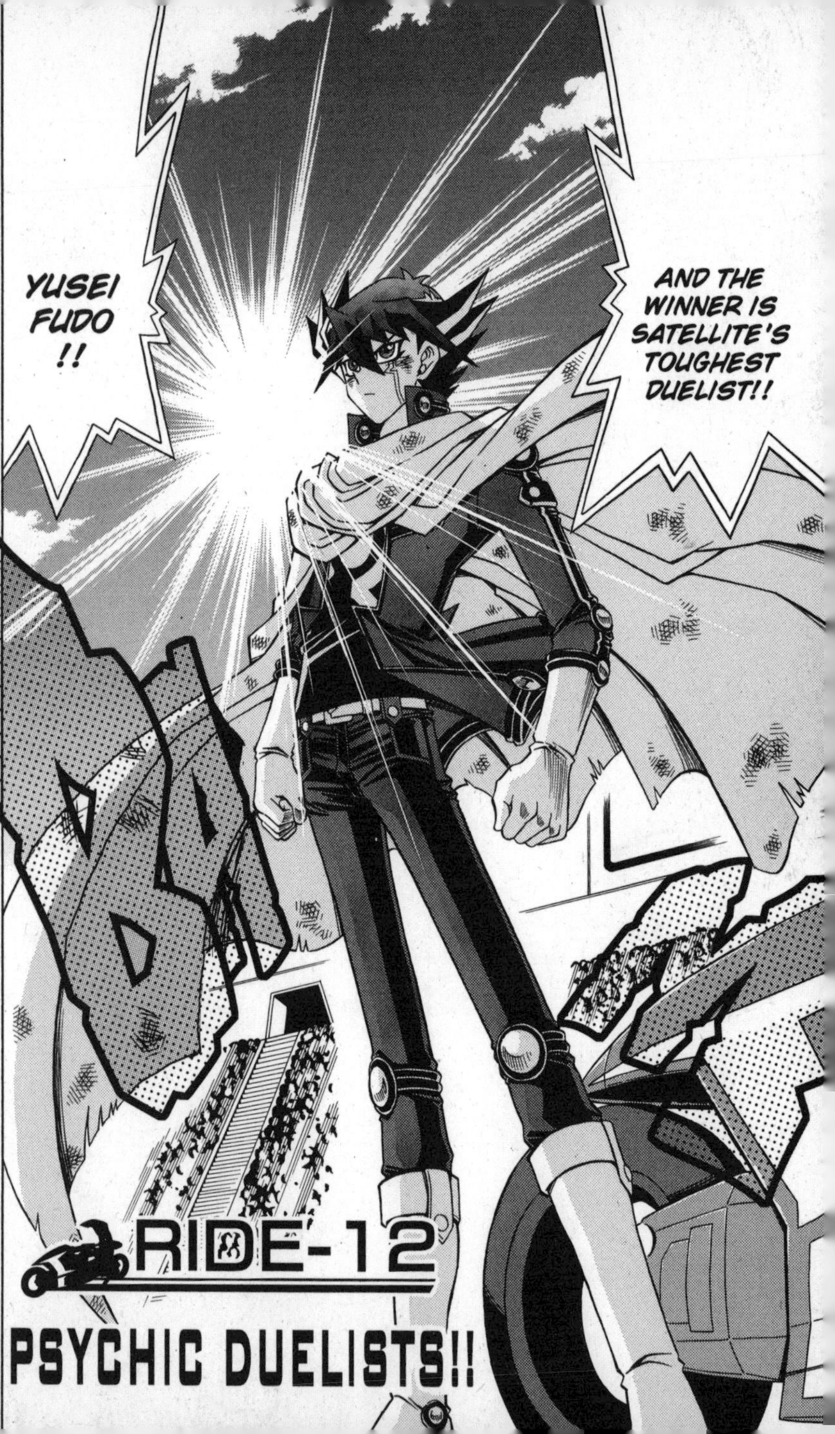
AND THE WINNER IS SATELLITE'S TOUGHEST DUELIST!!
YUSEI FUDO !!
RIDE-12
PSYCHIC DUELISTS!!

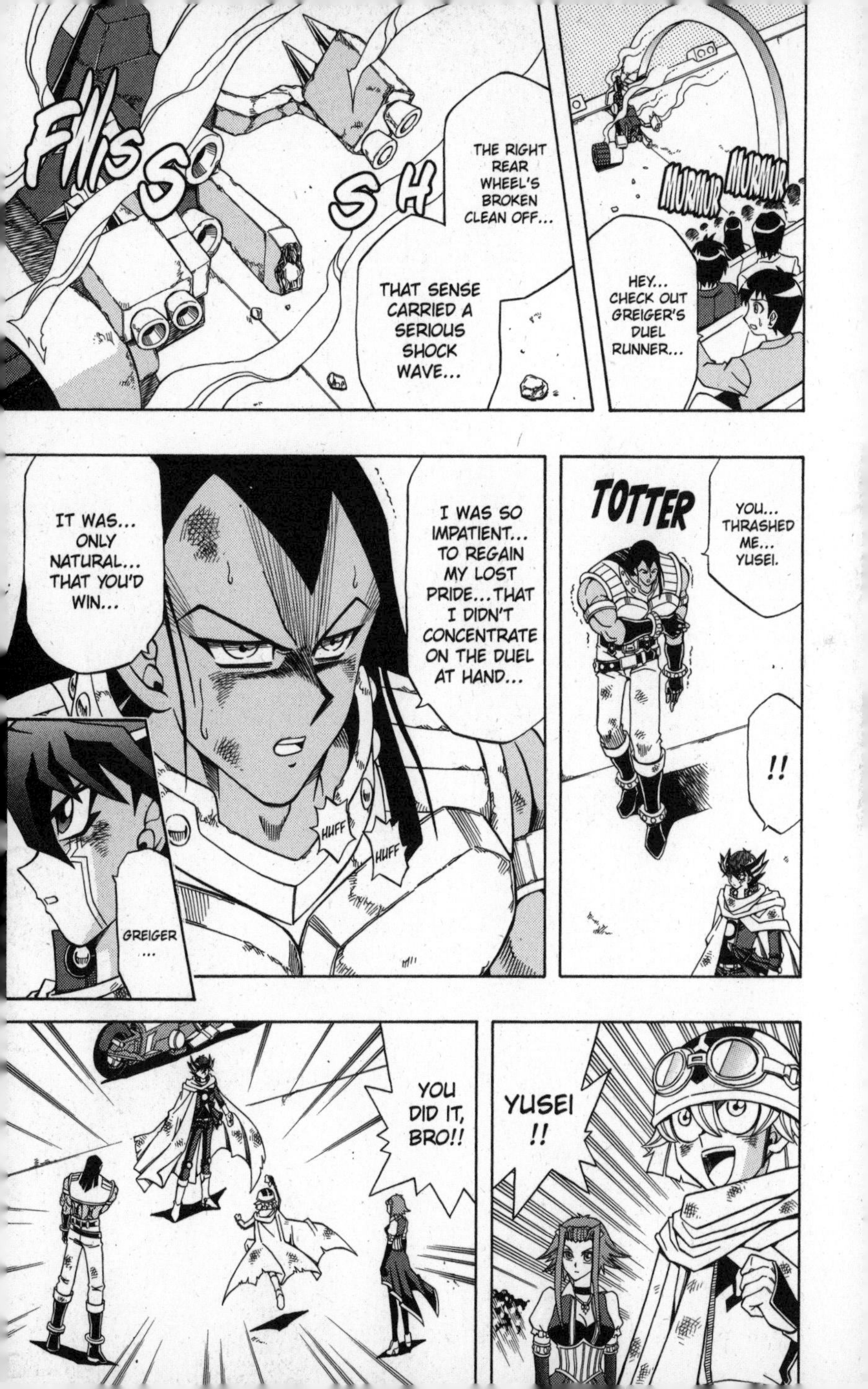
MURMUR
MURMUR
HEY... CHECK OUT GREIGER'S DUEL RUNNER...
THE RIGHT REAR WHEEL'S BROKEN CLEAN OFF...
THAT SENSE CARRIED A SERIOUS SHOCK WAVE...
FWISSSH
TOTTER
YOU... THRASHED ME... YUSEI.
!!
I WAS SO IMPATIENT... TO REGAIN MY LOST PRIDE...THAT I DIDN'T CONCENTRATE ON THE DUEL AT HAND...
IT WAS... ONLY NATURAL... THAT YOU'D WIN...
HUFF
HUFF
GREIGER ...
YUSEI !!
YOU DID IT, BRO!!

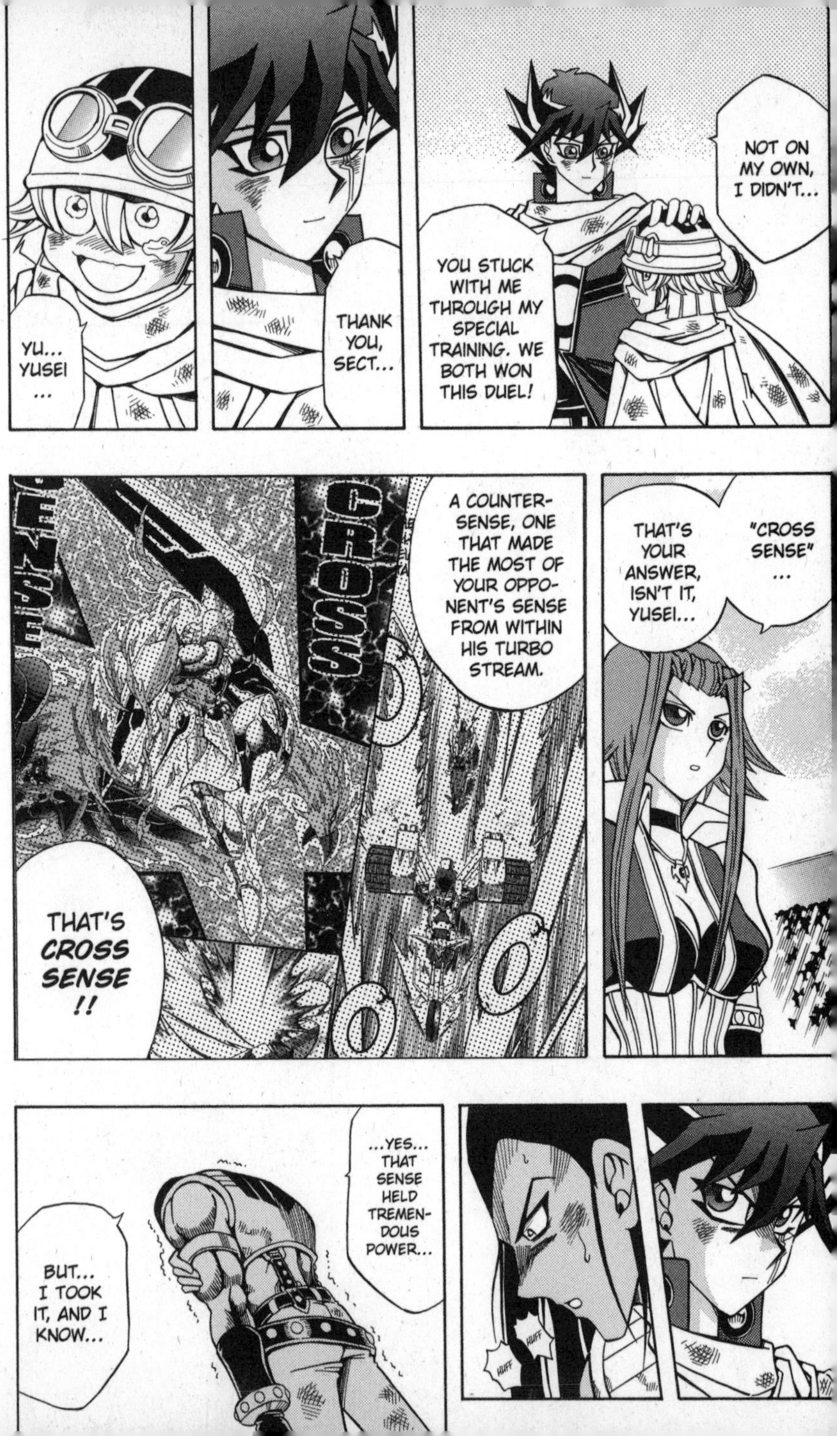

NOT ON MY OWN, I DIDN'T...
YOU STUCK WITH ME THROUGH MY SPECIAL TRAINING. WE BOTH WON THIS DUEL!
THANK YOU, SECT...
YU... YUSEI ...
"CROSS SENSE" ...
THAT'S YOUR ANSWER, ISN'T IT, YUSEI...
A COUNTER-SENSE, ONE THAT MADE THE MOST OF YOUR OPPONENT'S SENSE FROM WITHIN HIS TURBO STREAM.
CROSS
THAT'S CROSS SENSE !!
HUFF
HUFF
HUFF
...YES... THAT SENSE HELD TREMENDOUS POWER...
BUT... I TOOK IT, AND I KNOW...

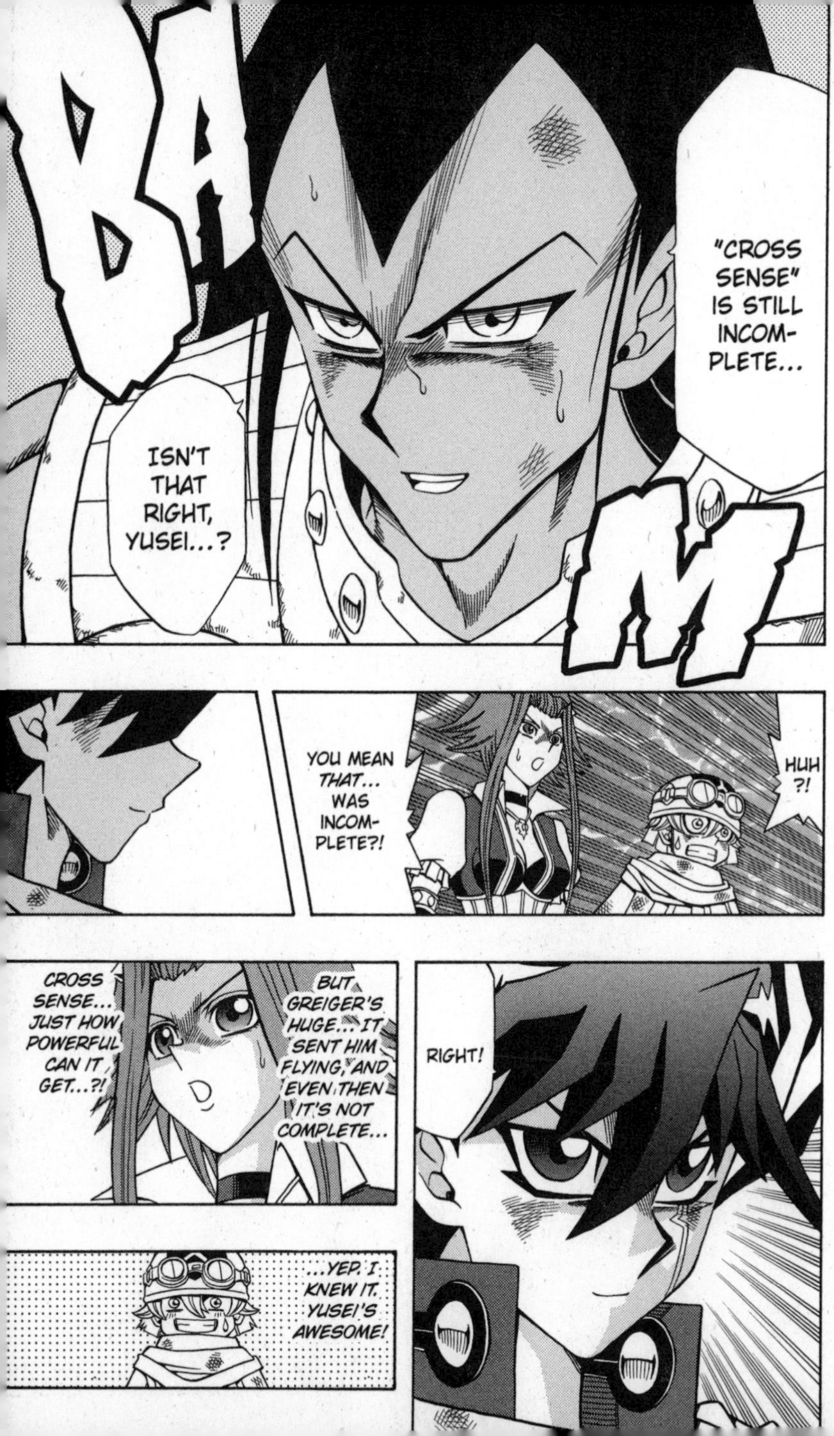
"CROSS SENSE" IS STILL INCOMPLETE...
BAM
ISN'T THAT RIGHT, YUSEI...?
HUH?!
YOU MEAN THAT... WAS INCOMPLETE?!
RIGHT!
BUT GREIGER'S HUGE... IT SENT HIM FLYING, AND EVEN THEN IT'S NOT COMPLETE...
CROSS SENSE... JUST HOW POWERFUL CAN IT GET...?!
...YEP. I KNEW IT. YUSEI'S AWESOME!

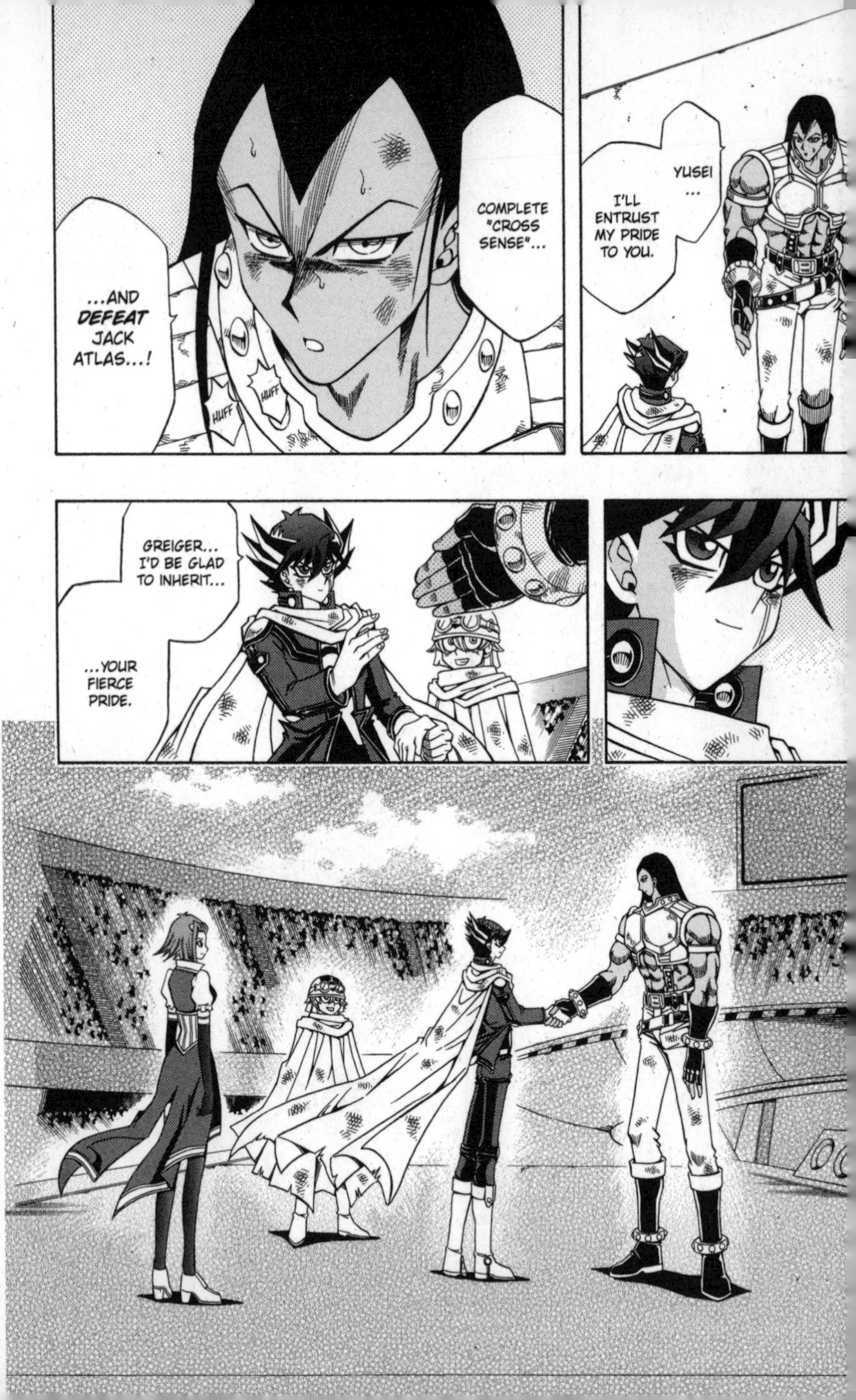
YUSEI...
I'LL ENTRUST MY PRIDE TO YOU.
COMPLETE "CROSS SENSE"...
HUFF
HUFF
...AND ***DEFEAT*** JACK ATLAS...!
GREIGER... I'D BE GLAD TO INHERIT...
...YOUR FIERCE PRIDE.

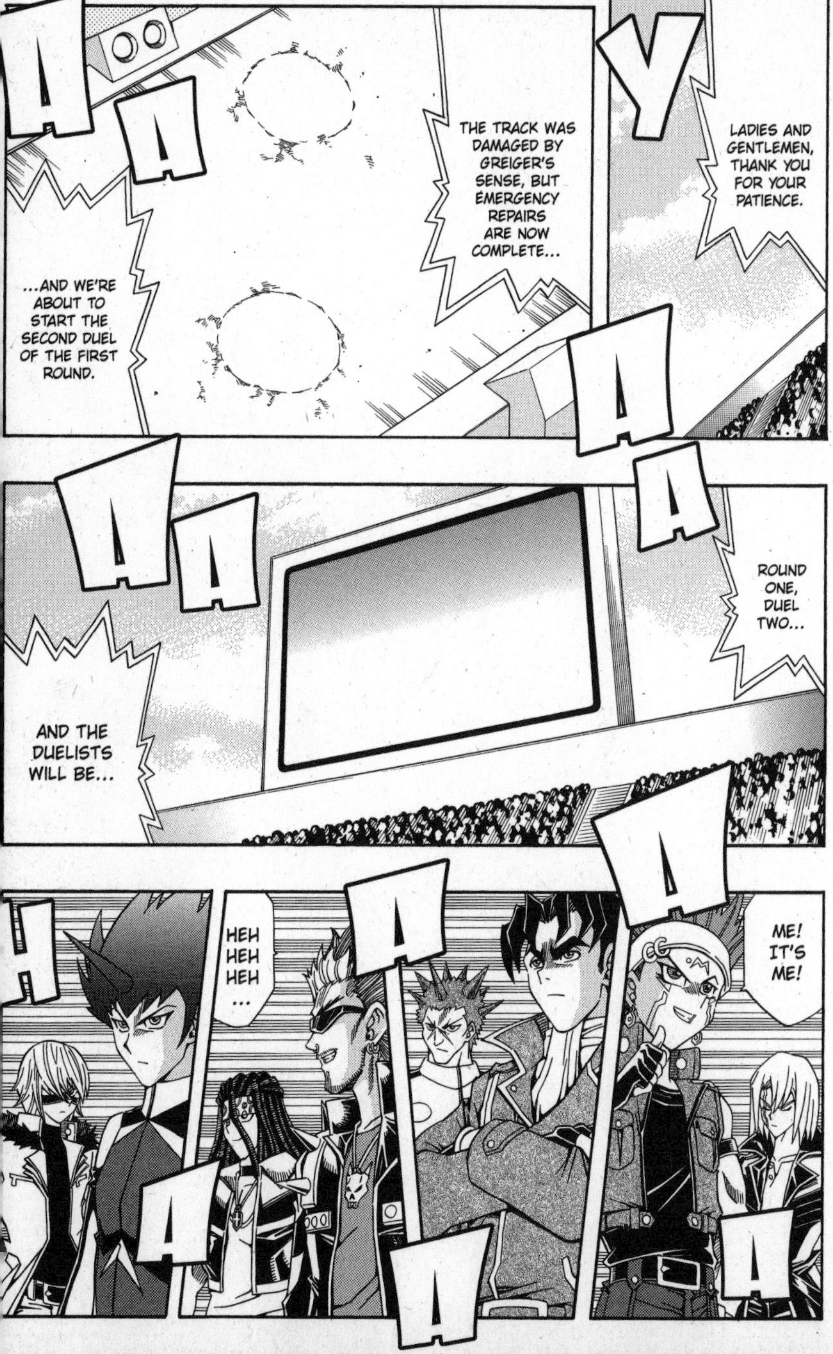
Y
LADIES AND GENTLEMEN, THANK YOU FOR YOUR PATIENCE.
A
A
A
THE TRACK WAS DAMAGED BY GREIGER'S SENSE, BUT EMERGENCY REPAIRS ARE NOW COMPLETE...
...AND WE'RE ABOUT TO START THE SECOND DUEL OF THE FIRST ROUND.
A
ROUND ONE, DUEL TWO...
A
A
AND THE DUELISTS WILL BE...
A
ME! IT'S ME!
A
A
A
HEH HEH HEH ...
A
H

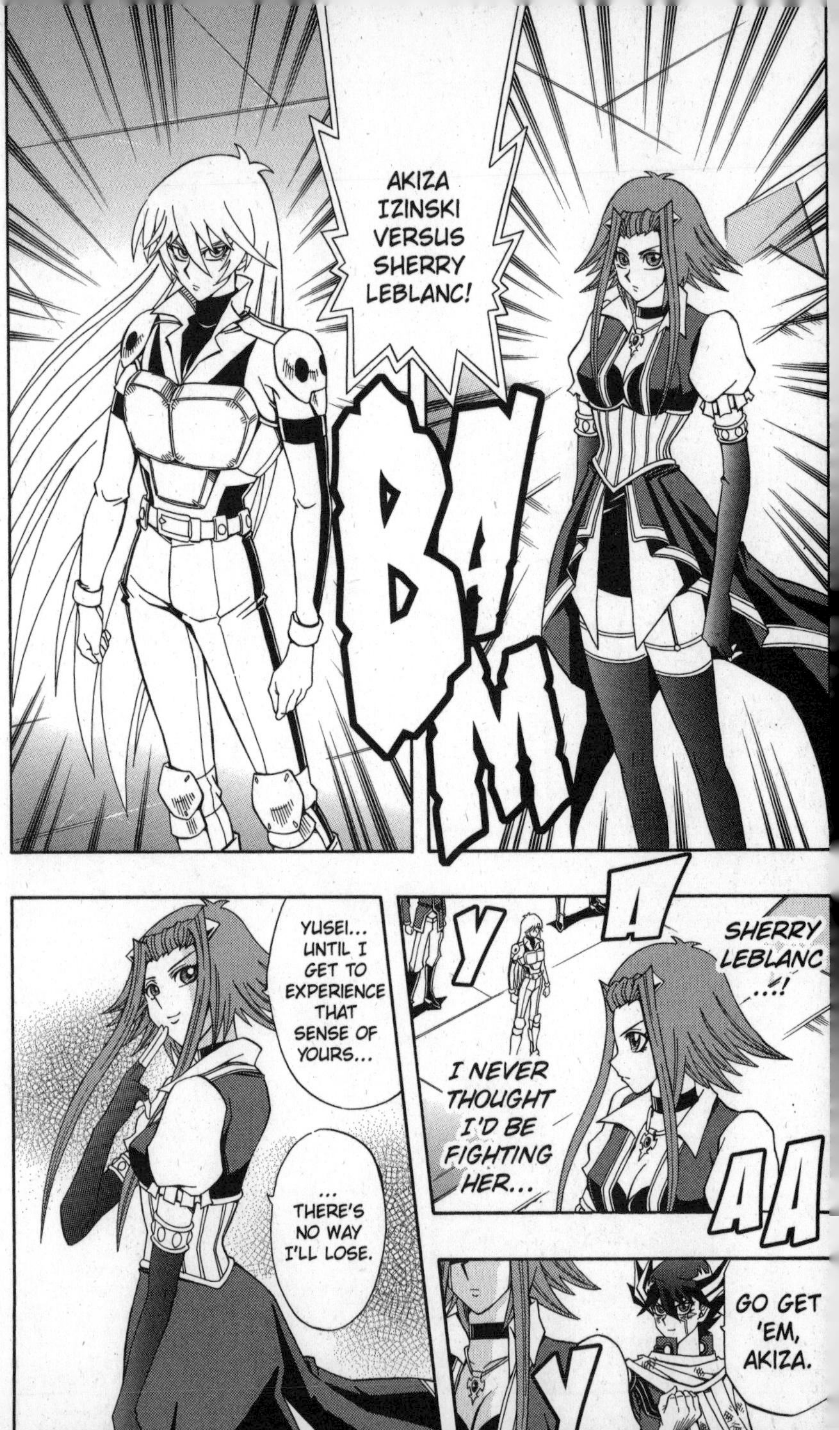
AKIZA IZINSKI VERSUS SHERRY LEBLANC!
BAM
SHERRY LEBLANC ...!
I NEVER THOUGHT I'D BE FIGHTING HER...
Y
A
AA
Y
GO GET 'EM, AKIZA.
YUSEI... UNTIL I GET TO EXPERIENCE THAT SENSE OF YOURS...
... THERE'S NO WAY I'LL LOSE.

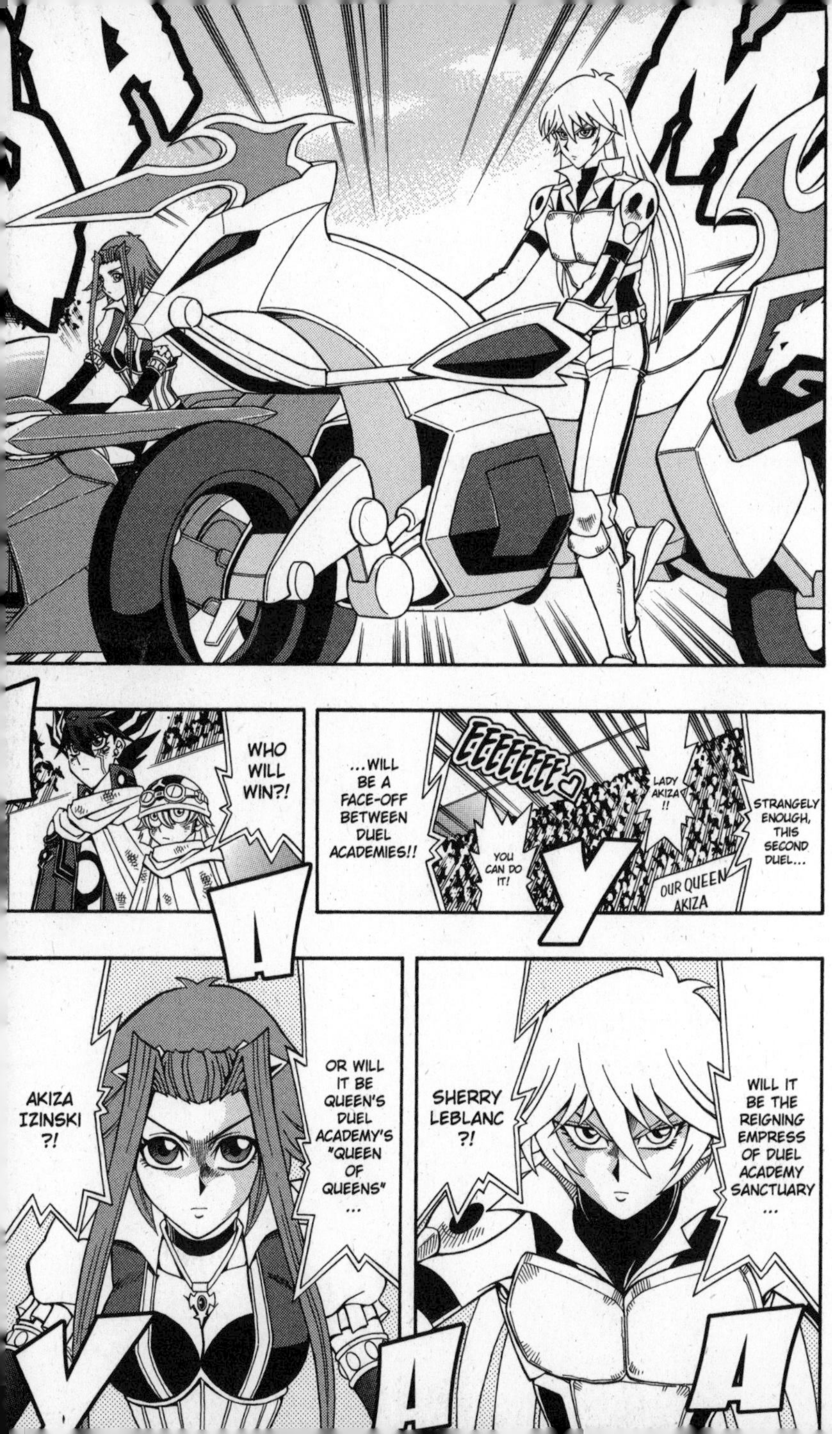
STRANGELY ENOUGH, THIS SECOND DUEL...
OUR QUEEN AKIZA
LADY AKIZA!!
EEEEEEEE♡
YOU CAN DO IT!
...WILL BE A FACE-OFF BETWEEN DUEL ACADEMIES!!
WHO WILL WIN?!
WILL IT BE THE REIGNING EMPRESS OF DUEL ACADEMY SANCTUARY...
SHERRY LEBLANC?!
OR WILL IT BE QUEEN'S DUEL ACADEMY'S "QUEEN OF QUEENS"...
AKIZA IZINSKI?!

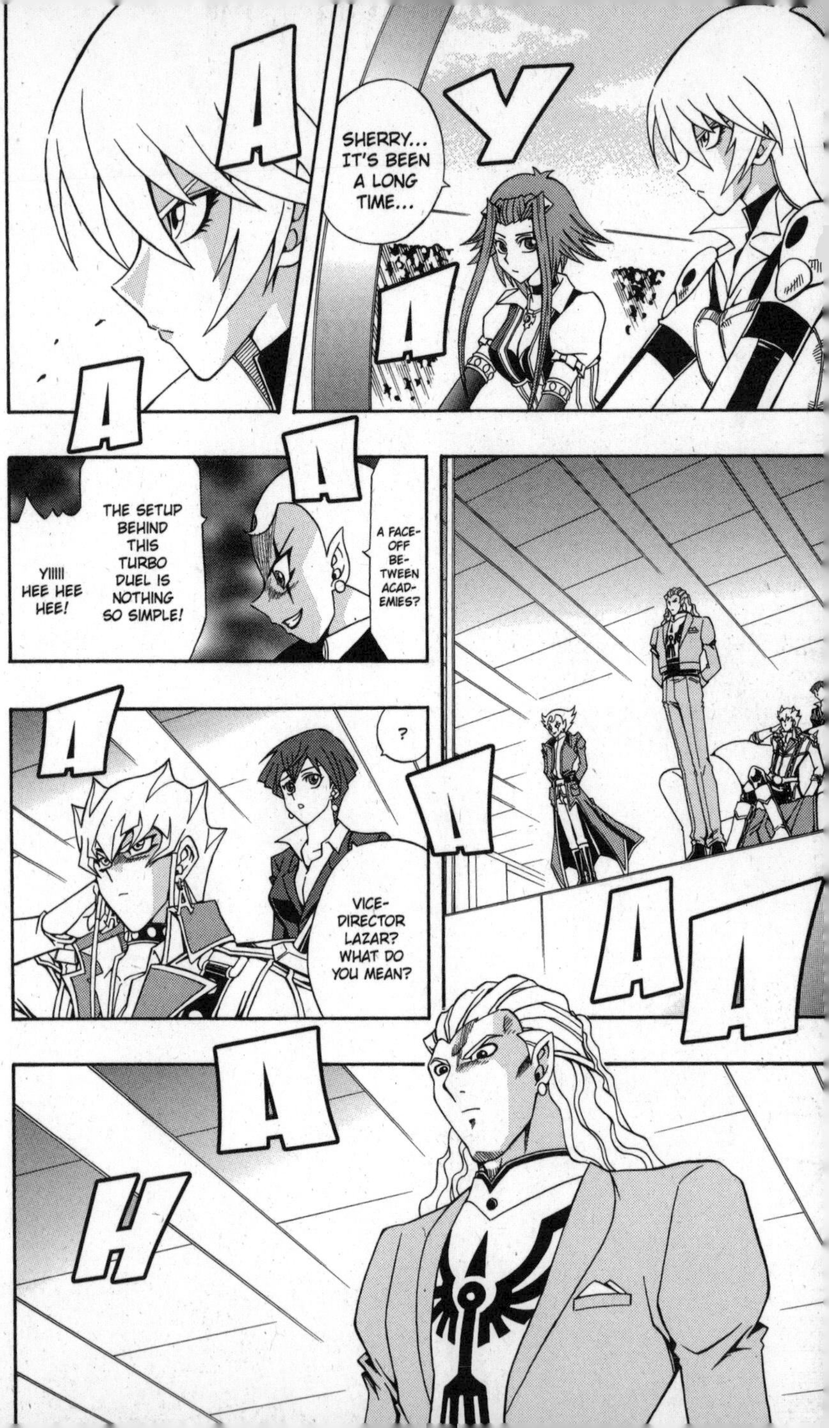
SHERRY... IT'S BEEN A LONG TIME...
A FACE-OFF BETWEEN ACADEMIES?
THE SETUP BEHIND THIS TURBO DUEL IS NOTHING SO SIMPLE!
YIIIII HEE HEE HEE!
?
VICE-DIRECTOR LAZAR? WHAT DO YOU MEAN?

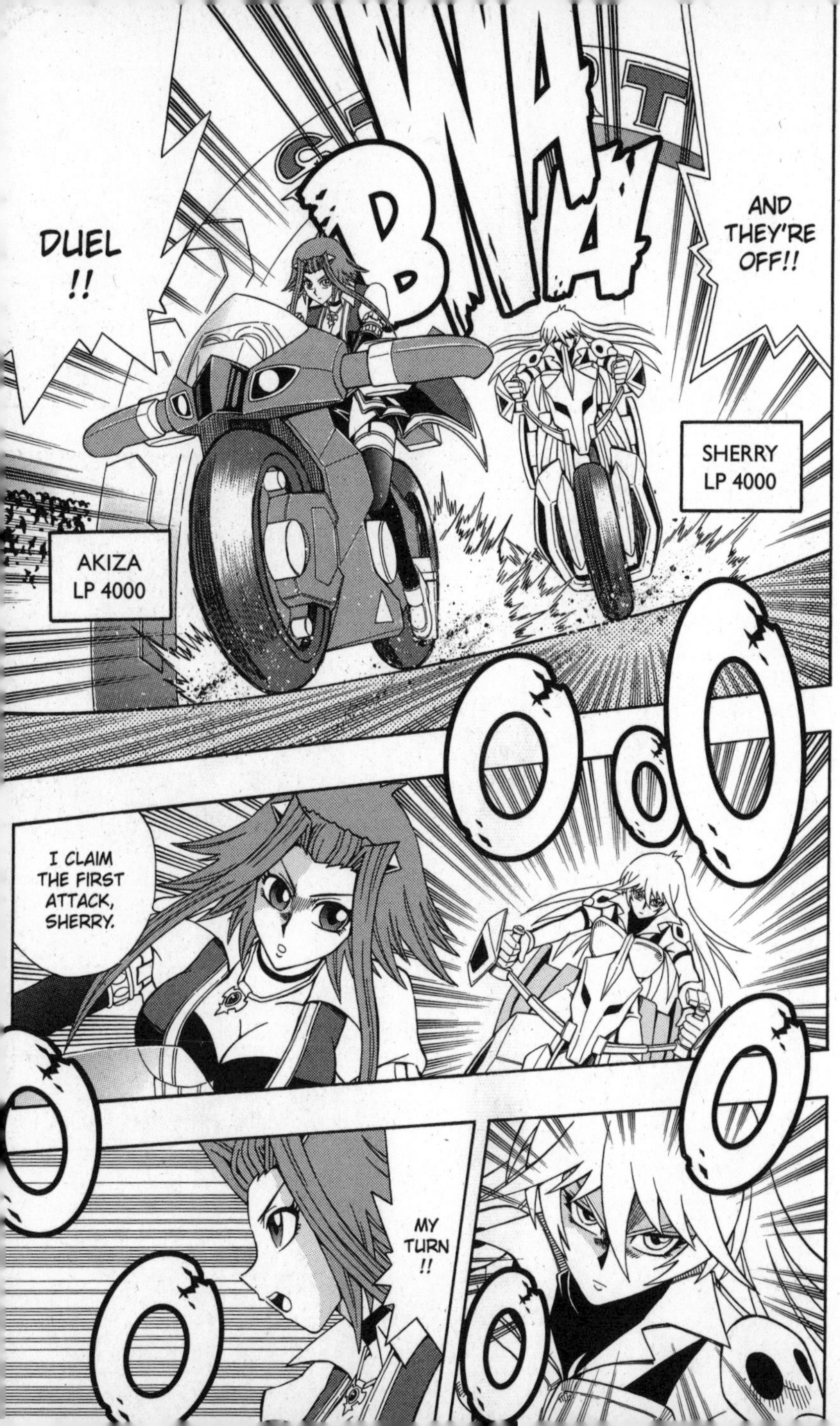
AND THEY'RE OFF!!
SHERRY LP 4000
DUEL!!
AKIZA LP 4000
I CLAIM THE FIRST ATTACK, SHERRY.
MY TURN!!

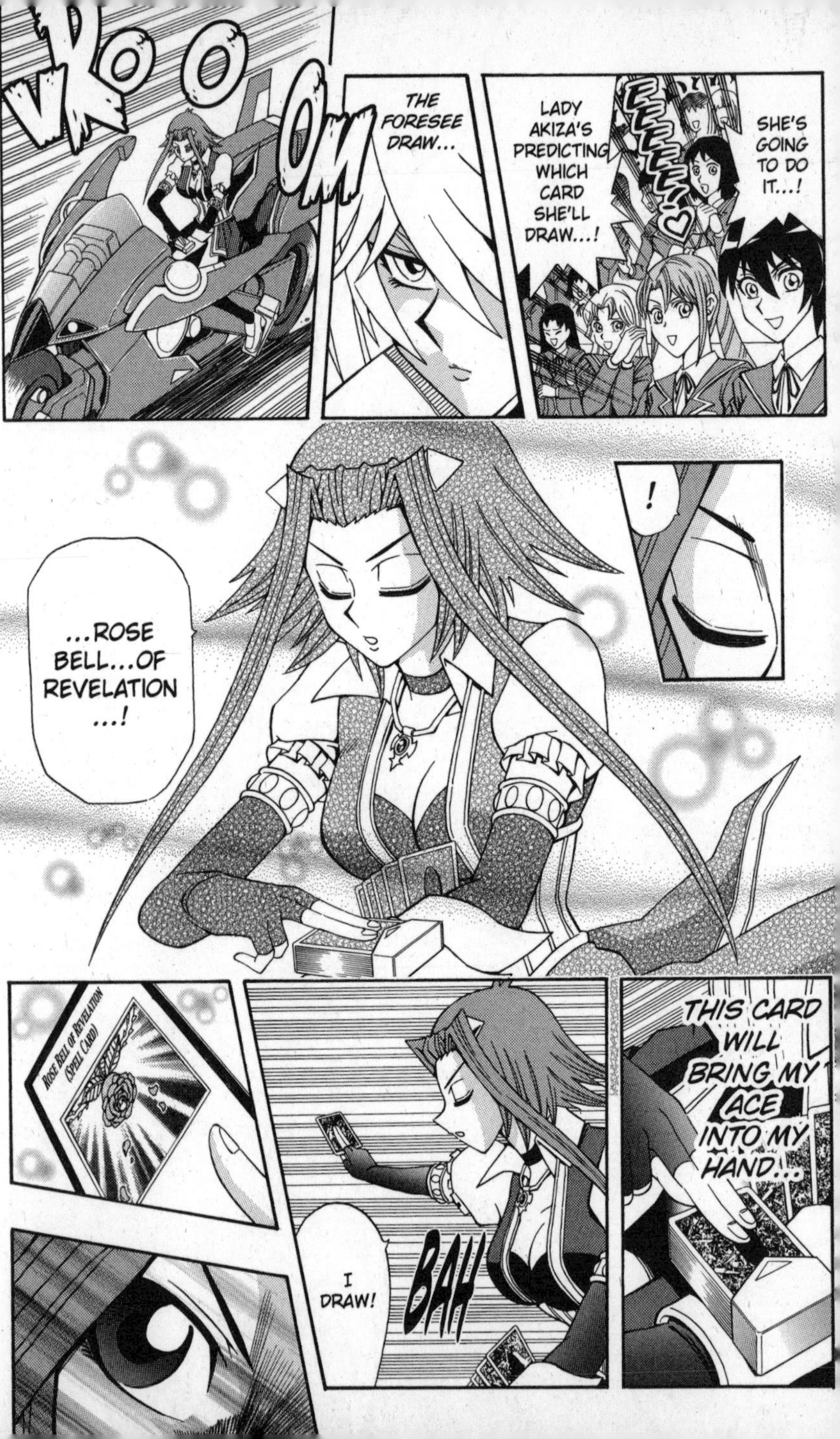
SHE'S GOING TO DO IT...!
LADY AKIZA'S PREDICTING WHICH CARD SHE'LL DRAW...!
THE FORESEE DRAW...
VROOOM
!
...ROSE BELL...OF REVELATION ...!
THIS CARD WILL BRING MY ACE INTO MY HAND...
BAH
I DRAW!
ROSE BELL OF REVELATION (SPELL CARD)

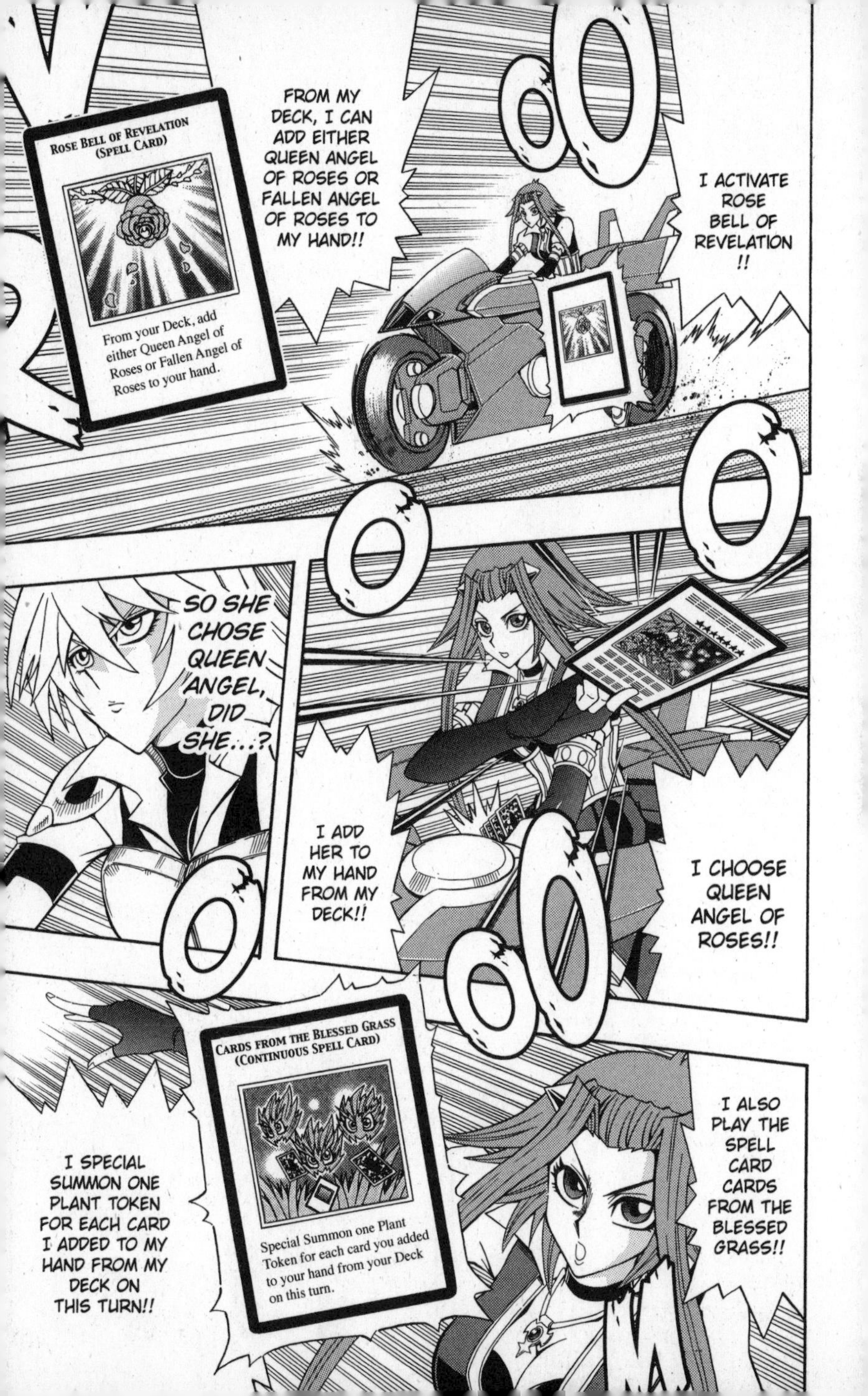
I ACTIVATE ROSE BELL OF REVELATION !!
FROM MY DECK, I CAN ADD EITHER QUEEN ANGEL OF ROSES OR FALLEN ANGEL OF ROSES TO MY HAND!!
ROSE BELL OF REVELATION (SPELL CARD)
From your Deck, add either Queen Angel of Roses or Fallen Angel of Roses to your hand.
I CHOOSE QUEEN ANGEL OF ROSES!!
I ADD HER TO MY HAND FROM MY DECK!!
SO SHE CHOSE QUEEN ANGEL, DID SHE...?
I ALSO PLAY THE SPELL CARD CARDS FROM THE BLESSED GRASS!!
CARDS FROM THE BLESSED GRASS (CONTINUOUS SPELL CARD)
Special Summon one Plant Token for each card you added to your hand from your Deck on this turn.
I SPECIAL SUMMON ONE PLANT TOKEN FOR EACH CARD I ADDED TO MY HAND FROM MY DECK ON THIS TURN!!

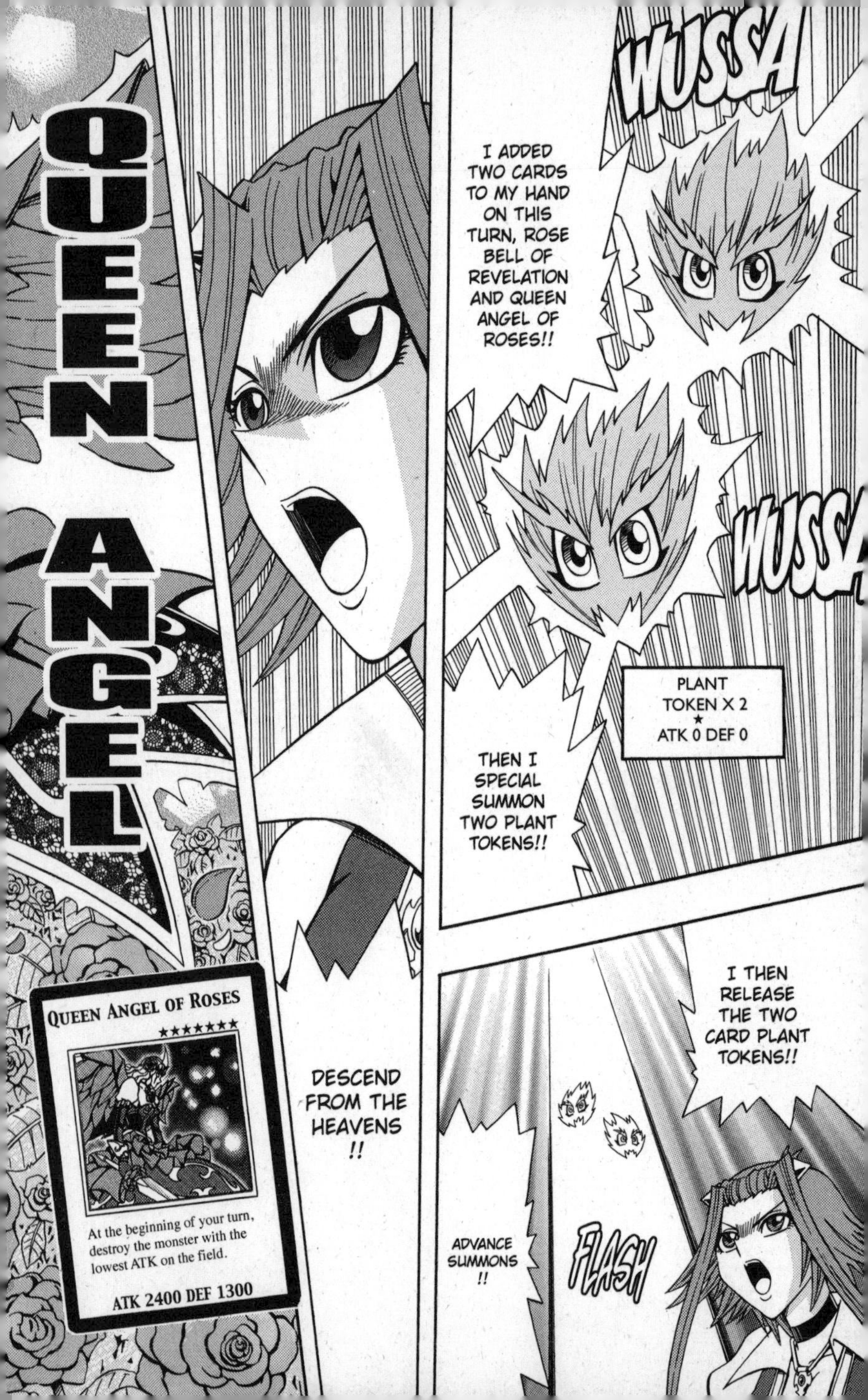
WUSSA
I ADDED TWO CARDS TO MY HAND ON THIS TURN, ROSE BELL OF REVELATION AND QUEEN ANGEL OF ROSES!!
WUSSA
PLANT TOKEN X 2 ★ ATK 0 DEF 0
THEN I SPECIAL SUMMON TWO PLANT TOKENS!!
I THEN RELEASE THE TWO CARD PLANT TOKENS!!
ADVANCE SUMMONS !!
FLASH
DESCEND FROM THE HEAVENS !!
QUEEN ANGEL
QUEEN ANGEL OF ROSES
★★★★★★★
At the beginning of your turn, destroy the monster with the lowest ATK on the field.
ATK 2400 DEF 1300

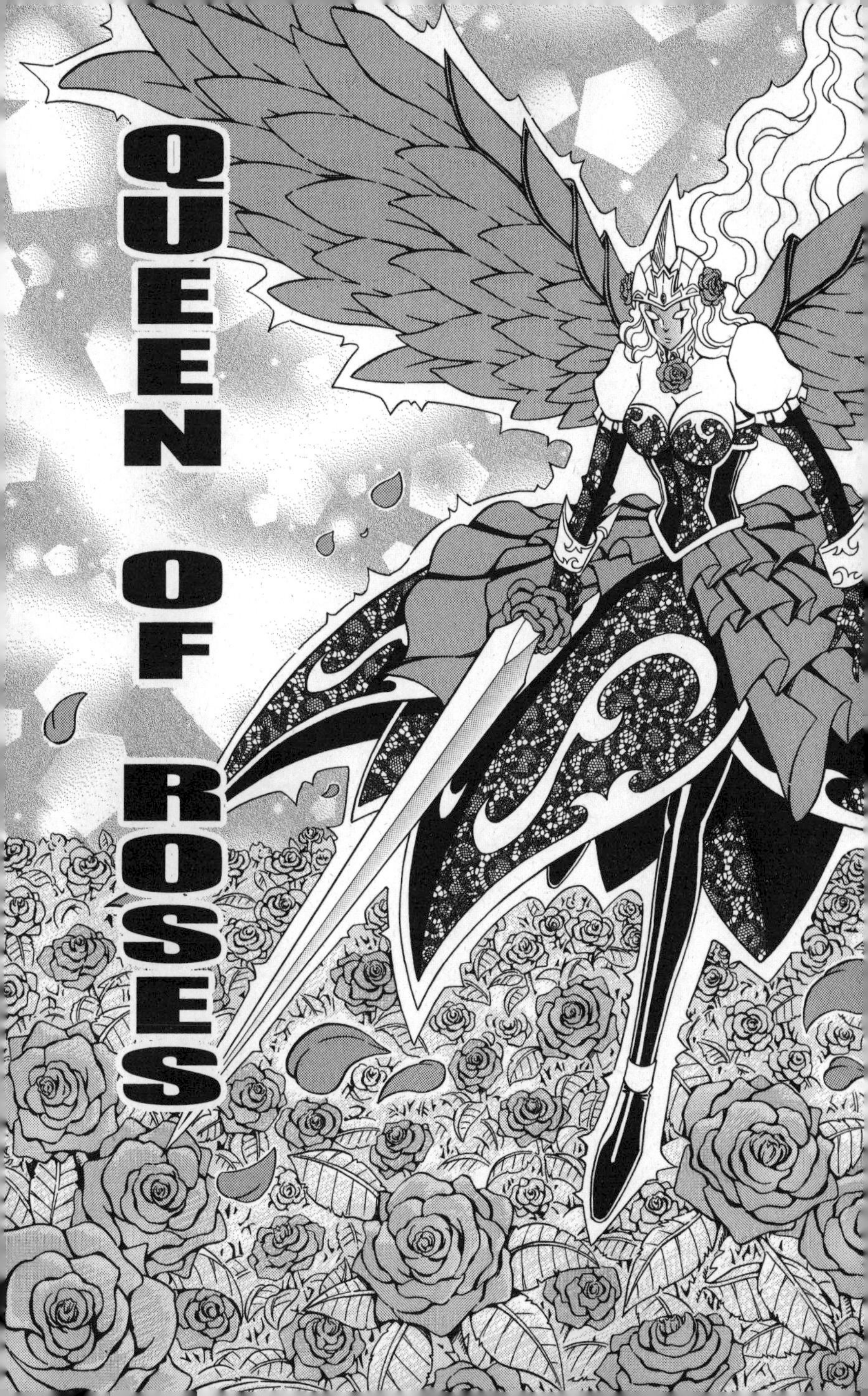
QUEEN OF ROSES

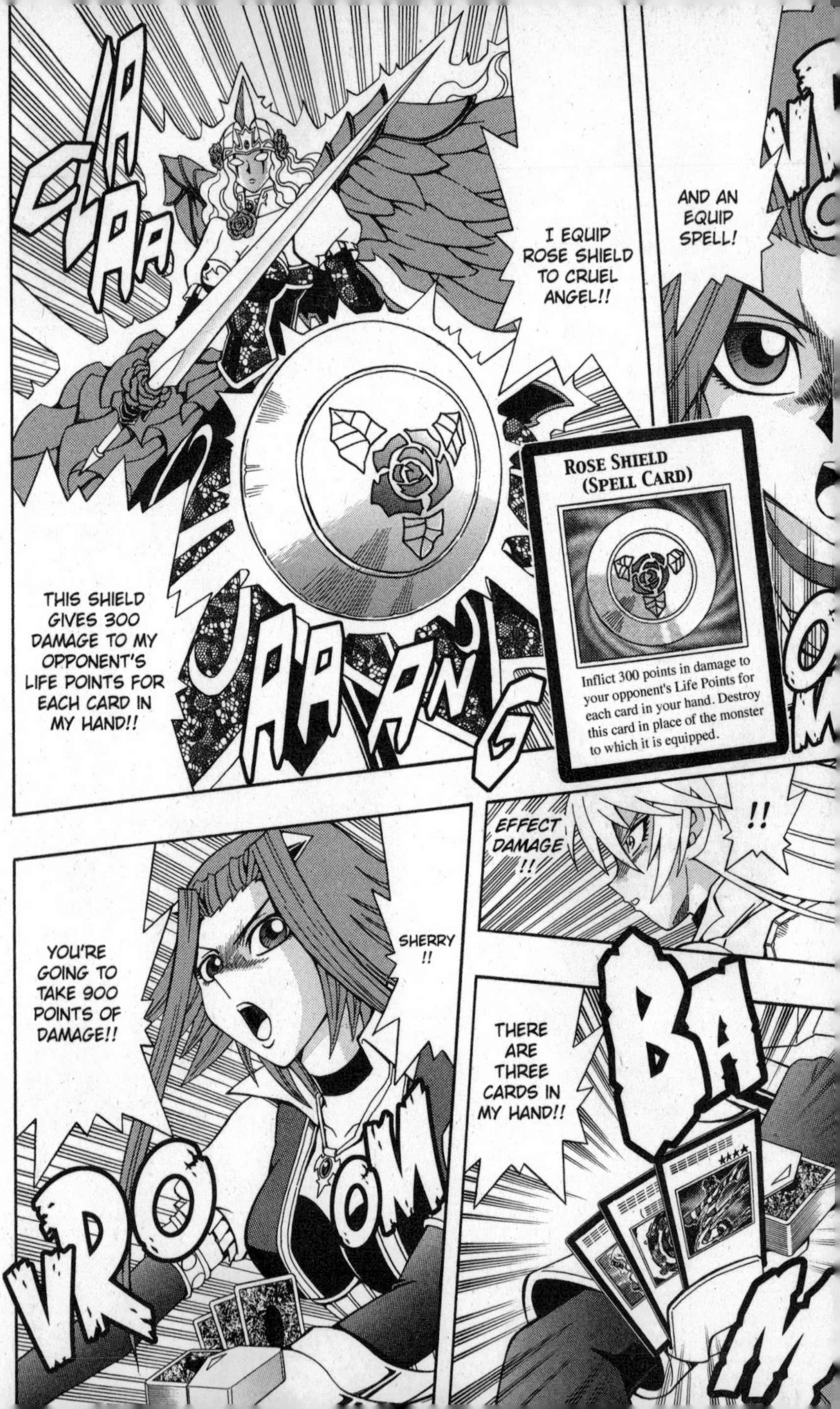
AND AN EQUIP SPELL!
CLAA
I EQUIP ROSE SHIELD TO CRUEL ANGEL!!
Rose Shield (Spell Card)
Inflict 300 points in damage to your opponent's Life Points for each card in your hand. Destroy this card in place of the monster to which it is equipped.
THIS SHIELD GIVES 300 DAMAGE TO MY OPPONENT'S LIFE POINTS FOR EACH CARD IN MY HAND!!
JAAANG
!!
EFFECT DAMAGE!!
BAM
THERE ARE THREE CARDS IN MY HAND!!
SHERRY!!
YOU'RE GOING TO TAKE 900 POINTS OF DAMAGE!!
VROOM

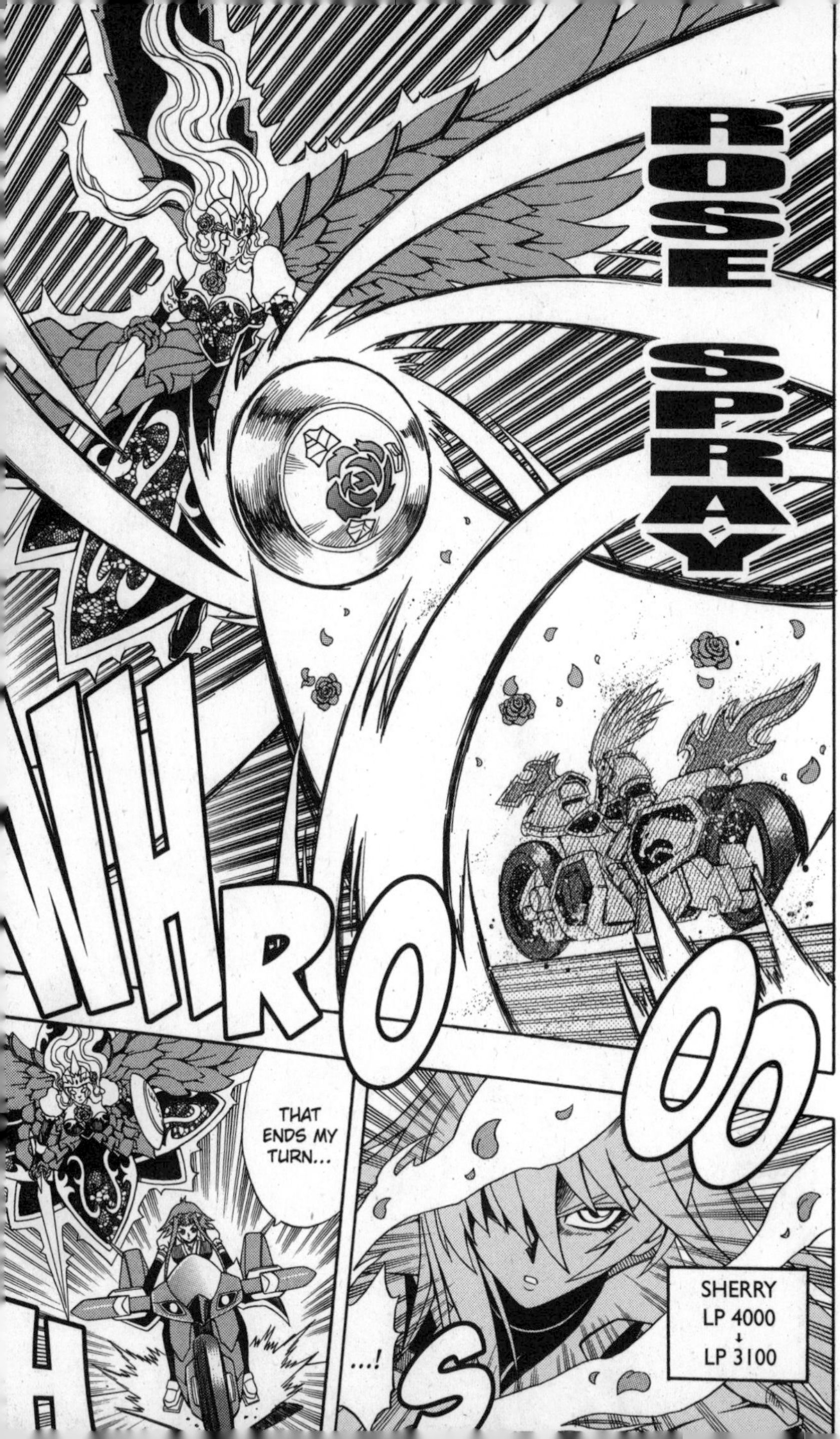
ROSE SPRAY
WHROOOO
SHERRY
LP 4000
↓
LP 3100
...!
THAT ENDS MY TURN...

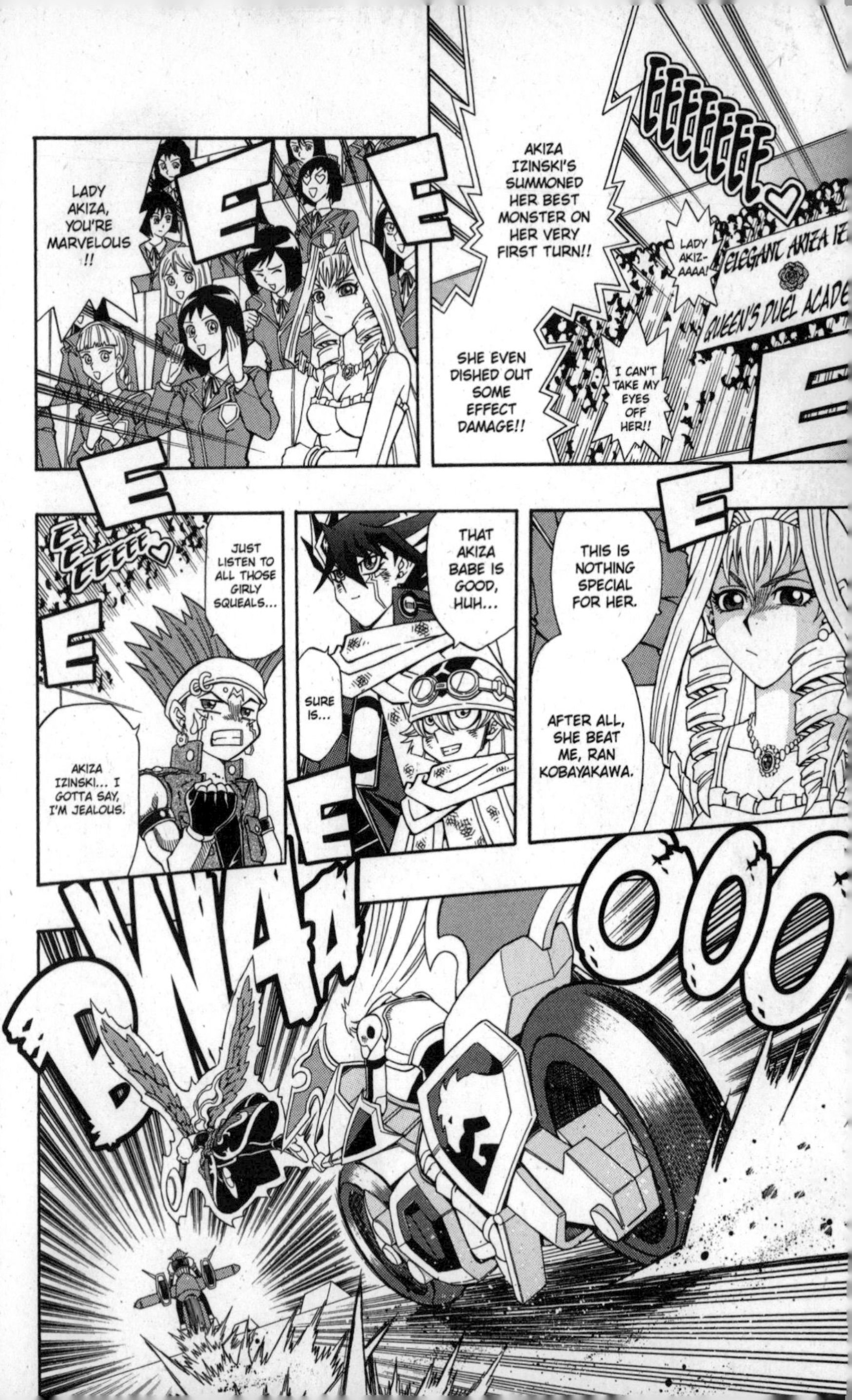
EEEEEEEE♥
AKIZA IZINSKI'S SUMMONED HER BEST MONSTER ON HER VERY FIRST TURN!!
LADY AKIZ-AAAA!
I CAN'T TAKE MY EYES OFF HER!!
SHE EVEN DISHED OUT SOME EFFECT DAMAGE!!
E
E E
LADY AKIZA, YOU'RE MARVELOUS!!
E
E
THIS IS NOTHING SPECIAL FOR HER.
AFTER ALL, SHE BEAT ME, RAN KOBAYAKAWA.
THAT AKIZA BABE IS GOOD, HUH...
SURE IS...
E
EEEEEEE♥
JUST LISTEN TO ALL THOSE GIRLY SQUEALS...
E
AKIZA IZINSKI... I GOTTA SAY, I'M JEALOUS.
BWAAOOO

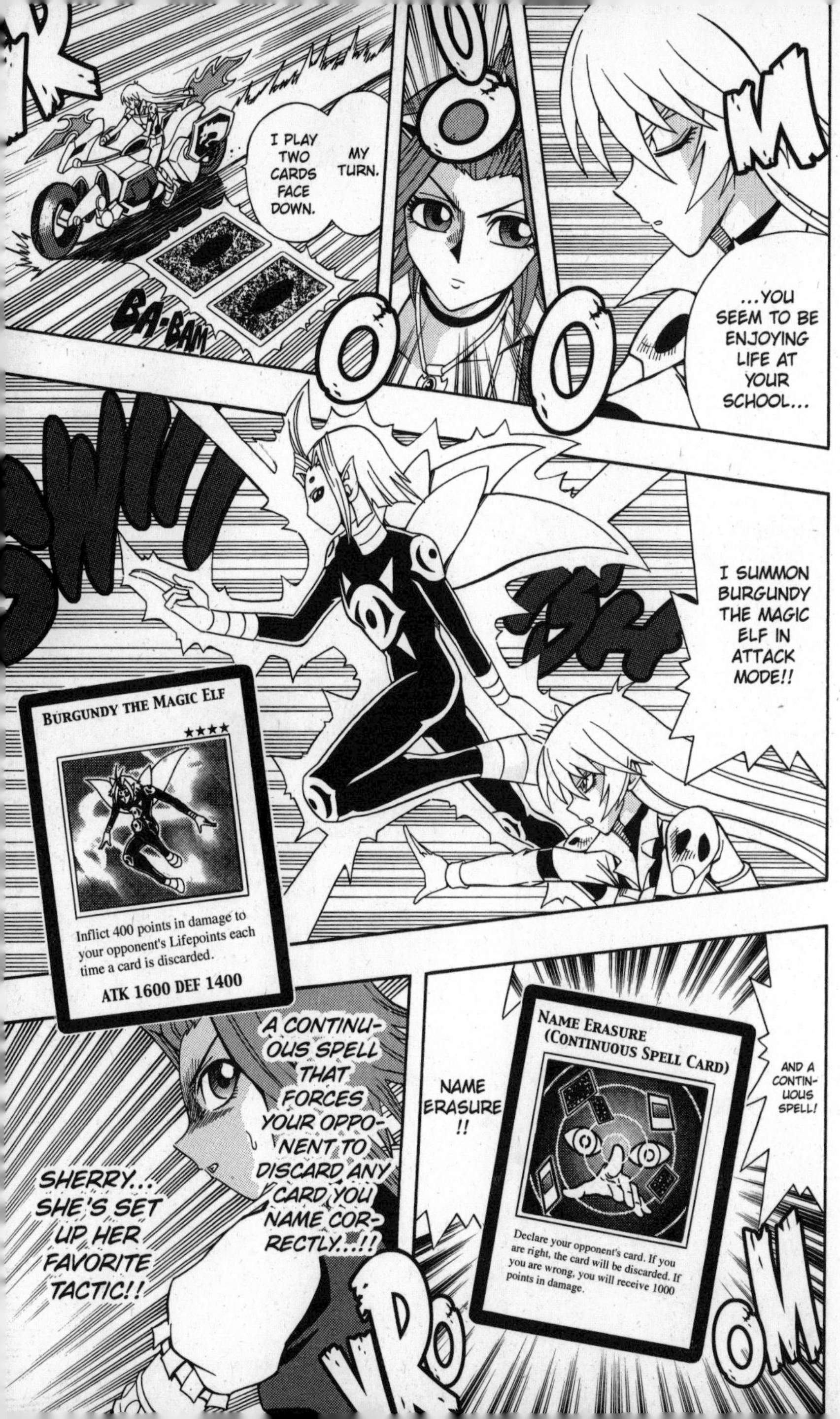
...YOU SEEM TO BE ENJOYING LIFE AT YOUR SCHOOL...
MY TURN.
I PLAY TWO CARDS FACE DOWN.
BA-BAM
I SUMMON BURGUNDY THE MAGIC ELF IN ATTACK MODE!!
BURGUNDY THE MAGIC ELF
Inflict 400 points in damage to your opponent's Lifepoints each time a card is discarded.
ATK 1600 DEF 1400
AND A CONTINUOUS SPELL!
NAME ERASURE!!
NAME ERASURE (CONTINUOUS SPELL CARD)
Declare your opponent's card. If you are right, the card will be discarded. If you are wrong, you will receive 1000 points in damage.
A CONTINUOUS SPELL THAT FORCES YOUR OPPONENT TO DISCARD ANY CARD YOU NAME CORRECTLY...!!
SHERRY... SHE'S SET UP HER FAVORITE TACTIC!!

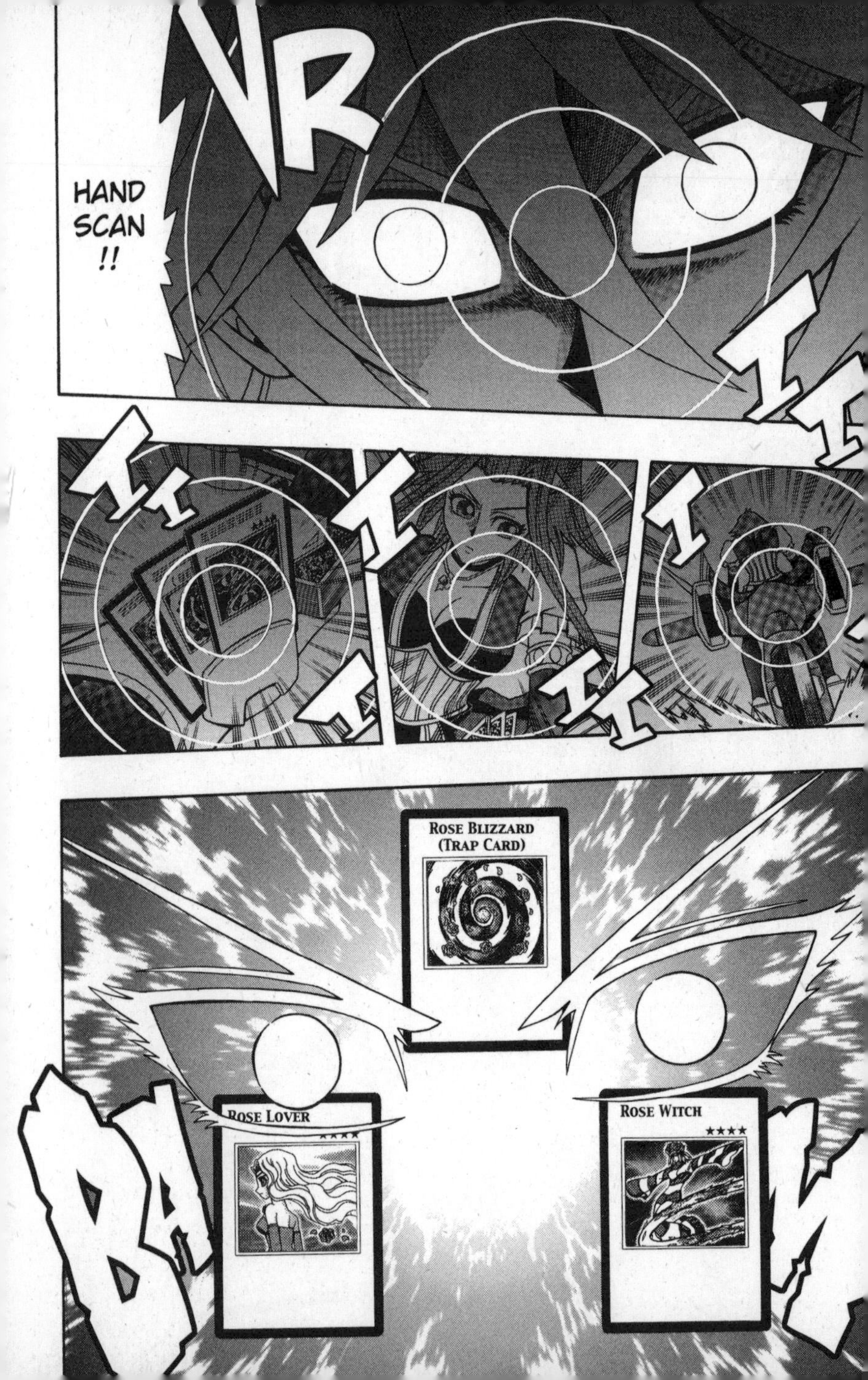
VR
HAND SCAN !!
ROSE BLIZZARD (TRAP CARD)
ROSE WITCH
ROSE LOVER

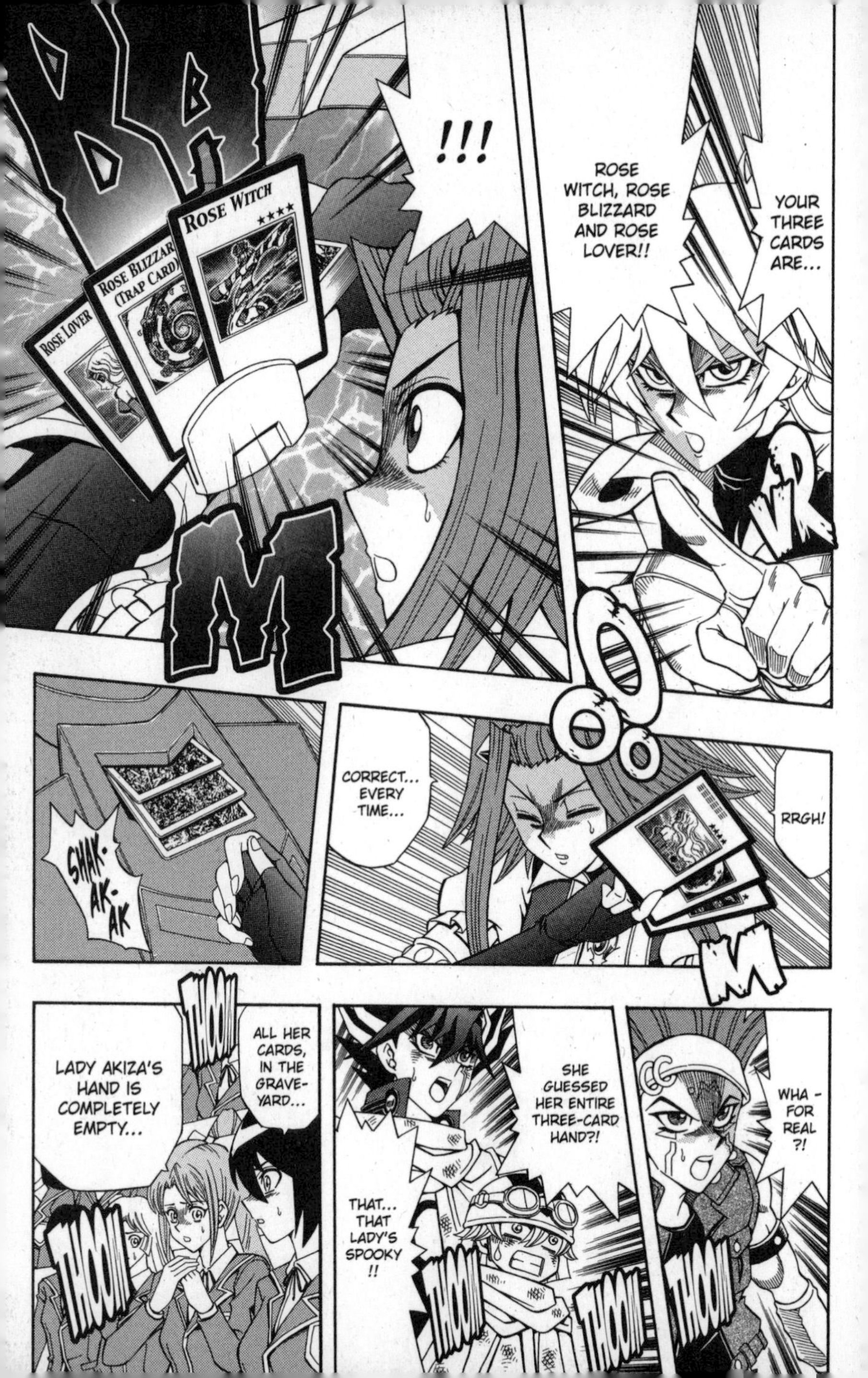
YOUR THREE CARDS ARE...
ROSE WITCH, ROSE BLIZZARD AND ROSE LOVER!!
!!!
ROSE WITCH
ROSE BLIZZAR (TRAP CARD)
ROSE LOVER
M
RRGH!
CORRECT... EVERY TIME...
SHAK-AK-AK
WHA- FOR REAL?!
THOOM
SHE GUESSED HER ENTIRE THREE-CARD HAND?!
THAT... THAT LADY'S SPOOKY!!
THOOM
THOOM
ALL HER CARDS, IN THE GRAVE-YARD...
LADY AKIZA'S HAND IS COMPLETELY EMPTY...
THOOM
THOOM

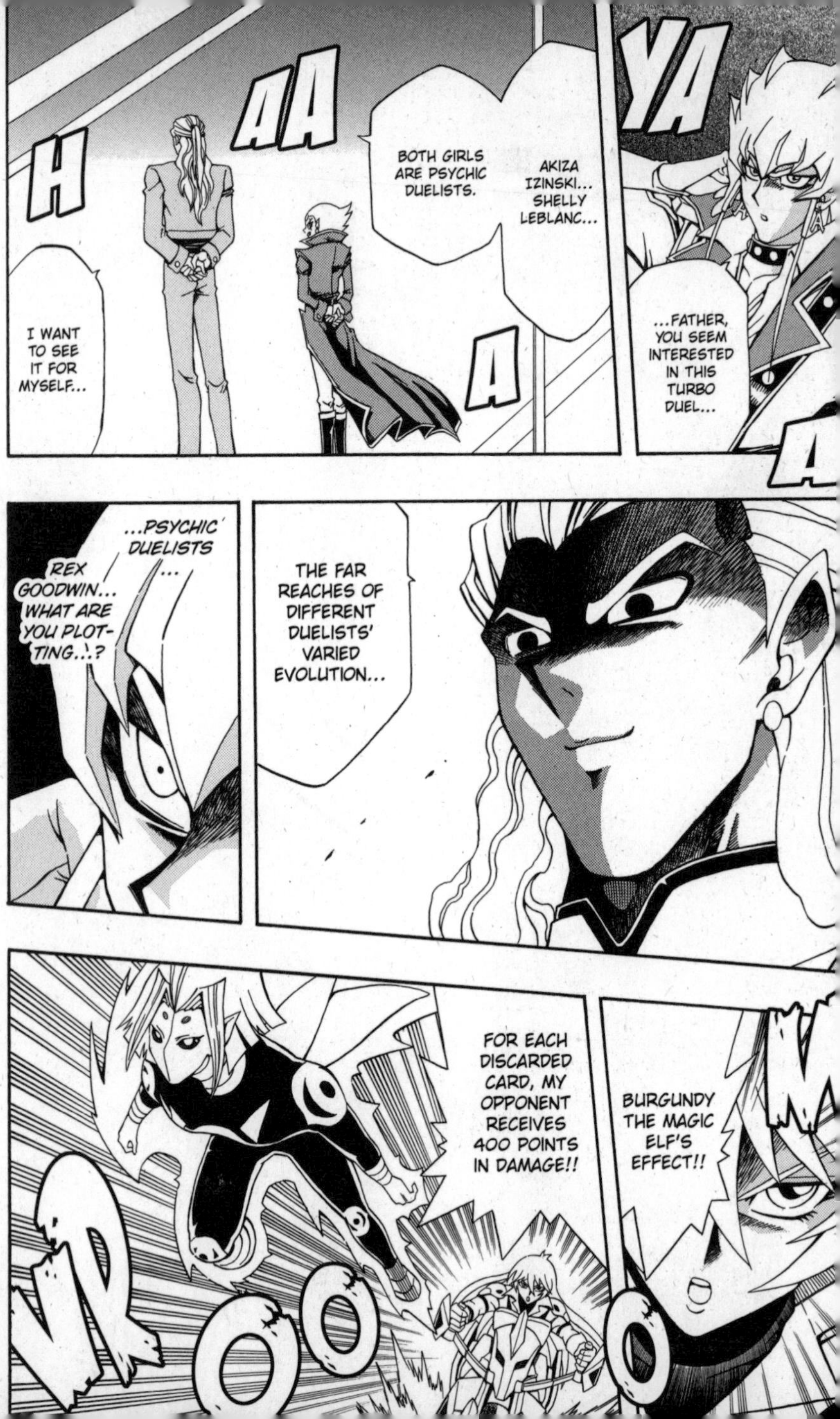
YA
...FATHER, YOU SEEM INTERESTED IN THIS TURBO DUEL...
A
AKIZA IZINSKI... SHELLY LEBLANC...
BOTH GIRLS ARE PSYCHIC DUELISTS.
AA
H
I WANT TO SEE IT FOR MYSELF...
A
THE FAR REACHES OF DIFFERENT DUELISTS' VARIED EVOLUTION...
...PSYCHIC DUELISTS...
REX GOODWIN... WHAT ARE YOU PLOTTING...?
BURGUNDY THE MAGIC ELF'S EFFECT!!
FOR EACH DISCARDED CARD, MY OPPONENT RECEIVES 400 POINTS IN DAMAGE!!
VROOOO

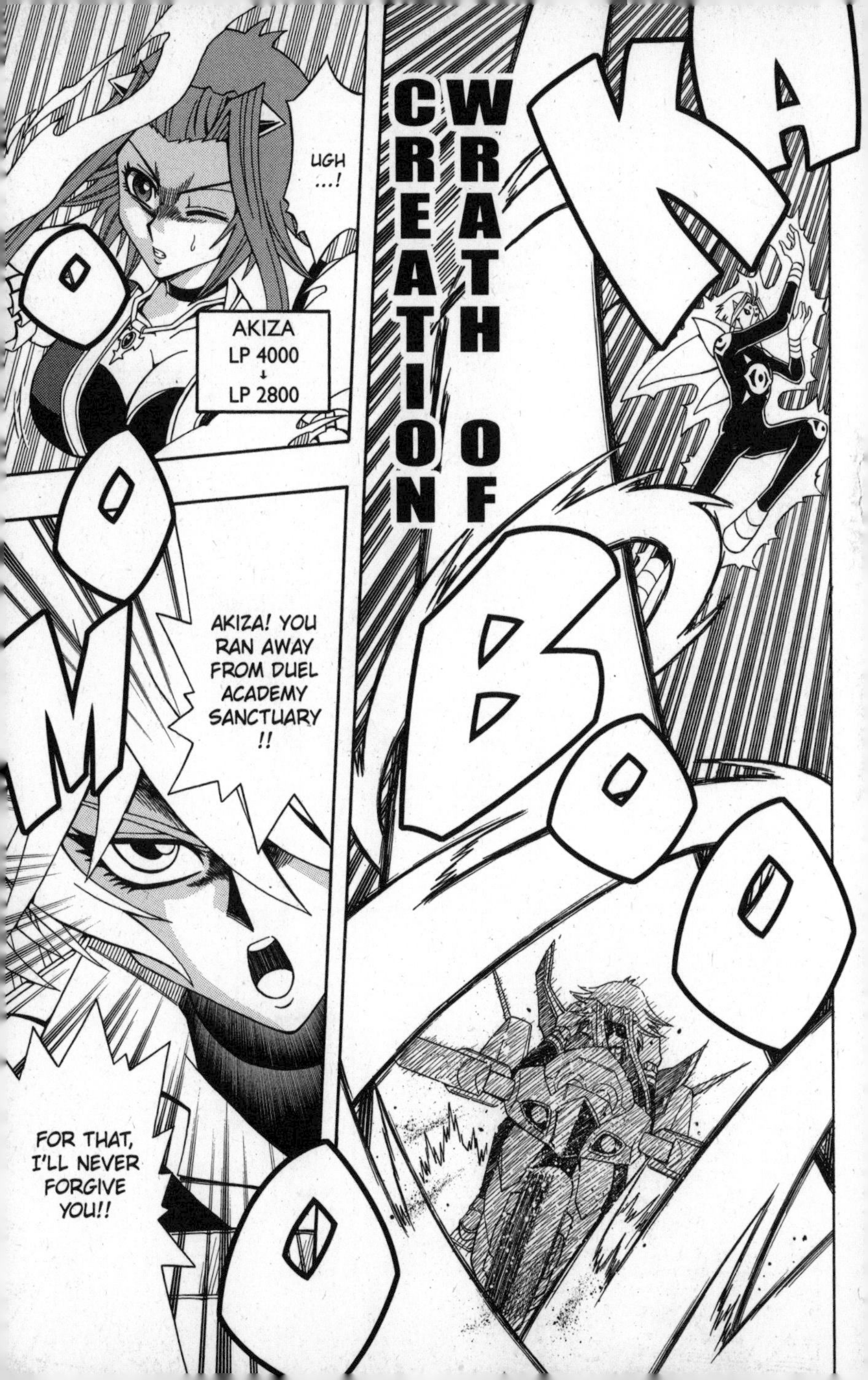
WRATH OF CREATION
UGH ...!
AKIZA LP 4000 ↓ LP 2800
AKIZA! YOU RAN AWAY FROM DUEL ACADEMY SANCTUARY !!
FOR THAT, I'LL NEVER FORGIVE YOU!!

5D's TRACKS

THE 12TH

BY SATOMASA

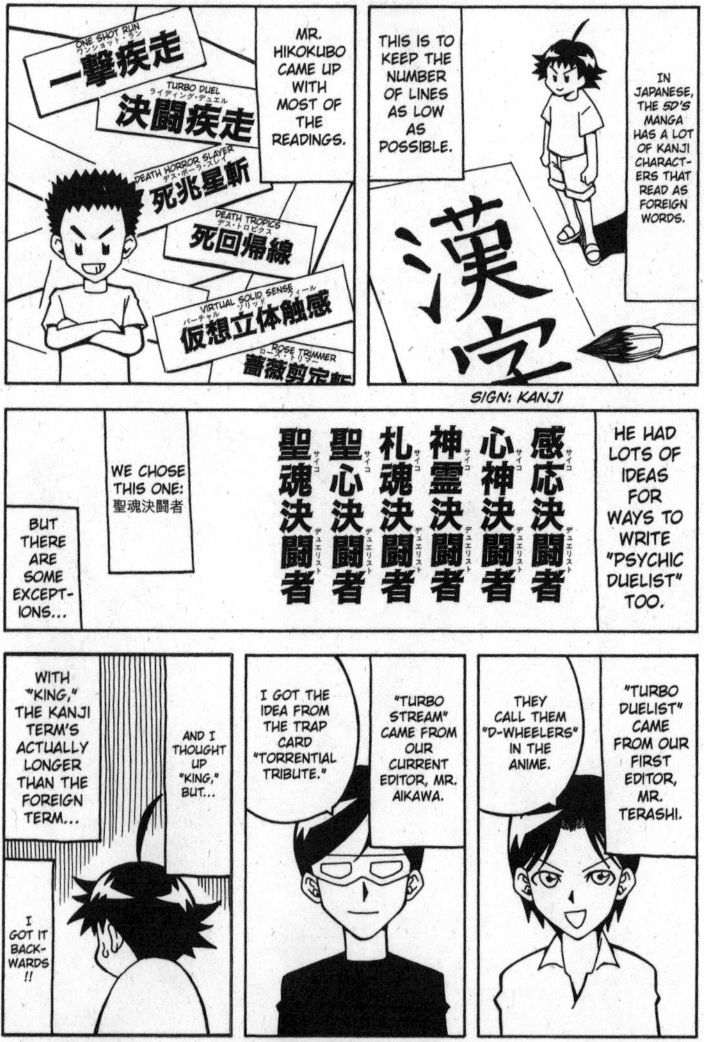
IN JAPANESE, THE 5D'S MANGA HAS A LOT OF KANJI CHARACTERS THAT READ AS FOREIGN WORDS.
THIS IS TO KEEP THE NUMBER OF LINES AS LOW AS POSSIBLE.
漢
SIGN: KANJI
MR. HIKOKUBO CAME UP WITH MOST OF THE READINGS.
ONE SHOT RUN ワンショット・ラン 一撃疾走
TURBO DUEL ライディング・デュエル 決闘疾走
DEATH HORROR SLAYER デス・ホーラ・スレイ 死兆星斬
DEATH TROPICS デス・トロピクス 死回帰線
VIRTUAL SOLID SENSE バーチャル・ソリッド・フィール 仮想立体触感
ROSE TRIMMER ローズ・トリマー
HE HAD LOTS OF IDEAS FOR WAYS TO WRITE "PSYCHIC DUELIST" TOO.
感応決闘者
心神決闘者
神霊決闘者
札魂決闘者
聖心決闘者
聖魂決闘者
WE CHOSE THIS ONE: 聖魂決闘者
BUT THERE ARE SOME EXCEPT-IONS...
"TURBO DUELIST" CAME FROM OUR FIRST EDITOR, MR. TERASHI.
THEY CALL THEM "D-WHEELERS" IN THE ANIME.
"TURBO STREAM" CAME FROM OUR CURRENT EDITOR, MR. AIKAWA.
I GOT THE IDEA FROM THE TRAP CARD "TORRENTIAL TRIBUTE."
AND I THOUGHT UP "KING," BUT...
WITH "KING," THE KANJI TERM'S ACTUALLY LONGER THAN THE FOREIGN TERM...
I GOT IT BACK-WARDS!!

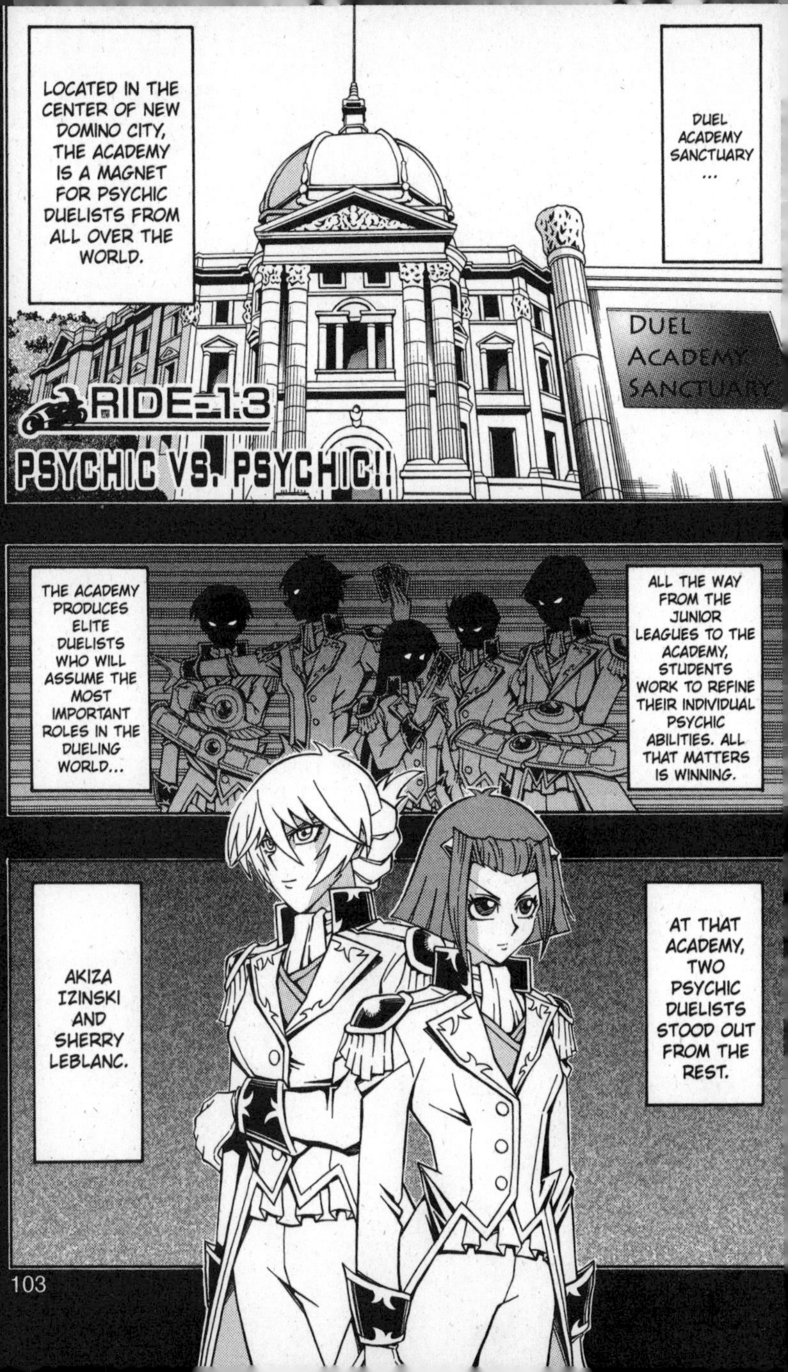
DUEL ACADEMY SANCTUARY ...
LOCATED IN THE CENTER OF NEW DOMINO CITY, THE ACADEMY IS A MAGNET FOR PSYCHIC DUELISTS FROM ALL OVER THE WORLD.
DUEL ACADEMY SANCTUARY
RIDE-13
PSYCHIC VS. PSYCHIC!!
ALL THE WAY FROM THE JUNIOR LEAGUES TO THE ACADEMY, STUDENTS WORK TO REFINE THEIR INDIVIDUAL PSYCHIC ABILITIES. ALL THAT MATTERS IS WINNING.
THE ACADEMY PRODUCES ELITE DUELISTS WHO WILL ASSUME THE MOST IMPORTANT ROLES IN THE DUELING WORLD...
AT THAT ACADEMY, TWO PSYCHIC DUELISTS STOOD OUT FROM THE REST.
AKIZA IZINSKI AND SHERRY LEBLANC.

RIDE 13

PSYCHIC VS. PSYCHIC

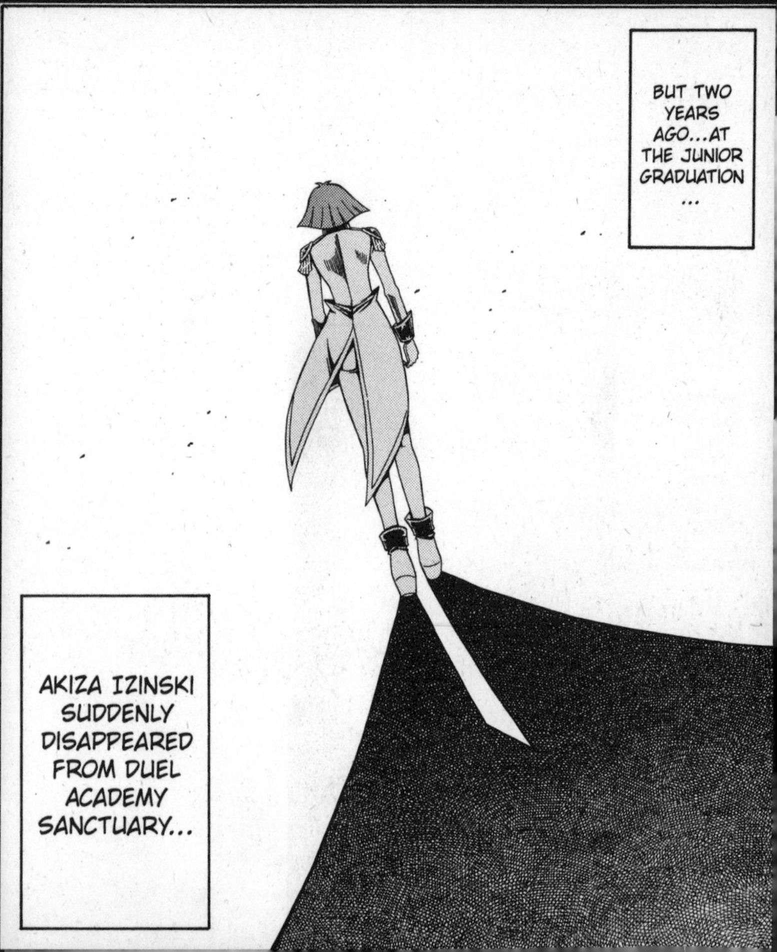
BUT TWO YEARS AGO...AT THE JUNIOR GRADUATION ...
AKIZA IZINSKI SUDDENLY DISAPPEARED FROM DUEL ACADEMY SANCTUARY...

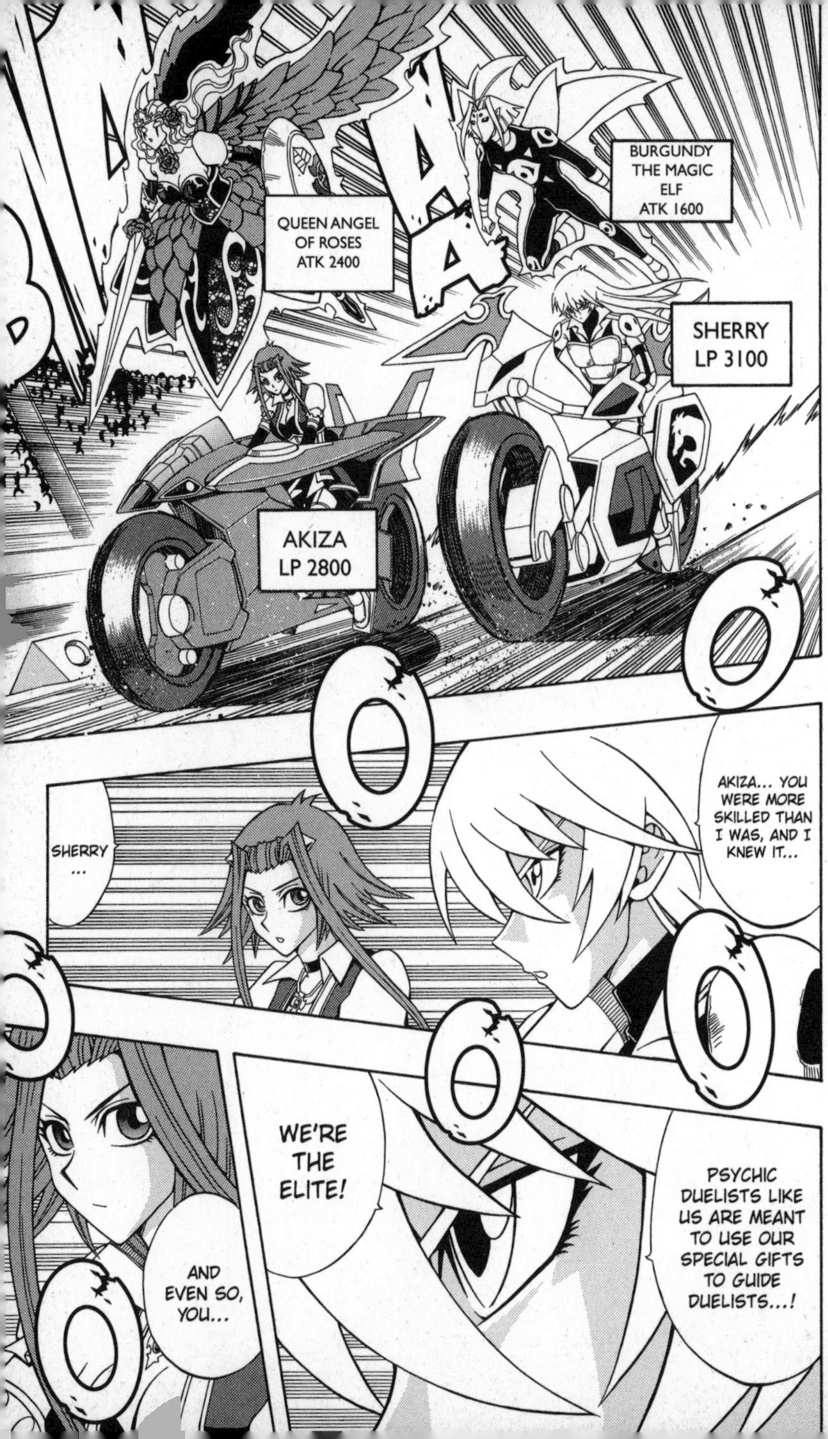
BURGUNDY THE MAGIC ELF ATK 1600
QUEEN ANGEL OF ROSES ATK 2400
SHERRY LP 3100
AKIZA LP 2800
AKIZA... YOU WERE MORE SKILLED THAN I WAS, AND I KNEW IT...
SHERRY ...
PSYCHIC DUELISTS LIKE US ARE MEANT TO USE OUR SPECIAL GIFTS TO GUIDE DUELISTS...!
WE'RE THE ELITE!
AND EVEN SO, YOU...

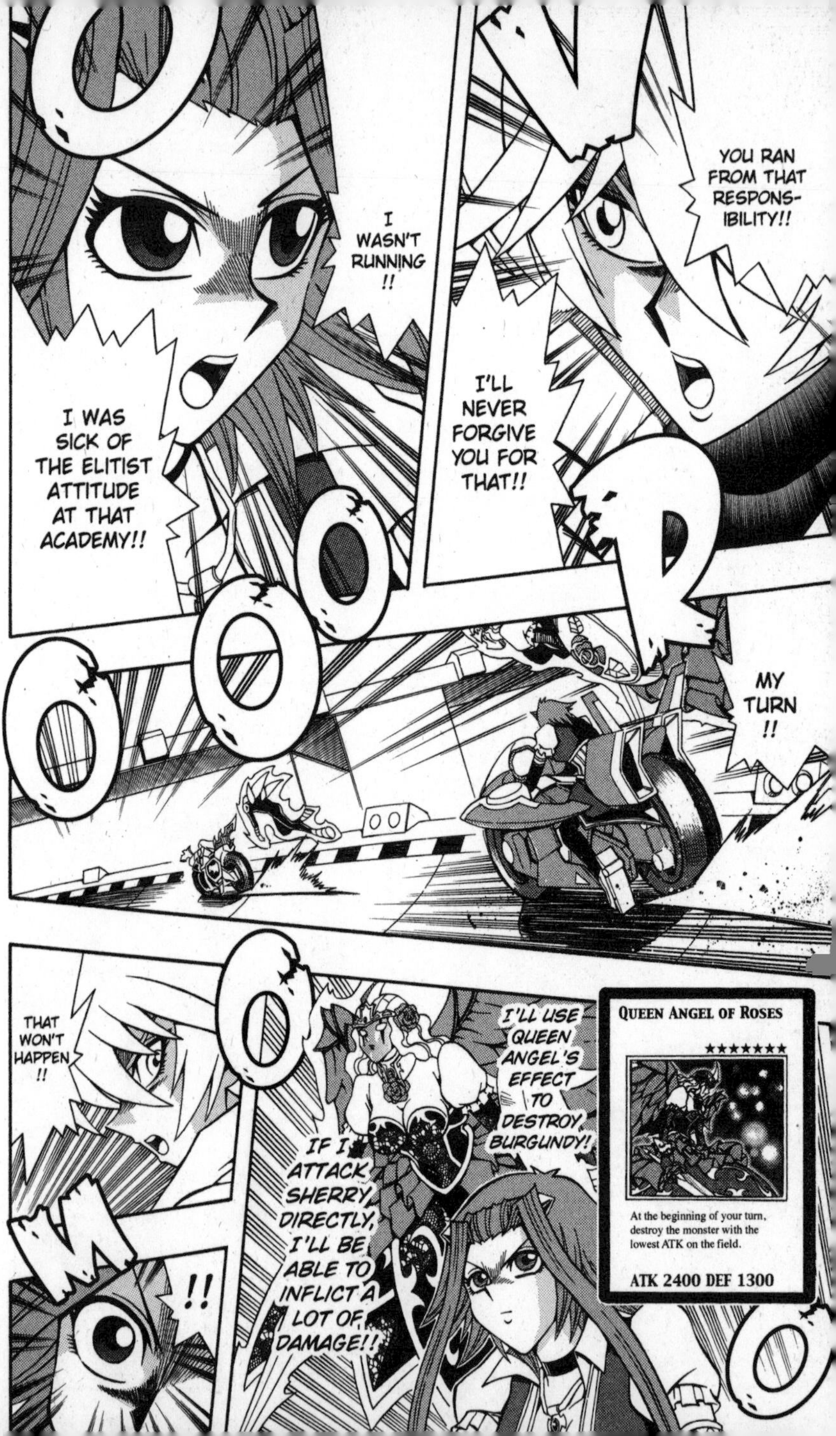
YOU RAN FROM THAT RESPONSIBILITY!!
I'LL NEVER FORGIVE YOU FOR THAT!!
I WASN'T RUNNING!!
I WAS SICK OF THE ELITIST ATTITUDE AT THAT ACADEMY!!
MY TURN!!
I'LL USE QUEEN ANGEL'S EFFECT TO DESTROY BURGUNDY!
IF I ATTACK SHERRY DIRECTLY, I'LL BE ABLE TO INFLICT A LOT OF DAMAGE!!
QUEEN ANGEL OF ROSES
★★★★★★★
At the beginning of your turn, destroy the monster with the lowest ATK on the field.
ATK 2400 DEF 1300
THAT WON'T HAPPEN!!
!!

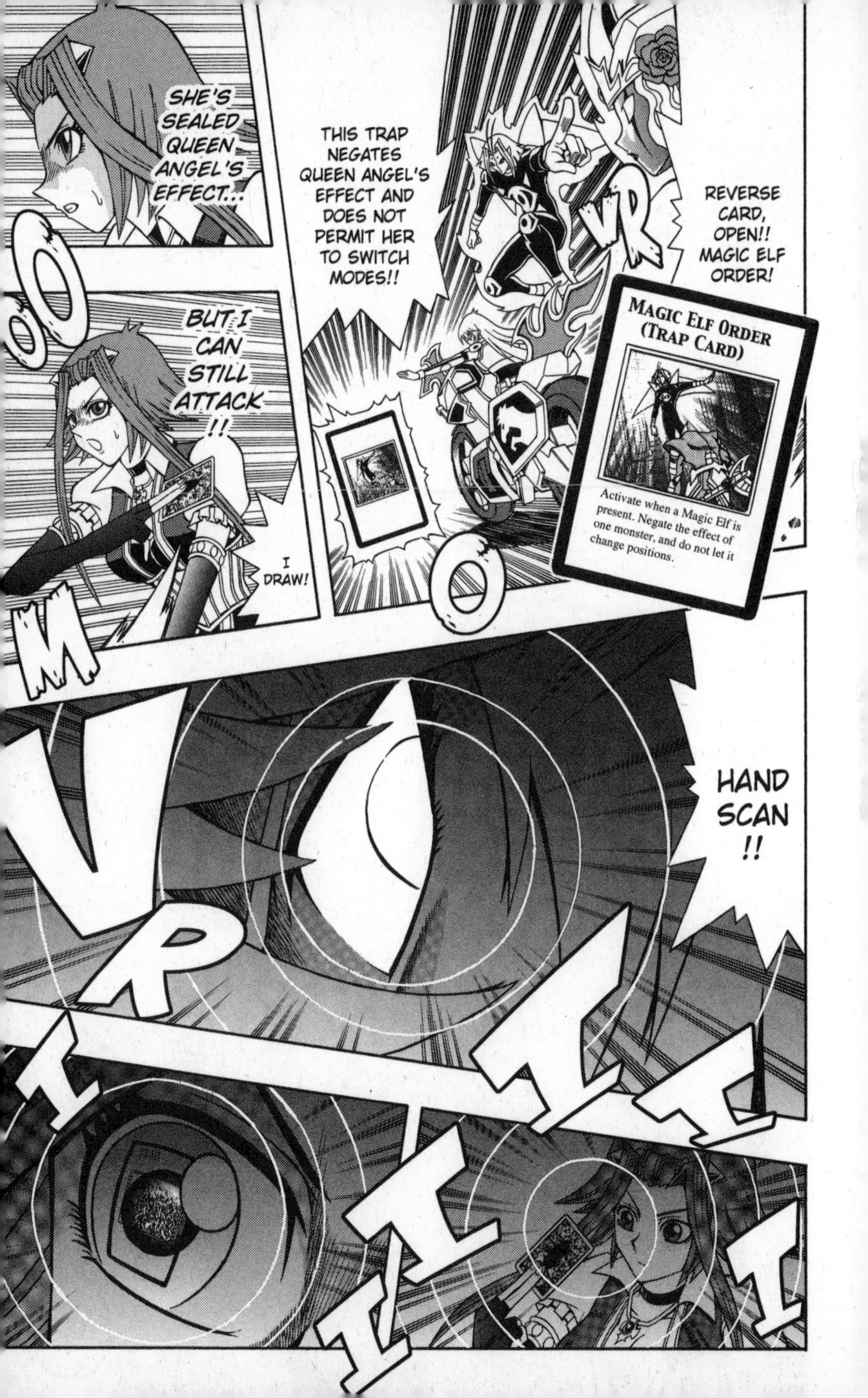
REVERSE CARD, OPEN!! MAGIC ELF ORDER!
MAGIC ELF ORDER (TRAP CARD)
Activate when a Magic Elf is present. Negate the effect of one monster, and do not let it change positions.
THIS TRAP NEGATES QUEEN ANGEL'S EFFECT AND DOES NOT PERMIT HER TO SWITCH MODES!!
SHE'S SEALED QUEEN ANGEL'S EFFECT...
BUT I CAN STILL ATTACK!!
I DRAW!
HAND SCAN!!

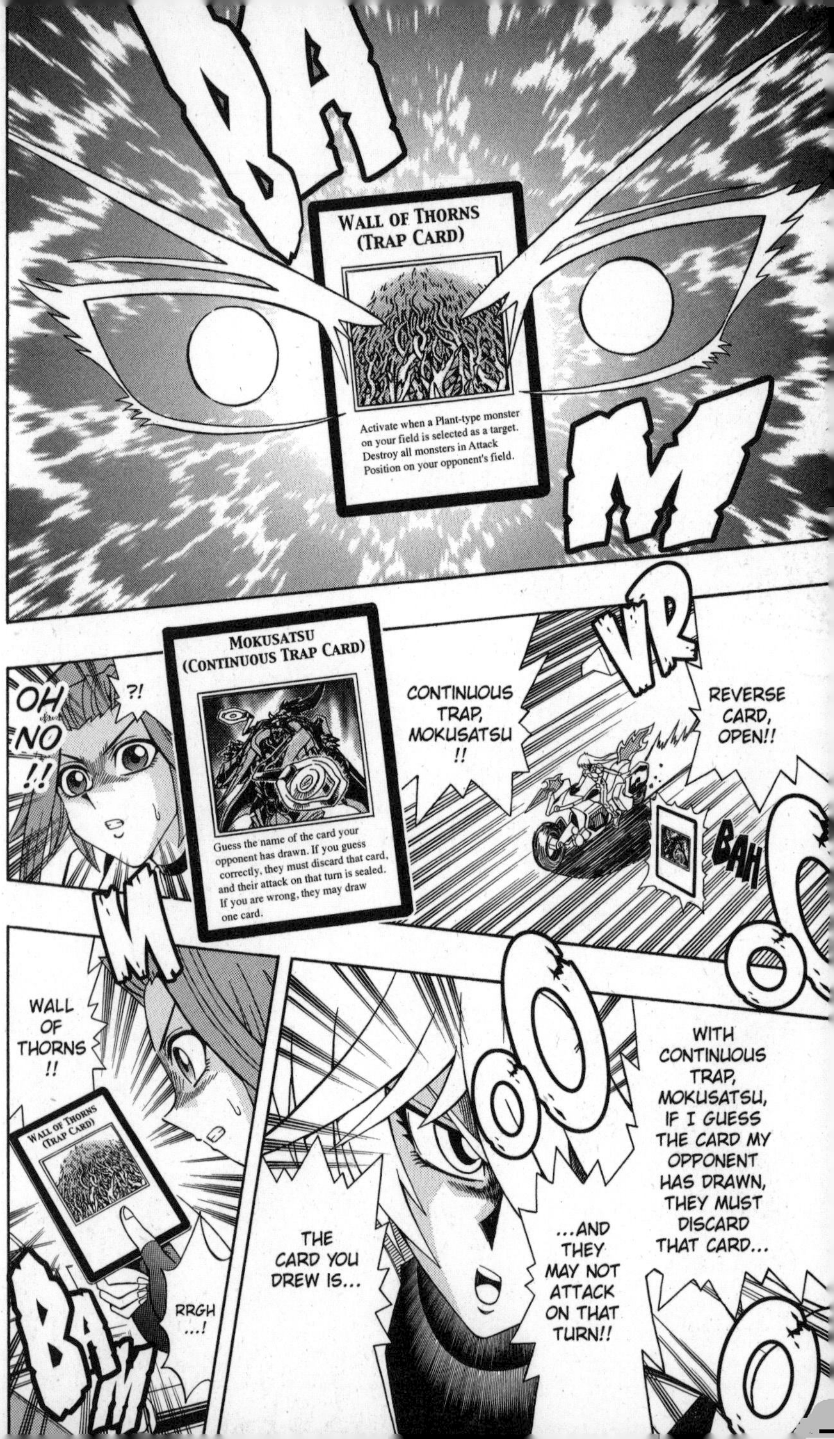

BA
WALL OF THORNS
(TRAP CARD)
Activate when a Plant-type monster on your field is selected as a target. Destroy all monsters in Attack Position on your opponent's field.
M
VR
REVERSE CARD, OPEN!!
BAM
CONTINUOUS TRAP, MOKUSATSU !!
MOKUSATSU
(CONTINUOUS TRAP CARD)
Guess the name of the card your opponent has drawn. If you guess correctly, they must discard that card, and their attack on that turn is sealed. If you are wrong, they may draw one card.
?!
OH NO !!
M
WITH CONTINUOUS TRAP, MOKUSATSU, IF I GUESS THE CARD MY OPPONENT HAS DRAWN, THEY MUST DISCARD THAT CARD...
...AND THEY MAY NOT ATTACK ON THAT TURN!!
THE CARD YOU DREW IS...
WALL OF THORNS !!
WALL OF THORNS
(TRAP CARD)
RRGH ...!
BAM

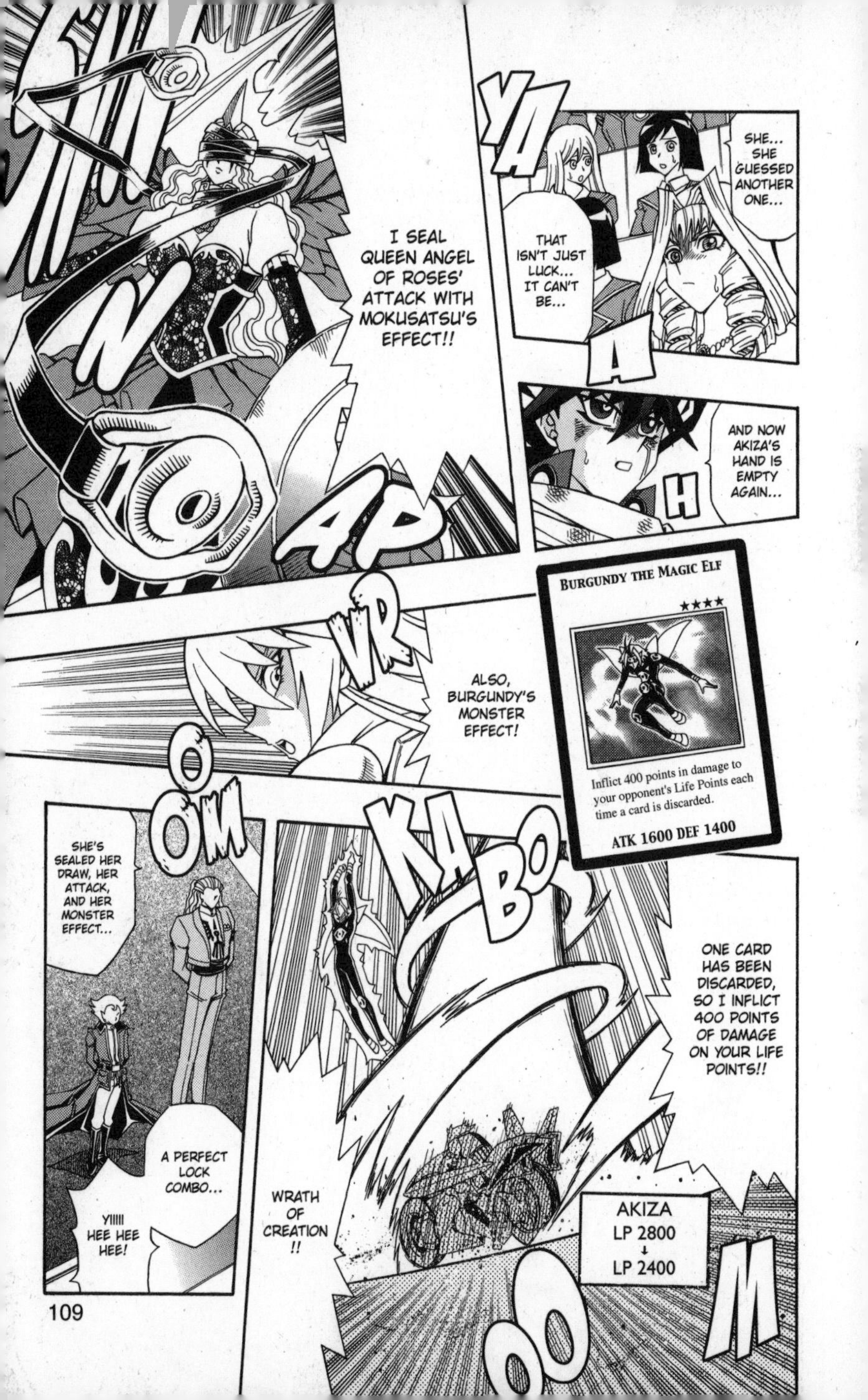
YA
SHE... SHE GUESSED ANOTHER ONE...
THAT ISN'T JUST LUCK... IT CAN'T BE...
A
AND NOW AKIZA'S HAND IS EMPTY AGAIN...
H
I SEAL QUEEN ANGEL OF ROSES' ATTACK WITH MOKUSATSU'S EFFECT!!
AP
BURGUNDY THE MAGIC ELF
★★★★
Inflict 400 points in damage to your opponent's Life Points each time a card is discarded.
ATK 1600 DEF 1400
ALSO, BURGUNDY'S MONSTER EFFECT!
VR
KA
BO
ONE CARD HAS BEEN DISCARDED, SO I INFLICT 400 POINTS OF DAMAGE ON YOUR LIFE POINTS!!
WRATH OF CREATION !!
AKIZA
LP 2800
↓
LP 2400
M
SHE'S SEALED HER DRAW, HER ATTACK, AND HER MONSTER EFFECT...
A PERFECT LOCK COMBO...
YIIIII HEE HEE HEE!

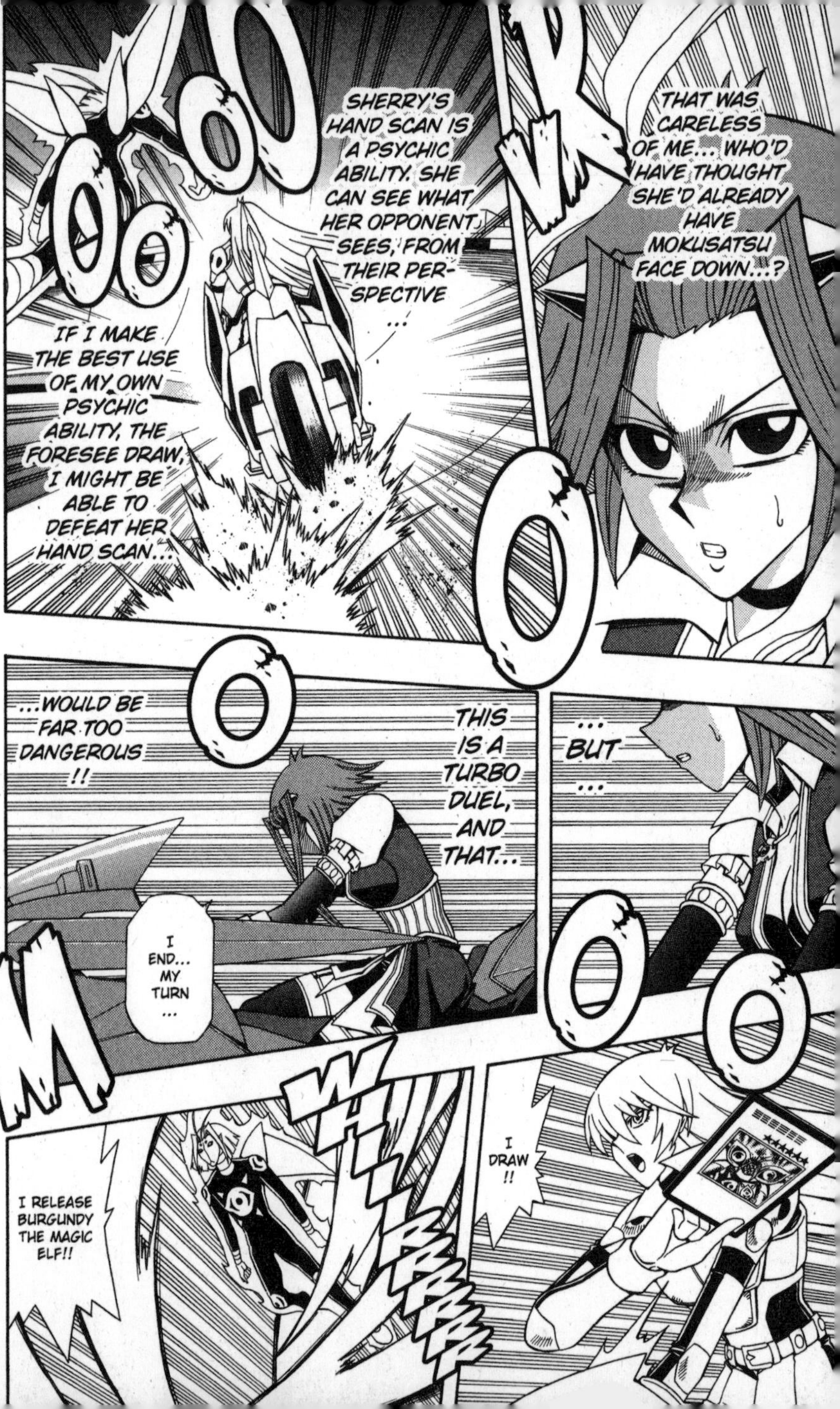
THAT WAS CARELESS OF ME... WHO'D HAVE THOUGHT SHE'D ALREADY HAVE MOKUSATSU FACE DOWN...?
SHERRY'S HAND SCAN IS A PSYCHIC ABILITY. SHE CAN SEE WHAT HER OPPONENT SEES, FROM THEIR PER-SPECTIVE ...
IF I MAKE THE BEST USE OF MY OWN PSYCHIC ABILITY, THE FORESEE DRAW, I MIGHT BE ABLE TO DEFEAT HER HAND SCAN...
... BUT ...
THIS IS A TURBO DUEL, AND THAT...
...WOULD BE FAR TOO DANGEROUS !!
I END... MY TURN ...
I DRAW !!
I RELEASE BURGUNDY THE MAGIC ELF!!

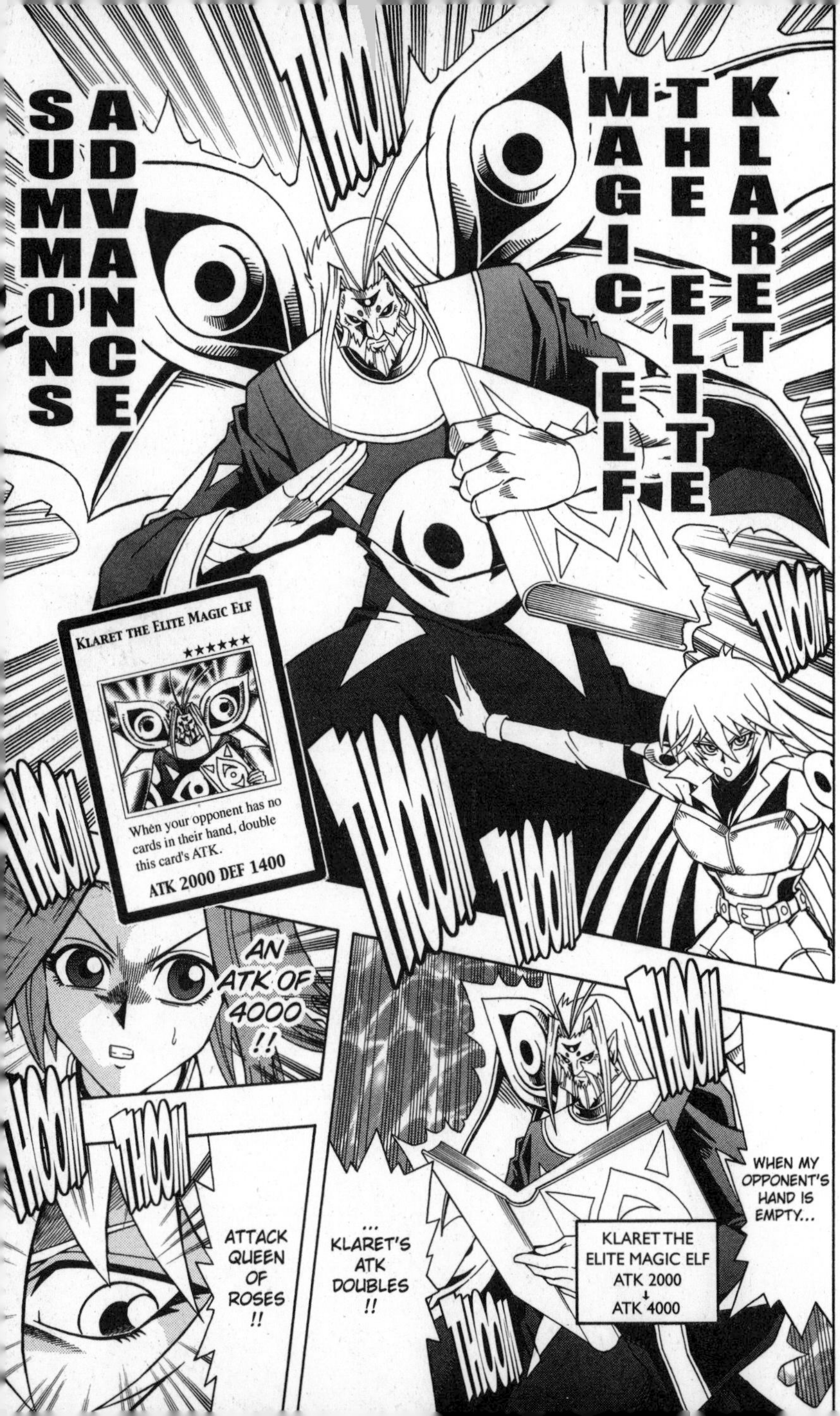
KLARET THE ELITE MAGIC ELF
ADVANCE SUMMONS
THOOM
KLARET THE ELITE MAGIC ELF
★★★★★★
When your opponent has no cards in their hand, double this card's ATK.
ATK 2000 DEF 1400
THOOM
THOOM
THOOM
THOOM
THOOM
WHEN MY OPPONENT'S HAND IS EMPTY...
KLARET THE ELITE MAGIC ELF ATK 2000 ATK 4000
... KLARET'S ATK DOUBLES !!
THOOM
AN ATK OF 4000 !!
THOOM
THOOM
ATTACK QUEEN OF ROSES !!

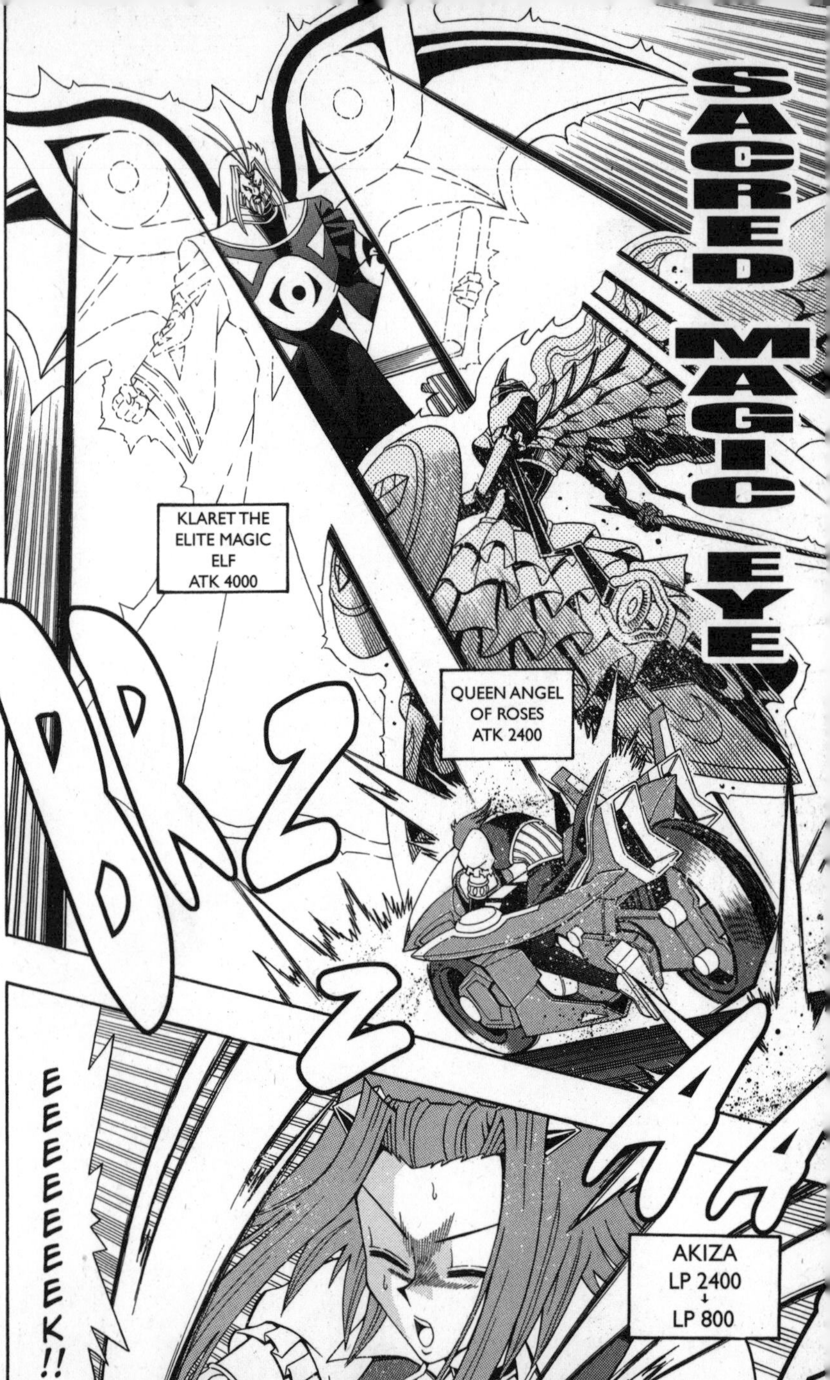
SACRED MAGIC EYE
KLARET THE ELITE MAGIC ELF ATK 4000
QUEEN ANGEL OF ROSES ATK 2400
BRZZ
AA
AKIZA LP 2400 → LP 800
EEEEEEEK!!

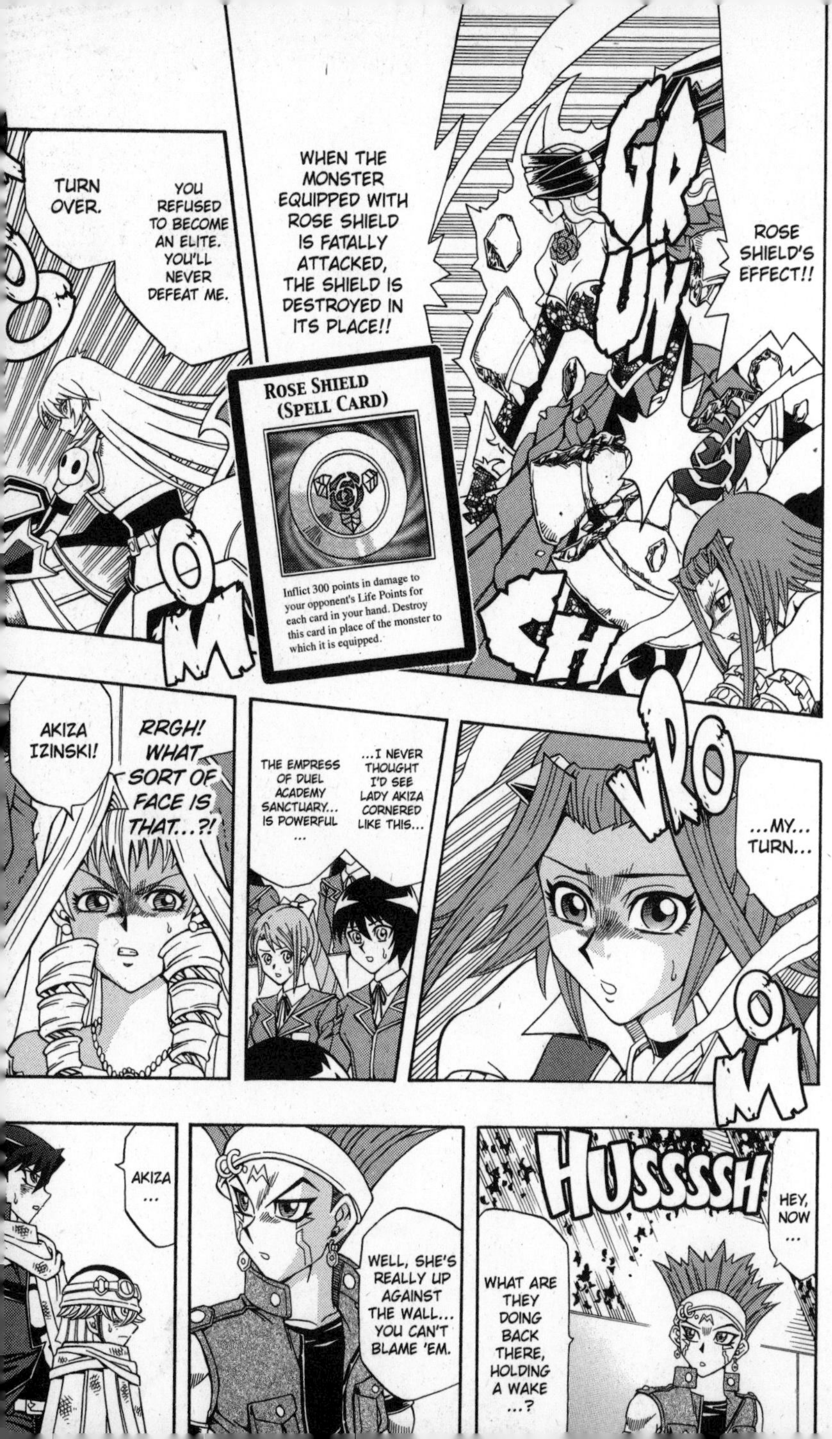
ROSE SHIELD'S EFFECT!!
CRUNCH
WHEN THE MONSTER EQUIPPED WITH ROSE SHIELD IS FATALLY ATTACKED, THE SHIELD IS DESTROYED IN ITS PLACE!!
ROSE SHIELD (SPELL CARD)
Inflict 300 points in damage to your opponent's Life Points for each card in your hand. Destroy this card in place of the monster to which it is equipped.
OOM
YOU REFUSED TO BECOME AN ELITE. YOU'LL NEVER DEFEAT ME.
TURN OVER.
VROOOM
...MY... TURN...
...I NEVER THOUGHT I'D SEE LADY AKIZA CORNERED LIKE THIS...
THE EMPRESS OF DUEL ACADEMY SANCTUARY... IS POWERFUL ...
RRGH! WHAT SORT OF FACE IS THAT...?!
AKIZA IZINSKI!
HUSSSSH
HEY, NOW ...
WHAT ARE THEY DOING BACK THERE, HOLDING A WAKE ...?
WELL, SHE'S REALLY UP AGAINST THE WALL... YOU CAN'T BLAME 'EM.
AKIZA ...

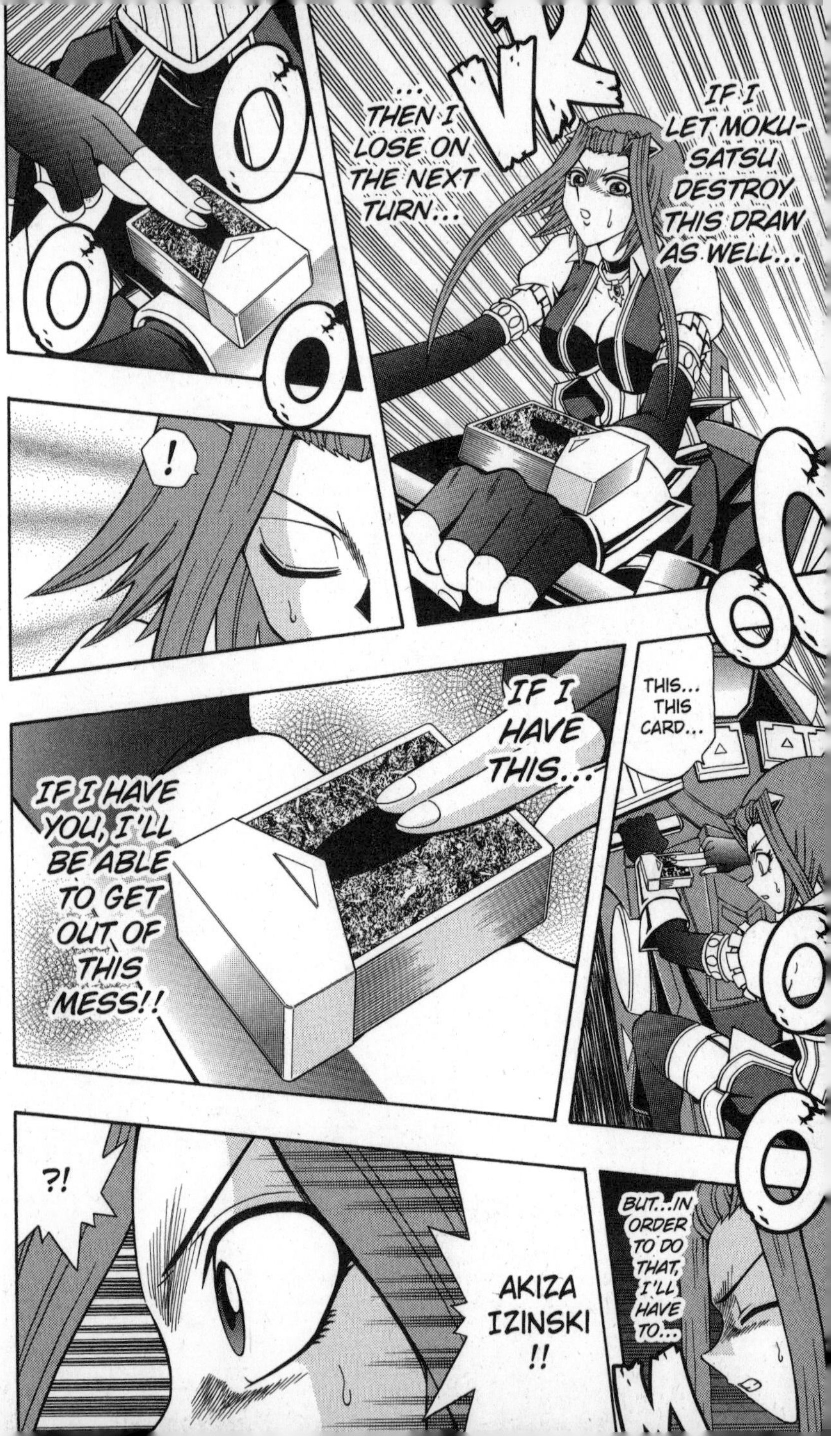
IF I LET MOKU-SATSU DESTROY THIS DRAW AS WELL...
...THEN I LOSE ON THE NEXT TURN...
!
THIS... THIS CARD...
IF I HAVE THIS...
IF I HAVE YOU, I'LL BE ABLE TO GET OUT OF THIS MESS!!
BUT...IN ORDER TO DO THAT, I'LL HAVE TO...
AKIZA IZINSKI !!
?!

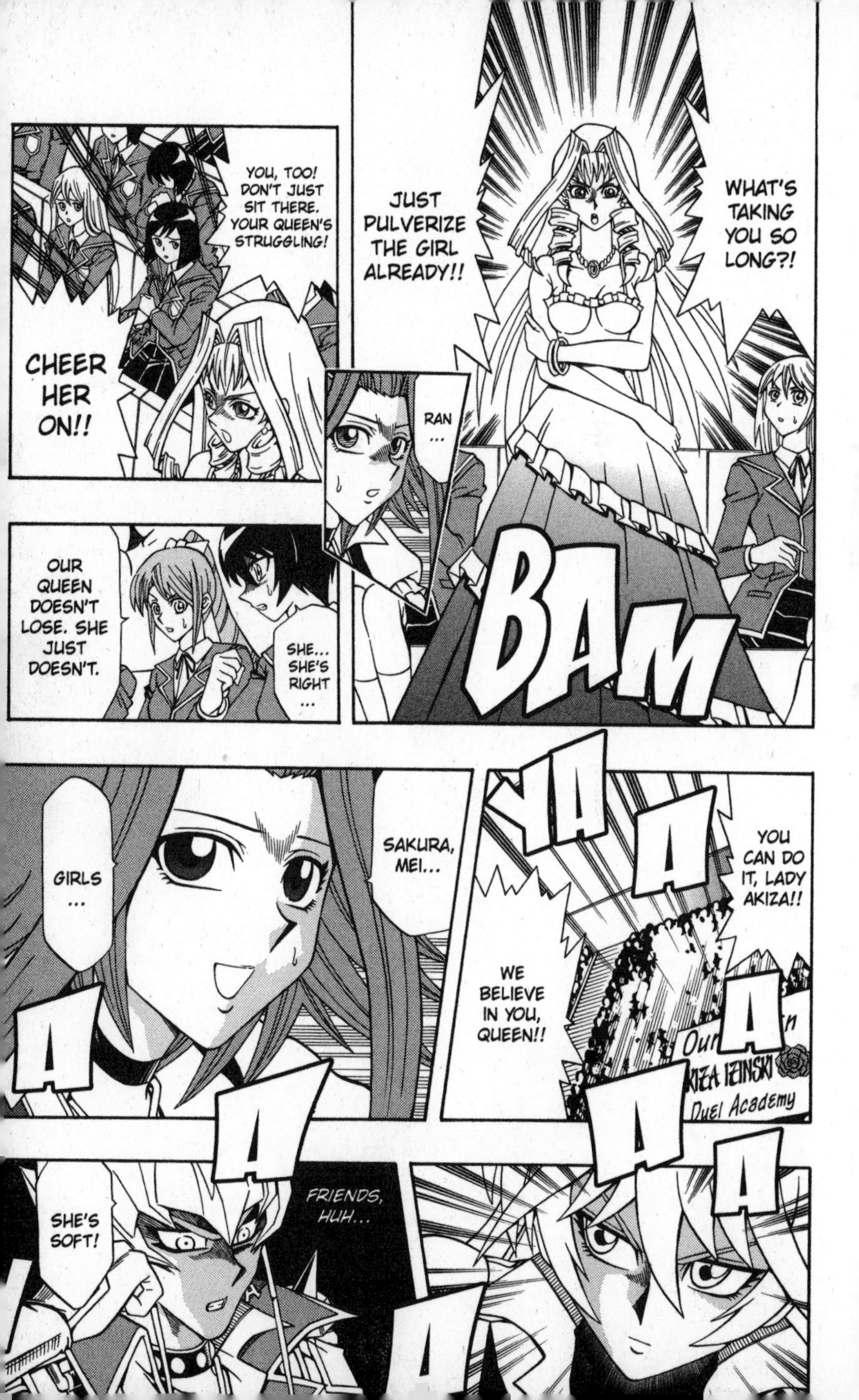
WHAT'S TAKING YOU SO LONG?!
JUST PULVERIZE THE GIRL ALREADY!!
BAM
RAN...
YOU, TOO! DON'T JUST SIT THERE. YOUR QUEEN'S STRUGGLING!
CHEER HER ON!!
SHE... SHE'S RIGHT...
OUR QUEEN DOESN'T LOSE. SHE JUST DOESN'T.
YA
A
YOU CAN DO IT, LADY AKIZA!!
WE BELIEVE IN YOU, QUEEN!!
A
Duel Academy
SAKURA, MEI...
GIRLS...
A
A
A
A
FRIENDS, HUH...
SHE'S SOFT!
A

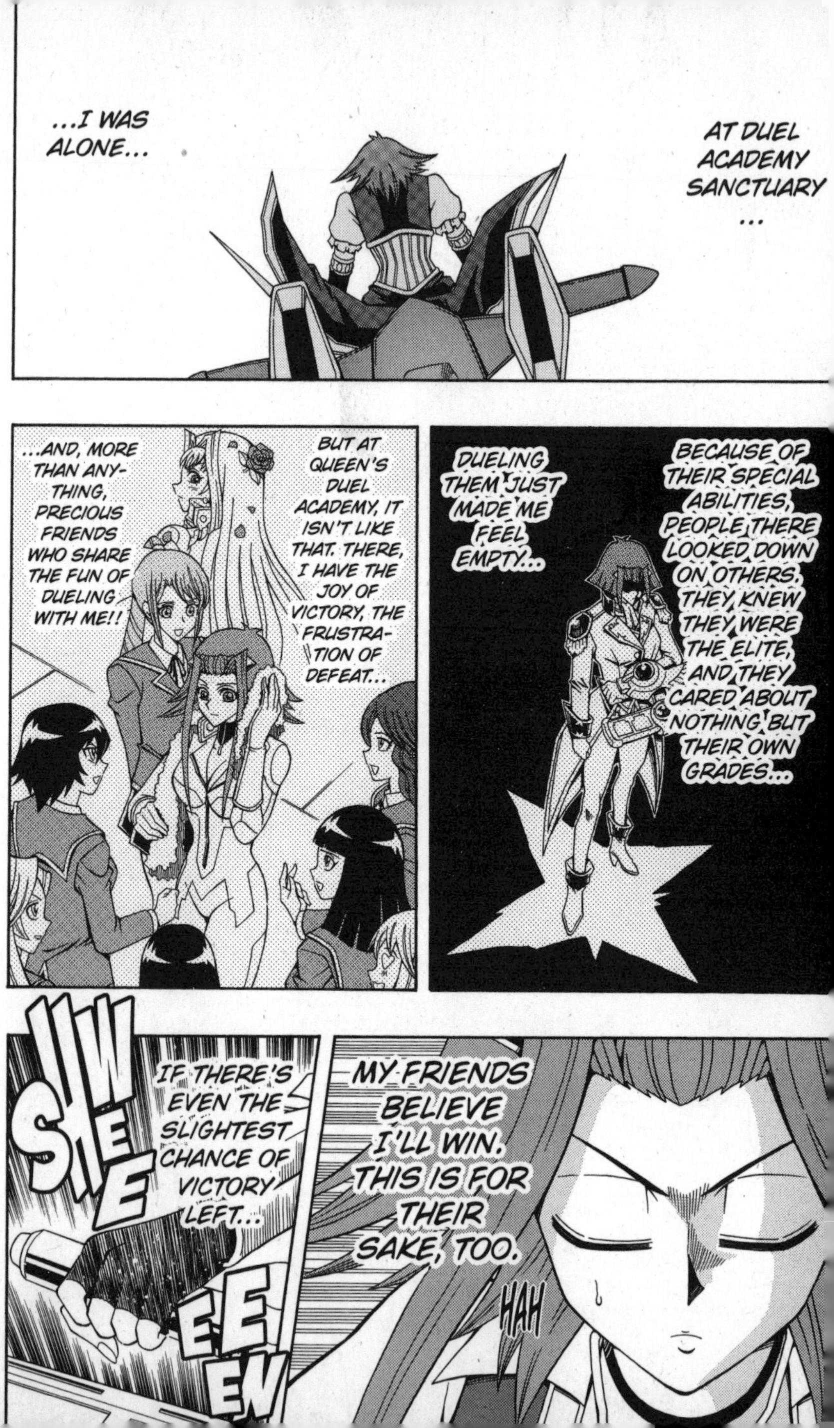
AT DUEL ACADEMY SANCTUARY...
...I WAS ALONE...
BECAUSE OF THEIR SPECIAL ABILITIES, PEOPLE THERE LOOKED DOWN ON OTHERS. THEY KNEW THEY WERE THE ELITE, AND THEY CARED ABOUT NOTHING BUT THEIR OWN GRADES...
DUELING THEM JUST MADE ME FEEL EMPTY...
BUT AT QUEEN'S DUEL ACADEMY, IT ISN'T LIKE THAT. THERE, I HAVE THE JOY OF VICTORY, THE FRUSTRATION OF DEFEAT...
...AND, MORE THAN ANYTHING, PRECIOUS FRIENDS WHO SHARE THE FUN OF DUELING WITH ME!!
MY FRIENDS BELIEVE I'LL WIN. THIS IS FOR THEIR SAKE, TOO.
HAH
IF THERE'S EVEN THE SLIGHTEST CHANCE OF VICTORY LEFT...

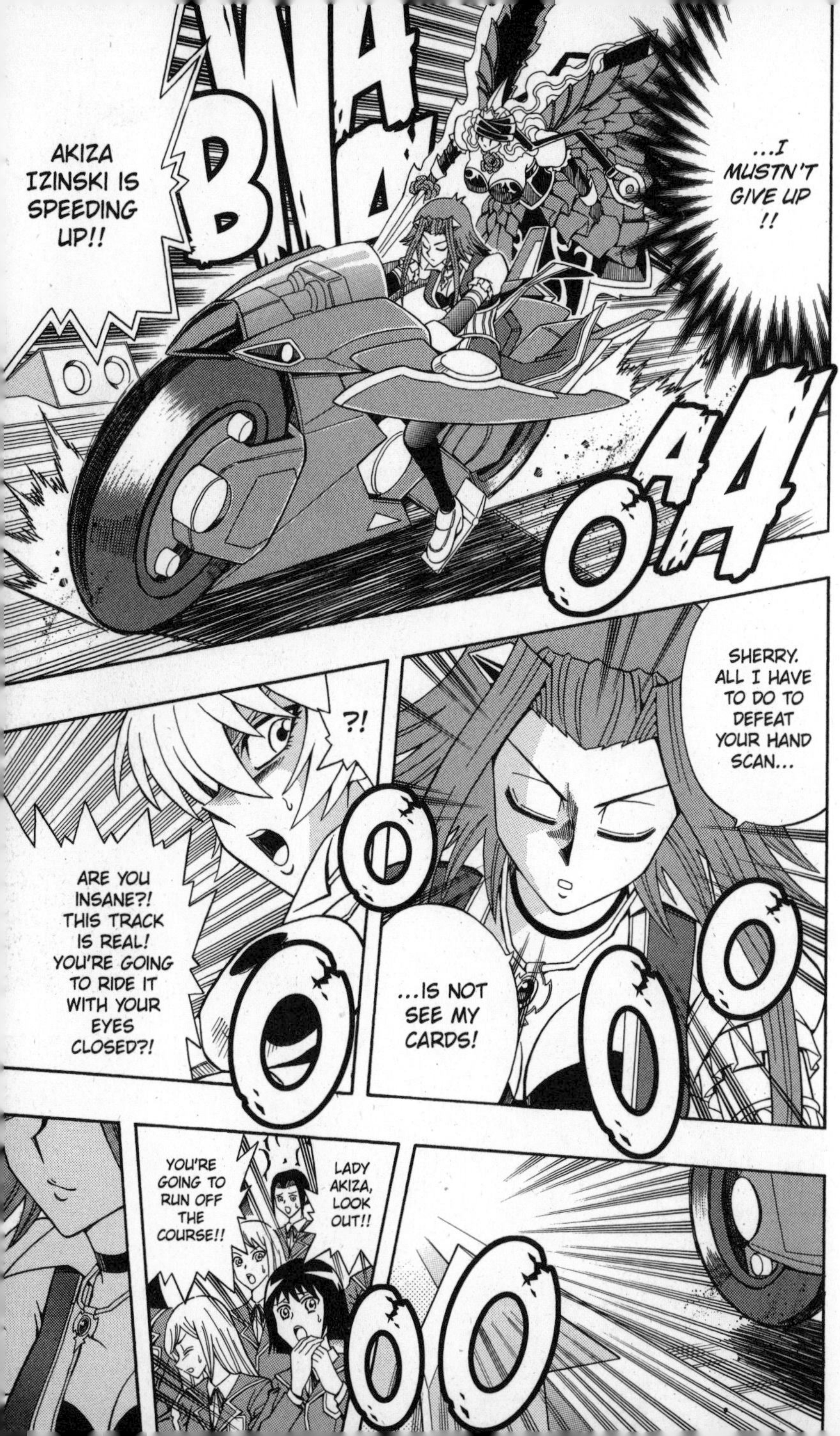
...I MUSTN'T GIVE UP !!
AKIZA IZINSKI IS SPEEDING UP!!
SHERRY. ALL I HAVE TO DO TO DEFEAT YOUR HAND SCAN...
...IS NOT SEE MY CARDS!
?!
ARE YOU INSANE?! THIS TRACK IS REAL! YOU'RE GOING TO RIDE IT WITH YOUR EYES CLOSED?!
LADY AKIZA, LOOK OUT!!
YOU'RE GOING TO RUN OFF THE COURSE!!

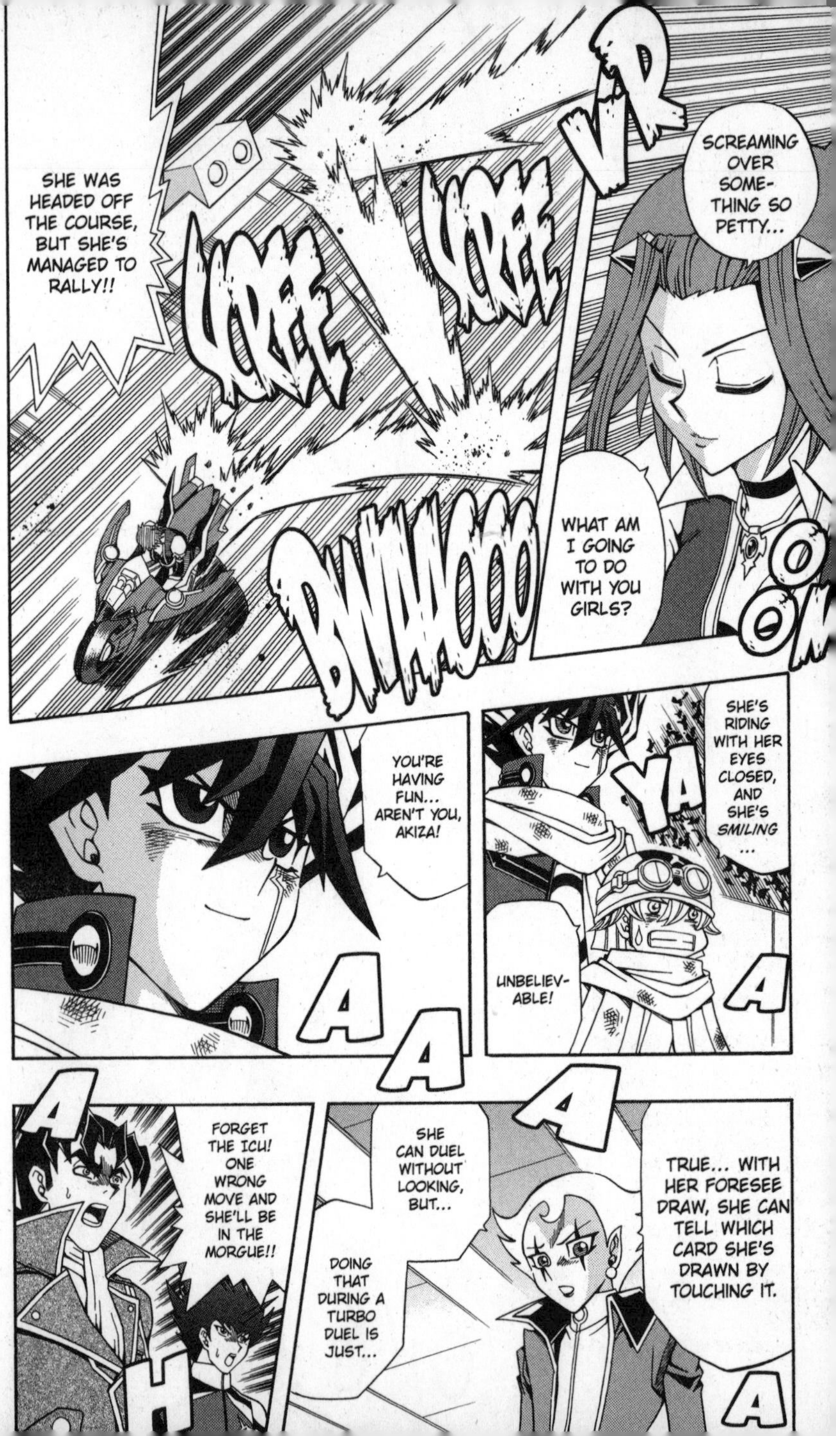

SCREAMING OVER SOME-THING SO PETTY...
WHAT AM I GOING TO DO WITH YOU GIRLS?
SHE WAS HEADED OFF THE COURSE, BUT SHE'S MANAGED TO RALLY!!
SHE'S RIDING WITH HER EYES CLOSED, AND SHE'S *SMILING*...
UNBELIEV-ABLE!
YOU'RE HAVING FUN... AREN'T YOU, AKIZA!
TRUE... WITH HER FORESEE DRAW, SHE CAN TELL WHICH CARD SHE'S DRAWN BY TOUCHING IT.
SHE CAN DUEL WITHOUT LOOKING, BUT...
DOING THAT DURING A TURBO DUEL IS JUST...
FORGET THE ICU! ONE WRONG MOVE AND SHE'LL BE IN THE MORGUE!!

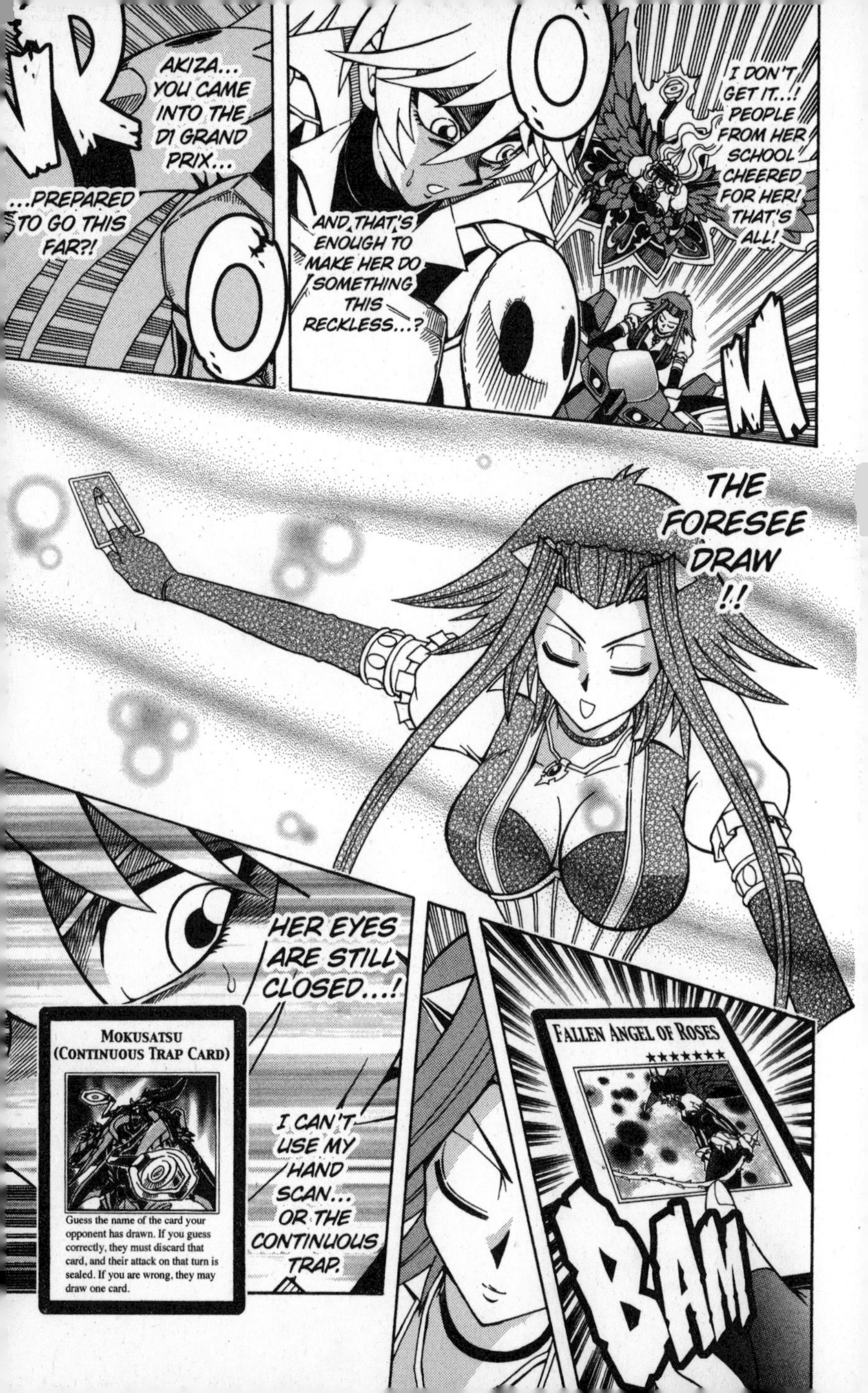
I DON'T GET IT...! PEOPLE FROM HER SCHOOL CHEERED FOR HER! THAT'S ALL!
AND THAT'S ENOUGH TO MAKE HER DO SOMETHING THIS RECKLESS...?
AKIZA... YOU CAME INTO THE D1 GRAND PRIX...
...PREPARED TO GO THIS FAR?!
THE FORESEE DRAW!!
FALLEN ANGEL OF ROSES
BAM
HER EYES ARE STILL CLOSED...!
MOKUSATSU (CONTINUOUS TRAP CARD)
Guess the name of the card your opponent has drawn. If you guess correctly, they must discard that card, and their attack on that turn is sealed. If you are wrong, they may draw one card.
I CAN'T USE MY HAND SCAN... OR THE CONTINUOUS TRAP.

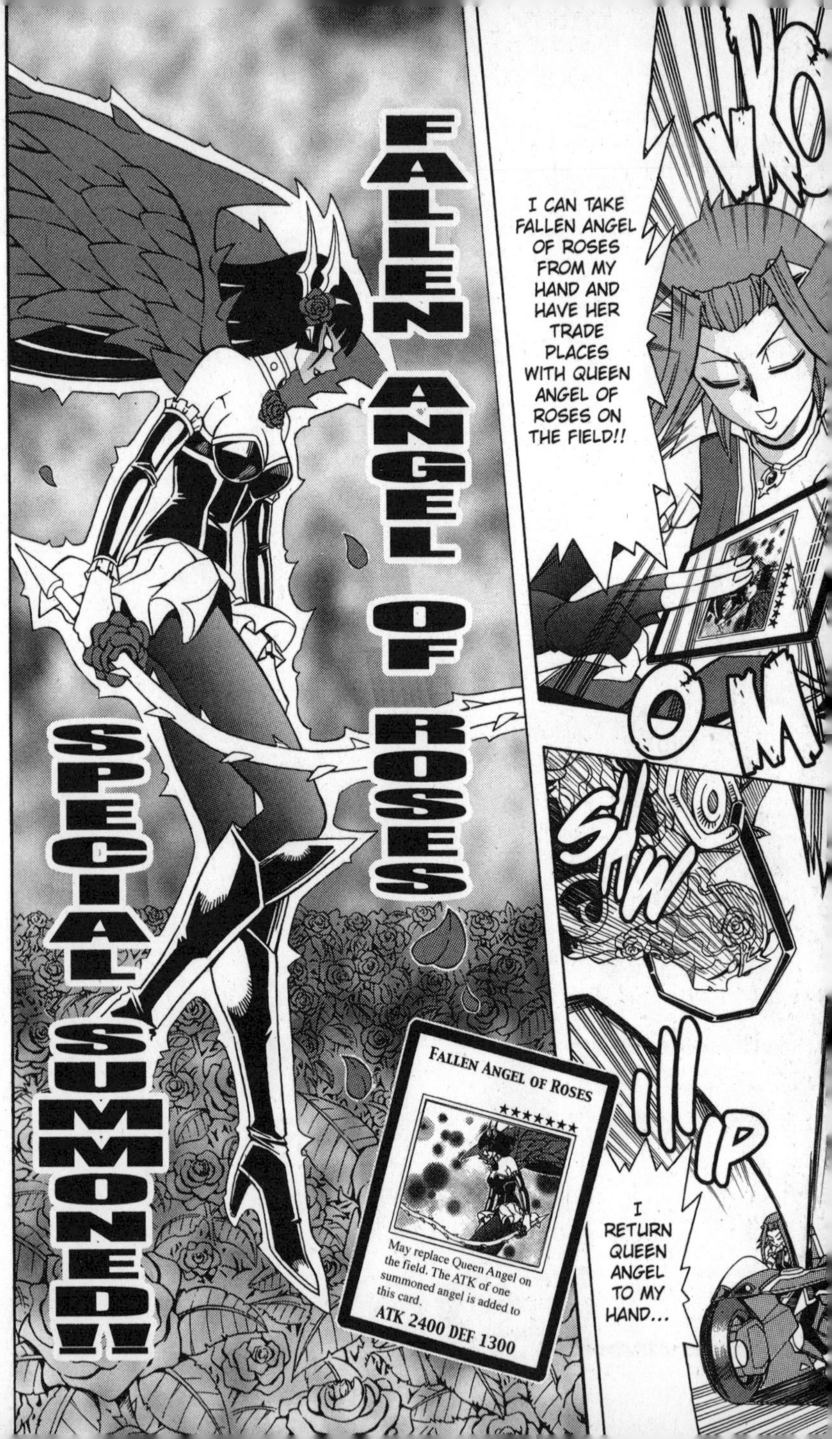

VROOOM
I CAN TAKE FALLEN ANGEL OF ROSES FROM MY HAND AND HAVE HER TRADE PLACES WITH QUEEN ANGEL OF ROSES ON THE FIELD!!
SHWOO
ZIP
I RETURN QUEEN ANGEL TO MY HAND...
FALLEN ANGEL OF ROSES
SPECIAL SUMMONED!!
FALLEN ANGEL OF ROSES
May replace Queen Angel on the field. The ATK of one summoned angel is added to this card.
ATK 2400 DEF 1300

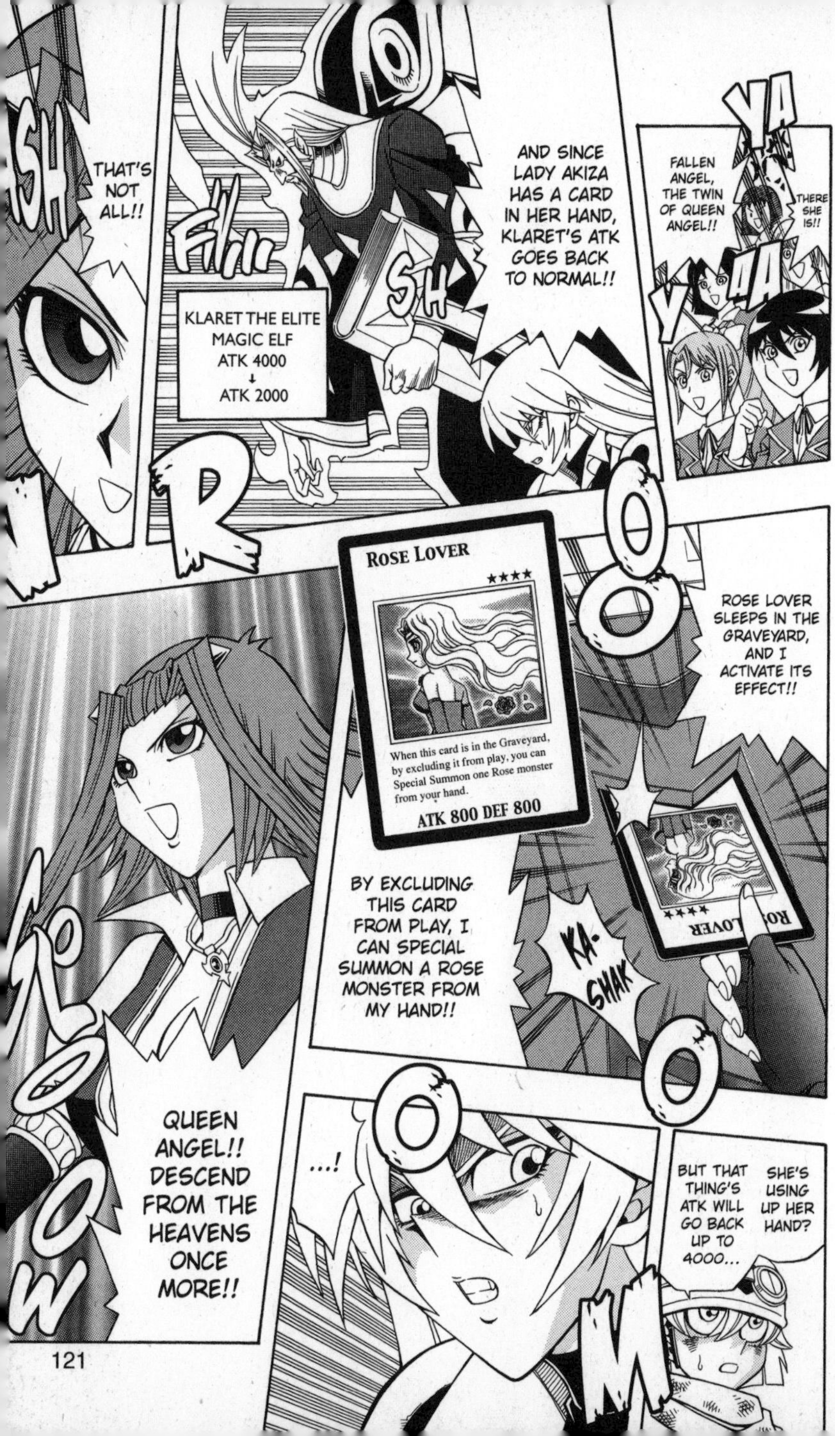

FALLEN ANGEL, THE TWIN OF QUEEN ANGEL!!
THERE SHE IS!!
AND SINCE LADY AKIZA HAS A CARD IN HER HAND, KLARET'S ATK GOES BACK TO NORMAL!!
KLARET THE ELITE MAGIC ELF
ATK 4000
↓
ATK 2000
THAT'S NOT ALL!!
ROSE LOVER SLEEPS IN THE GRAVEYARD, AND I ACTIVATE ITS EFFECT!!
ROSE LOVER
★★★★
When this card is in the Graveyard, by excluding it from play, you can Special Summon one Rose monster from your hand.
ATK 800 DEF 800
BY EXCLUDING THIS CARD FROM PLAY, I CAN SPECIAL SUMMON A ROSE MONSTER FROM MY HAND!!
KA-SHAK
SHE'S USING UP HER HAND?
BUT THAT THING'S ATK WILL GO BACK UP TO 4000...
...!
QUEEN ANGEL!! DESCEND FROM THE HEAVENS ONCE MORE!!

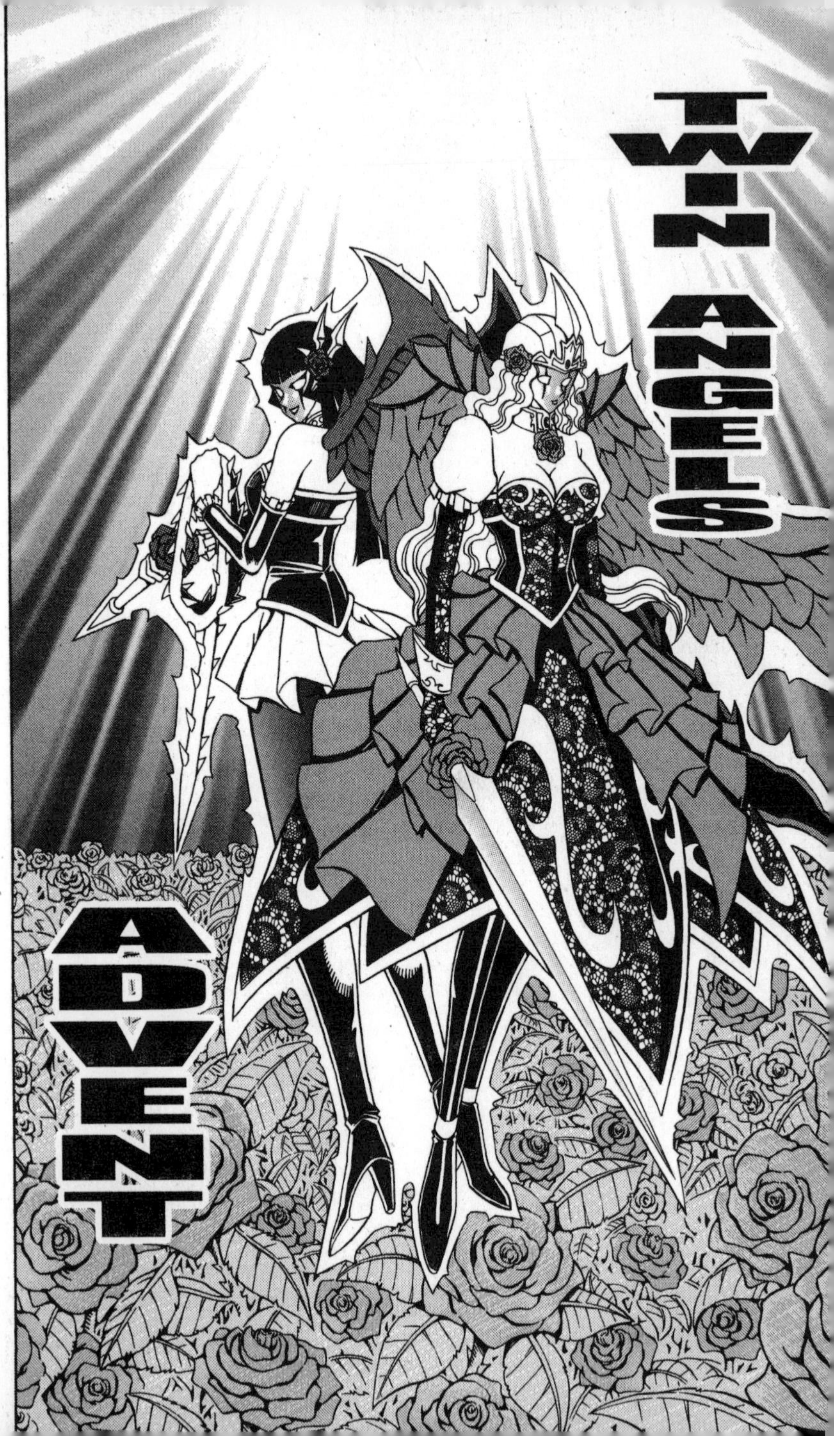
TWIN ANGELS
ADVENT

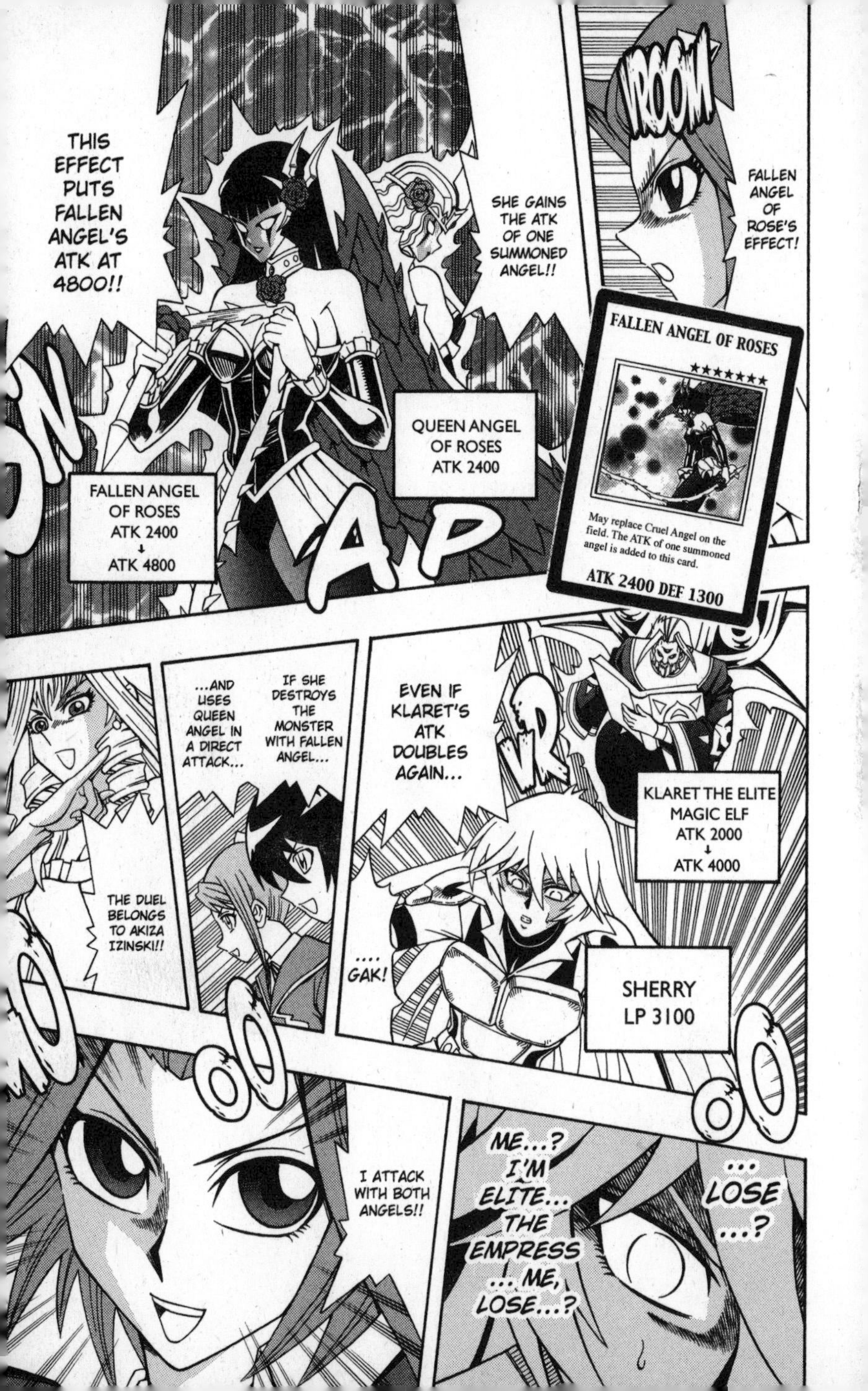
VROOM
FALLEN ANGEL OF ROSE'S EFFECT!
FALLEN ANGEL OF ROSES
May replace Cruel Angel on the field. The ATK of one summoned angel is added to this card.
ATK 2400 DEF 1300
SHE GAINS THE ATK OF ONE SUMMONED ANGEL!!
THIS EFFECT PUTS FALLEN ANGEL'S ATK AT 4800!!
QUEEN ANGEL OF ROSES ATK 2400
FALLEN ANGEL OF ROSES ATK 2400 ↓ ATK 4800
KLARET THE ELITE MAGIC ELF ATK 2000 ↓ ATK 4000
EVEN IF KLARET'S ATK DOUBLES AGAIN...
.... GAK!
SHERRY LP 3100
IF SHE DESTROYS THE MONSTER WITH FALLEN ANGEL...
...AND USES QUEEN ANGEL IN A DIRECT ATTACK...
THE DUEL BELONGS TO AKIZA IZINSKI!!
... LOSE ...?
ME...? I'M ELITE... THE EMPRESS ... ME, LOSE...?
I ATTACK WITH BOTH ANGELS!!

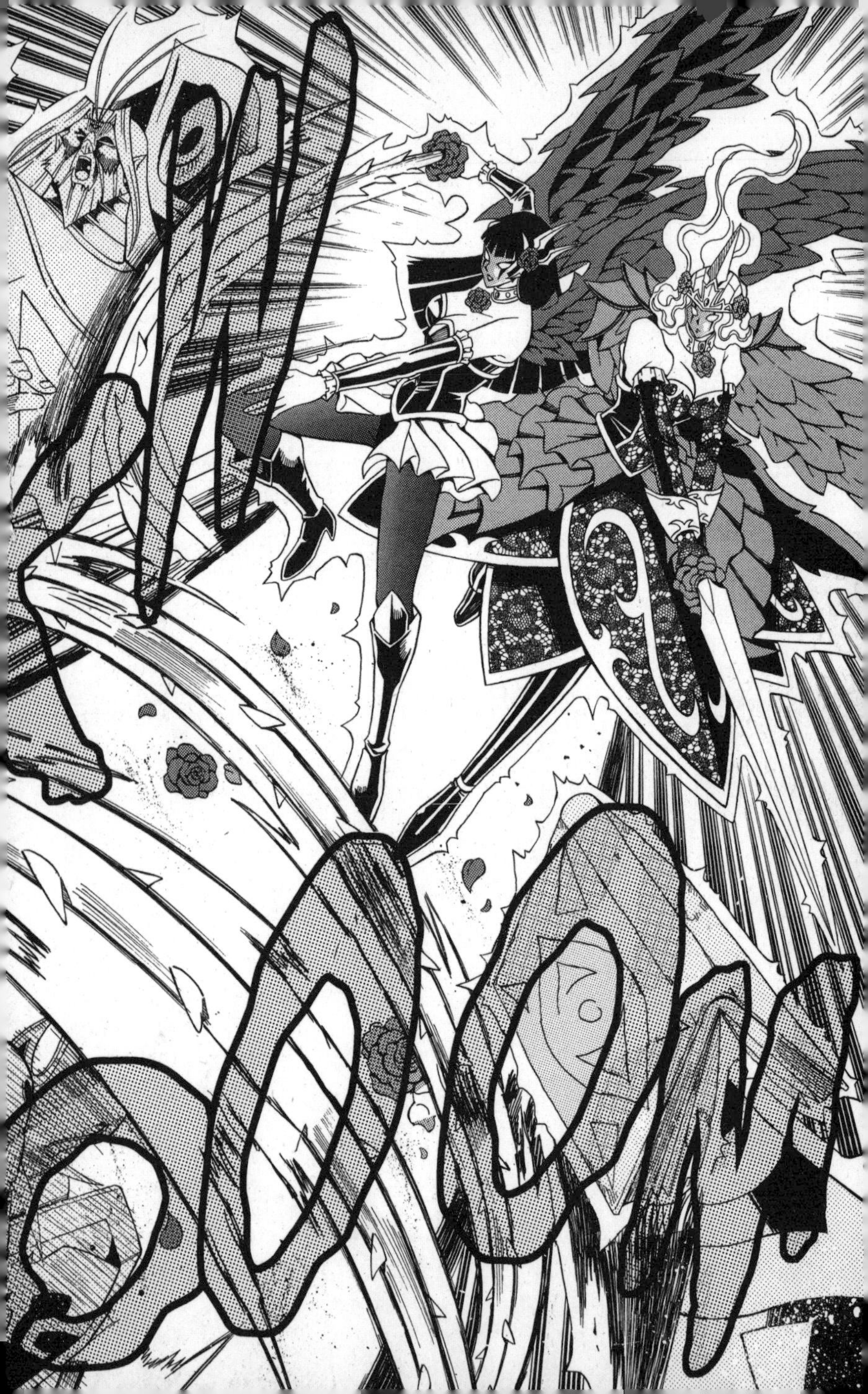

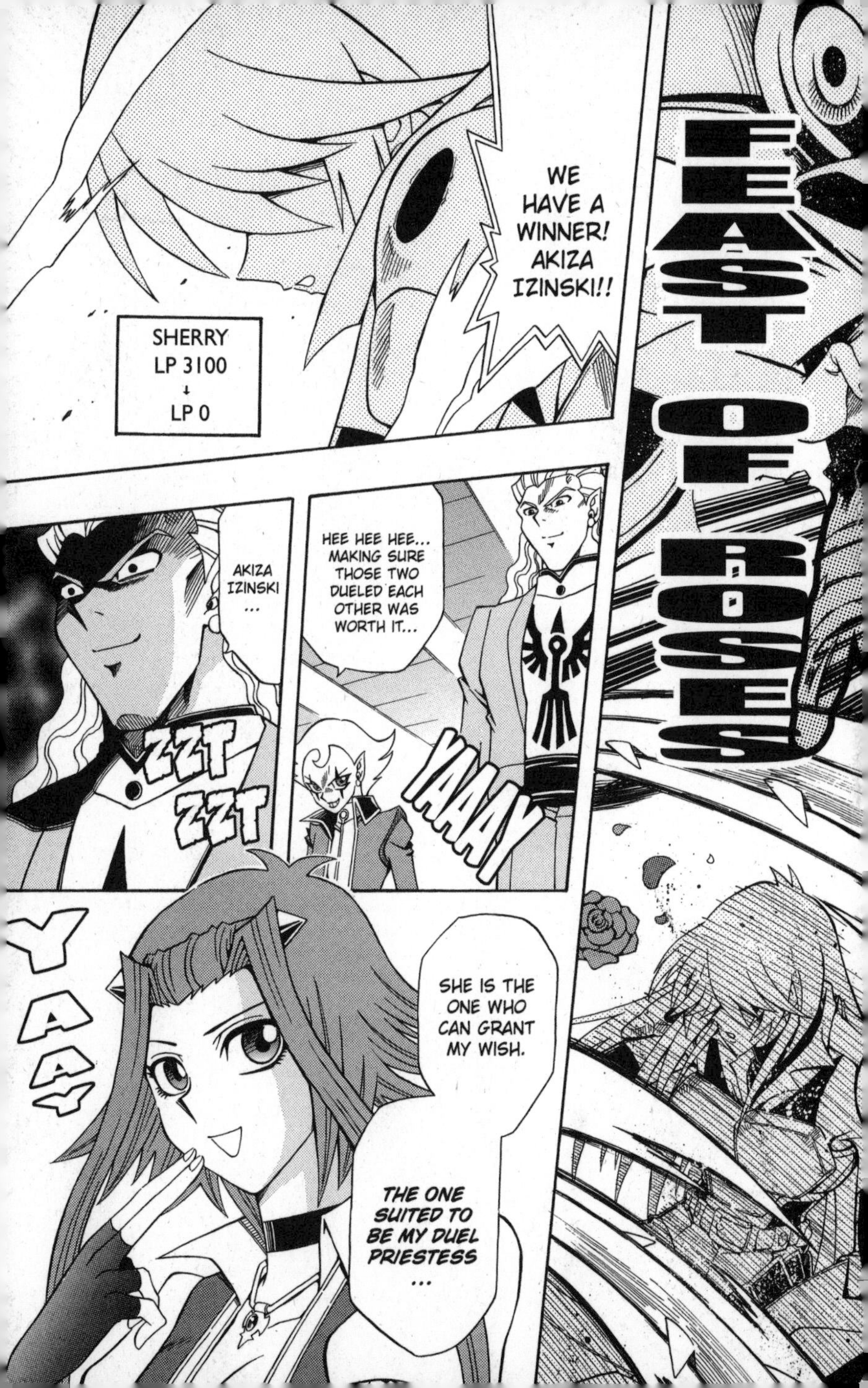
FEAST OF ROSES
WE HAVE A WINNER! AKIZA IZINSKI!!
SHERRY LP 3100 ↓ LP 0
HEE HEE HEE... MAKING SURE THOSE TWO DUELED EACH OTHER WAS WORTH IT...
YAAAY
AKIZA IZINSKI ...
ZZT
ZZT
SHE IS THE ONE WHO CAN GRANT MY WISH.
THE ONE SUITED TO BE MY DUEL PRIESTESS ...
YAAAY

5D's TRACKS BY SATOMASA

THE 13TH

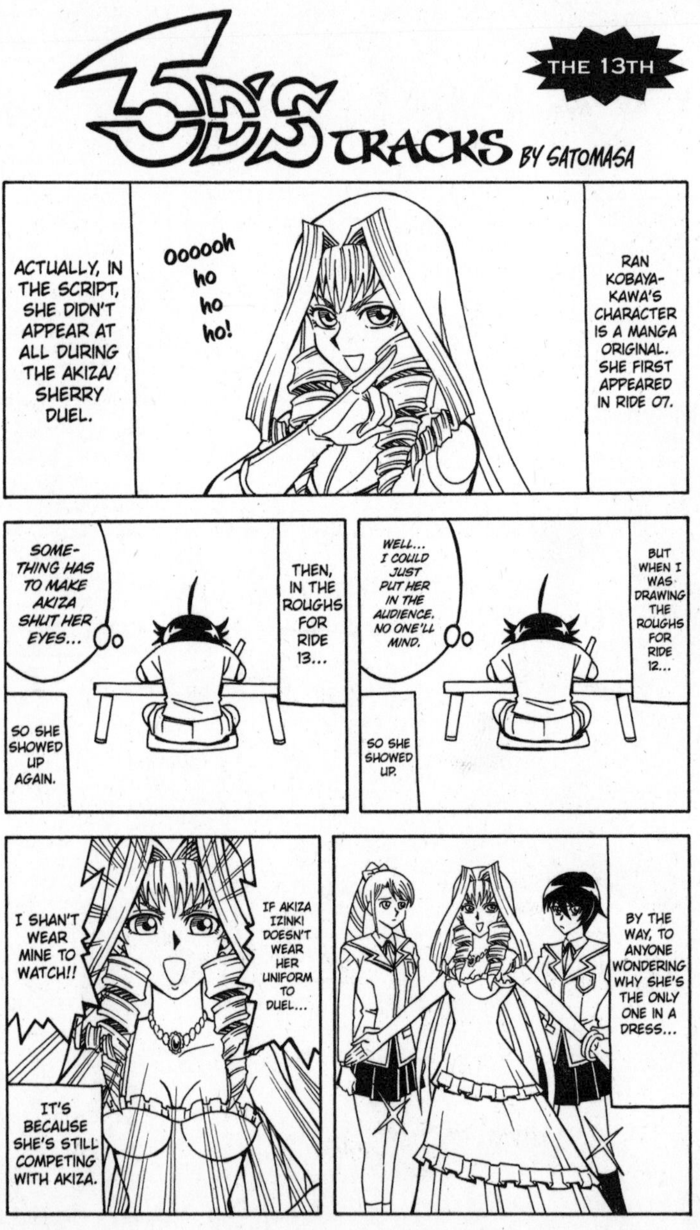
RAN KOBAYAKAWA'S CHARACTER IS A MANGA ORIGINAL. SHE FIRST APPEARED IN RIDE 07.
Oooooh ho ho ho!
ACTUALLY, IN THE SCRIPT, SHE DIDN'T APPEAR AT ALL DURING THE AKIZA/SHERRY DUEL.
BUT WHEN I WAS DRAWING THE ROUGHS FOR RIDE 12...
WELL... I COULD JUST PUT HER IN THE AUDIENCE. NO ONE'LL MIND.
SO SHE SHOWED UP.
THEN, IN THE ROUGHS FOR RIDE 13...
SOMETHING HAS TO MAKE AKIZA SHUT HER EYES...
SO SHE SHOWED UP AGAIN.
BY THE WAY, TO ANYONE WONDERING WHY SHE'S THE ONLY ONE IN A DRESS...
IF AKIZA IZINKI DOESN'T WEAR HER UNIFORM TO DUEL...
I SHAN'T WEAR MINE TO WATCH!!
IT'S BECAUSE SHE'S STILL COMPETING WITH AKIZA.

RIDE-14

RIVALS!!

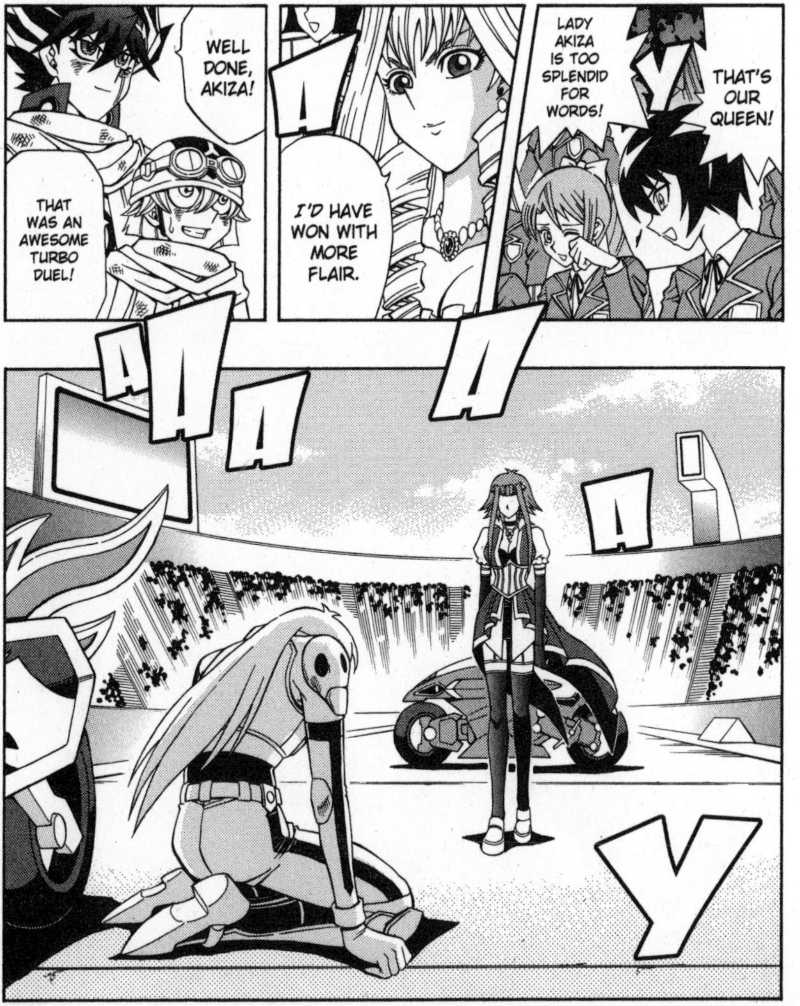
THAT'S OUR QUEEN!
LADY AKIZA IS TOO SPLENDID FOR WORDS!
I'D HAVE WON WITH MORE FLAIR.
WELL DONE, AKIZA!
THAT WAS AN AWESOME TURBO DUEL!
YAAAAA

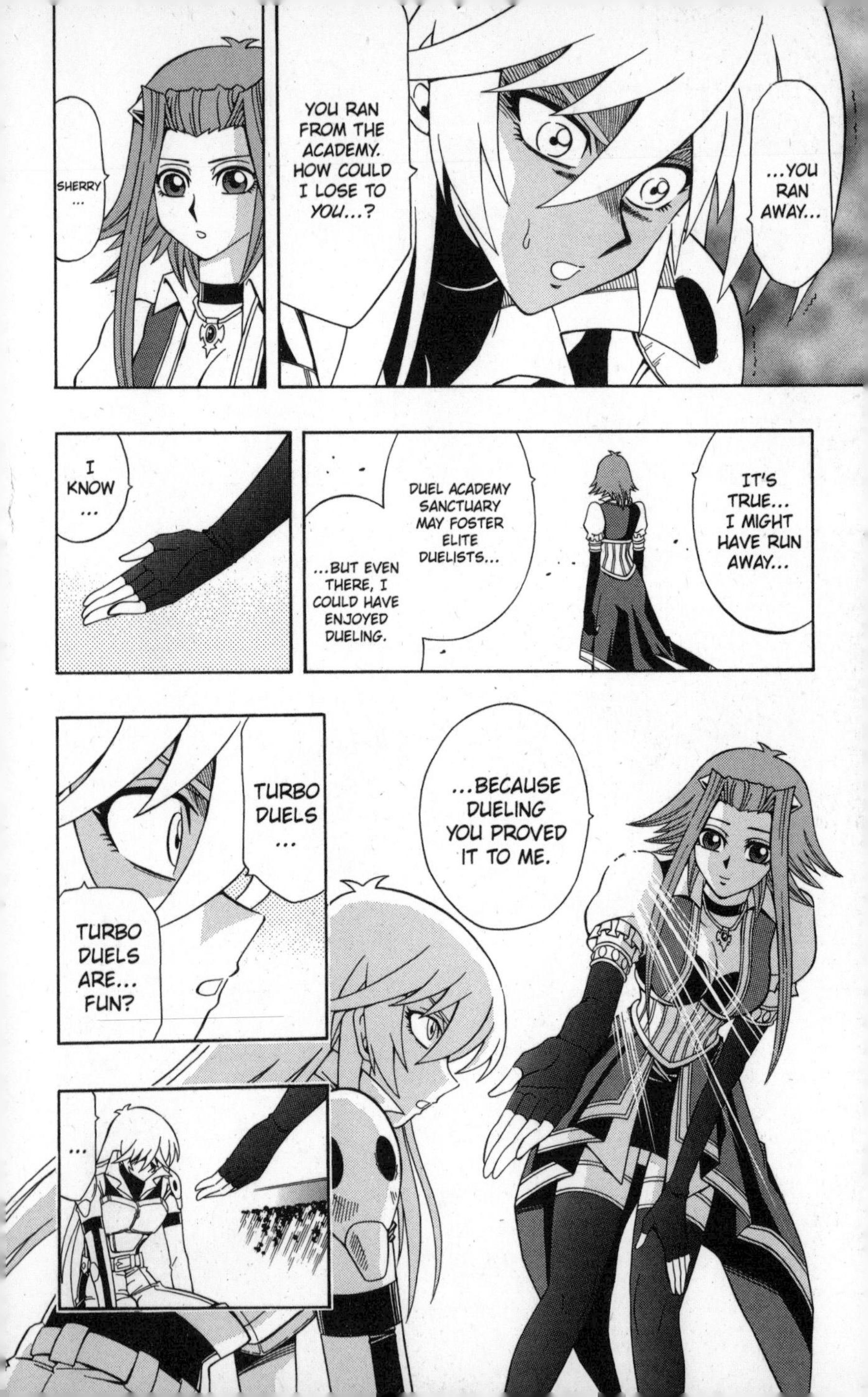
...YOU RAN AWAY...
YOU RAN FROM THE ACADEMY. HOW COULD I LOSE TO YOU...?
SHERRY...
IT'S TRUE... I MIGHT HAVE RUN AWAY...
DUEL ACADEMY SANCTUARY MAY FOSTER ELITE DUELISTS...
...BUT EVEN THERE, I COULD HAVE ENJOYED DUELING.
I KNOW...
...BECAUSE DUELING YOU PROVED IT TO ME.
TURBO DUELS...
TURBO DUELS ARE... FUN?
...

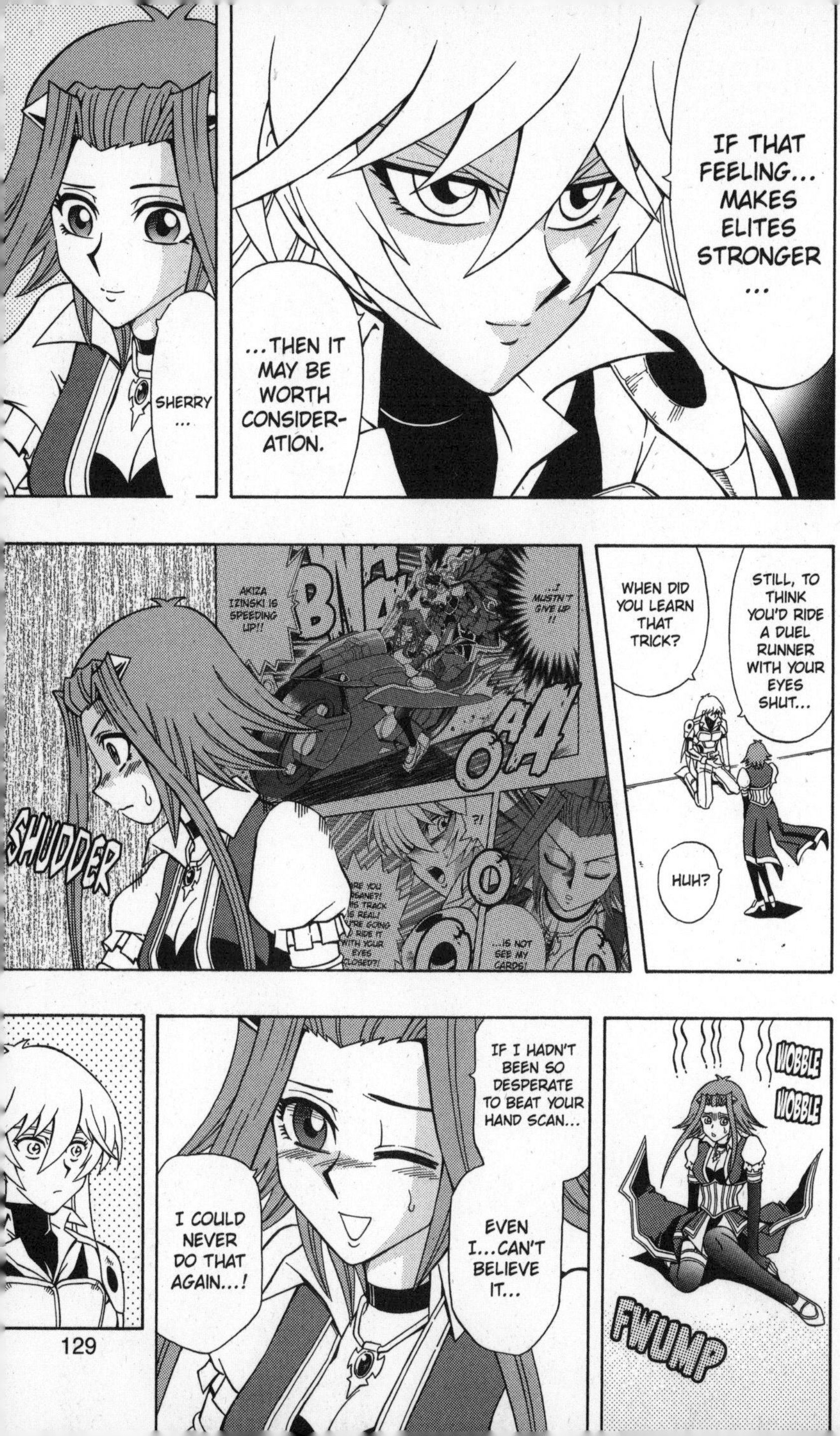
IF THAT FEELING... MAKES ELITES STRONGER ...
...THEN IT MAY BE WORTH CONSIDER-ATION.
SHERRY ...
STILL, TO THINK YOU'D RIDE A DUEL RUNNER WITH YOUR EYES SHUT...
WHEN DID YOU LEARN THAT TRICK?
HUH?
...I MUSTN'T GIVE UP !!
AKIZA IZINSKI IS SPEEDING UP!!
SHUDDER
WOBBLE WOBBLE
FWUMP
IF I HADN'T BEEN SO DESPERATE TO BEAT YOUR HAND SCAN...
EVEN I...CAN'T BELIEVE IT...
I COULD NEVER DO THAT AGAIN...!

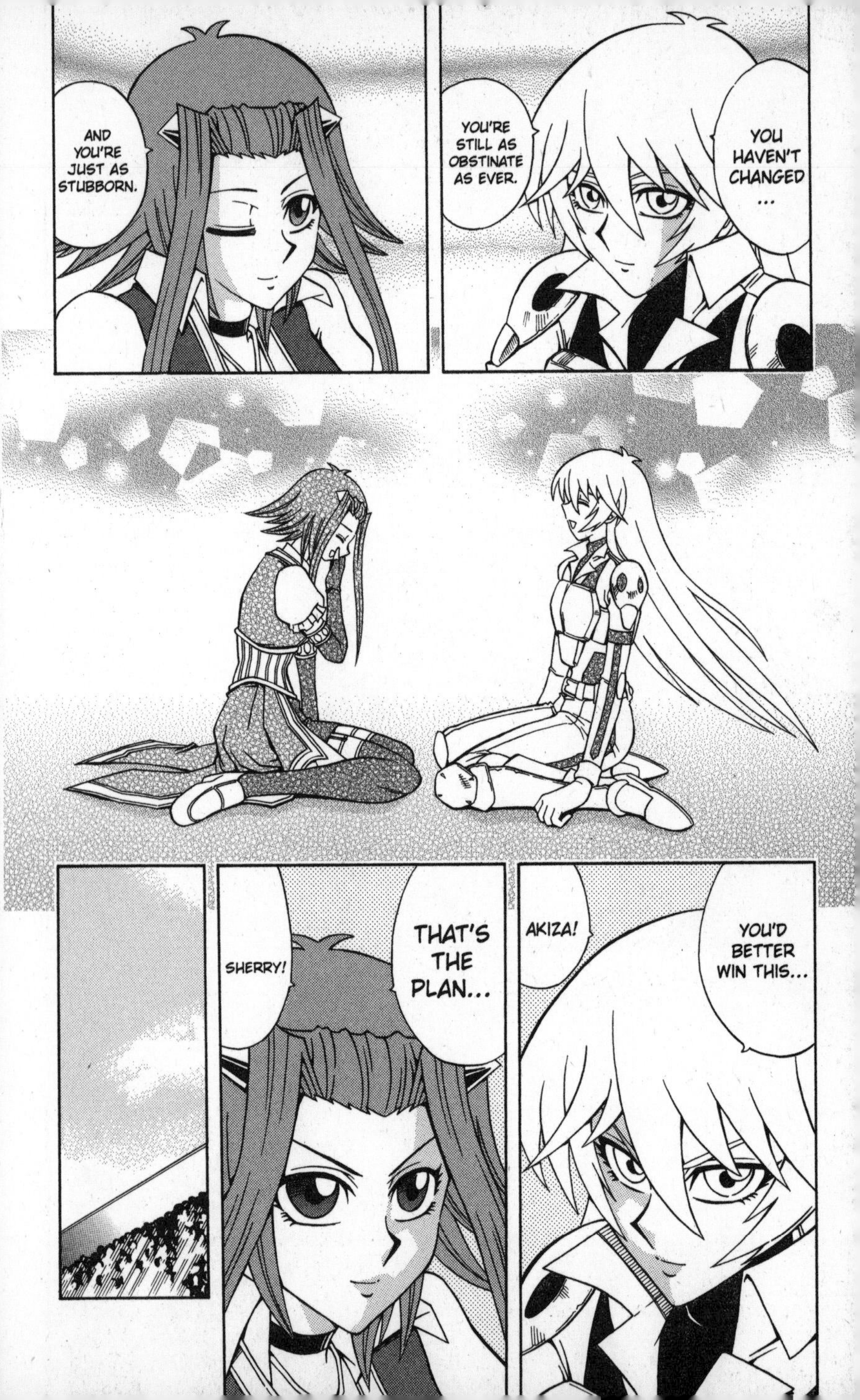
YOU HAVEN'T CHANGED ...
YOU'RE STILL AS OBSTINATE AS EVER.
AND YOU'RE JUST AS STUBBORN.
YOU'D BETTER WIN THIS...
AKIZA!
THAT'S THE PLAN...
SHERRY!

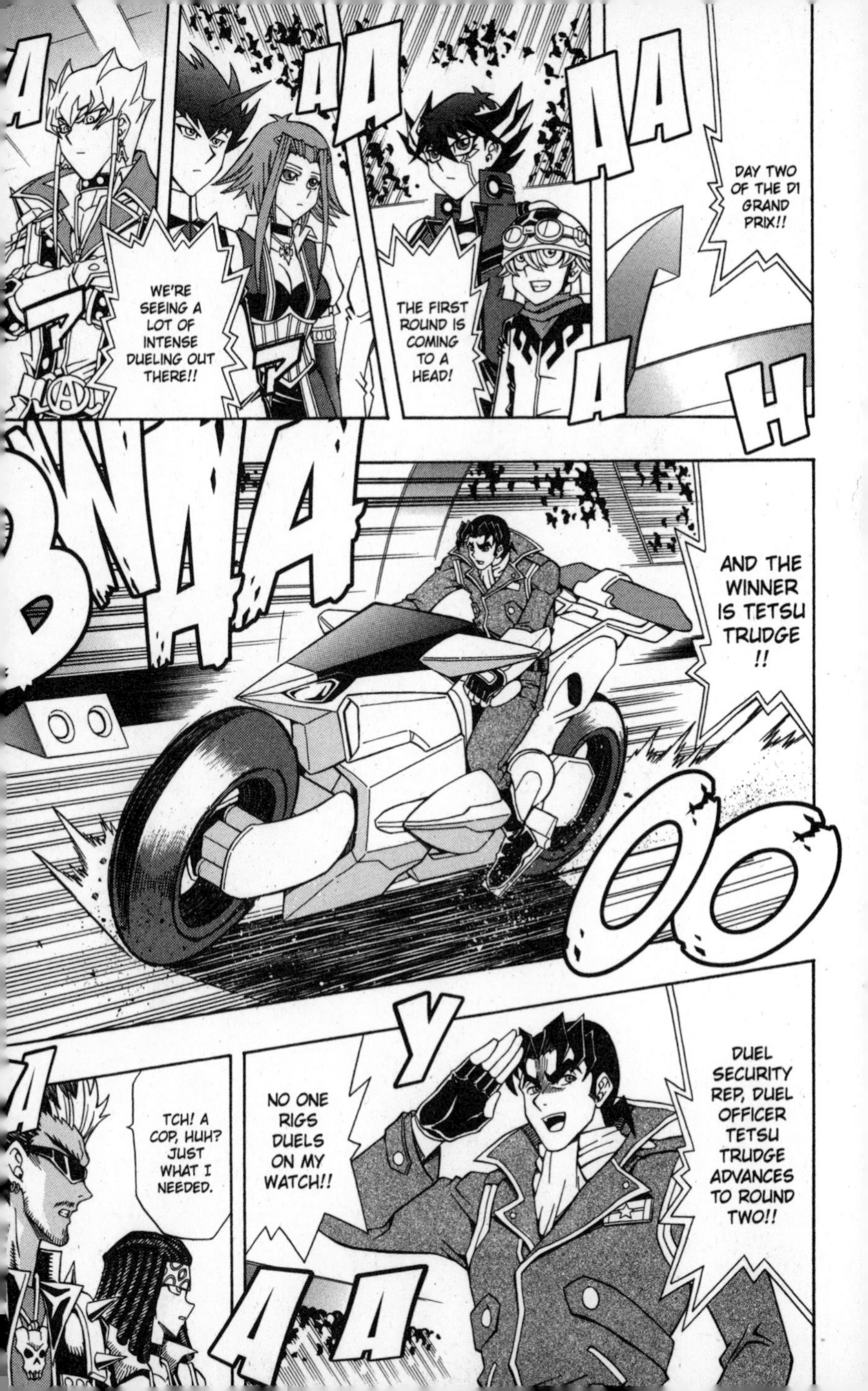
DAY TWO OF THE D1 GRAND PRIX!!
THE FIRST ROUND IS COMING TO A HEAD!
WE'RE SEEING A LOT OF INTENSE DUELING OUT THERE!!
AND THE WINNER IS TETSU TRUDGE !!
DUEL SECURITY REP, DUEL OFFICER TETSU TRUDGE ADVANCES TO ROUND TWO!!
NO ONE RIGS DUELS ON MY WATCH!!
TCH! A COP, HUH? JUST WHAT I NEEDED.

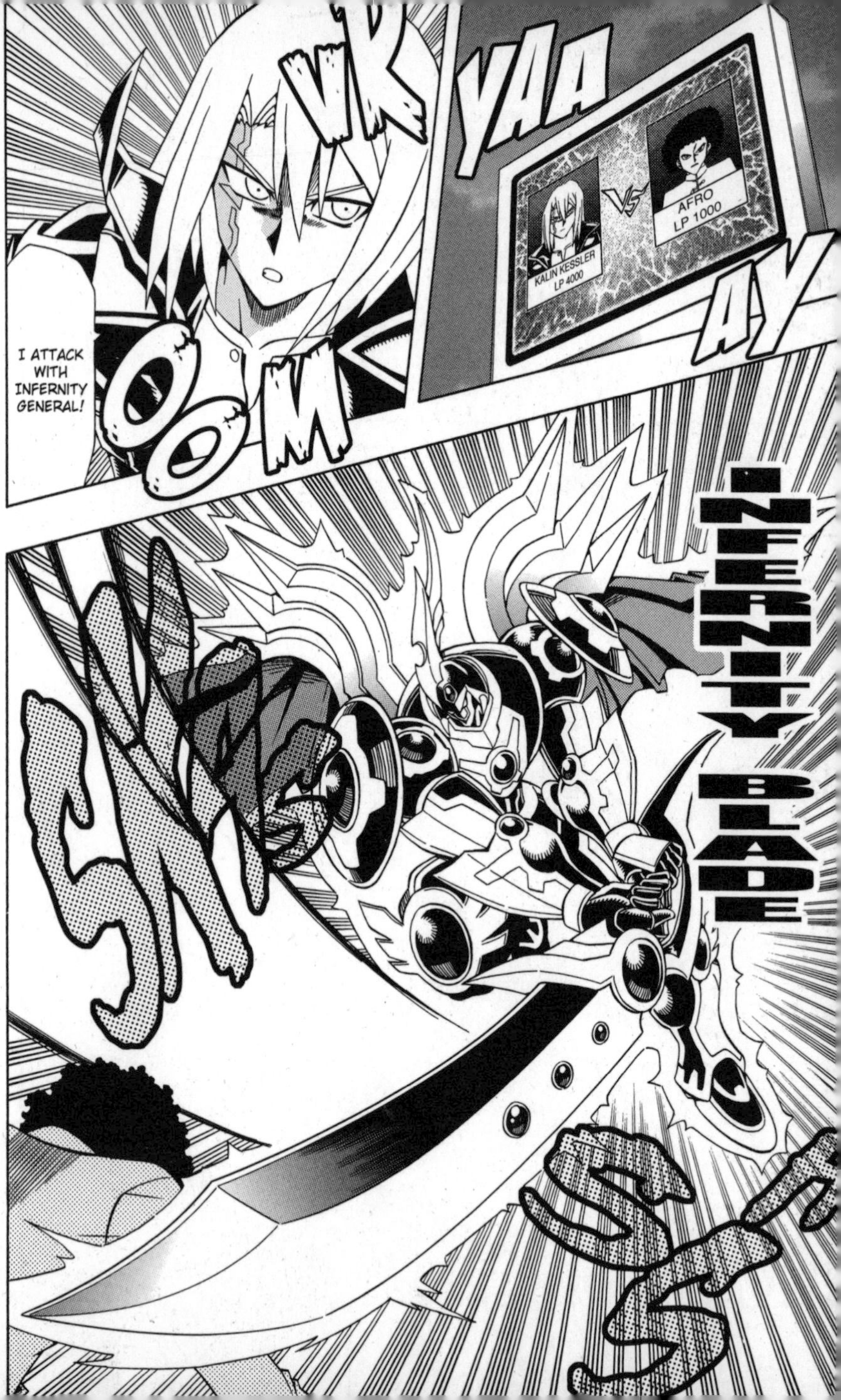

YAA
AY
AFRO
LP 1000
VS
KALIN KESSLER
LP 4000
VR
OOM
I ATTACK WITH INFERNITY GENERAL!
INFERNITY BLADE

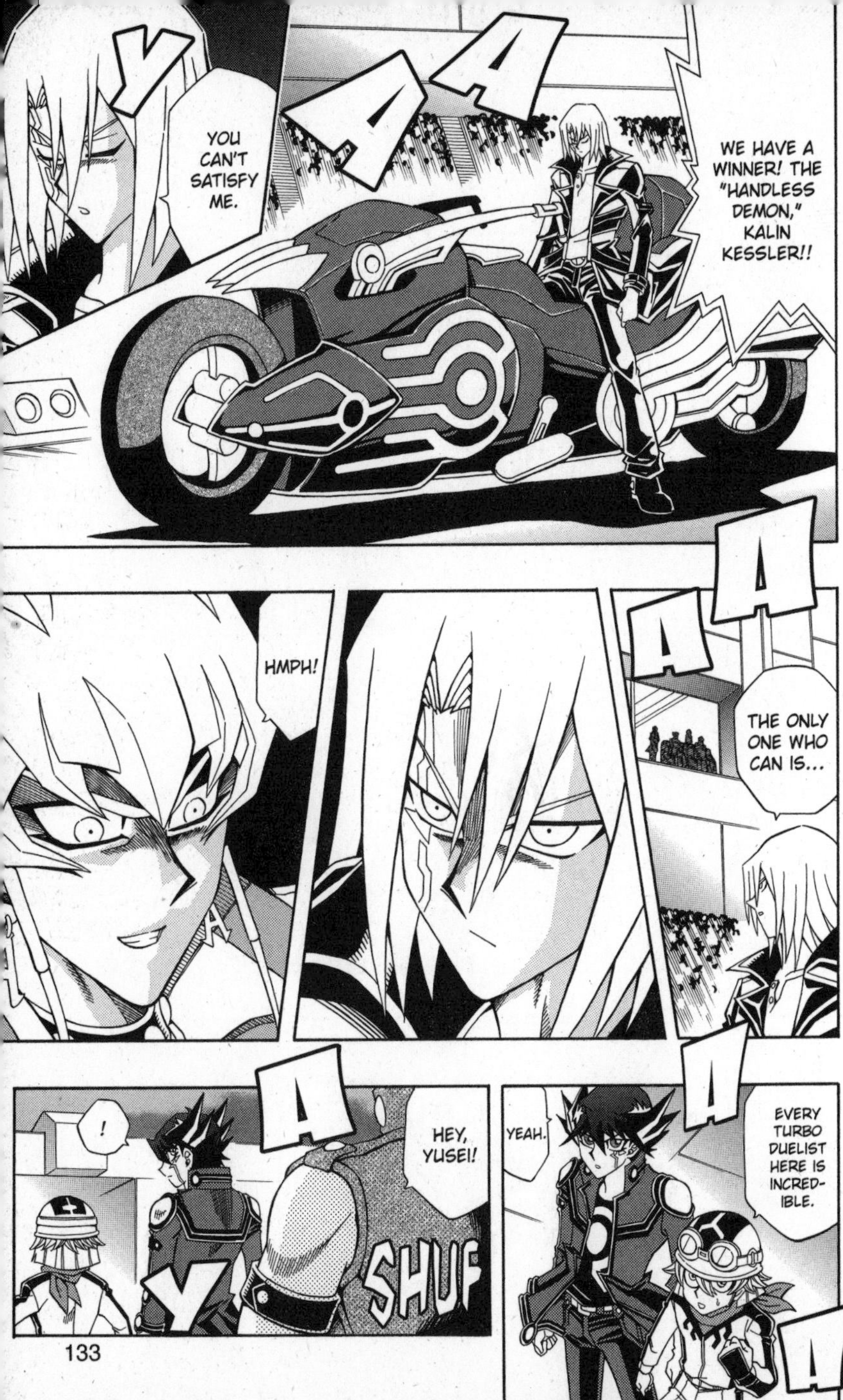
YAAA
WE HAVE A WINNER! THE "HANDLESS DEMON," KALIN KESSLER!!
YOU CAN'T SATISFY ME.
AA
THE ONLY ONE WHO CAN IS...
HMPH!
AA
EVERY TURBO DUELIST HERE IS INCREDIBLE.
YEAH.
A
HEY, YUSEI!
!
SHUF
Y

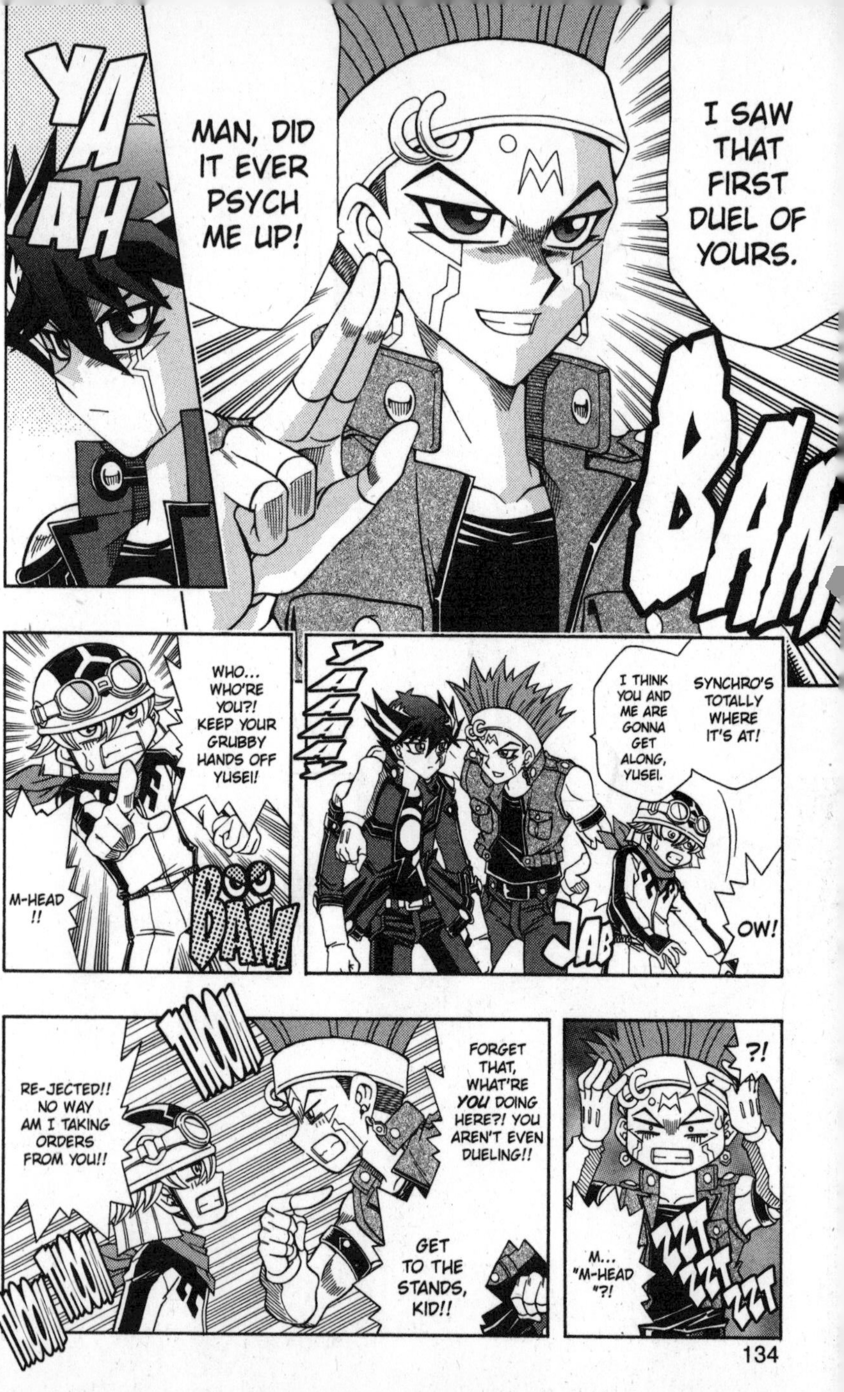

I SAW THAT FIRST DUEL OF YOURS.
BAM
MAN, DID IT EVER PSYCH ME UP!
YA AH
SYNCHRO'S TOTALLY WHERE IT'S AT!
I THINK YOU AND ME ARE GONNA GET ALONG, YUSEI.
JAB
OW!
WHO... WHO'RE YOU?! KEEP YOUR GRUBBY HANDS OFF YUSEI!
BAM
M-HEAD !!
?!
M... "M-HEAD"?!
ZZZT ZZZT ZZZT
FORGET THAT, WHAT'RE *YOU* DOING HERE?! YOU AREN'T EVEN DUELING!!
THOOM
GET TO THE STANDS, KID!!
RE-JECTED!! NO WAY AM I TAKING ORDERS FROM YOU!!
THOOM THOOM

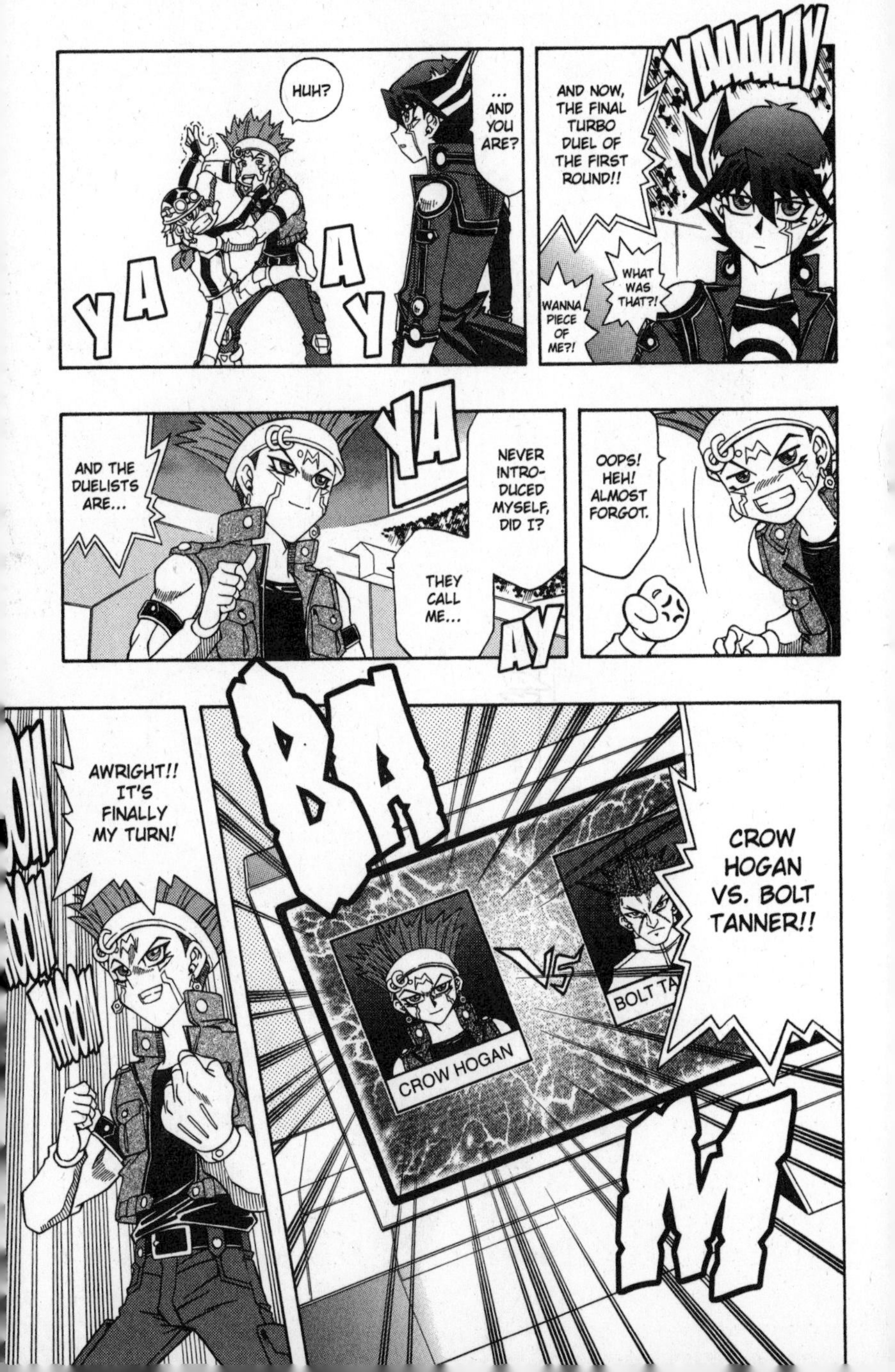
YAAAAAY!
AND NOW, THE FINAL TURBO DUEL OF THE FIRST ROUND!!
WHAT WAS THAT?!
WANNA PIECE OF ME?!
... AND YOU ARE?
HUH?
Y A A Y
OOPS! HEH! ALMOST FORGOT.
YA
NEVER INTRO-DUCED MYSELF, DID I?
THEY CALL ME...
AY
AND THE DUELISTS ARE...
BA
M
CROW HOGAN VS. BOLT TANNER!!
CROW HOGAN
VS
BOLT TA
AWRIGHT!! IT'S FINALLY MY TURN!
THOOM

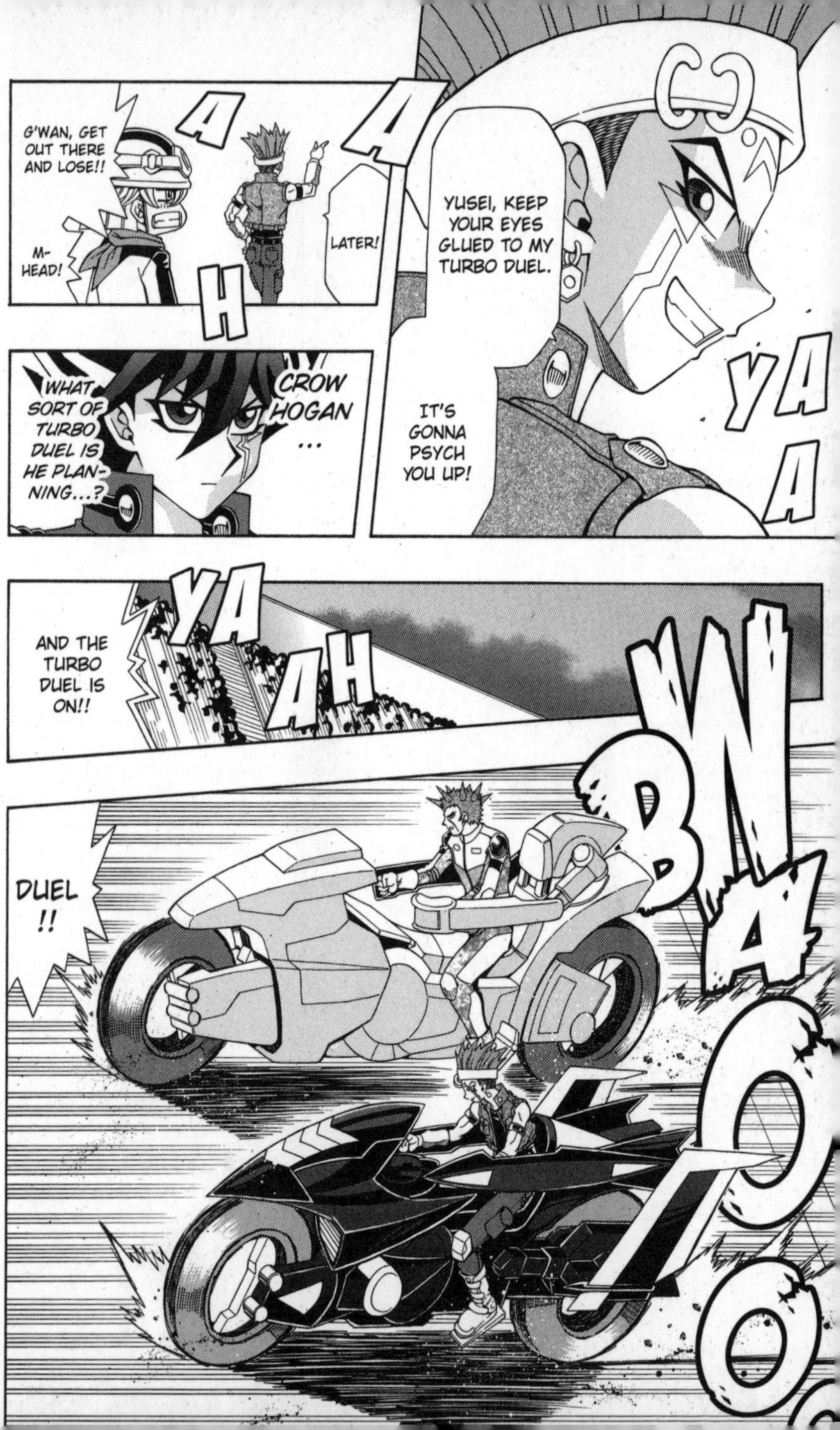
YUSEI, KEEP YOUR EYES GLUED TO MY TURBO DUEL.
IT'S GONNA PSYCH YOU UP!
YAAA
AAH
LATER!
G'WAN, GET OUT THERE AND LOSE!!
M-HEAD!
CROW HOGAN...
WHAT SORT OF TURBO DUEL IS HE PLANNING...?
YAAH
AND THE TURBO DUEL IS ON!!
DUEL!!

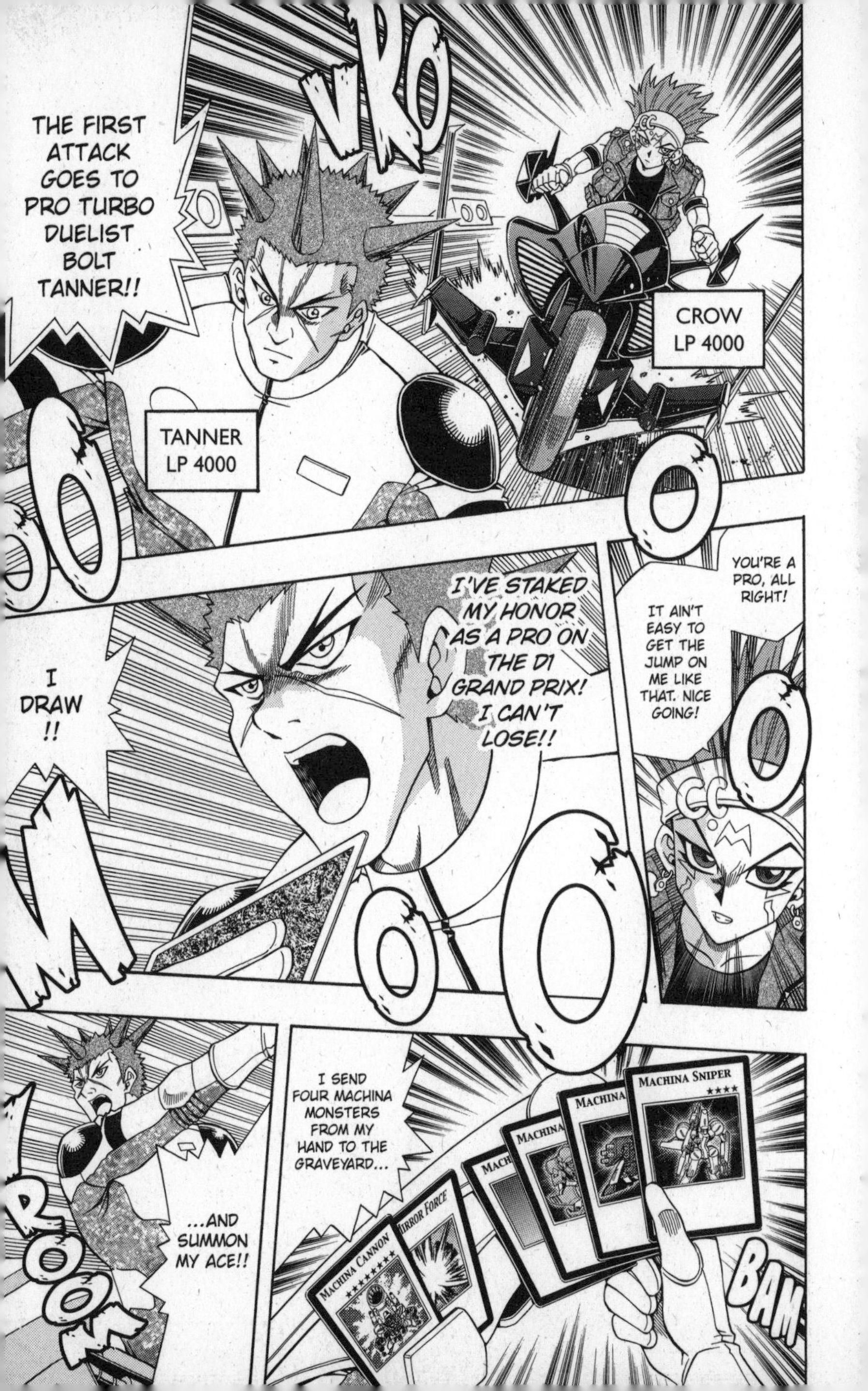
VRO
THE FIRST ATTACK GOES TO PRO TURBO DUELIST BOLT TANNER!!
CROW LP 4000
TANNER LP 4000
YOU'RE A PRO, ALL RIGHT!
IT AIN'T EASY TO GET THE JUMP ON ME LIKE THAT. NICE GOING!
I'VE STAKED MY HONOR AS A PRO ON THE D1 GRAND PRIX! I CAN'T LOSE!!
I DRAW!!
I SEND FOUR MACHINA MONSTERS FROM MY HAND TO THE GRAVEYARD...
...AND SUMMON MY ACE!!
MACHINA SNIPER
MACHINA CANNON
BAM
ROOO

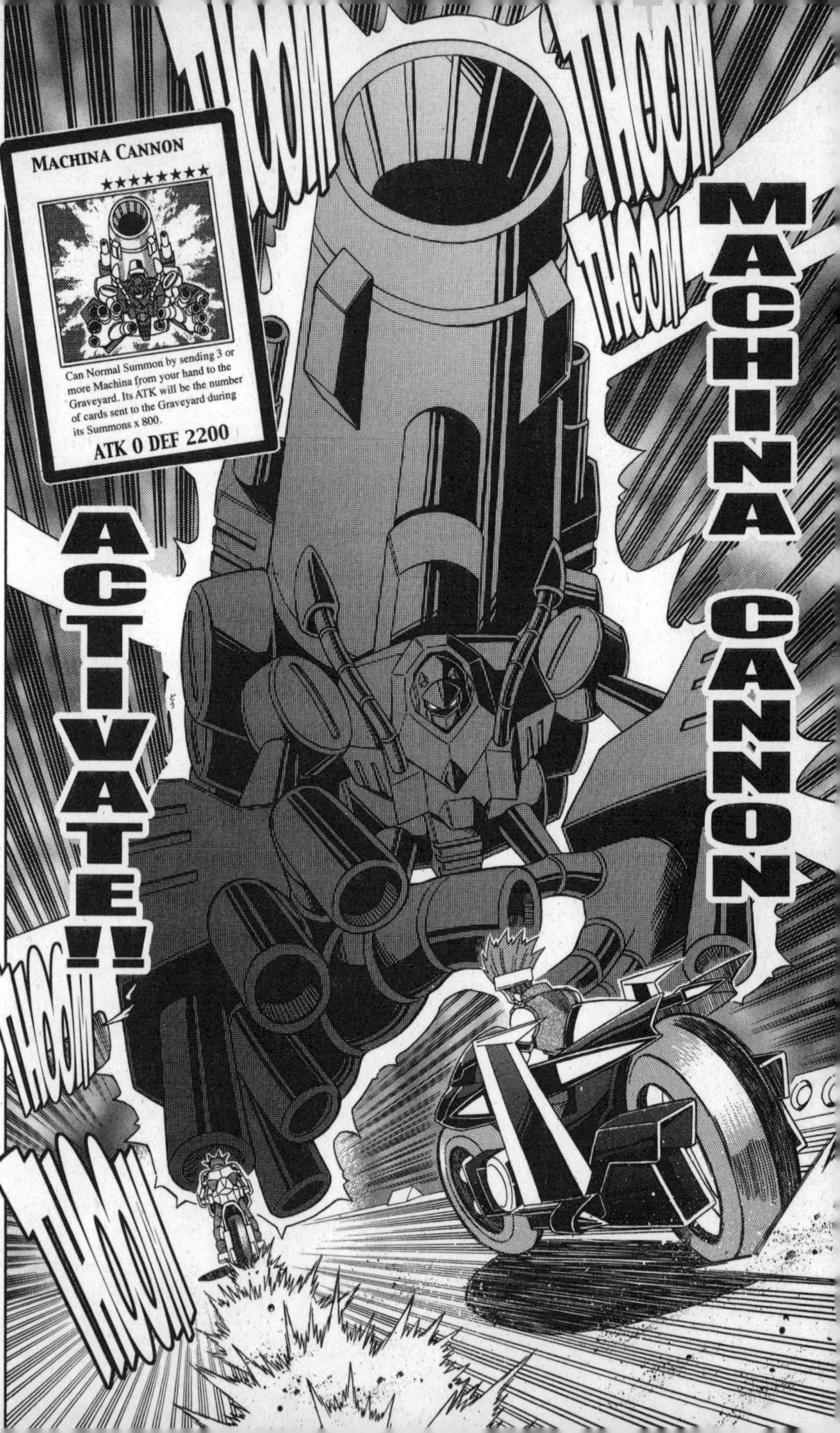
THOOM
THOOM
MACHINA CANNON
MACHINA CANNON
★★★★★★★★★
Can Normal Summon by sending 3 or more Machina from your hand to the Graveyard. Its ATK will be the number of cards sent to the Graveyard during its Summons x 800.
ATK 0 DEF 2200
ACTIVATE!!
THOOM
THOOM

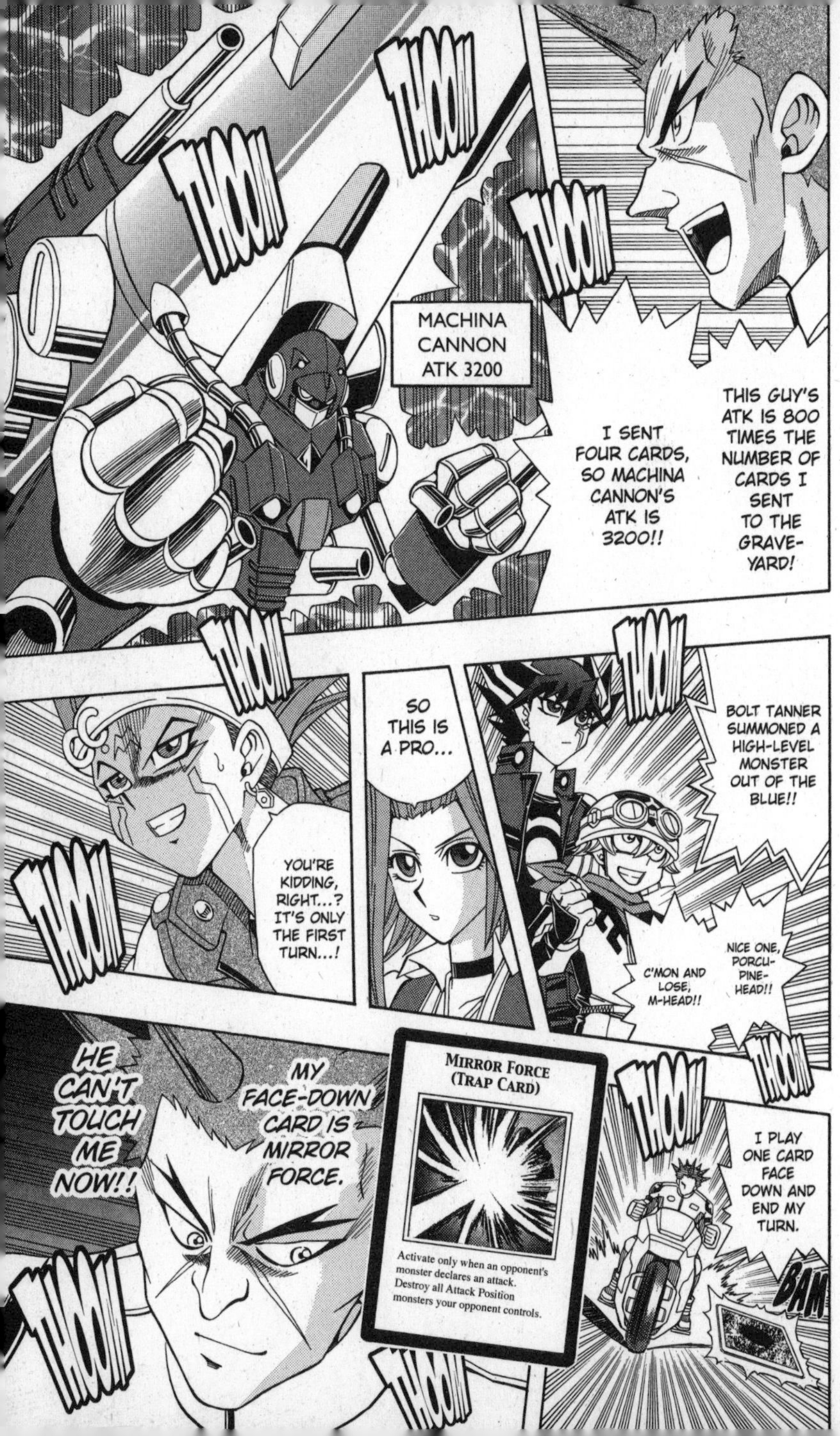
THOOM
THIS GUY'S ATK IS 800 TIMES THE NUMBER OF CARDS I SENT TO THE GRAVEYARD!
I SENT FOUR CARDS, SO MACHINA CANNON'S ATK IS 3200!!
THOOM
THOOM
MACHINA CANNON ATK 3200
THOOM
BOLT TANNER SUMMONED A HIGH-LEVEL MONSTER OUT OF THE BLUE!!
NICE ONE, PORCUPINE-HEAD!!
C'MON AND LOSE, M-HEAD!!
THOOM
SO THIS IS A PRO...
THOOM
YOU'RE KIDDING, RIGHT...? IT'S ONLY THE FIRST TURN...!
THOOM
THOOM
I PLAY ONE CARD FACE DOWN AND END MY TURN.
BAM
MIRROR FORCE (TRAP CARD)
Activate only when an opponent's monster declares an attack. Destroy all Attack Position monsters your opponent controls.
THOOM
MY FACE-DOWN CARD IS MIRROR FORCE.
HE CAN'T TOUCH ME NOW!!
THOOM

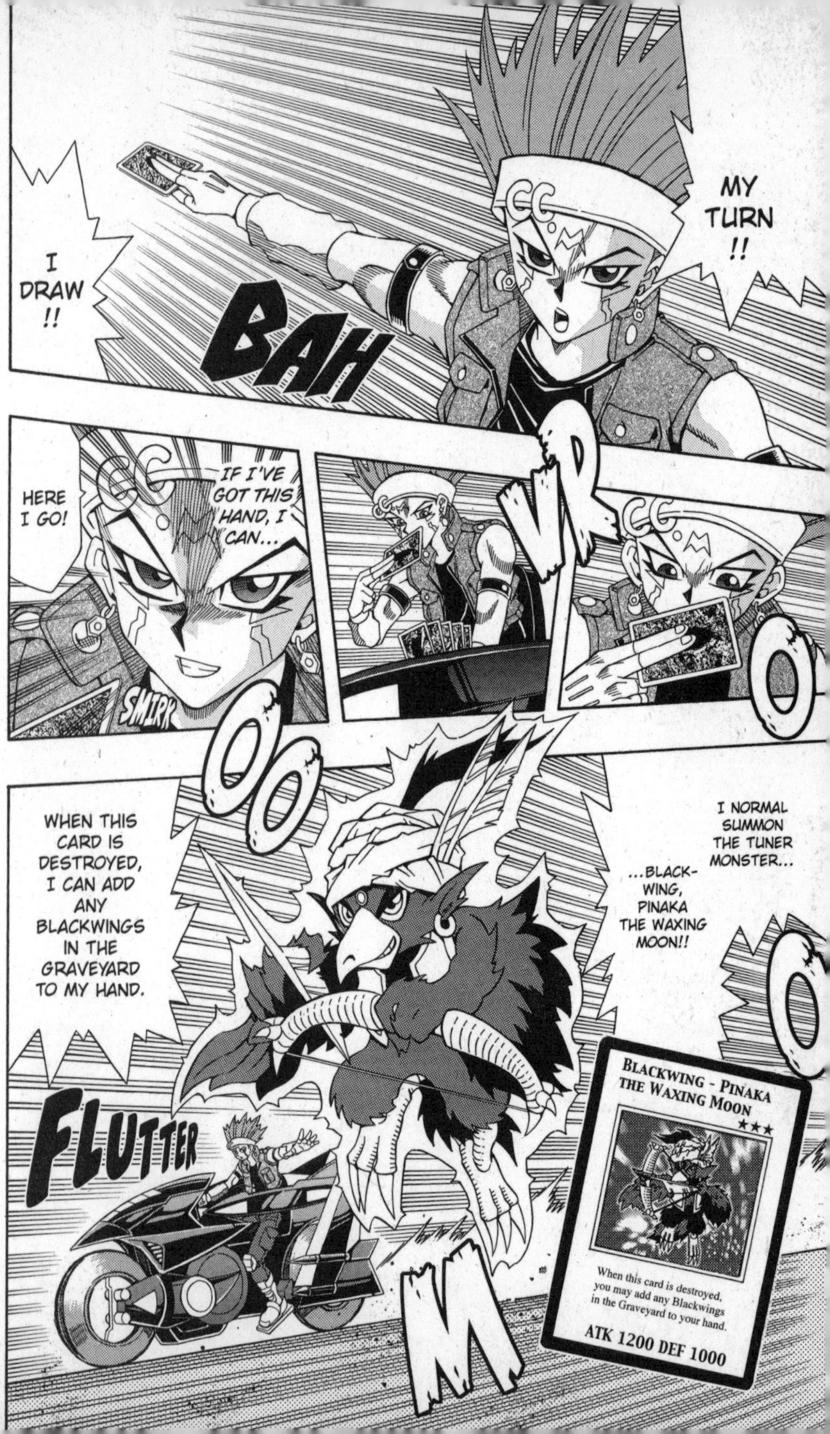
MY TURN!!
I DRAW!!
BAH
IF I'VE GOT THIS HAND, I CAN...
HERE I GO!
SMIRK
VROOOOM
I NORMAL SUMMON THE TUNER MONSTER...
...BLACK-WING, PINAKA THE WAXING MOON!!
WHEN THIS CARD IS DESTROYED, I CAN ADD ANY BLACKWINGS IN THE GRAVEYARD TO MY HAND.
FLUTTER
BLACKWING - PINAKA THE WAXING MOON
When this card is destroyed, you may add any Blackwings in the Graveyard to your hand.
ATK 1200 DEF 1000

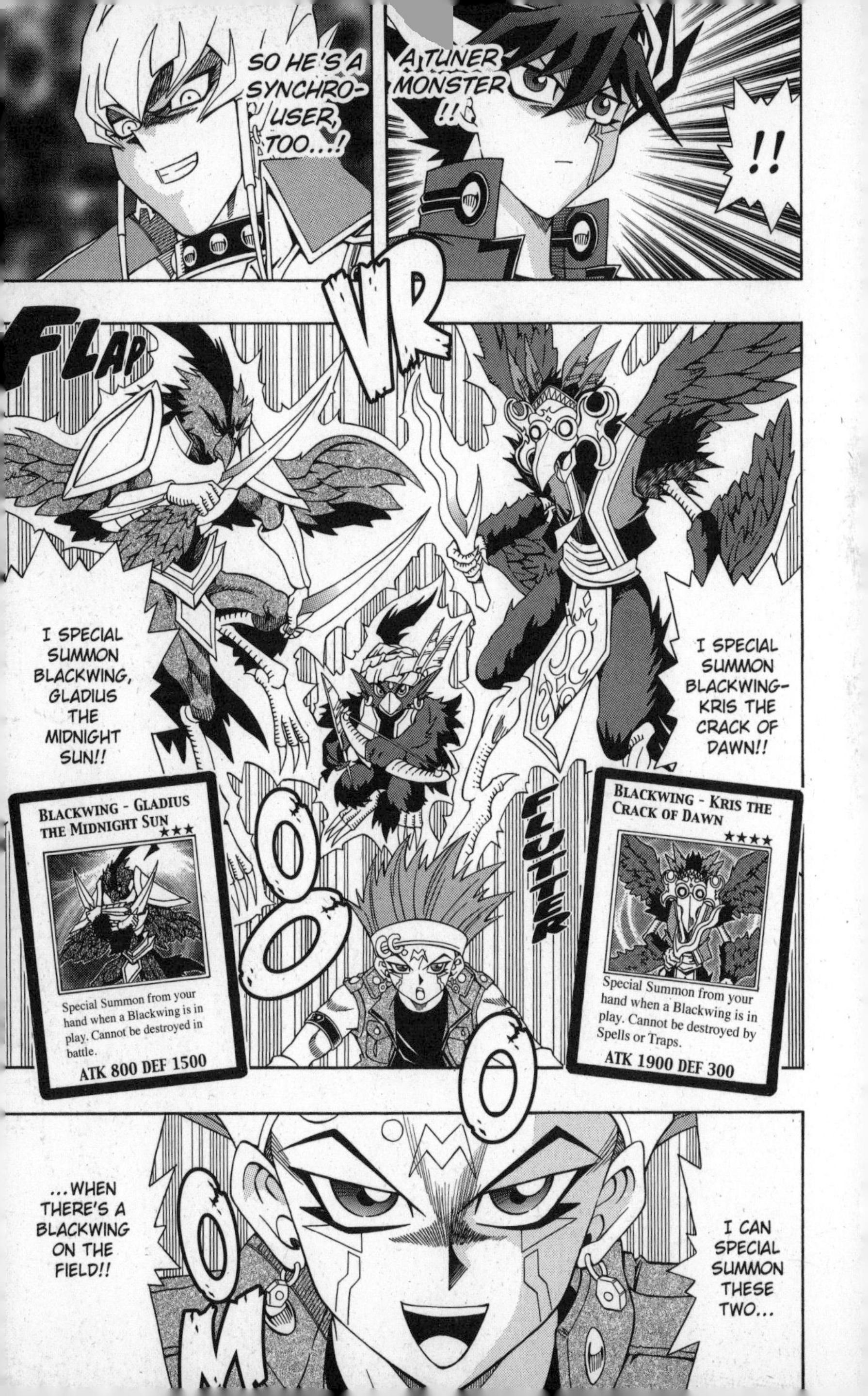

!!
A TUNER MONSTER !!
SO HE'S A SYNCHRO-USER, TOO...!
VR
I SPECIAL SUMMON BLACKWING-KRIS THE CRACK OF DAWN!!
BLACKWING - KRIS THE CRACK OF DAWN
★★★★
Special Summon from your hand when a Blackwing is in play. Cannot be destroyed by Spells or Traps.
ATK 1900 DEF 300
FLUTTER
FLAP
I SPECIAL SUMMON BLACKWING, GLADIUS THE MIDNIGHT SUN!!
BLACKWING - GLADIUS THE MIDNIGHT SUN
★★★
Special Summon from your hand when a Blackwing is in play. Cannot be destroyed in battle.
ATK 800 DEF 1500
I CAN SPECIAL SUMMON THESE TWO...
...WHEN THERE'S A BLACKWING ON THE FIELD!!

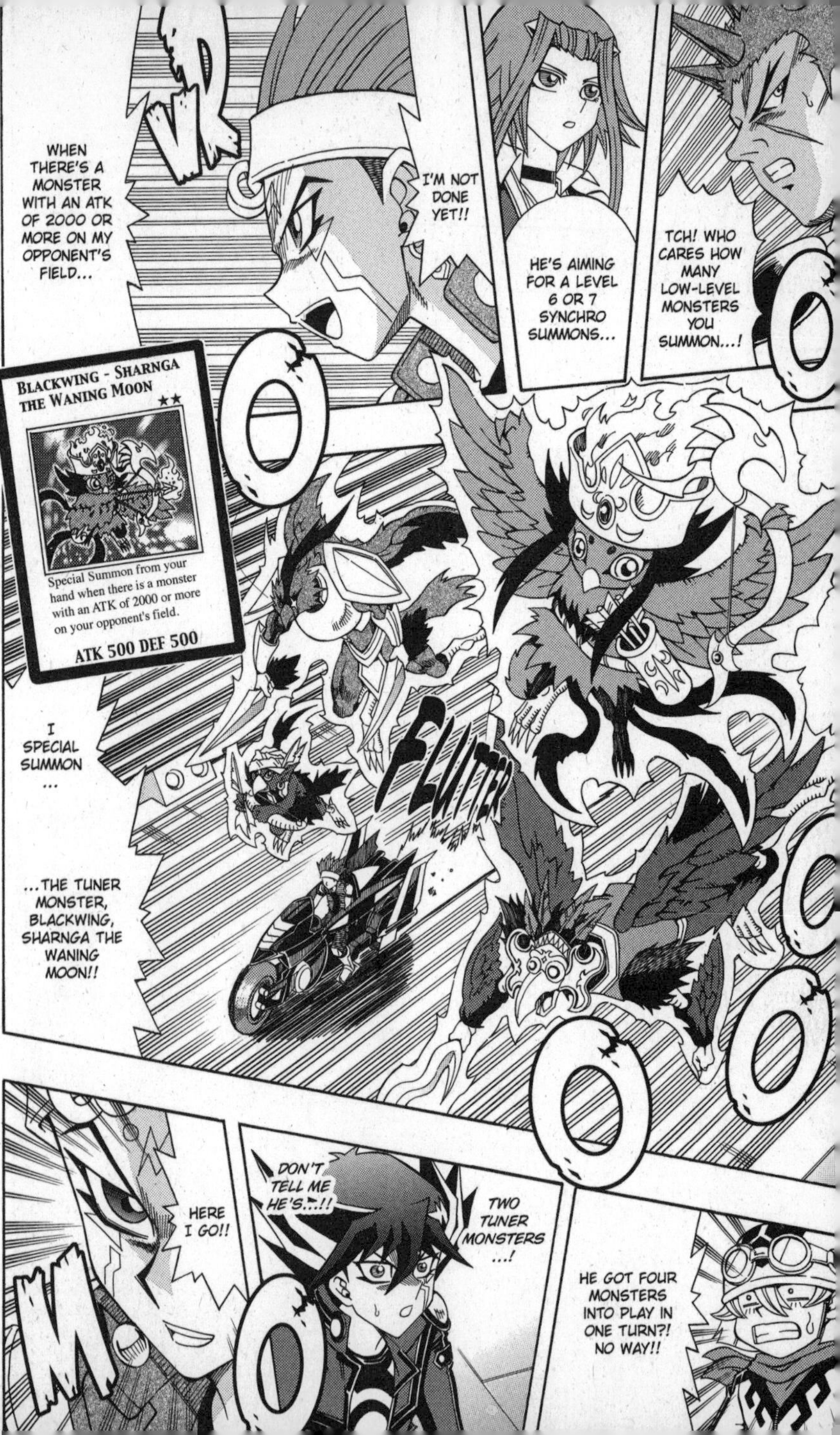
TCH! WHO CARES HOW MANY LOW-LEVEL MONSTERS YOU SUMMON...!
HE'S AIMING FOR A LEVEL 6 OR 7 SYNCHRO SUMMONS...
I'M NOT DONE YET!!
WHEN THERE'S A MONSTER WITH AN ATK OF 2000 OR MORE ON MY OPPONENT'S FIELD...
BLACKWING - SHARNGA THE WANING MOON
Special Summon from your hand when there is a monster with an ATK of 2000 or more on your opponent's field.
ATK 500 DEF 500
I SPECIAL SUMMON...
...THE TUNER MONSTER, BLACKWING, SHARNGA THE WANING MOON!!
FLUTTER
HE GOT FOUR MONSTERS INTO PLAY IN ONE TURN?! NO WAY!!
TWO TUNER MONSTERS...!
DON'T TELL ME HE'S...!!
HERE I GO!!

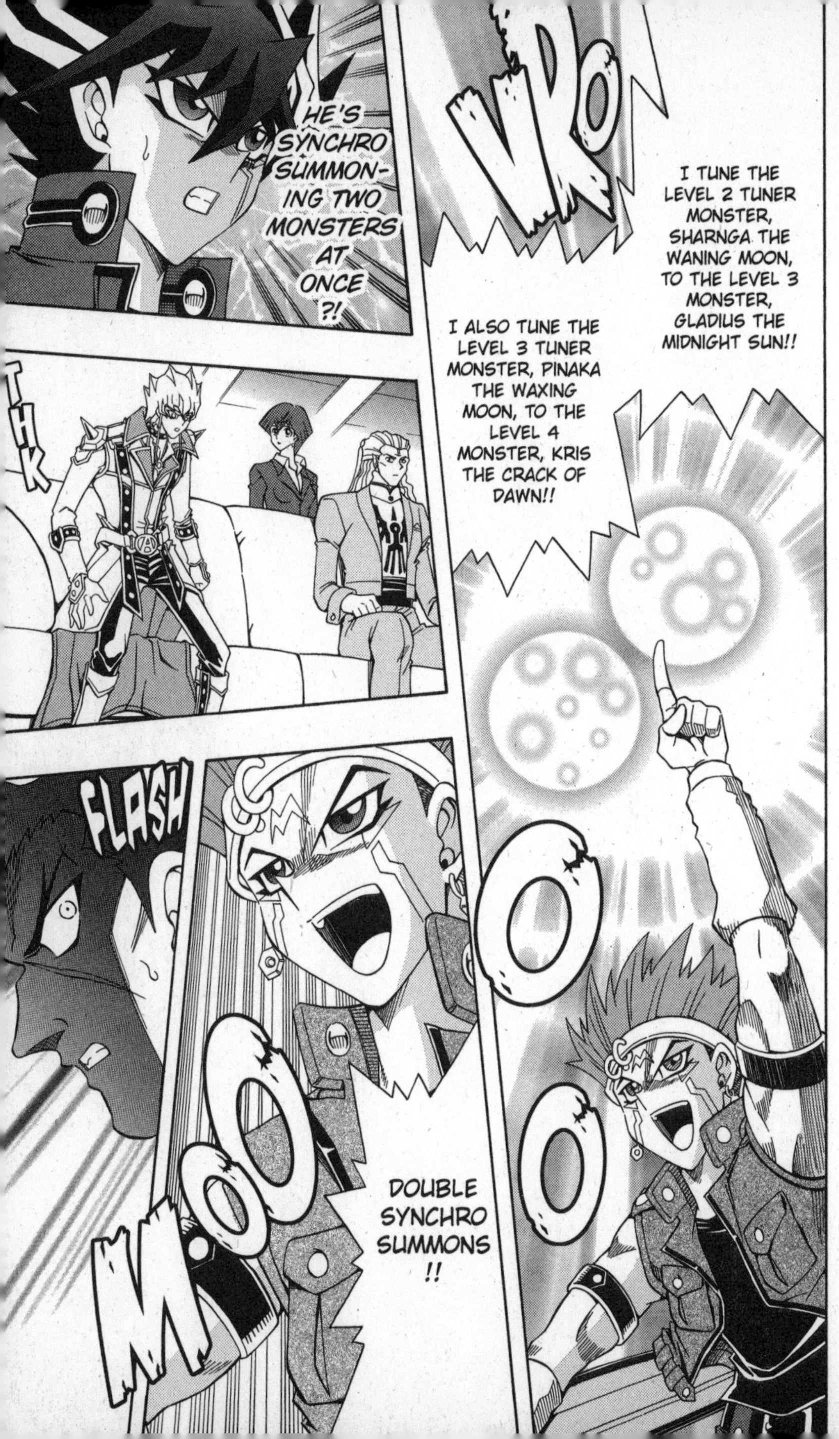
I TUNE THE LEVEL 2 TUNER MONSTER, SHARNGA THE WANING MOON, TO THE LEVEL 3 MONSTER, GLADIUS THE MIDNIGHT SUN!!
I ALSO TUNE THE LEVEL 3 TUNER MONSTER, PINAKA THE WAXING MOON, TO THE LEVEL 4 MONSTER, KRIS THE CRACK OF DAWN!!
HE'S SYNCHRO SUMMONING TWO MONSTERS AT ONCE ?!
THK
DOUBLE SYNCHRO SUMMONS !!
FLASH

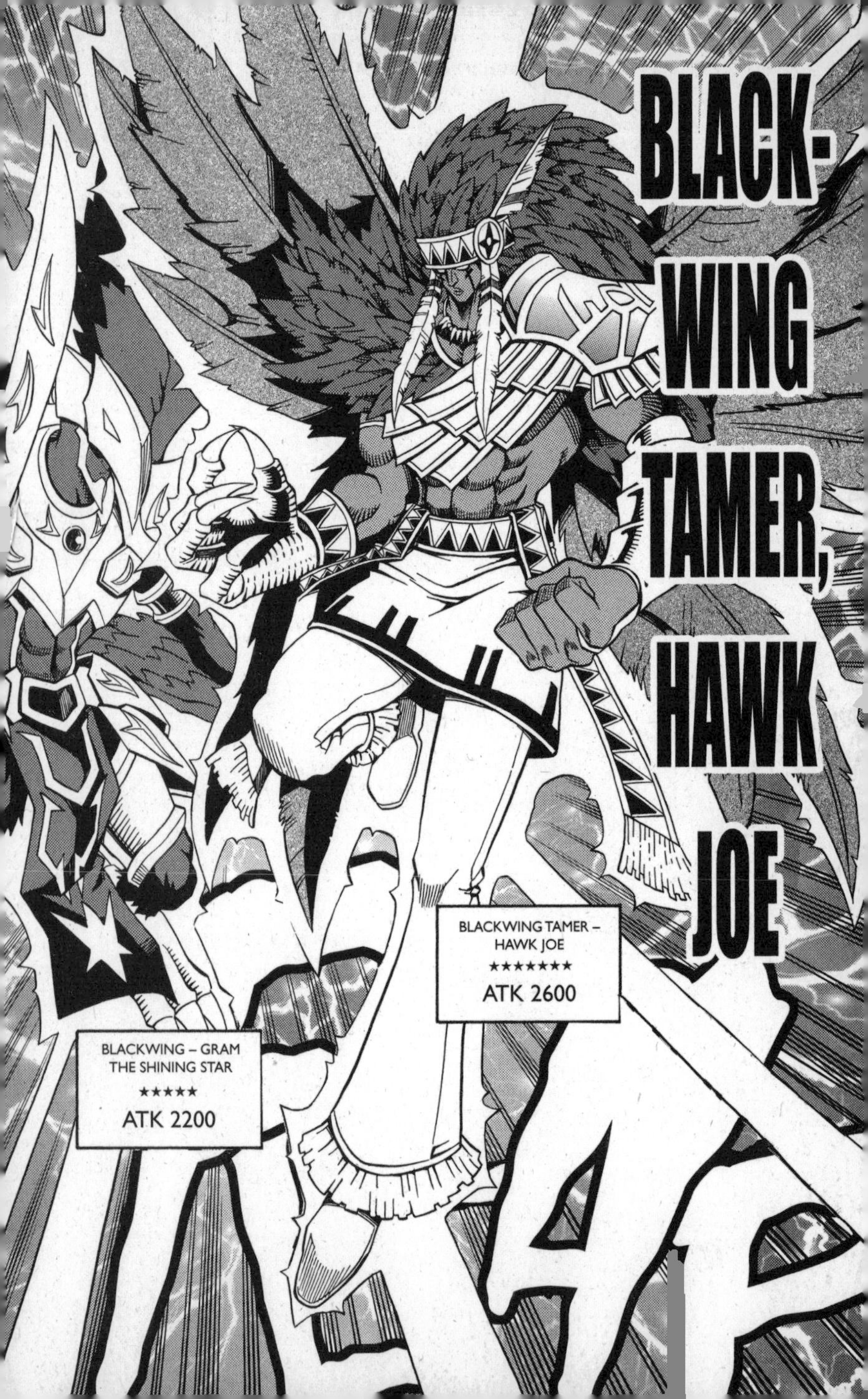
BLACK-WING TAMER, HAWK JOE
BLACKWING TAMER – HAWK JOE
★★★★★★★
ATK 2600
BLACKWING – GRAM THE SHINING STAR
★★★★★
ATK 2200

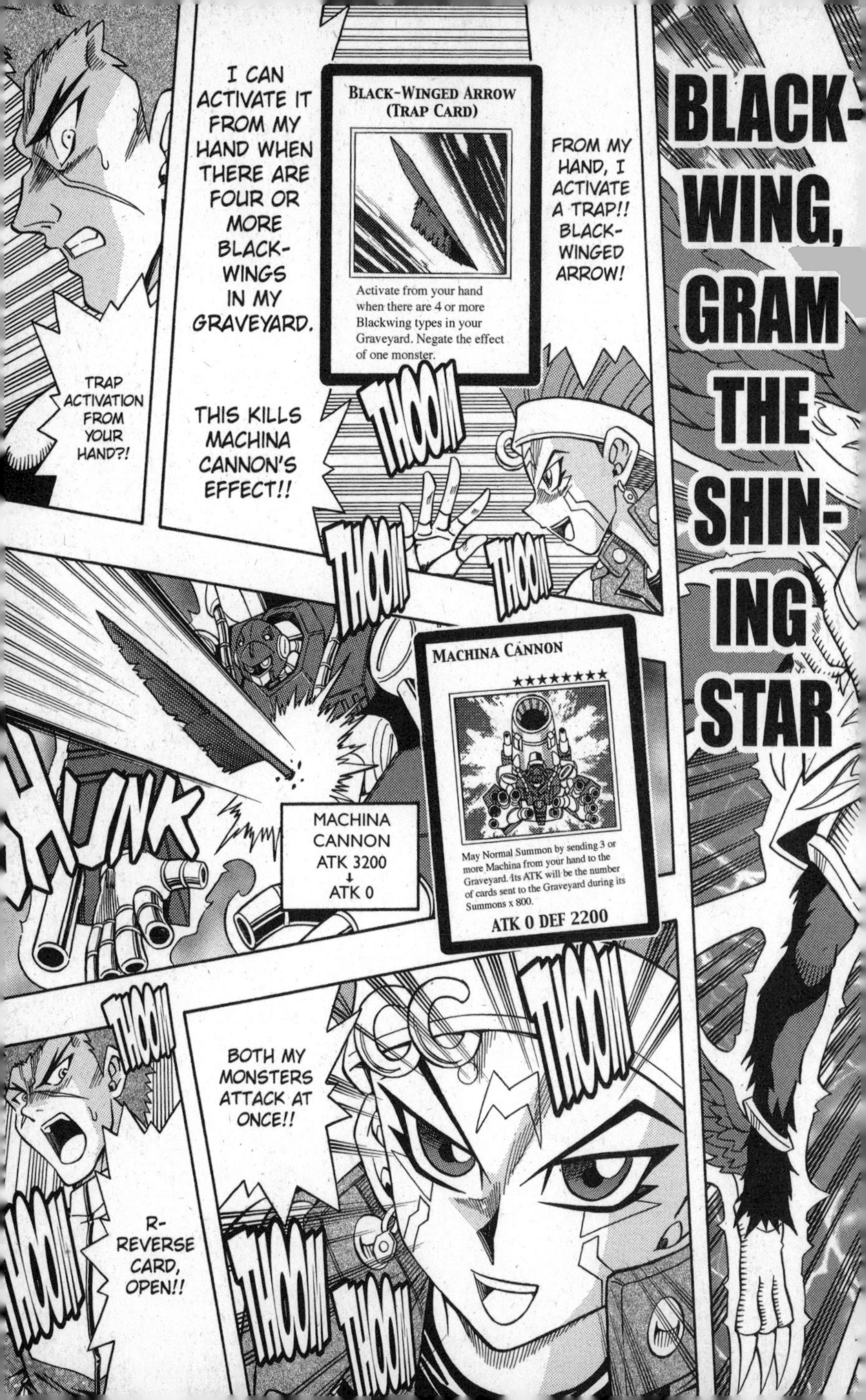
BLACK-WING, GRAM THE SHIN-ING STAR
FROM MY HAND, I ACTIVATE A TRAP!! BLACK-WINGED ARROW!
BLACK-WINGED ARROW (TRAP CARD)
Activate from your hand when there are 4 or more Blackwing types in your Graveyard. Negate the effect of one monster.
I CAN ACTIVATE IT FROM MY HAND WHEN THERE ARE FOUR OR MORE BLACK-WINGS IN MY GRAVEYARD.
THOOM
THIS KILLS MACHINA CANNON'S EFFECT!!
THOOM
THOOM
TRAP ACTIVATION FROM YOUR HAND?!
MACHINA CANNON
May Normal Summon by sending 3 or more Machina from your hand to the Graveyard. Its ATK will be the number of cards sent to the Graveyard during its Summons x 800.
ATK 0 DEF 2200
MACHINA CANNON ATK 3200 ↓ ATK 0
HUNK
THOOM
BOTH MY MONSTERS ATTACK AT ONCE!!
THOOM
THOOM
THOOM
R-REVERSE CARD, OPEN!!
THOOM

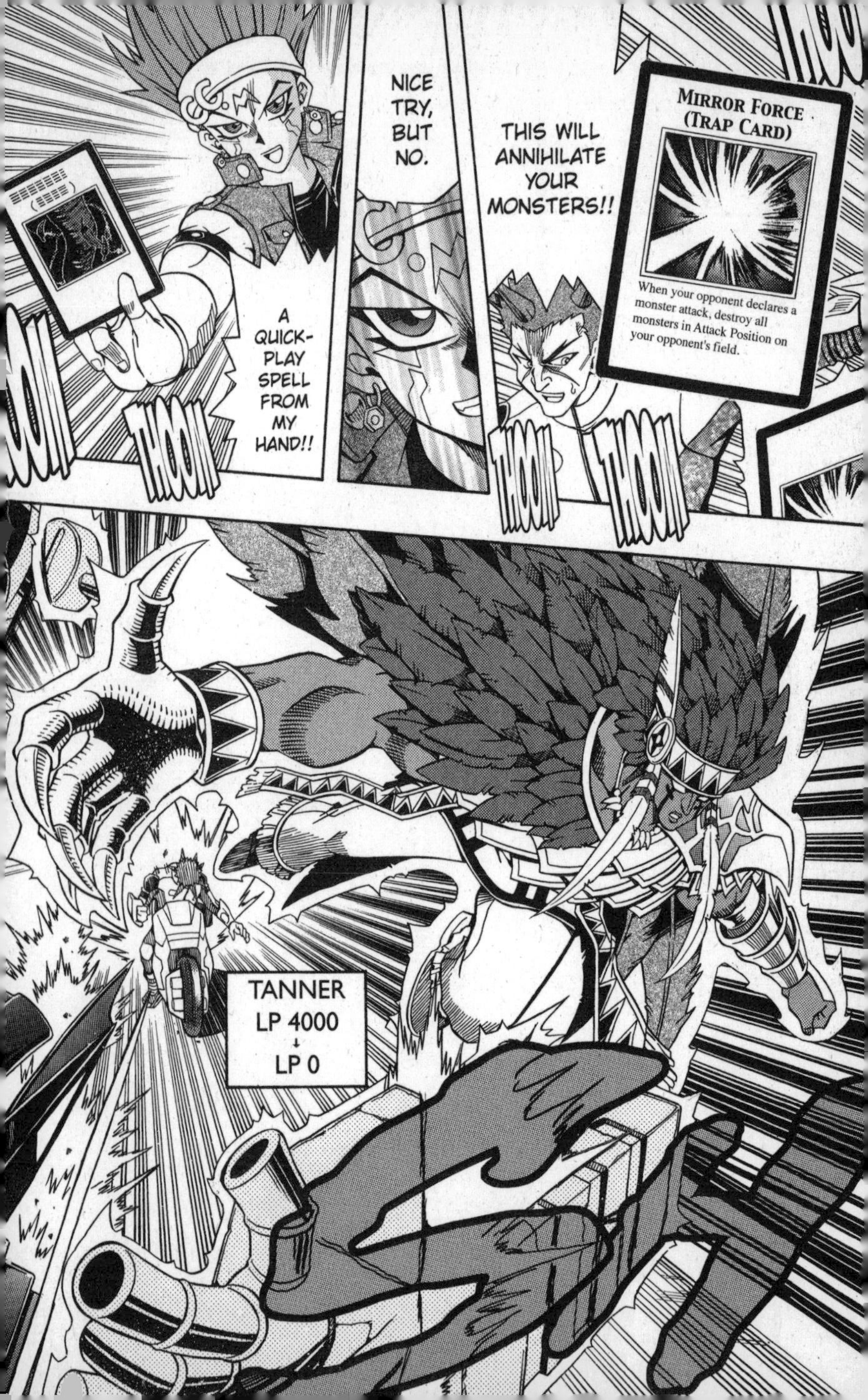
THIS WILL ANNIHILATE YOUR MONSTERS!!
MIRROR FORCE (TRAP CARD)
When your opponent declares a monster attack, destroy all monsters in Attack Position on your opponent's field.
THOOM
THOOM
NICE TRY, BUT NO.
A QUICK-PLAY SPELL FROM MY HAND!!
THOOM
TANNER LP 4000 ↓ LP 0

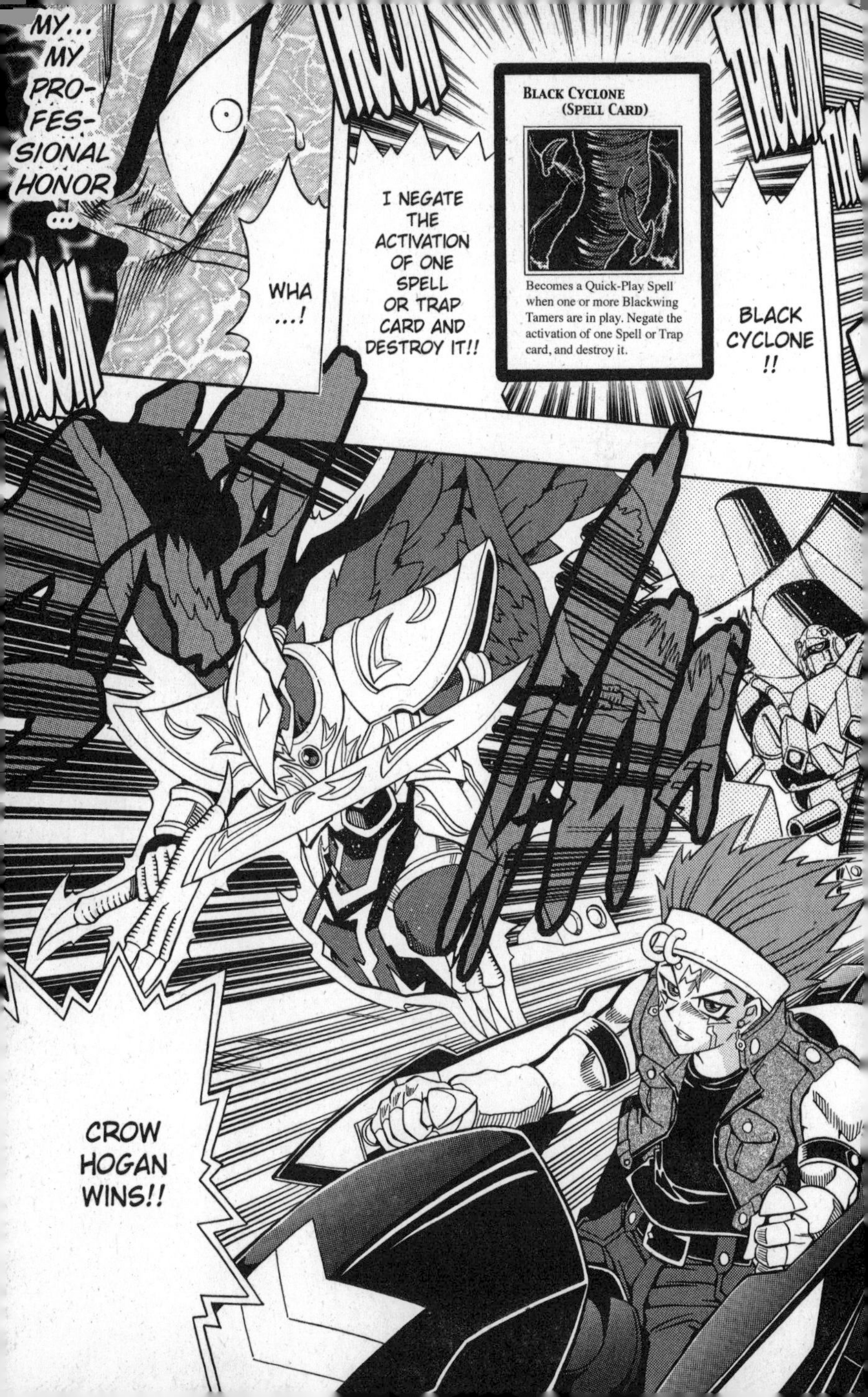
THOOM
BLACK CYCLONE !!
BLACK CYCLONE
(SPELL CARD)
Becomes a Quick-Play Spell when one or more Blackwing Tamers are in play. Negate the activation of one Spell or Trap card, and destroy it.
THOOM
I NEGATE THE ACTIVATION OF ONE SPELL OR TRAP CARD AND DESTROY IT!!
WHA ...!
MY... MY PRO-FES-SIONAL HONOR ...
THOOM
CROW HOGAN WINS!!

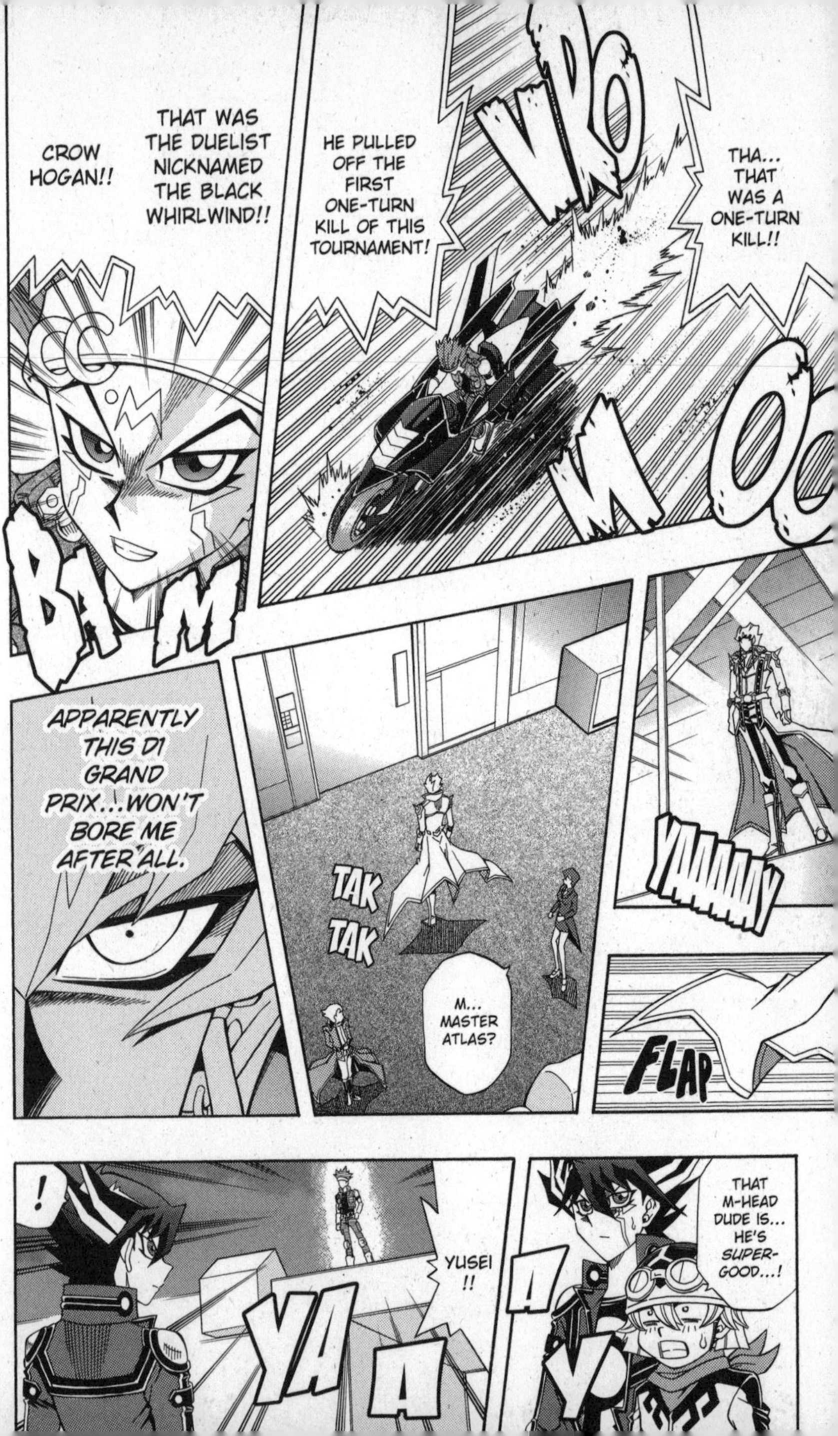
THA... THAT WAS A ONE-TURN KILL!!
VROOOM
HE PULLED OFF THE FIRST ONE-TURN KILL OF THIS TOURNAMENT!
THAT WAS THE DUELIST NICKNAMED THE BLACK WHIRLWIND!!
CROW HOGAN!!
BAM
YAAAAAY
FLAP
TAK TAK
M... MASTER ATLAS?
APPARENTLY THIS D1 GRAND PRIX...WON'T BORE ME AFTER ALL.
THAT M-HEAD DUDE IS... HE'S SUPER-GOOD...!
YUSEI!!
!
YAAAY

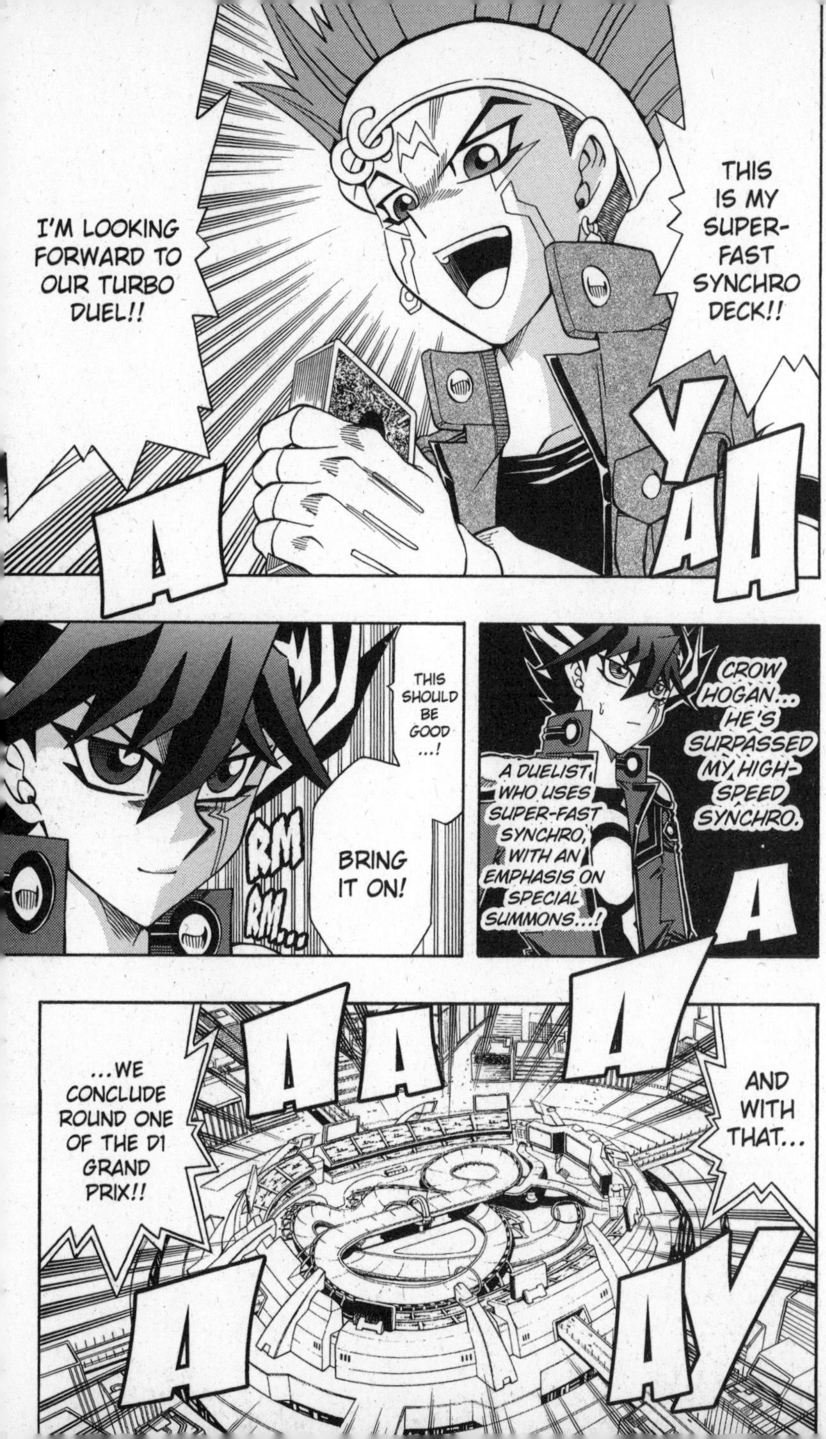
THIS IS MY SUPER-FAST SYNCHRO DECK!!
I'M LOOKING FORWARD TO OUR TURBO DUEL!!
YAAA
A
CROW HOGAN... HE'S SURPASSED MY HIGH-SPEED SYNCHRO.
A DUELIST WHO USES SUPER-FAST SYNCHRO, WITH AN EMPHASIS ON SPECIAL SUMMONS...!
A
THIS SHOULD BE GOOD...!
BRING IT ON!
RM RM RM...
AND WITH THAT...
...WE CONCLUDE ROUND ONE OF THE D1 GRAND PRIX!!
AAAA
AAY

5D's TRACKS

THE 14TH

BY SATOMASA

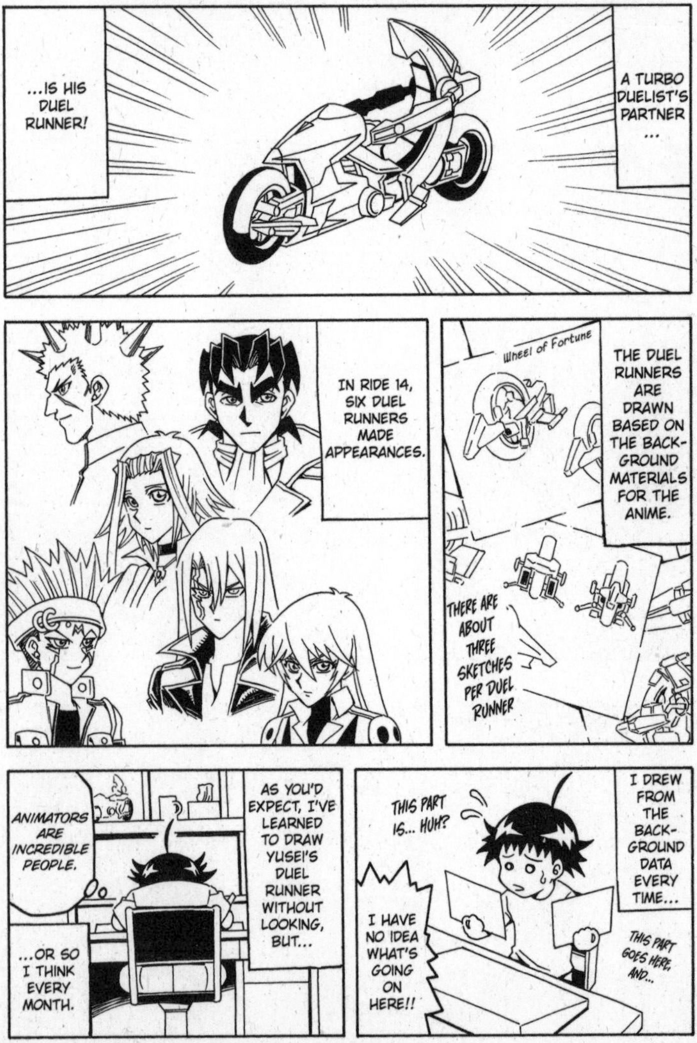
A TURBO DUELIST'S PARTNER ...
...IS HIS DUEL RUNNER!
THE DUEL RUNNERS ARE DRAWN BASED ON THE BACK-GROUND MATERIALS FOR THE ANIME.
Wheel of Fortune
THERE ARE ABOUT THREE SKETCHES PER DUEL RUNNER
IN RIDE 14, SIX DUEL RUNNERS MADE APPEARANCES.
I DREW FROM THE BACK-GROUND DATA EVERY TIME...
THIS PART IS... HUH?
THIS PART GOES HERE, AND...
I HAVE NO IDEA WHAT'S GOING ON HERE!!
AS YOU'D EXPECT, I'VE LEARNED TO DRAW YUSEI'S DUEL RUNNER WITHOUT LOOKING, BUT...
ANIMATORS ARE INCREDIBLE PEOPLE.
...OR SO I THINK EVERY MONTH.

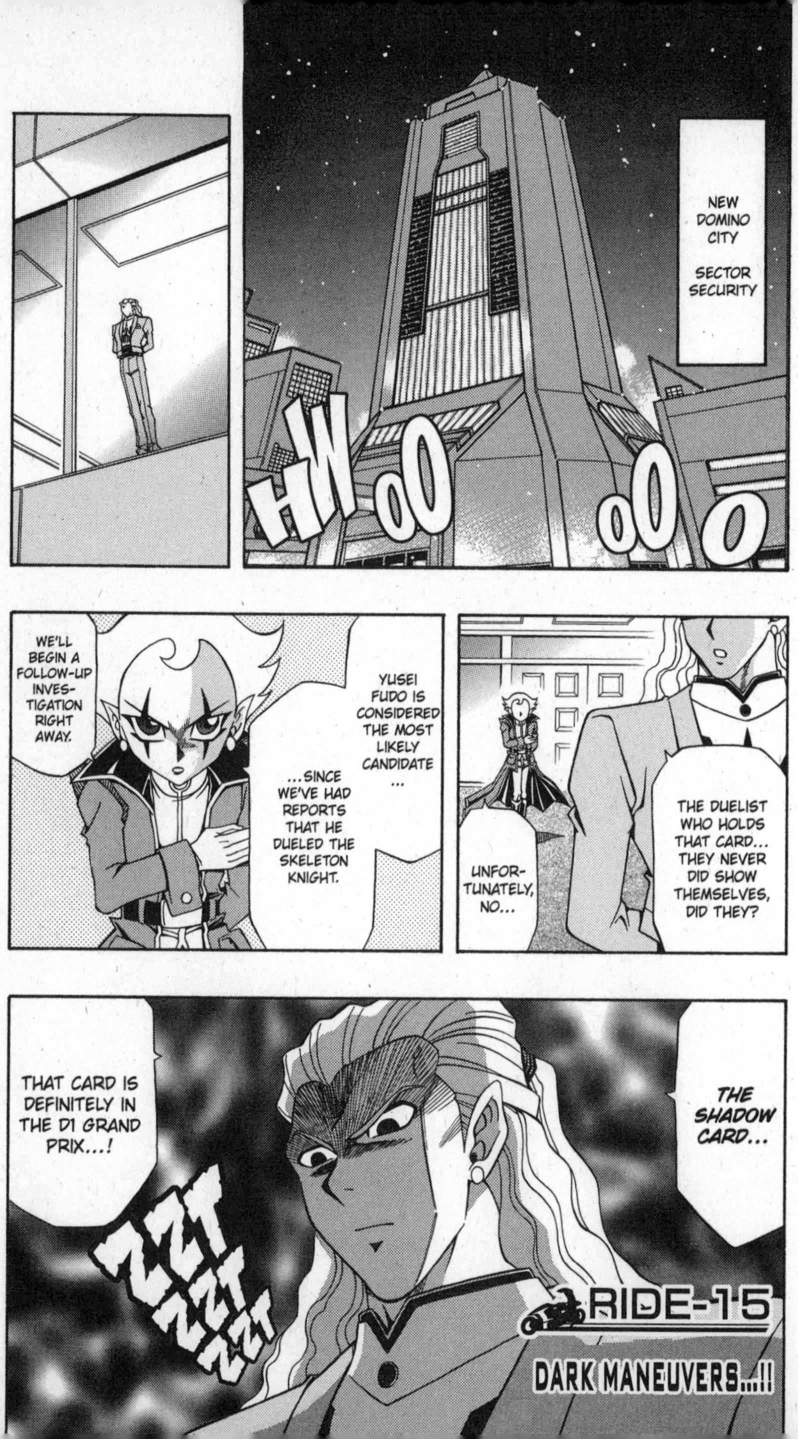
NEW DOMINO CITY

SECTOR SECURITY
HWOOO
OOO
THE DUELIST WHO HOLDS THAT CARD... THEY NEVER DID SHOW THEMSELVES, DID THEY?
UNFORTUNATELY, NO...
YUSEI FUDO IS CONSIDERED THE MOST LIKELY CANDIDATE...
...SINCE WE'VE HAD REPORTS THAT HE DUELED THE SKELETON KNIGHT.
WE'LL BEGIN A FOLLOW-UP INVESTIGATION RIGHT AWAY.
THE SHADOW CARD...
THAT CARD IS DEFINITELY IN THE D1 GRAND PRIX...!
ZZZT ZZZT ZZZT
RIDE-15
DARK MANEUVERS...!!

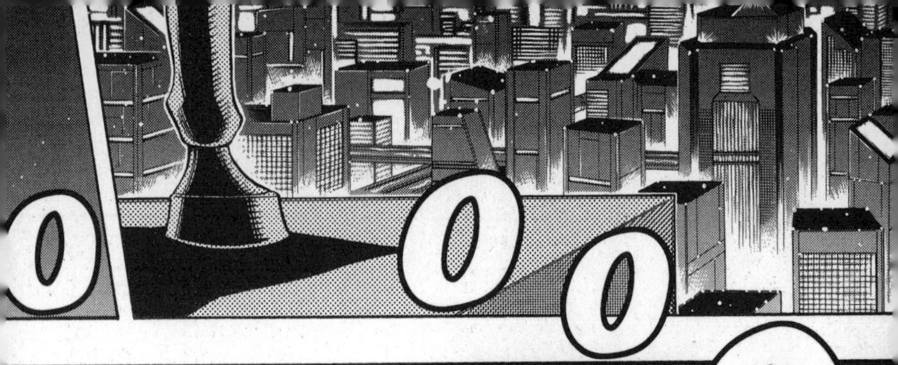
O
O
O
O
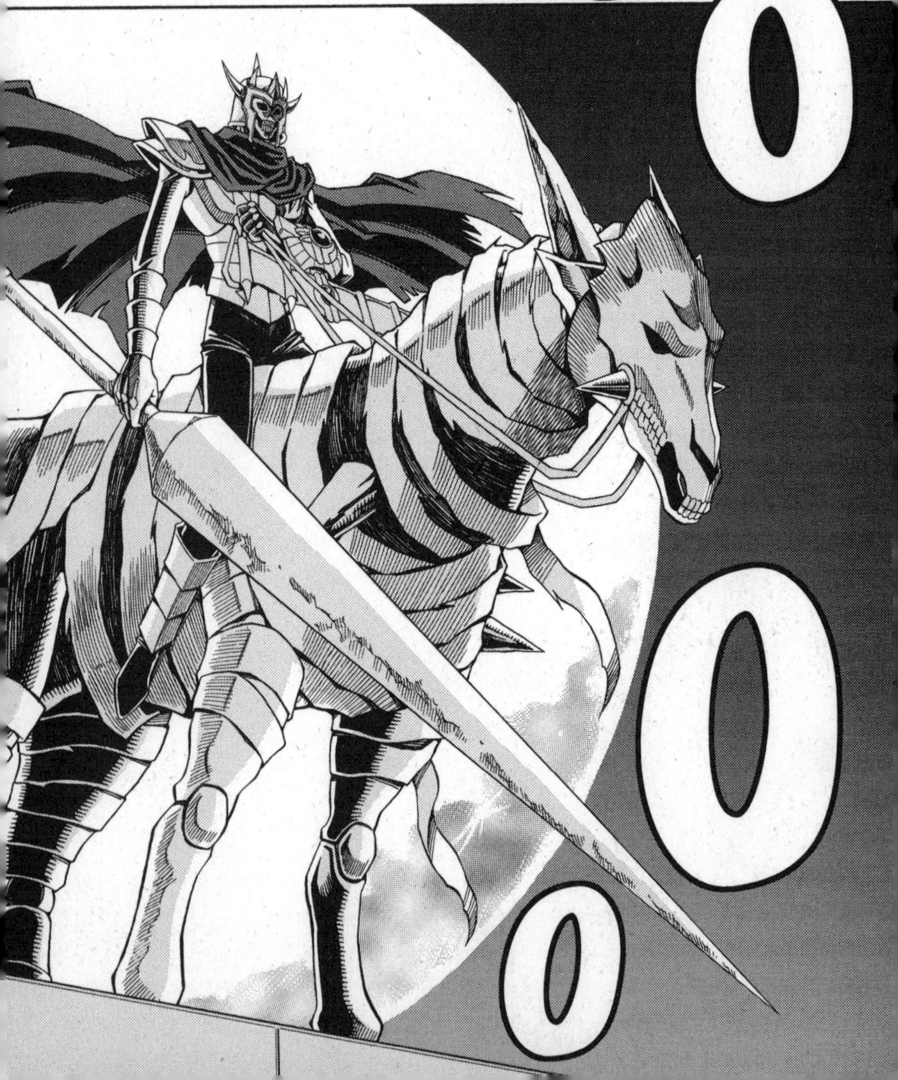
O
O
O

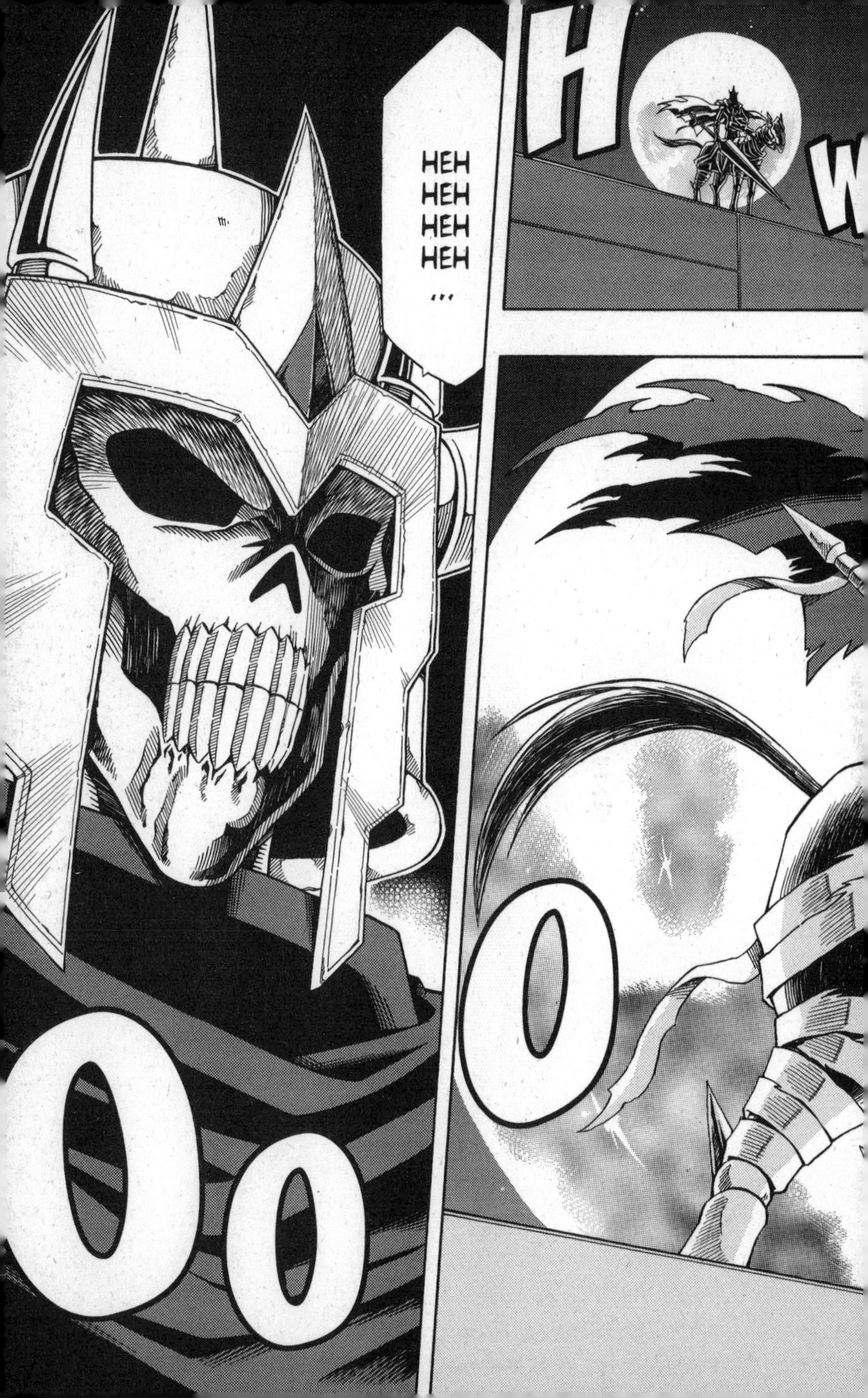
H
W
O
HEH HEH HEH HEH ...
OO

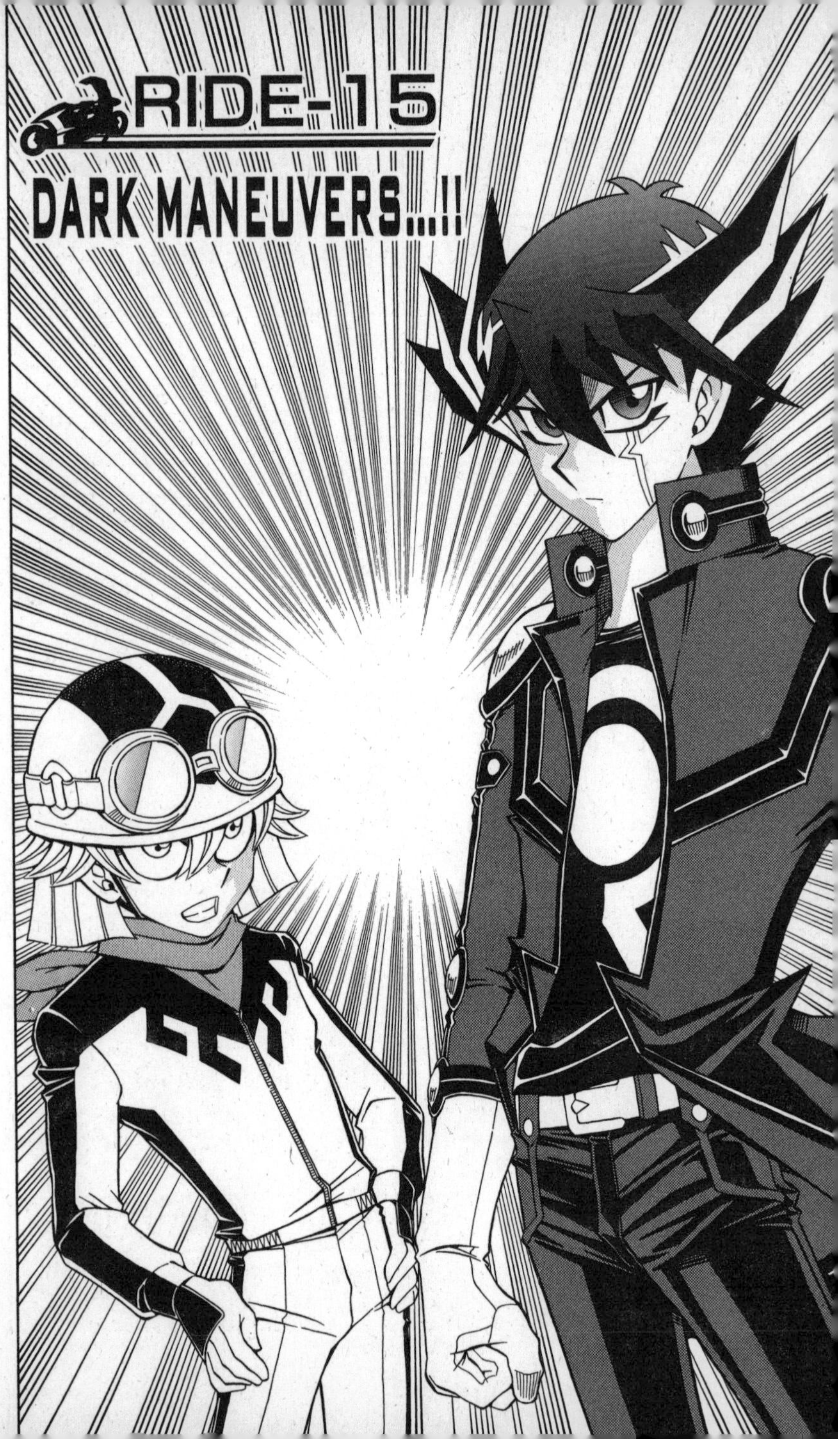
RIDE-15
DARK MANEUVERS...!!

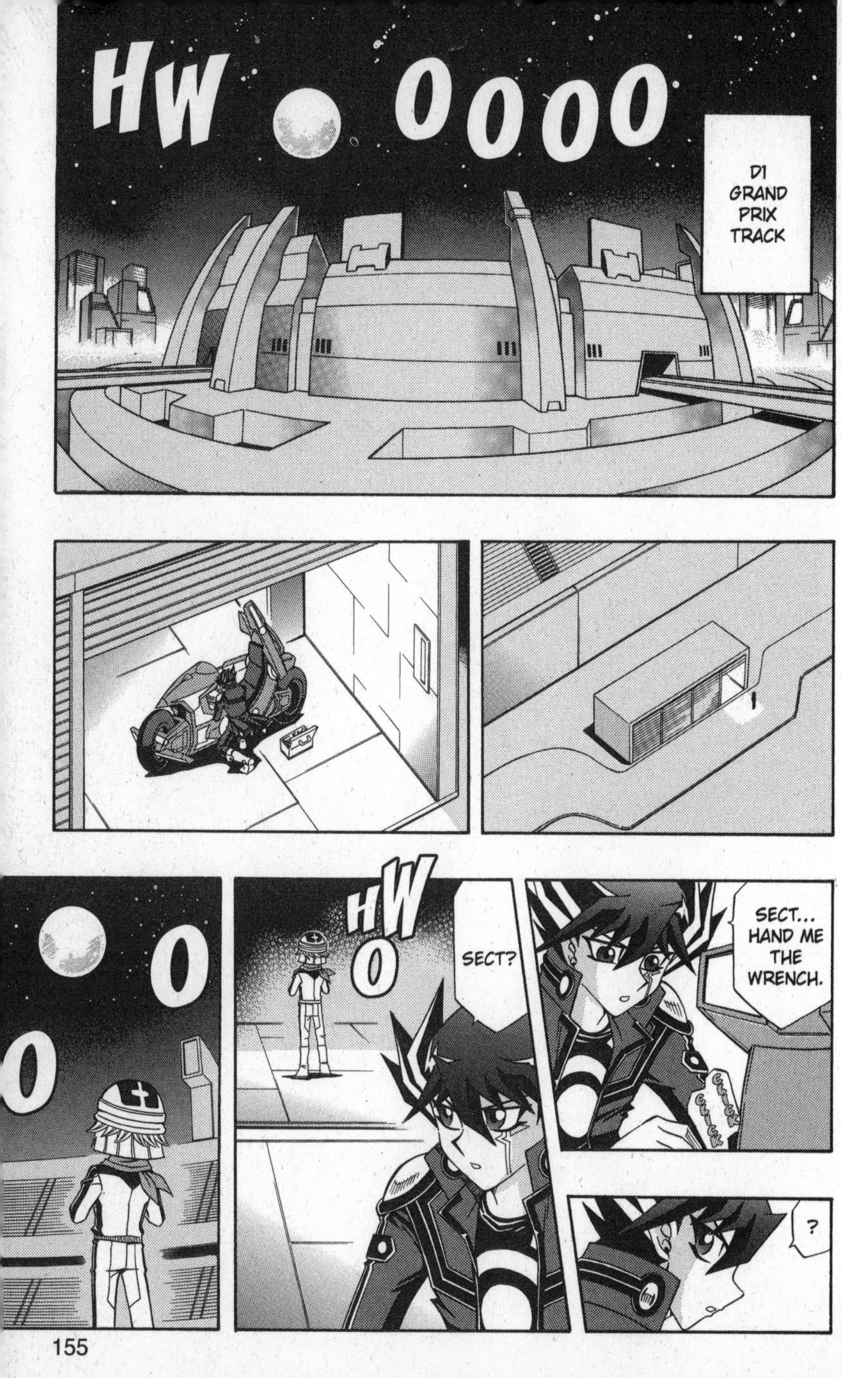
HW OOOO
D1 GRAND PRIX TRACK
SECT... HAND ME THE WRENCH.
?
HW O
SECT?
O O

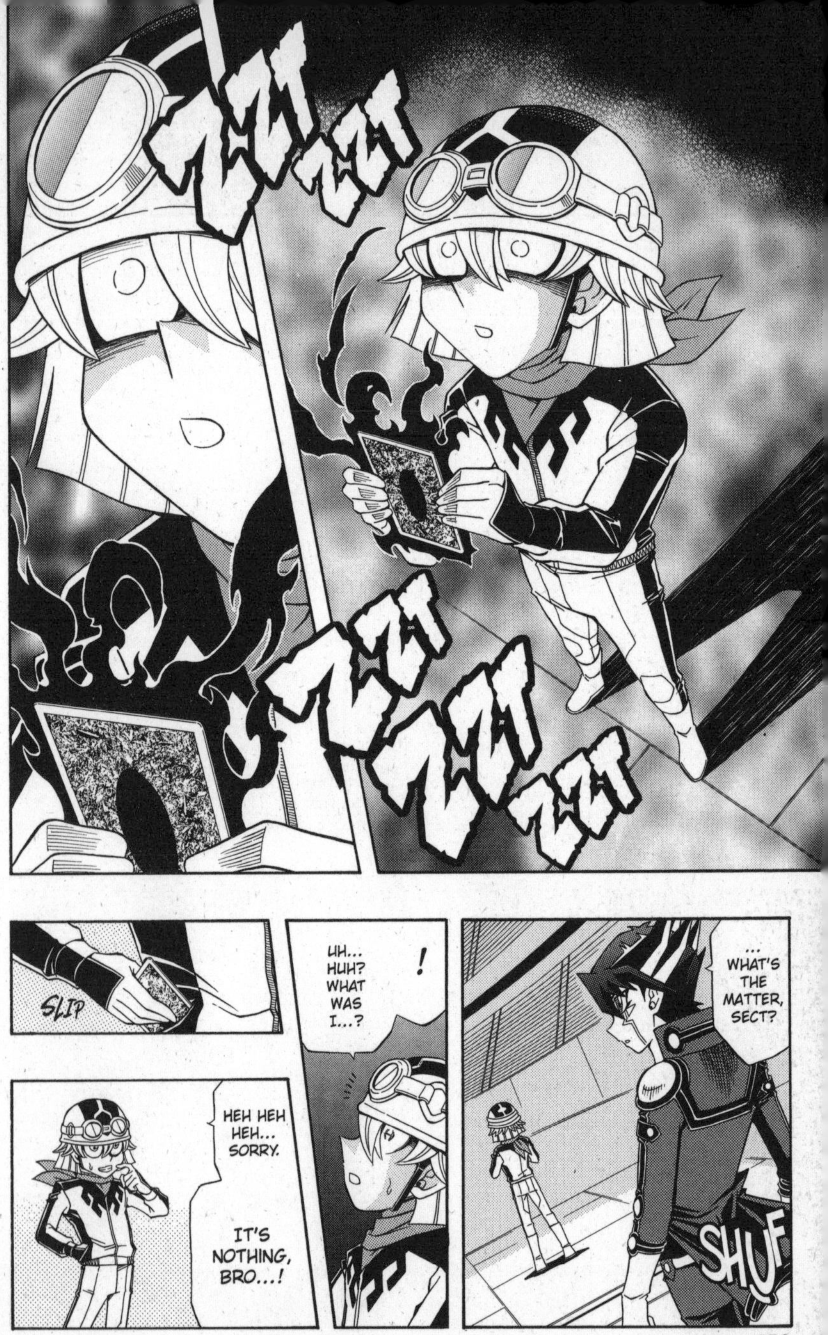
ZZZT
ZZZT
ZZZT
ZZZT
ZZZT
ZZZT ZZZT
... WHAT'S THE MATTER, SECT?
SHUF
!
UH... HUH? WHAT WAS I...?
SLIP
HEH HEH HEH... SORRY.
IT'S NOTHING, BRO...!

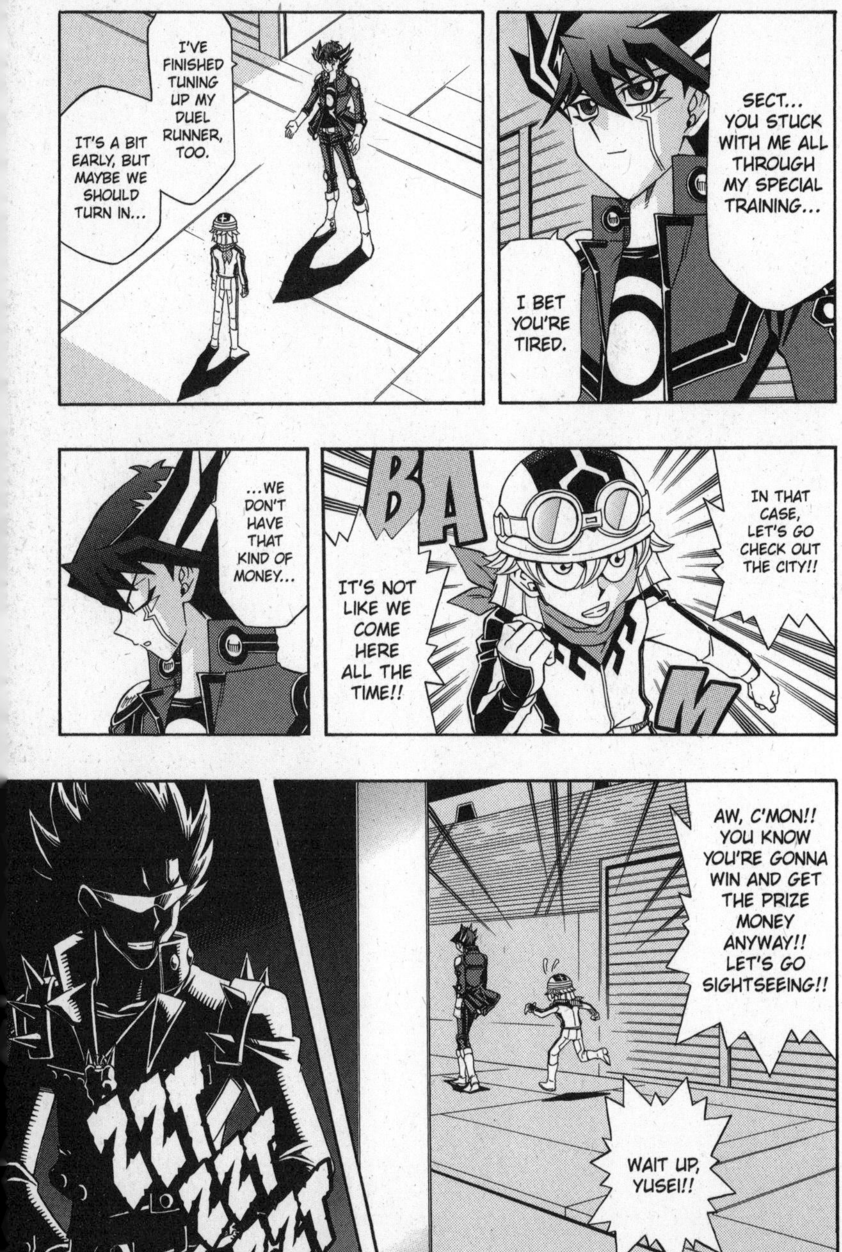
SECT... YOU STUCK WITH ME ALL THROUGH MY SPECIAL TRAINING...
I BET YOU'RE TIRED.
I'VE FINISHED TUNING UP MY DUEL RUNNER, TOO.
IT'S A BIT EARLY, BUT MAYBE WE SHOULD TURN IN...
BAM
IN THAT CASE, LET'S GO CHECK OUT THE CITY!!
IT'S NOT LIKE WE COME HERE ALL THE TIME!!
...WE DON'T HAVE THAT KIND OF MONEY...
AW, C'MON!! YOU KNOW YOU'RE GONNA WIN AND GET THE PRIZE MONEY ANYWAY!! LET'S GO SIGHTSEEING!!
WAIT UP, YUSEI!!
ZZZT ZZZT ZZZT

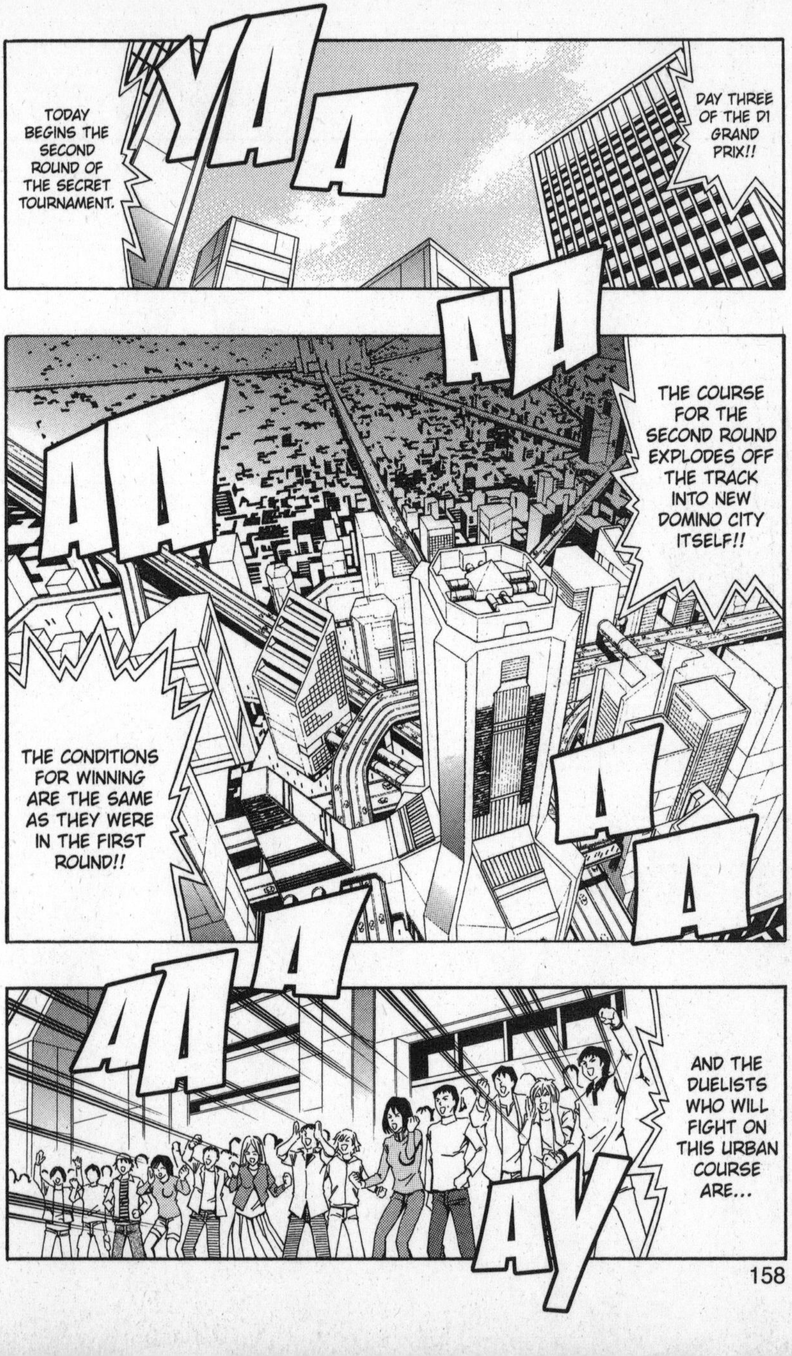
DAY THREE OF THE D1 GRAND PRIX!!
TODAY BEGINS THE SECOND ROUND OF THE SECRET TOURNAMENT.
YAA
AA
THE COURSE FOR THE SECOND ROUND EXPLODES OFF THE TRACK INTO NEW DOMINO CITY ITSELF!!
AA
AA
A
THE CONDITIONS FOR WINNING ARE THE SAME AS THEY WERE IN THE FIRST ROUND!!
A
AA
AND THE DUELISTS WHO WILL FIGHT ON THIS URBAN COURSE ARE...
AY

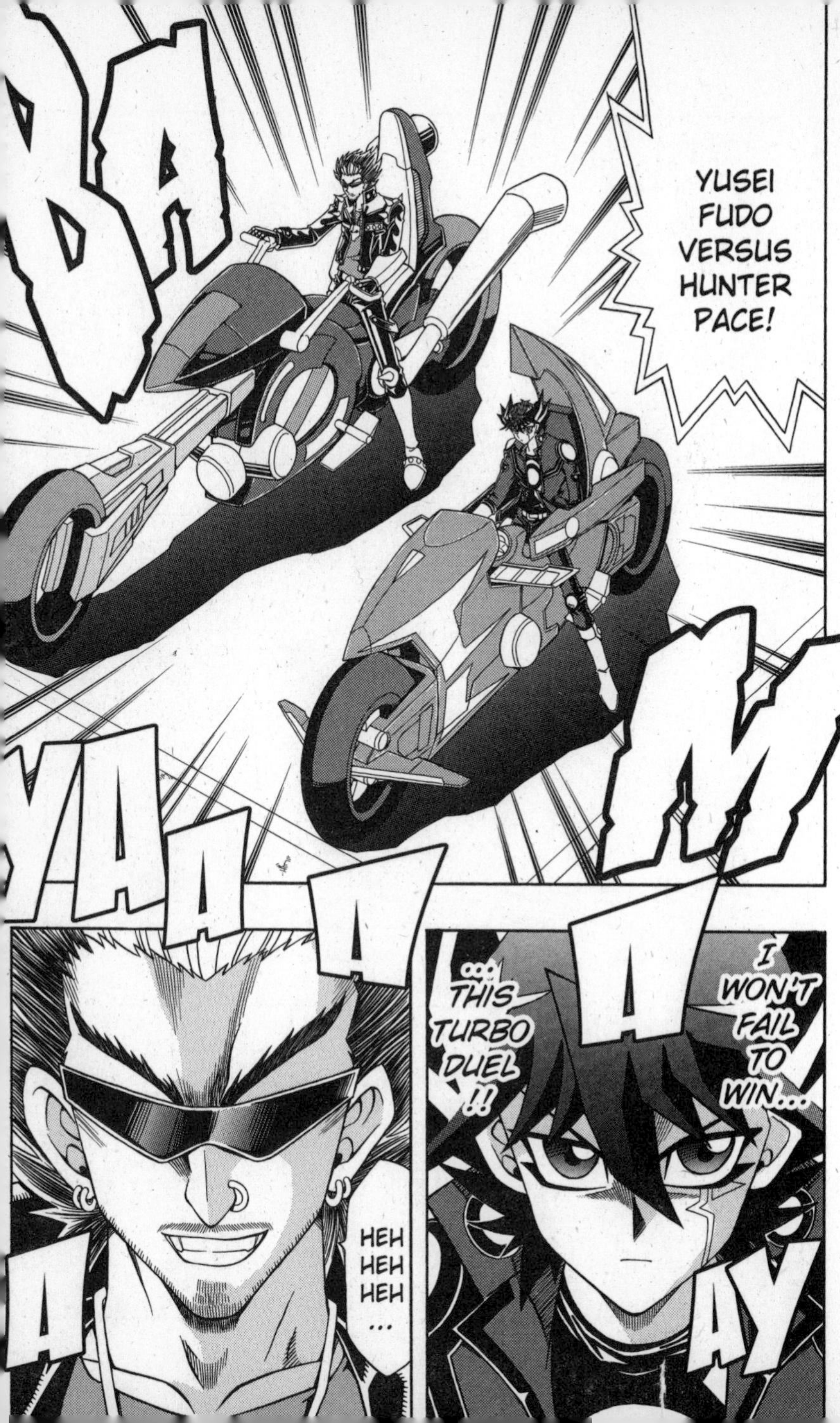
YUSEI FUDO VERSUS HUNTER PACE!
I WON'T FAIL TO WIN...
...THIS TURBO DUEL!!
HEH HEH HEH...

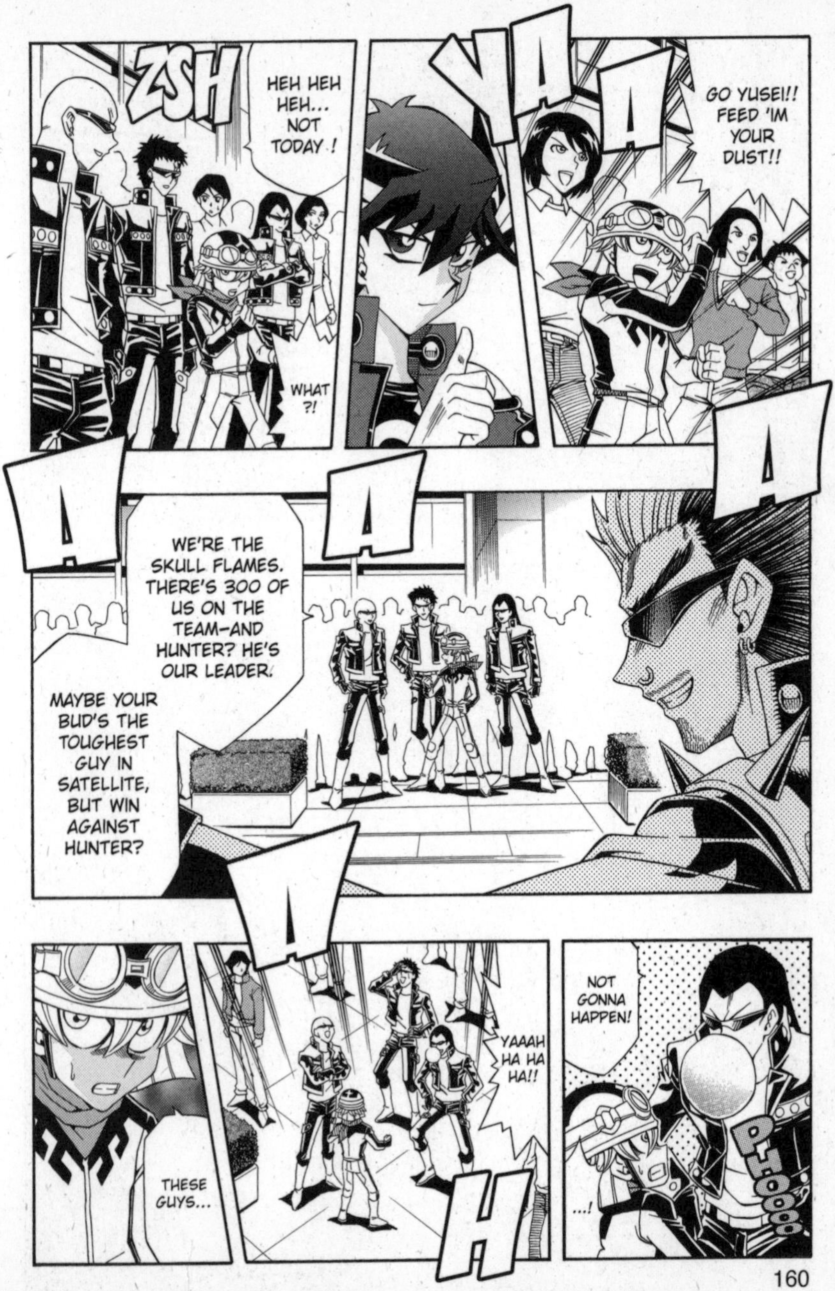
GO YUSEI!! FEED 'IM YOUR DUST!!
ZSH
HEH HEH HEH... NOT TODAY!
WHAT?!
WE'RE THE SKULL FLAMES. THERE'S 300 OF US ON THE TEAM—AND HUNTER? HE'S OUR LEADER.
MAYBE YOUR BUD'S THE TOUGHEST GUY IN SATELLITE, BUT WIN AGAINST HUNTER?
NOT GONNA HAPPEN!
...!
YAAAH HA HA HA!!
THESE GUYS...

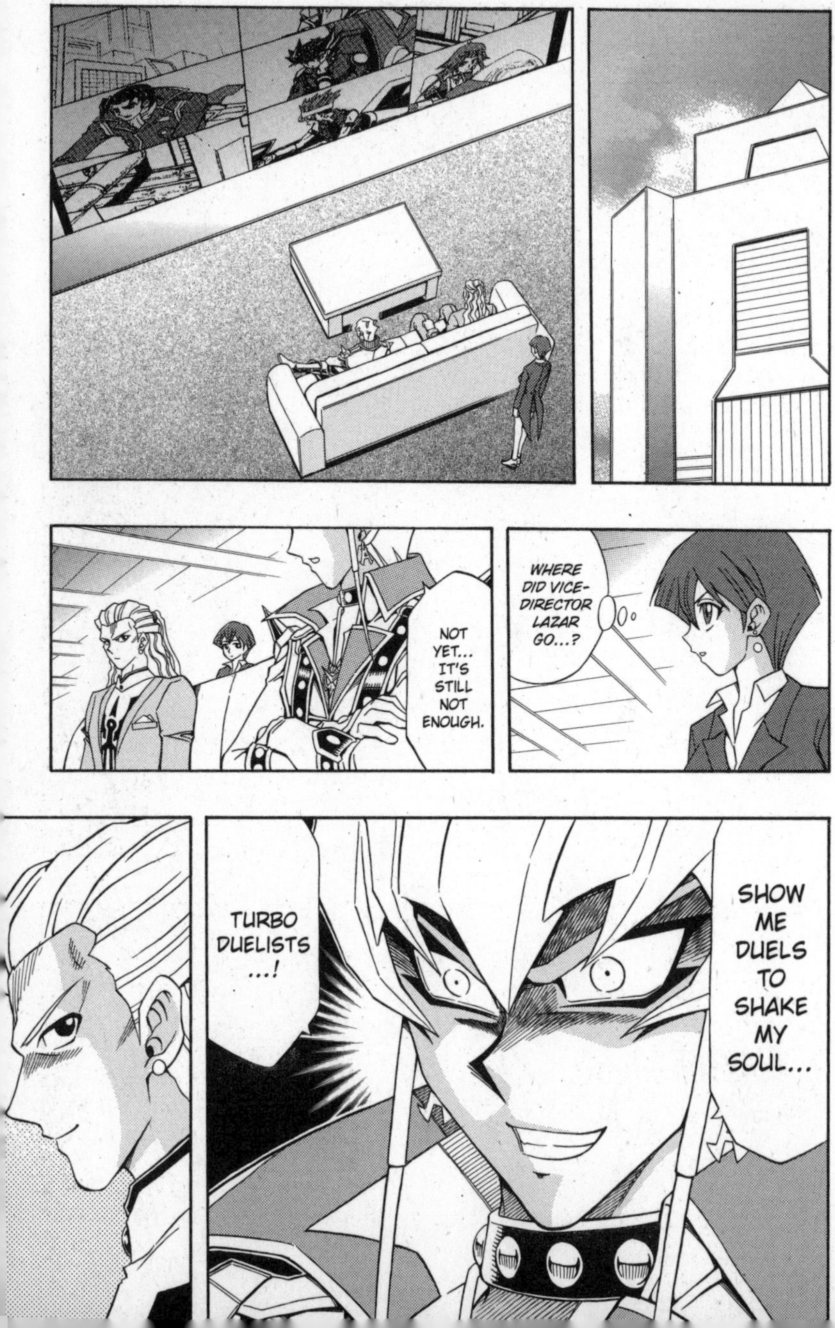
WHERE DID VICE-DIRECTOR LAZAR GO...?
NOT YET... IT'S STILL NOT ENOUGH.
SHOW ME DUELS TO SHAKE MY SOUL...
TURBO DUELISTS ...!

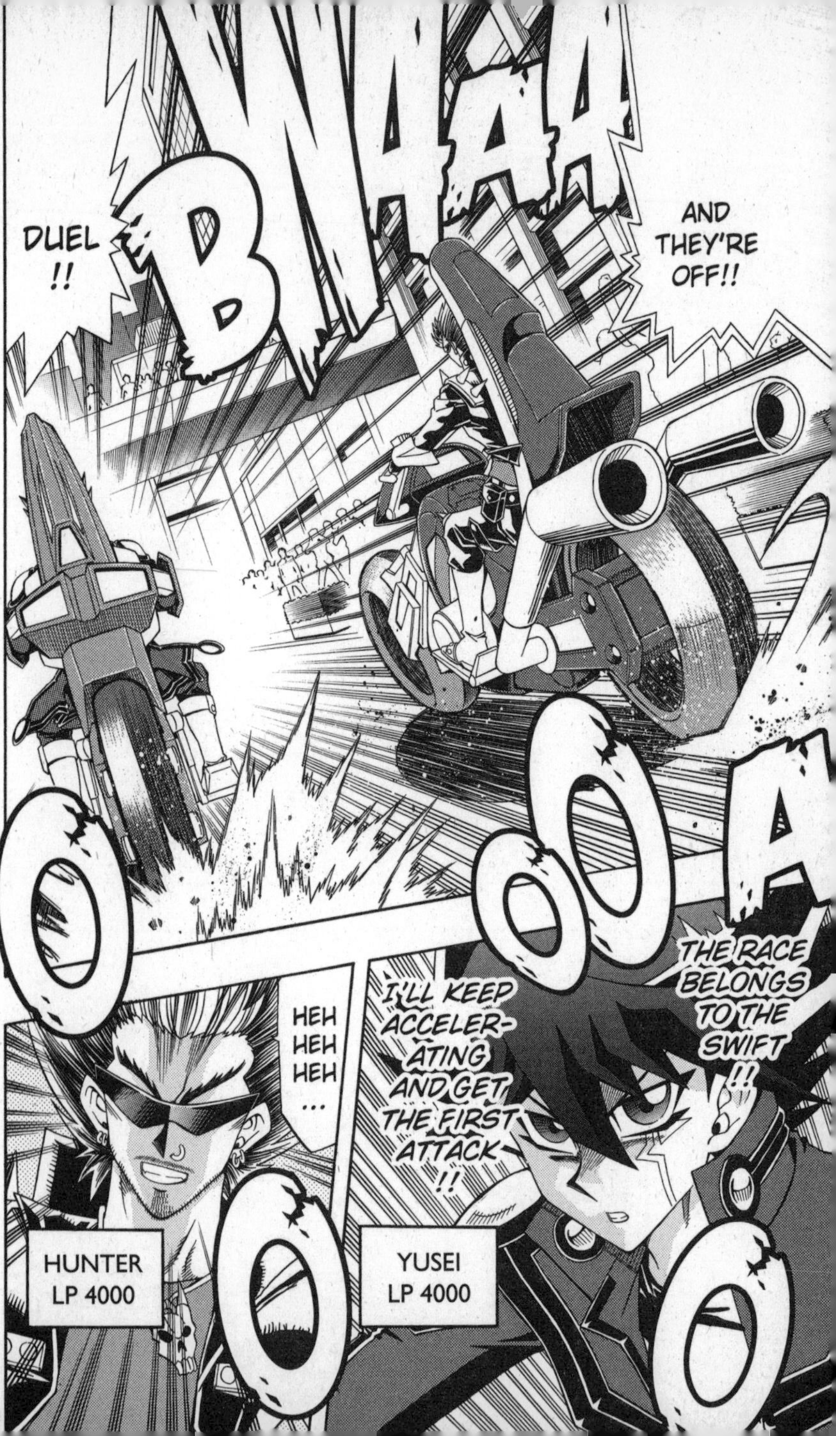

AND THEY'RE OFF!!
DUEL!!
BWAAA
OOOOA
THE RACE BELONGS TO THE SWIFT!!
I'LL KEEP ACCELER-ATING AND GET THE FIRST ATTACK!!
YUSEI LP 4000
HEH HEH HEH...
HUNTER LP 4000
BOOOO

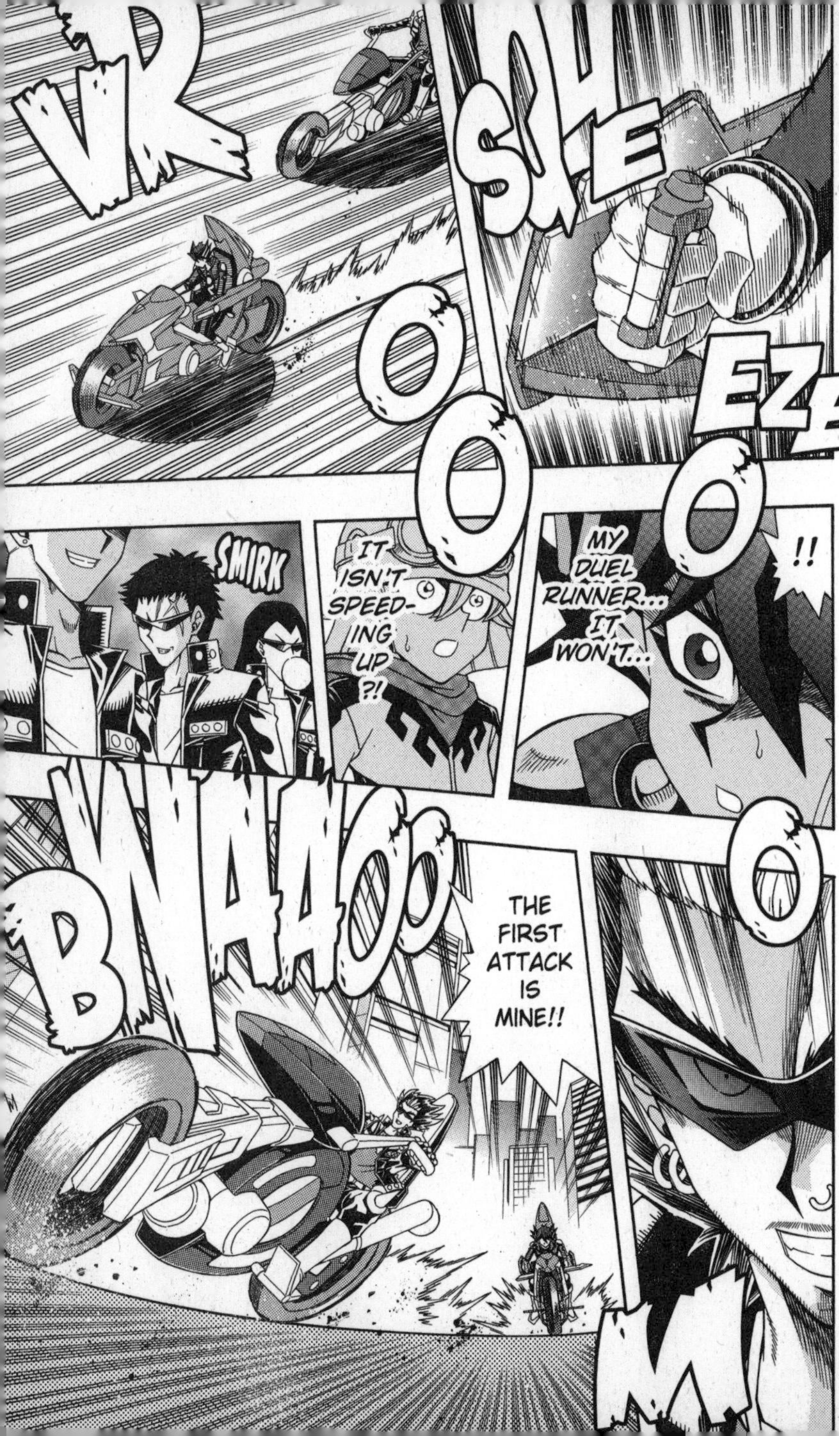

EZE
!!
MY DUEL RUNNER... IT WON'T...
IT ISN'T SPEEDING UP?!
SMIRK
THE FIRST ATTACK IS MINE!!

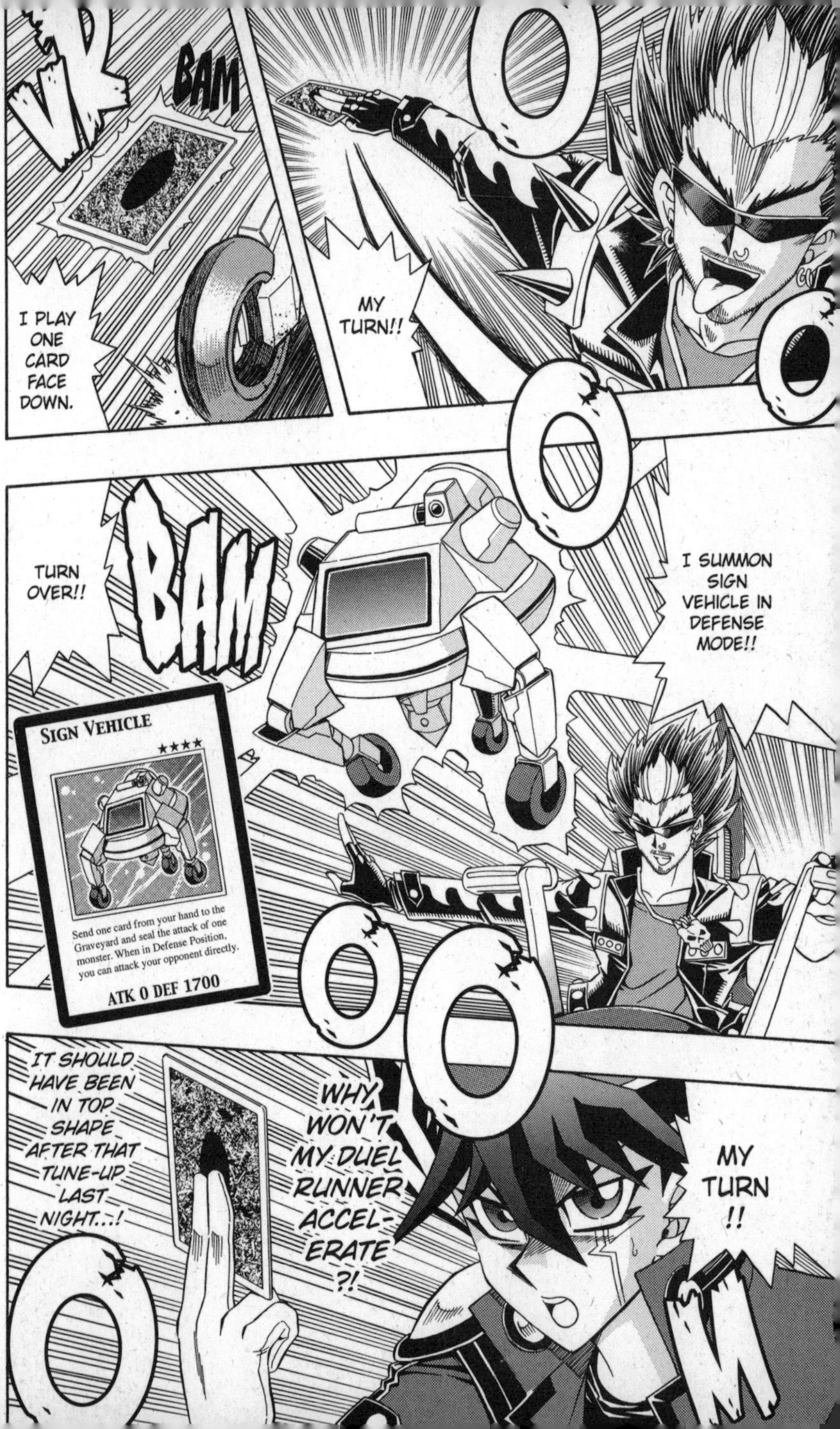
MY TURN!!
BAM
I PLAY ONE CARD FACE DOWN.
I SUMMON SIGN VEHICLE IN DEFENSE MODE!!
BAM
TURN OVER!!
SIGN VEHICLE
Send one card from your hand to the Graveyard and seal the attack of one monster. When in Defense Position, you can attack your opponent directly.
ATK 0 DEF 1700
MY TURN!!
WHY WON'T MY DUEL RUNNER ACCELERATE?!
IT SHOULD HAVE BEEN IN TOP SHAPE AFTER THAT TUNE-UP LAST NIGHT...!

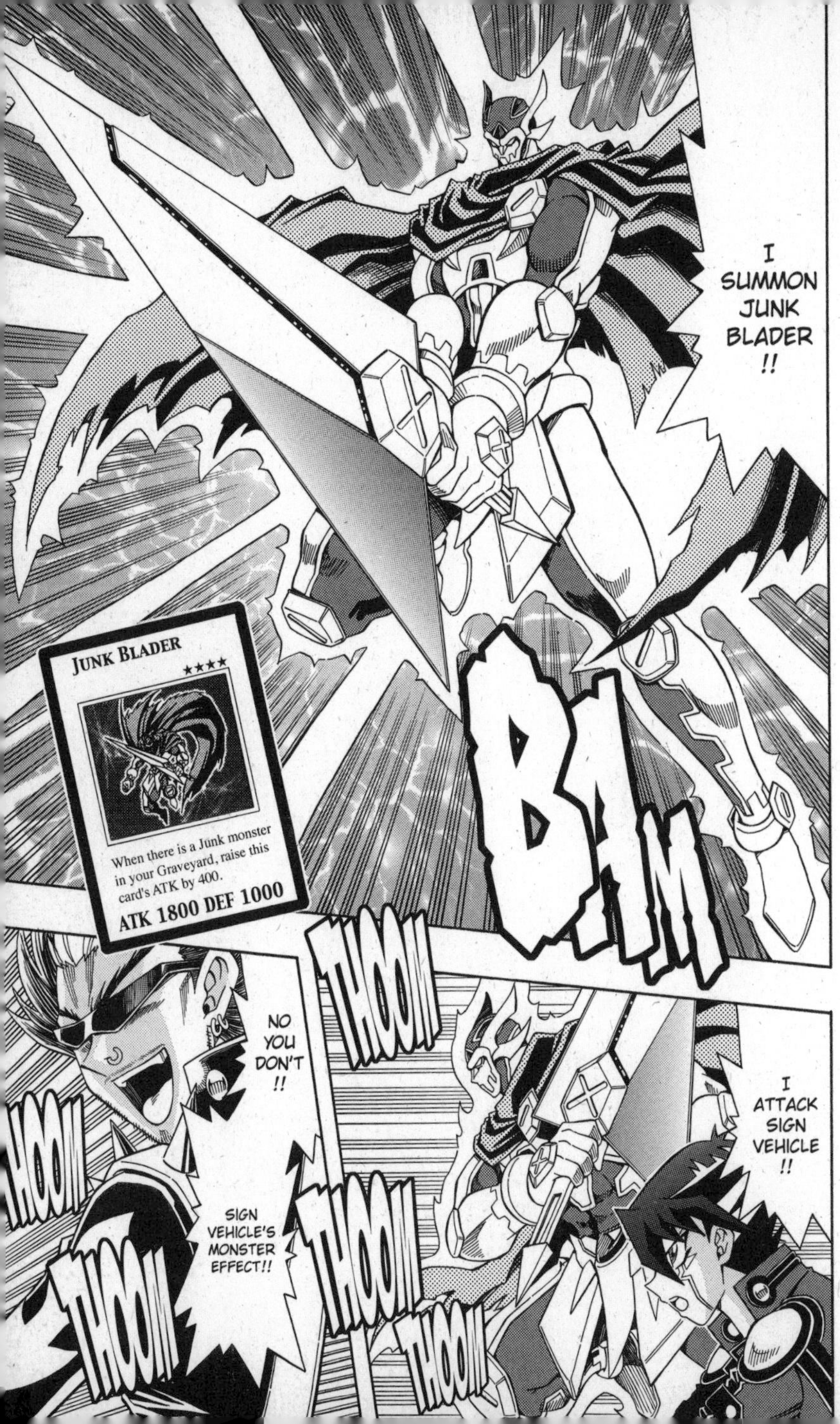
I SUMMON JUNK BLADER !!
BAM
JUNK BLADER
★★★★
When there is a Junk monster in your Graveyard, raise this card's ATK by 400.
ATK 1800 DEF 1000
I ATTACK SIGN VEHICLE !!
THOOM
THOOM
THOOM
NO YOU DON'T !!
SIGN VEHICLE'S MONSTER EFFECT!!
THOOM
THOOM

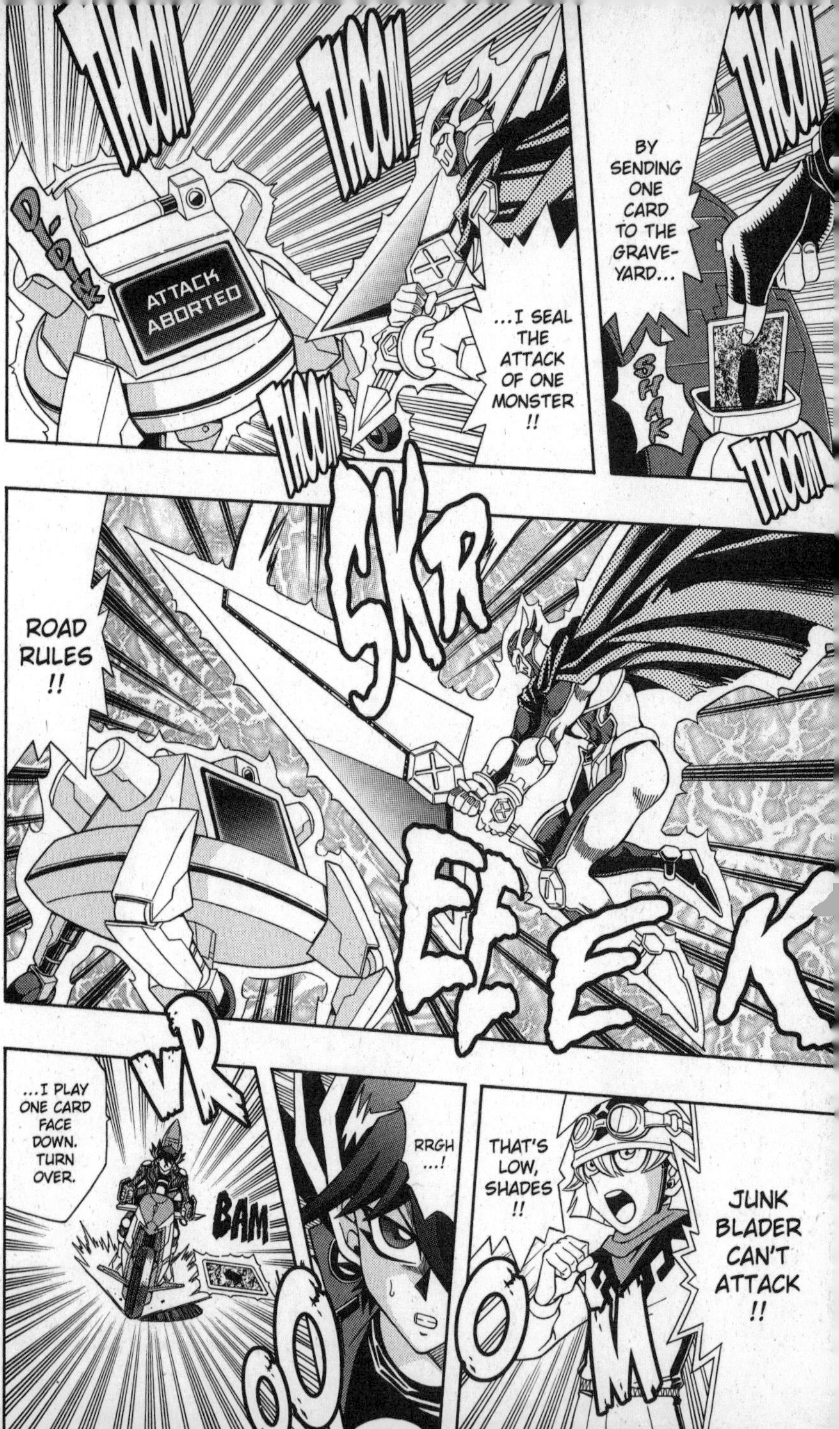
BY SENDING ONE CARD TO THE GRAVEYARD...
SHAK
THOOM
THOOM
THOOM
...I SEAL THE ATTACK OF ONE MONSTER!!
ATTACK ABORTED
THOOM
SKR
EEEK
ROAD RULES!!
JUNK BLADER CAN'T ATTACK!!
THAT'S LOW, SHADES!!
RRGH...!
VROOM
...I PLAY ONE CARD FACE DOWN. TURN OVER.
BAM

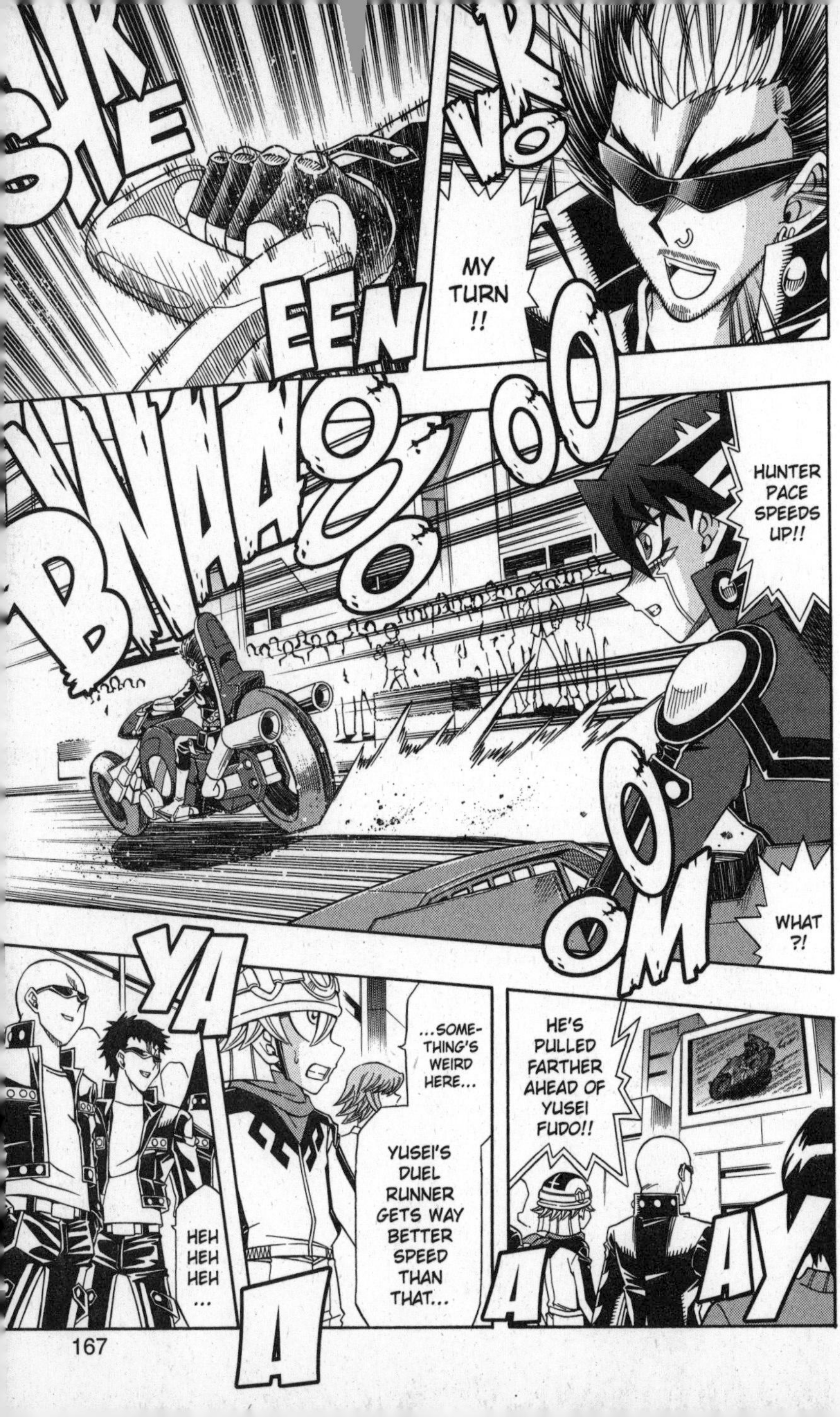
MY TURN !!
HUNTER PACE SPEEDS UP!!
WHAT ?!
HE'S PULLED FARTHER AHEAD OF YUSEI FUDO!!
...SOME-THING'S WEIRD HERE...
YUSEI'S DUEL RUNNER GETS WAY BETTER SPEED THAN THAT...
HEH HEH HEH ...

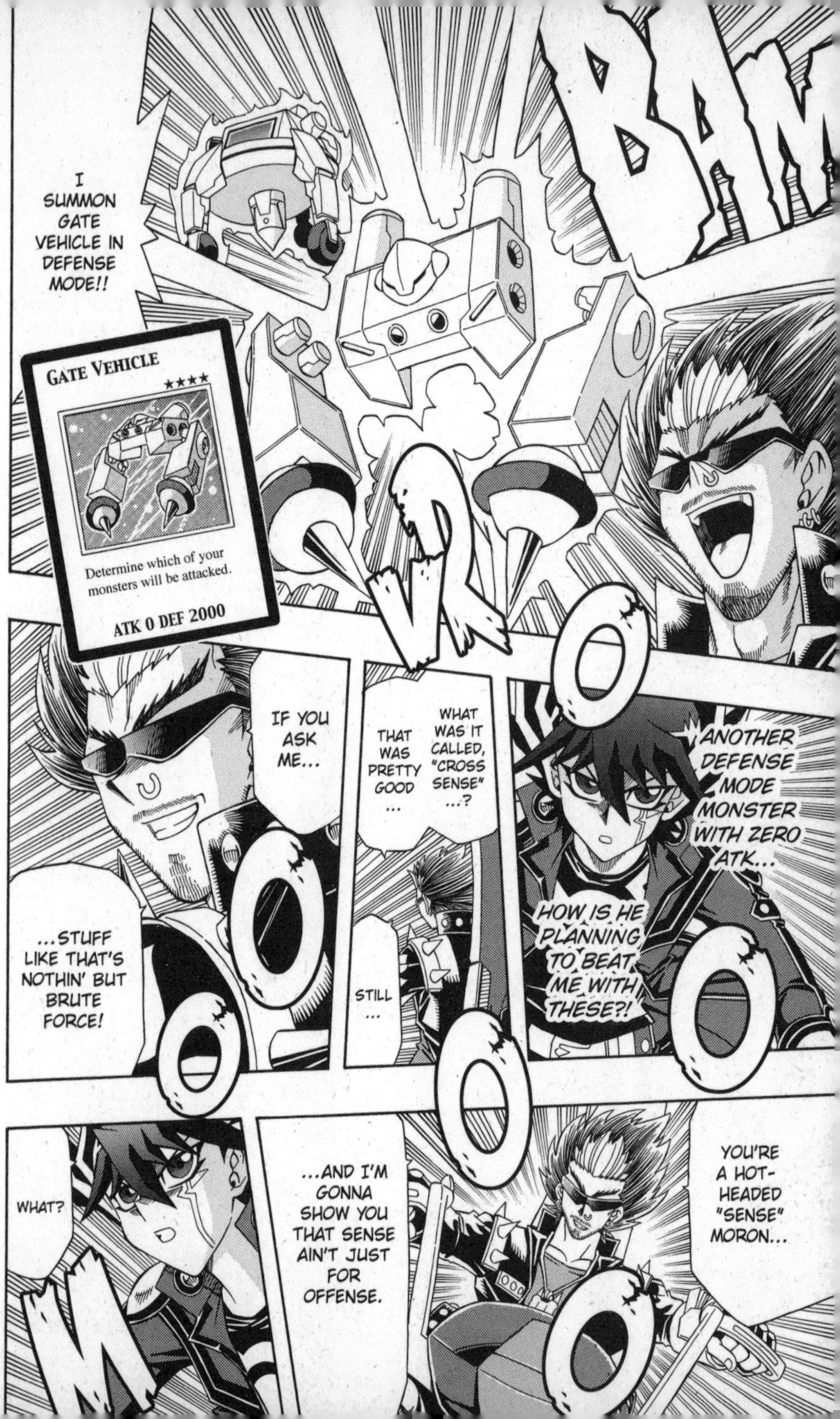
BAM
I SUMMON GATE VEHICLE IN DEFENSE MODE!!
GATE VEHICLE
★★★★
Determine which of your monsters will be attacked.
ATK 0 DEF 2000
ANOTHER DEFENSE MODE MONSTER WITH ZERO ATK...
HOW IS HE PLANNING TO BEAT ME WITH THESE?!
WHAT WAS IT CALLED, "CROSS SENSE"...?
THAT WAS PRETTY GOOD...
STILL...
IF YOU ASK ME...
...STUFF LIKE THAT'S NOTHIN' BUT BRUTE FORCE!
YOU'RE A HOT-HEADED "SENSE" MORON...
...AND I'M GONNA SHOW YOU THAT SENSE AIN'T JUST FOR OFFENSE.
WHAT?

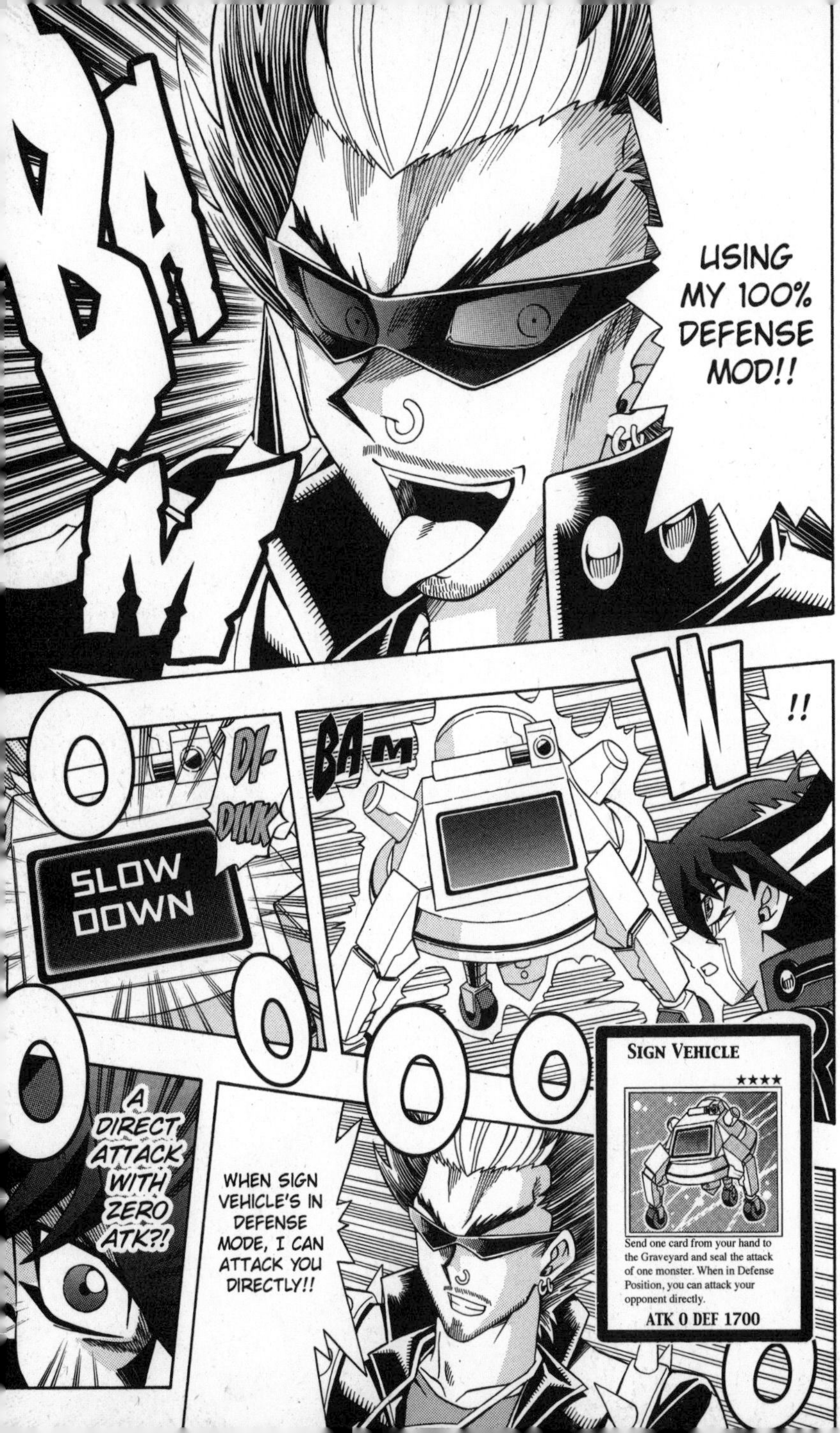
USING MY 100% DEFENSE MOD!!
BAM
W !!
BAM
DI-DINK
SLOW DOWN
SIGN VEHICLE
★★★★
Send one card from your hand to the Graveyard and seal the attack of one monster. When in Defense Position, you can attack your opponent directly.
ATK 0 DEF 1700
WHEN SIGN VEHICLE'S IN DEFENSE MODE, I CAN ATTACK YOU DIRECTLY!!
A DIRECT ATTACK WITH ZERO ATK?!

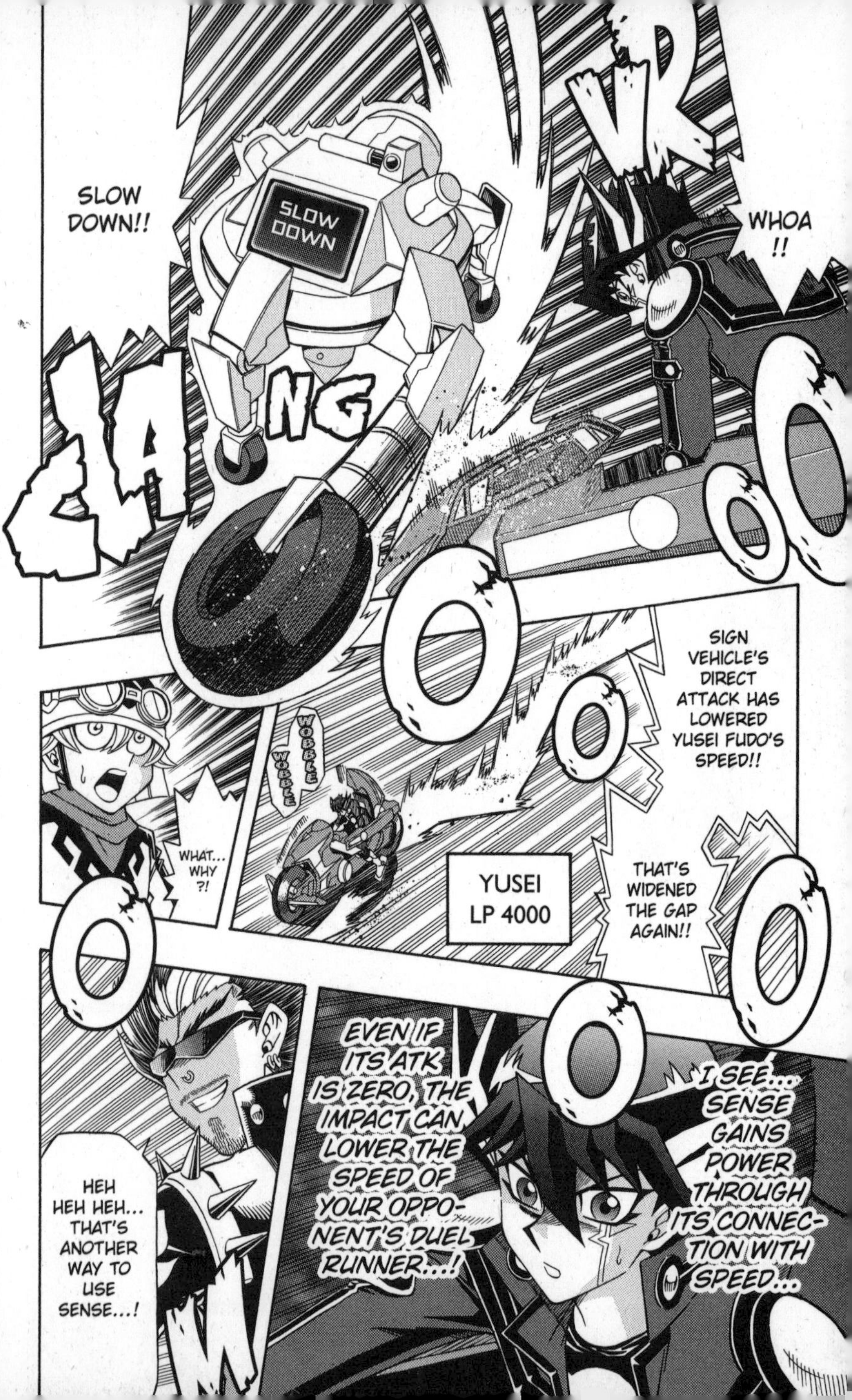
VR
WHOA!!
SLOW DOWN
SLOW DOWN!!
CLANG
SIGN VEHICLE'S DIRECT ATTACK HAS LOWERED YUSEI FUDO'S SPEED!!
THAT'S WIDENED THE GAP AGAIN!!
YUSEI LP 4000
WOBBLE WOBBLE
WHAT... WHY?!
I SEE... SENSE GAINS POWER THROUGH ITS CONNECTION WITH SPEED...
EVEN IF ITS ATK IS ZERO, THE IMPACT CAN LOWER THE SPEED OF YOUR OPPONENT'S DUEL RUNNER...!
HEH HEH HEH... THAT'S ANOTHER WAY TO USE SENSE...!

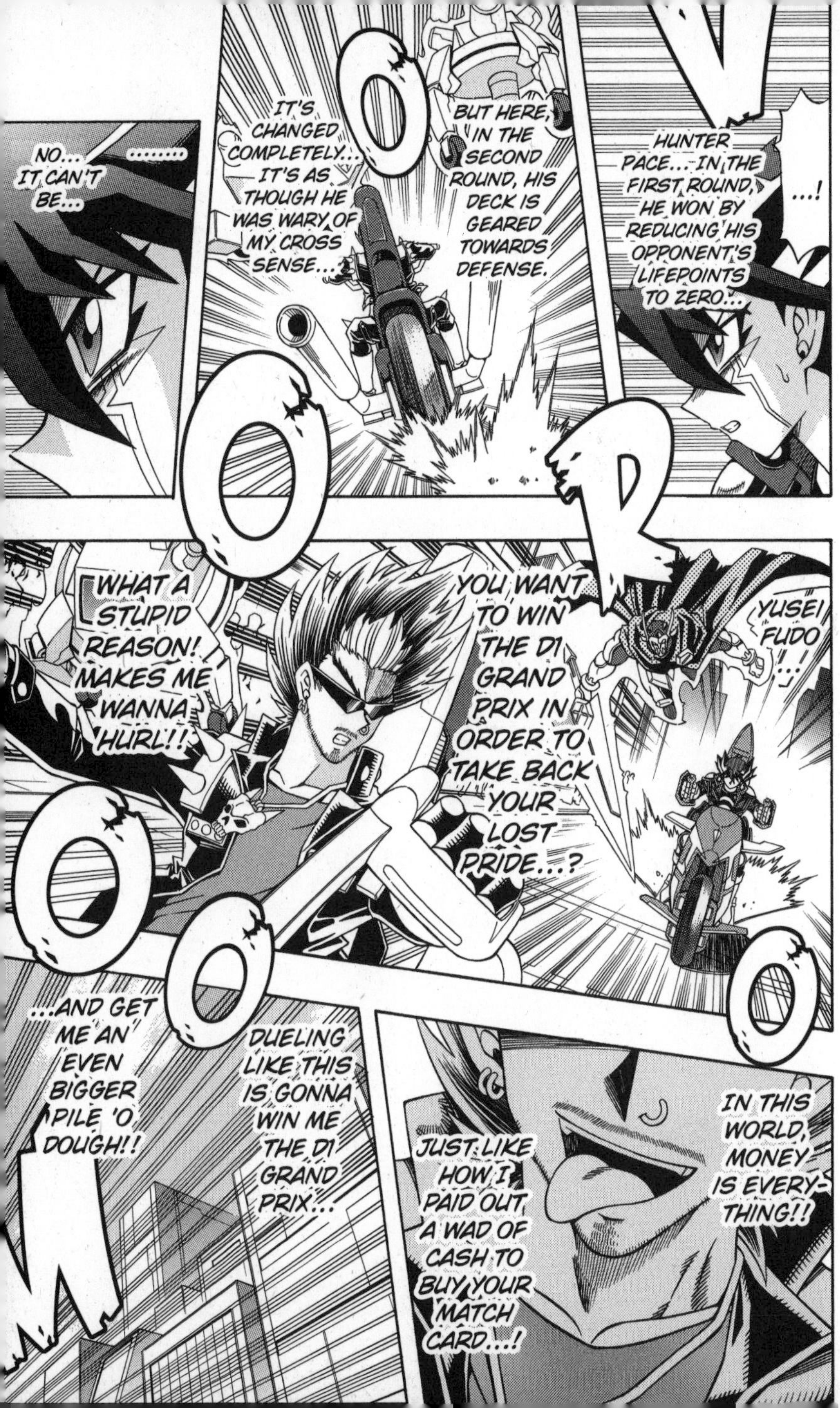
HUNTER PACE... IN THE FIRST ROUND, HE WON BY REDUCING HIS OPPONENT'S LIFEPOINTS TO ZERO...
...!
BUT HERE, IN THE SECOND ROUND, HIS DECK IS GEARED TOWARDS DEFENSE.
IT'S CHANGED COMPLETELY... IT'S AS THOUGH HE WAS WARY OF MY CROSS SENSE...
....
NO... IT CAN'T BE...
YUSEI FUDO...!
YOU WANT TO WIN THE D1 GRAND PRIX IN ORDER TO TAKE BACK YOUR LOST PRIDE...?
WHAT A STUPID REASON! MAKES ME WANNA HURL!!
IN THIS WORLD, MONEY IS EVERYTHING!!
JUST LIKE HOW I PAID OUT A WAD OF CASH TO BUY YOUR MATCH CARD...!
DUELING LIKE THIS IS GONNA WIN ME THE D1 GRAND PRIX...
...AND GET ME AN EVEN BIGGER PILE 'O DOUGH!!

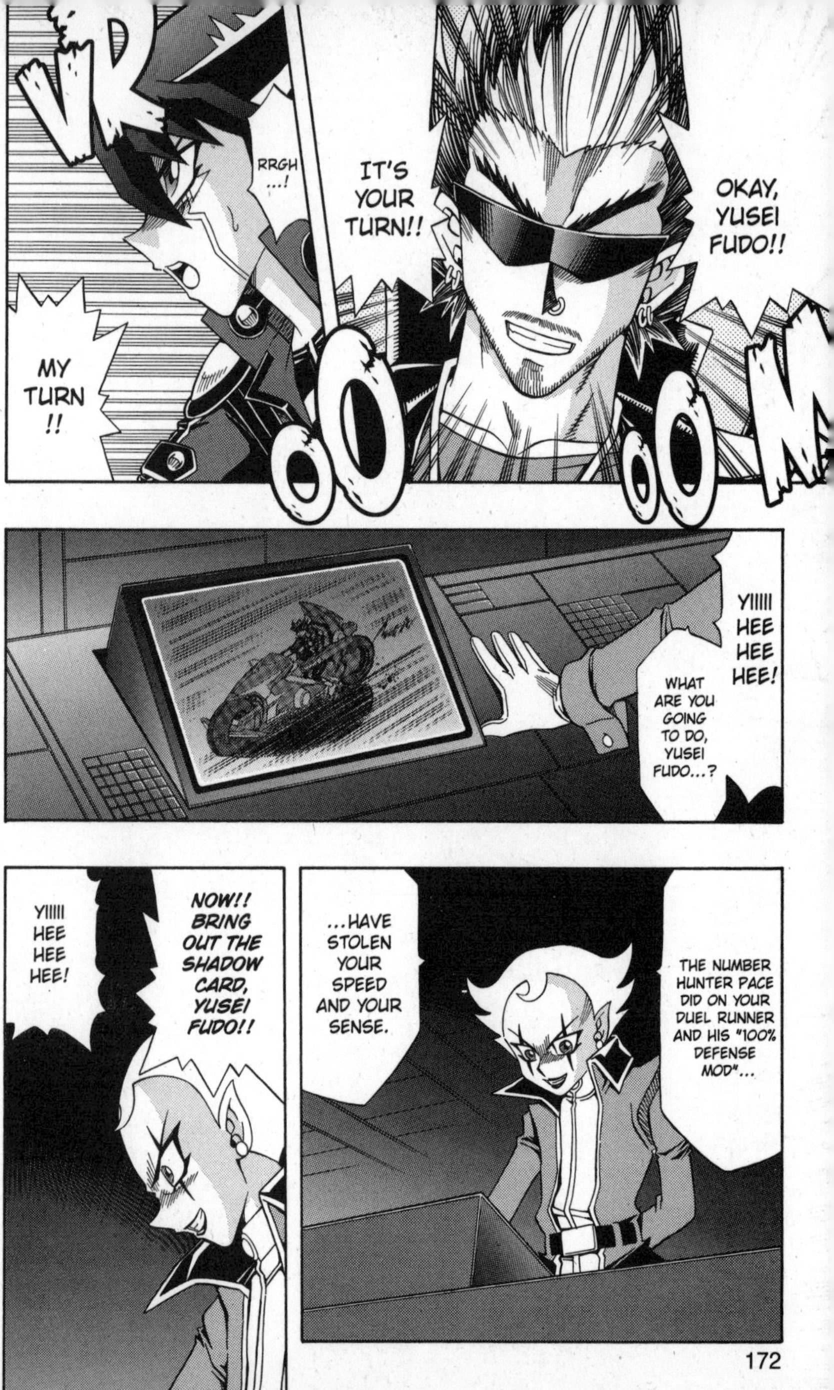
OKAY, YUSEI FUDO!!
IT'S YOUR TURN!!
RRGH ...!
MY TURN !!
YIIIII HEE HEE HEE!
WHAT ARE YOU GOING TO DO, YUSEI FUDO...?
THE NUMBER HUNTER PACE DID ON YOUR DUEL RUNNER AND HIS "100% DEFENSE MOD"...
...HAVE STOLEN YOUR SPEED AND YOUR SENSE.
NOW!! BRING OUT THE SHADOW CARD, YUSEI FUDO!!
YIIIII HEE HEE HEE!

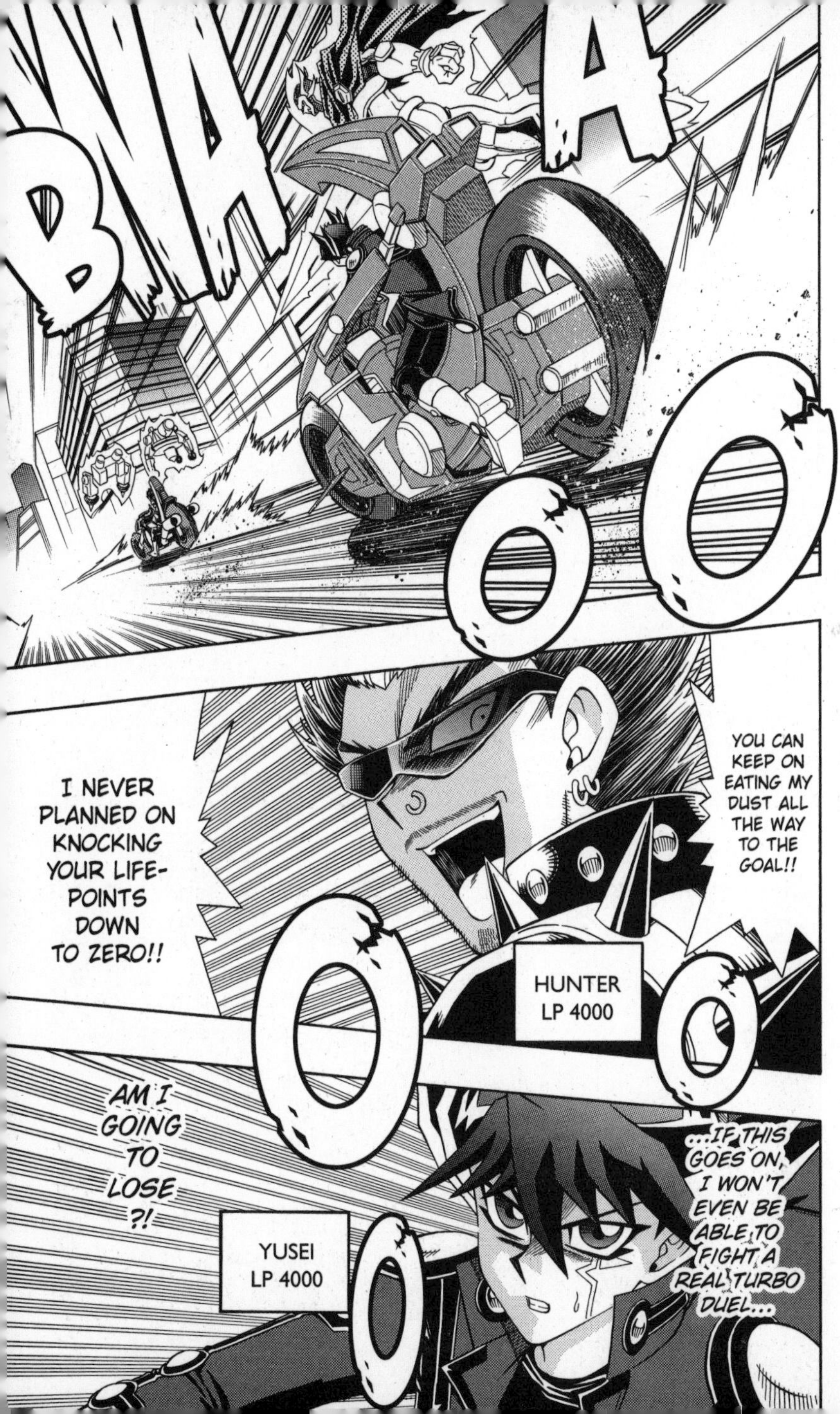
BWAAOO
YOU CAN KEEP ON EATING MY DUST ALL THE WAY TO THE GOAL!!
I NEVER PLANNED ON KNOCKING YOUR LIFE-POINTS DOWN TO ZERO!!
HUNTER LP 4000
...IF THIS GOES ON, I WON'T EVEN BE ABLE TO FIGHT A REAL TURBO DUEL...
AM I GOING TO LOSE?!
YUSEI LP 4000

5D's TRACKS

THE 15TH

BY SATOMASA

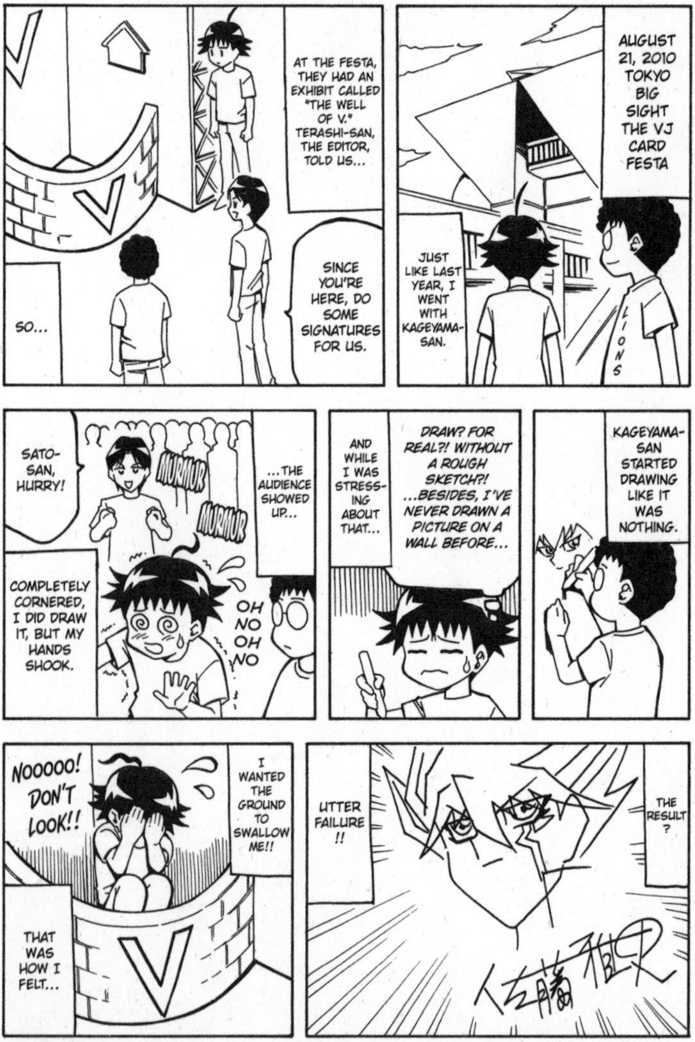
AUGUST 21, 2010 TOKYO BIG SIGHT THE VJ CARD FESTA
JUST LIKE LAST YEAR, I WENT WITH KAGEYAMA-SAN.
LIONS
AT THE FESTA, THEY HAD AN EXHIBIT CALLED "THE WELL OF V." TERASHI-SAN, THE EDITOR, TOLD US...
SINCE YOU'RE HERE, DO SOME SIGNATURES FOR US.
SO...
KAGEYAMA-SAN STARTED DRAWING LIKE IT WAS NOTHING.
DRAW? FOR REAL?! WITHOUT A ROUGH SKETCH?! ...BESIDES, I'VE NEVER DRAWN A PICTURE ON A WALL BEFORE...
AND WHILE I WAS STRESSING ABOUT THAT...
...THE AUDIENCE SHOWED UP...
SATO-SAN, HURRY!
MURMUR
MURMUR
OH NO OH NO
COMPLETELY CORNERED, I DID DRAW IT, BUT MY HANDS SHOOK.
THE RESULT?
UTTER FAILURE!!
I WANTED THE GROUND TO SWALLOW ME!!
NOOOOO! DON'T LOOK!!
THAT WAS HOW I FELT...

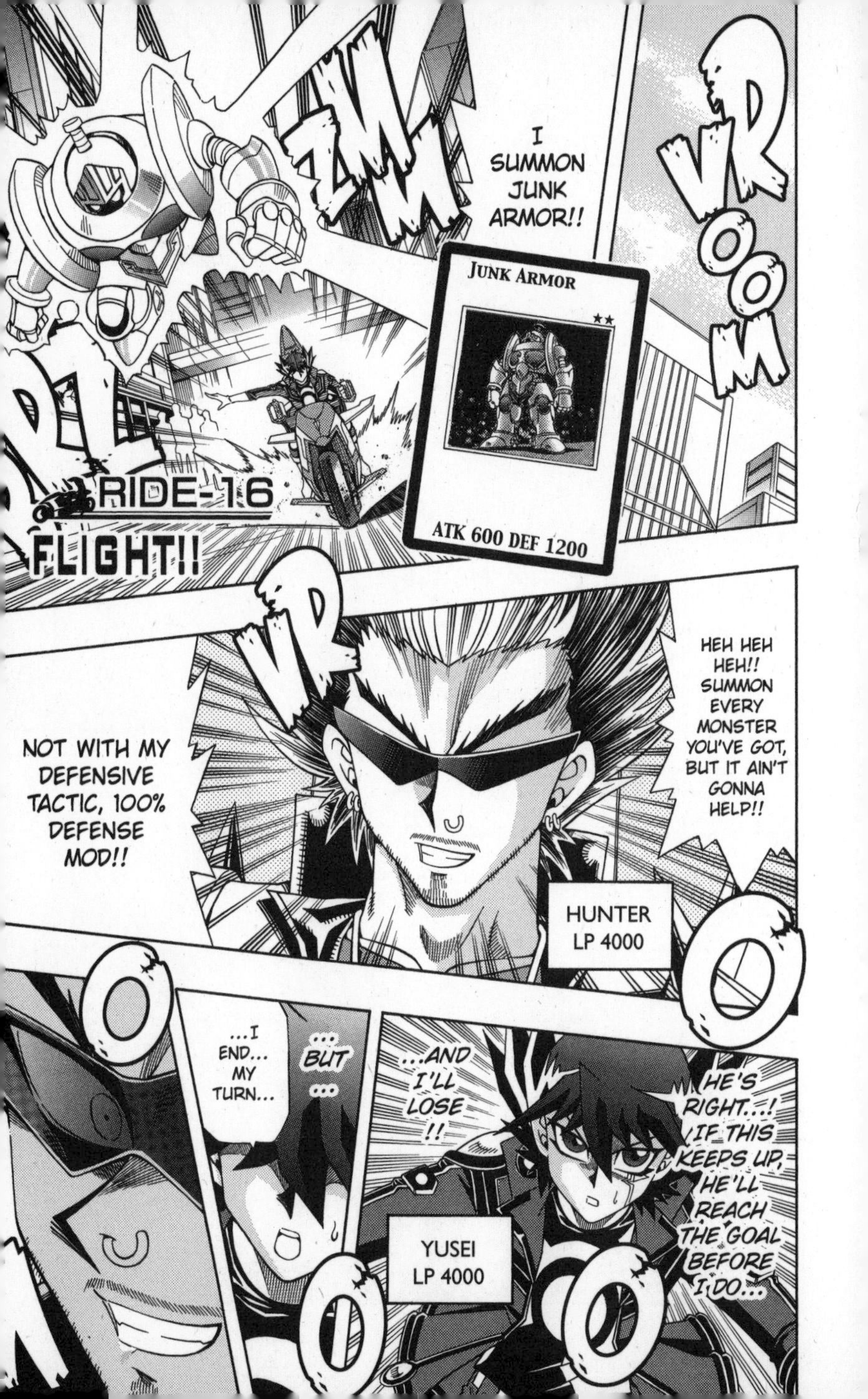
VROOOM
I SUMMON JUNK ARMOR!!
ZWM
JUNK ARMOR
ATK 600 DEF 1200
RIDE-16
FLIGHT!!
VR
HEH HEH HEH!! SUMMON EVERY MONSTER YOU'VE GOT, BUT IT AIN'T GONNA HELP!!
NOT WITH MY DEFENSIVE TACTIC, 100% DEFENSE MOD!!
HUNTER LP 4000
HE'S RIGHT...! IF THIS KEEPS UP, HE'LL REACH THE GOAL BEFORE I DO...
...AND I'LL LOSE!!
...BUT...
YUSEI LP 4000
...I END... MY TURN...

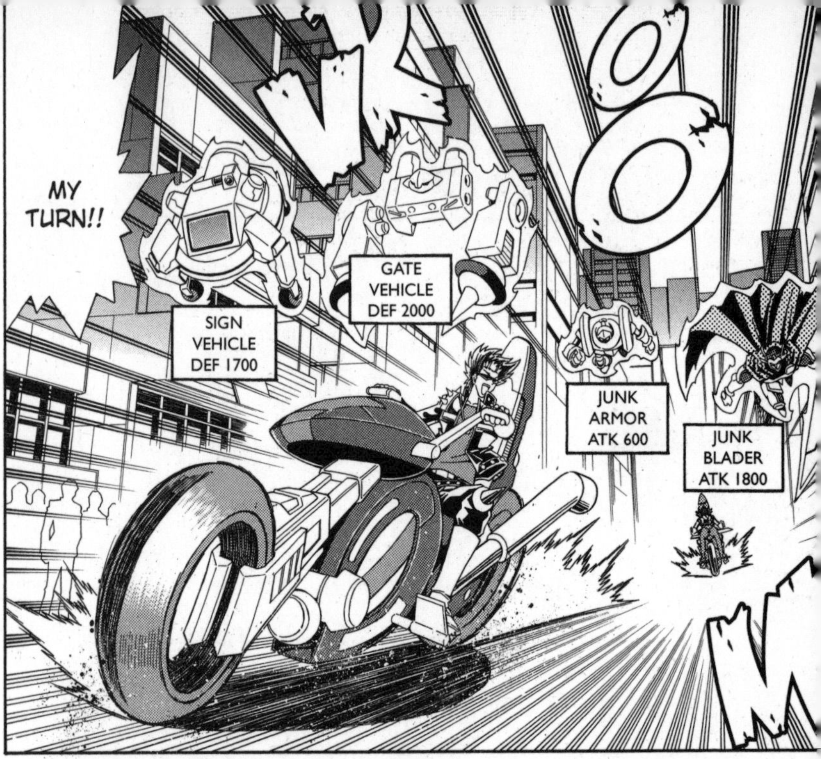
MY TURN!!
GATE VEHICLE DEF 2000
SIGN VEHICLE DEF 1700
JUNK BLADER ATK 1800
JUNK ARMOR ATK 600

RIDE-16

FLIGHT!!

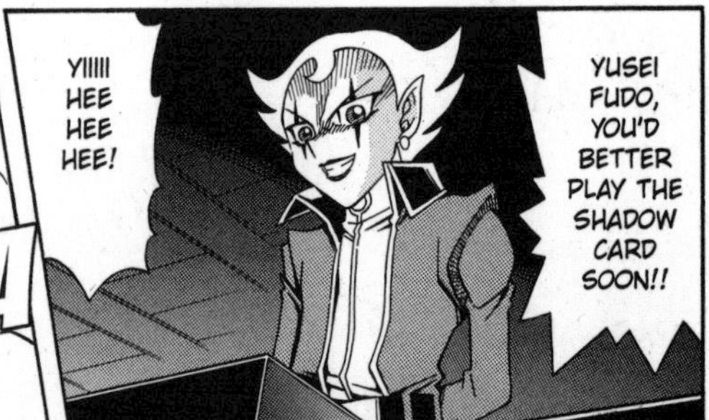
YUSEI FUDO, YOU'D BETTER PLAY THE SHADOW CARD SOON!!
YIIIII HEE HEE HEE!

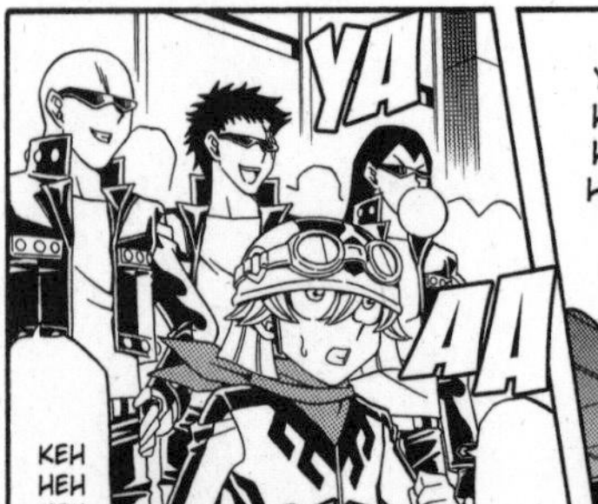
YUSEI ...
KEH HEH HEH ...

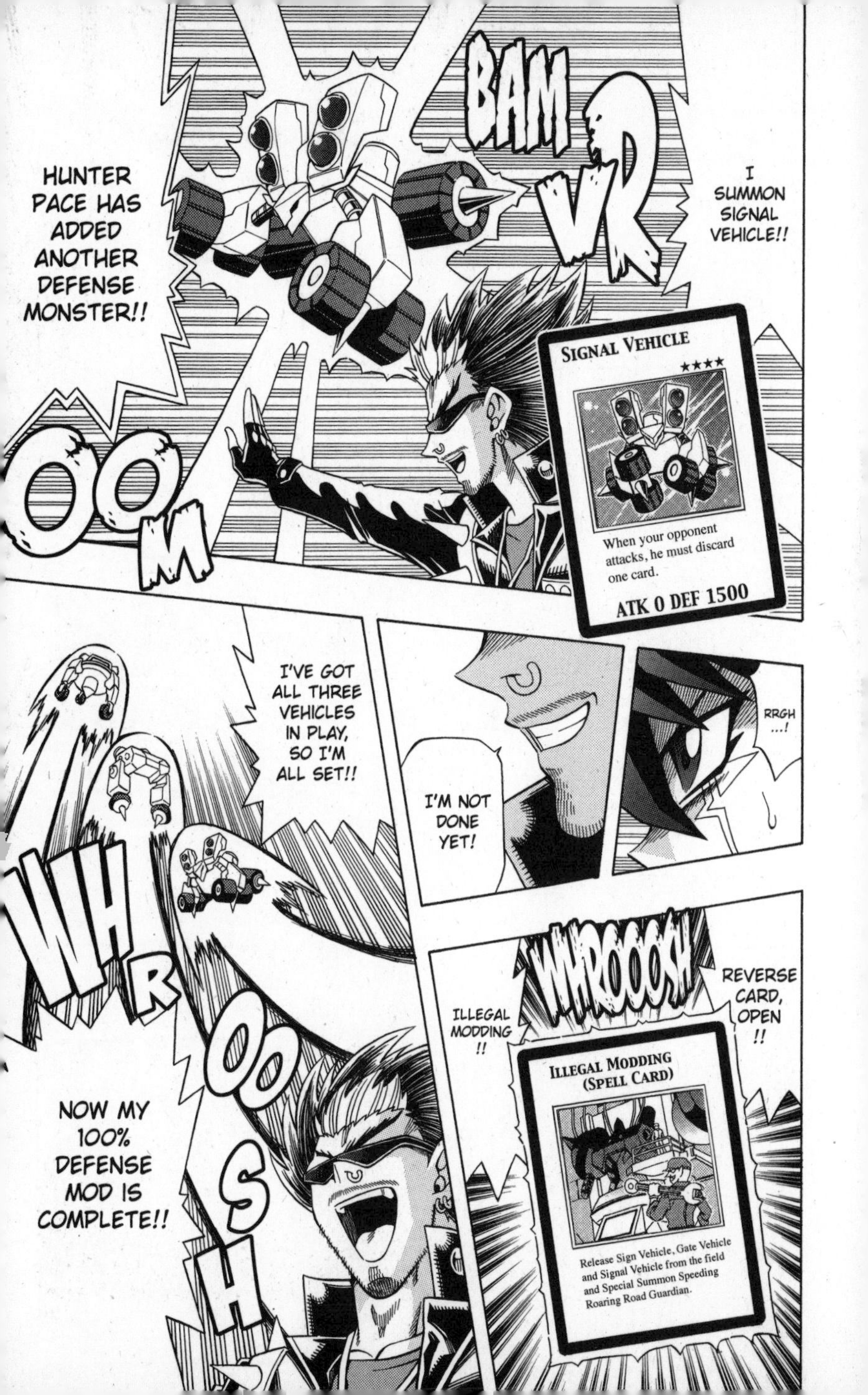
I SUMMON SIGNAL VEHICLE!!
BAM
VROOM
SIGNAL VEHICLE
★★★★
When your opponent attacks, he must discard one card.
ATK 0 DEF 1500
HUNTER PACE HAS ADDED ANOTHER DEFENSE MONSTER!!
RRGH ...!
I'M NOT DONE YET!
REVERSE CARD, OPEN!!
WHROOOSH
ILLEGAL MODDING!!
ILLEGAL MODDING (SPELL CARD)
Release Sign Vehicle, Gate Vehicle and Signal Vehicle from the field and Special Summon Speeding Roaring Road Guardian.
I'VE GOT ALL THREE VEHICLES IN PLAY, SO I'M ALL SET!!
WHRROOOSH
NOW MY 100% DEFENSE MOD IS COMPLETE!!

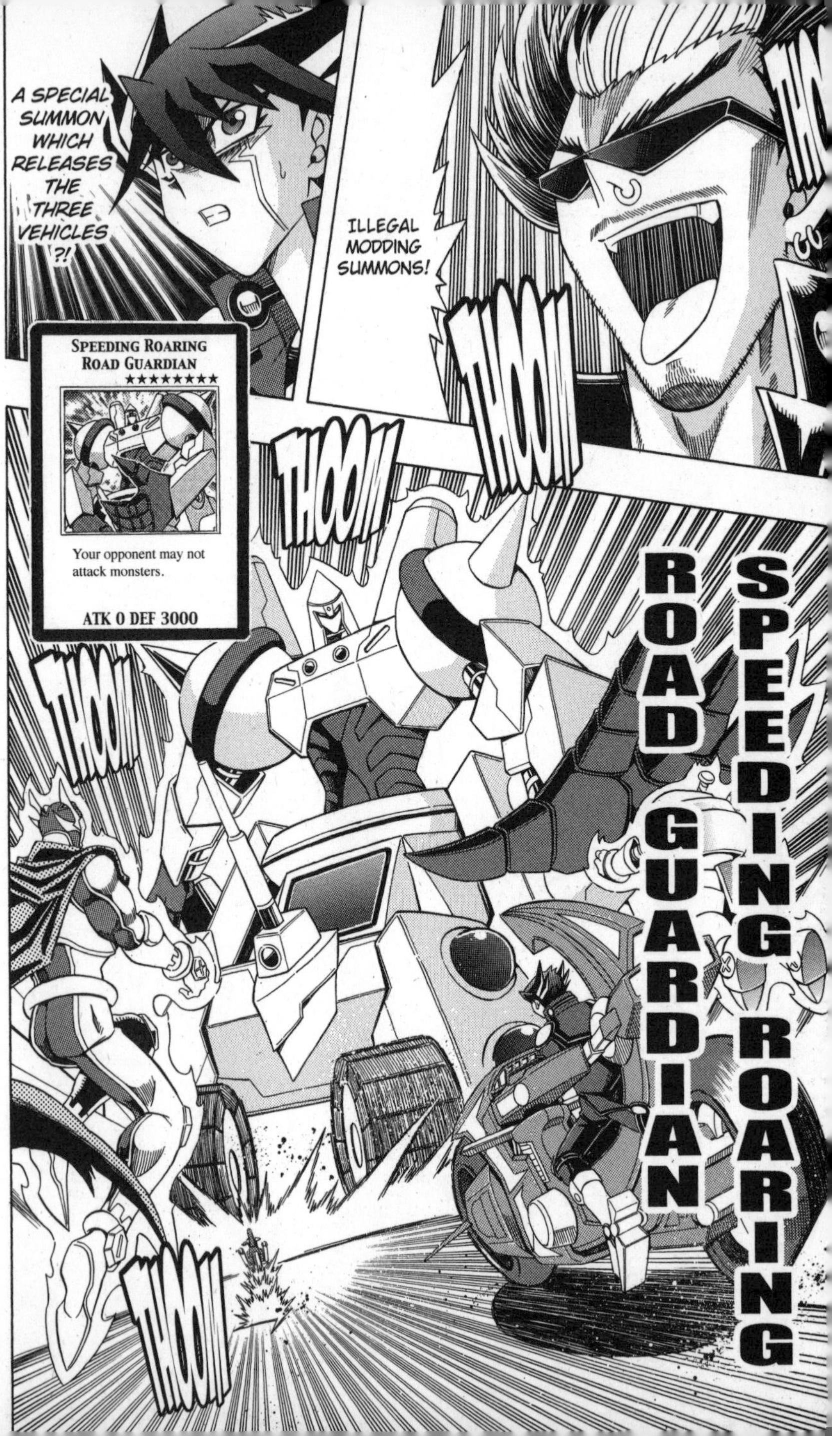
ILLEGAL MODDING SUMMONS!
THOOM
A SPECIAL SUMMON WHICH RELEASES THE THREE VEHICLES ?!
SPEEDING ROARING
ROAD GUARDIAN
THOOM
THOOM
SPEEDING ROARING ROAD GUARDIAN
★★★★★★★★★
Your opponent may not attack monsters.
ATK 0 DEF 3000
THOOM
THOOM

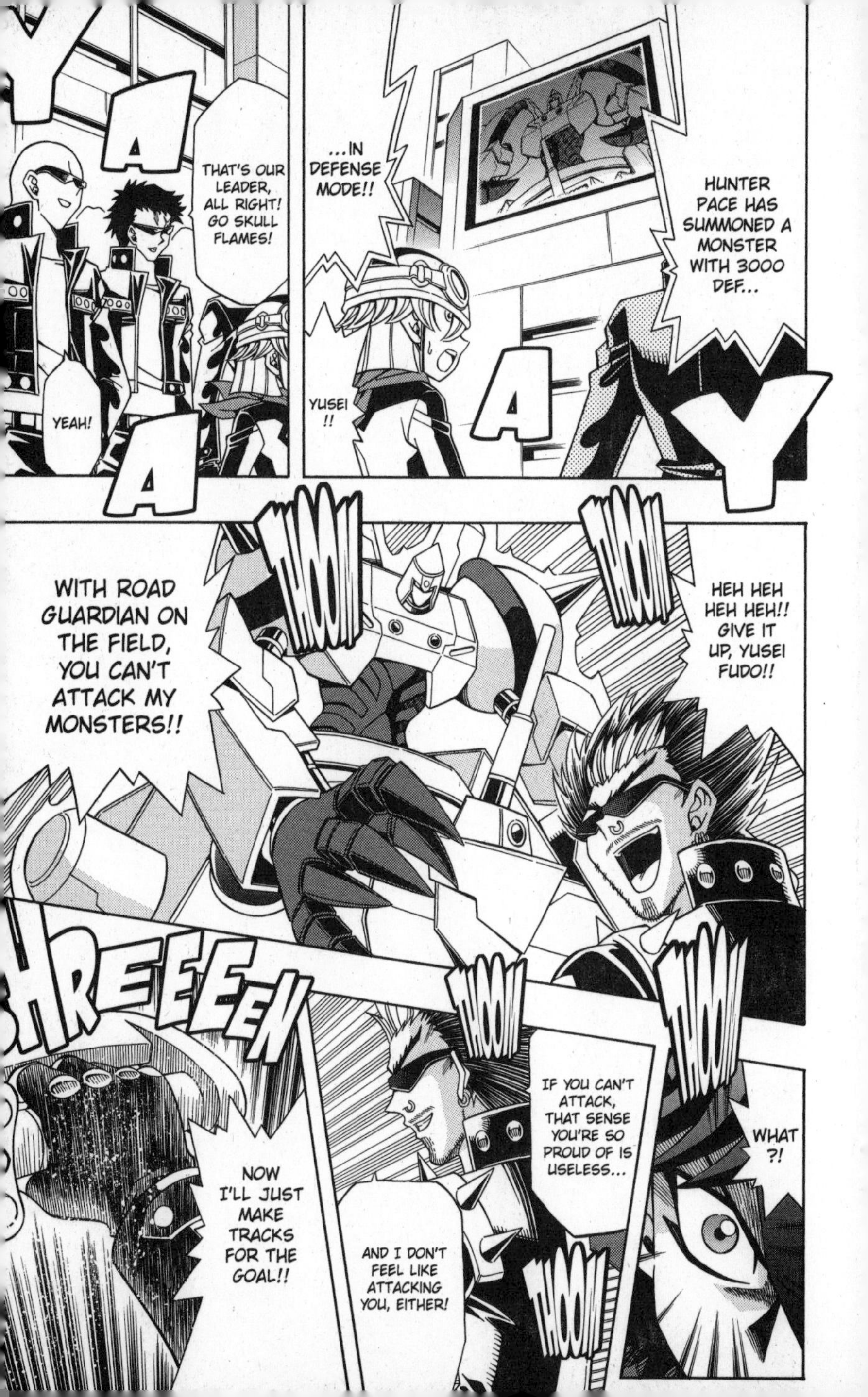

HUNTER PACE HAS SUMMONED A MONSTER WITH 3000 DEF...
...IN DEFENSE MODE!!
YUSEI!!
YAAAY
THAT'S OUR LEADER, ALL RIGHT! GO SKULL FLAMES!
YEAH!
THOOM
THOOM
HEH HEH HEH HEH!! GIVE IT UP, YUSEI FUDO!!
WITH ROAD GUARDIAN ON THE FIELD, YOU CAN'T ATTACK MY MONSTERS!!
THOOM
THOOM
WHAT?!
THOOM
IF YOU CAN'T ATTACK, THAT SENSE YOU'RE SO PROUD OF IS USELESS...
AND I DON'T FEEL LIKE ATTACKING YOU, EITHER!
NOW I'LL JUST MAKE TRACKS FOR THE GOAL!!
SHREEEEN

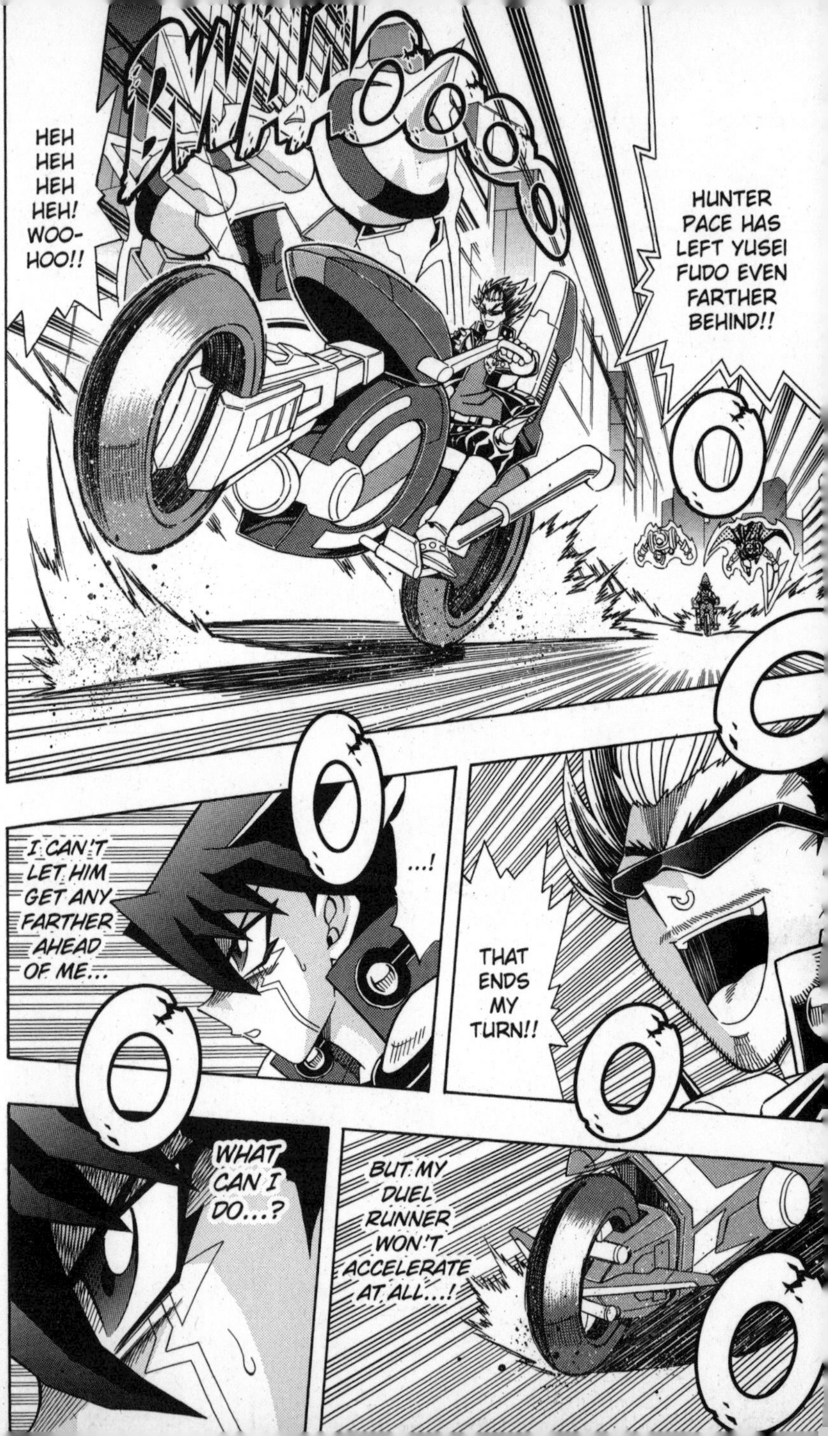
HUNTER PACE HAS LEFT YUSEI FUDO EVEN FARTHER BEHIND!!
HEH HEH HEH HEH! WOO-HOO!!
THAT ENDS MY TURN!!
...!
I CAN'T LET HIM GET ANY FARTHER AHEAD OF ME...
BUT MY DUEL RUNNER WON'T ACCELERATE AT ALL...!
WHAT CAN I DO...?

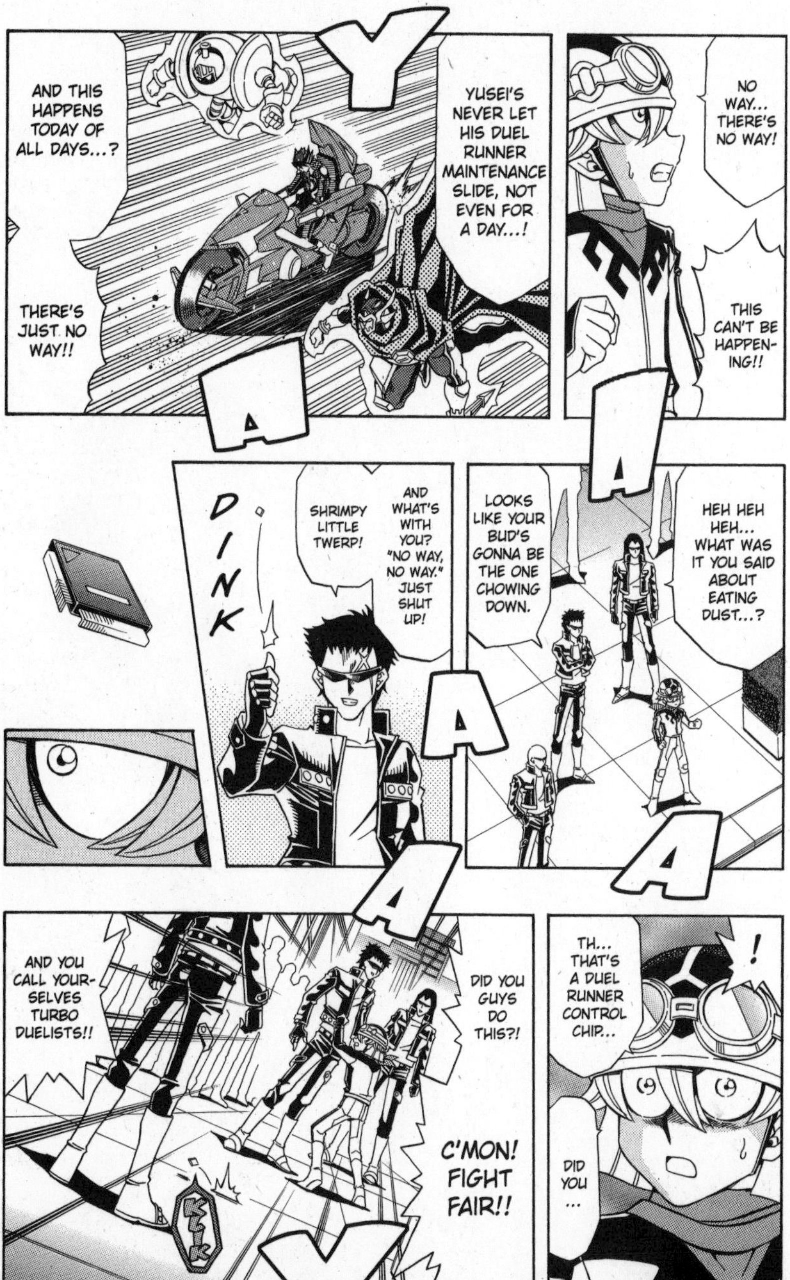
YAAAAAY
NO WAY... THERE'S NO WAY!
THIS CAN'T BE HAPPENING!!
YUSEI'S NEVER LET HIS DUEL RUNNER MAINTENANCE SLIDE, NOT EVEN FOR A DAY...!
AND THIS HAPPENS TODAY OF ALL DAYS...?
THERE'S JUST NO WAY!!
HEH HEH HEH... WHAT WAS IT YOU SAID ABOUT EATING DUST...?
LOOKS LIKE YOUR BUD'S GONNA BE THE ONE CHOWING DOWN.
AND WHAT'S WITH YOU? "NO WAY, NO WAY." JUST SHUT UP!
SHRIMPY LITTLE TWERP!
DINK
!
TH... THAT'S A DUEL RUNNER CONTROL CHIP...
DID YOU ...
DID YOU GUYS DO THIS?!
C'MON! FIGHT FAIR!!
AND YOU CALL YOURSELVES TURBO DUELISTS!!
KLIK

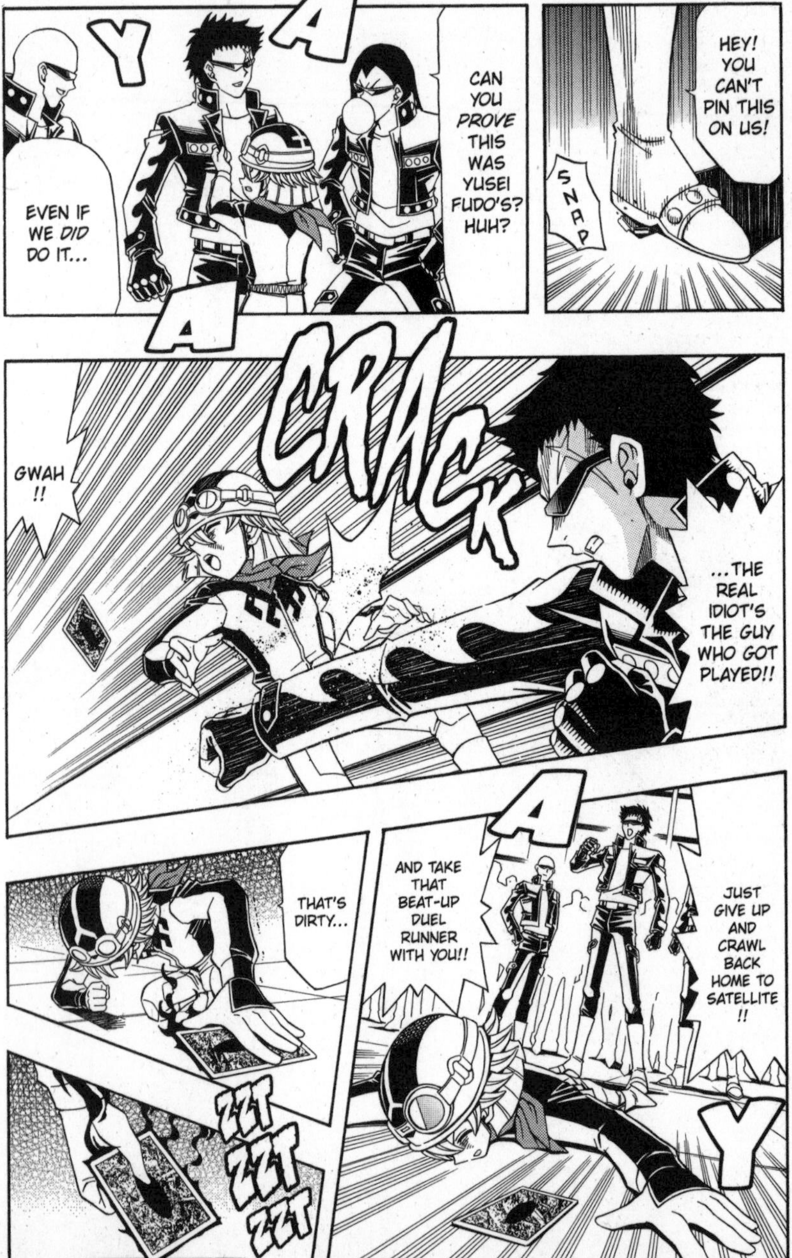
HEY! YOU CAN'T PIN THIS ON US!
SNAP
A
CAN YOU *PROVE* THIS WAS YUSEI FUDO'S? HUH?
Y
EVEN IF WE *DID* DO IT...
A
CRACK
...THE REAL IDIOT'S THE GUY WHO GOT PLAYED!!
GWAH !!
JUST GIVE UP AND CRAWL BACK HOME TO SATELLITE !!
A
AND TAKE THAT BEAT-UP DUEL RUNNER WITH YOU!!
Y
THAT'S DIRTY...
ZZT ZZT ZZT ZZT

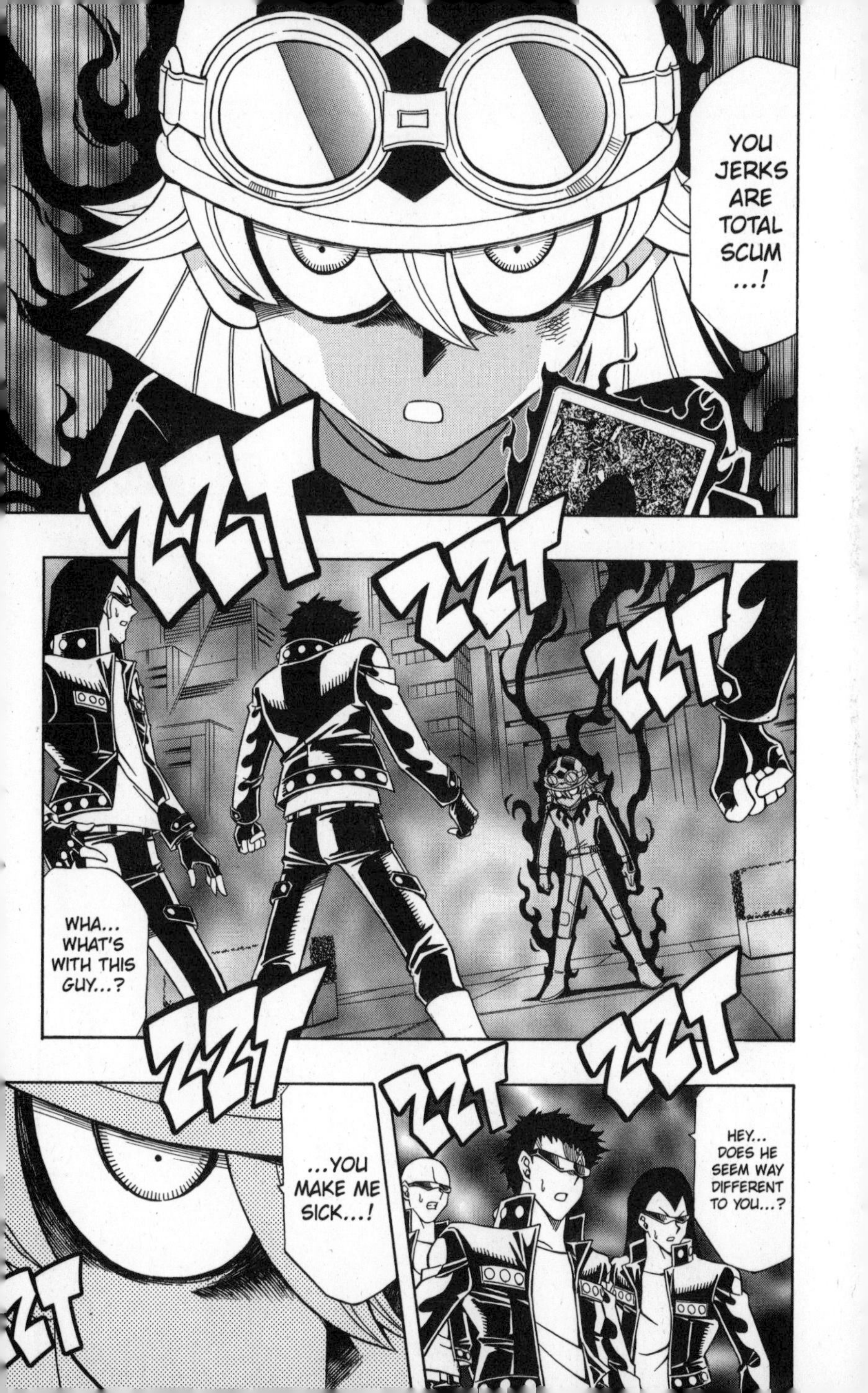
YOU JERKS ARE TOTAL SCUM...!
ZZZT
ZZZT
ZZZT
WHA... WHAT'S WITH THIS GUY...?
ZZZT
ZZZT
ZZZT
HEY... DOES HE SEEM WAY DIFFERENT TO YOU...?
...YOU MAKE ME SICK...!

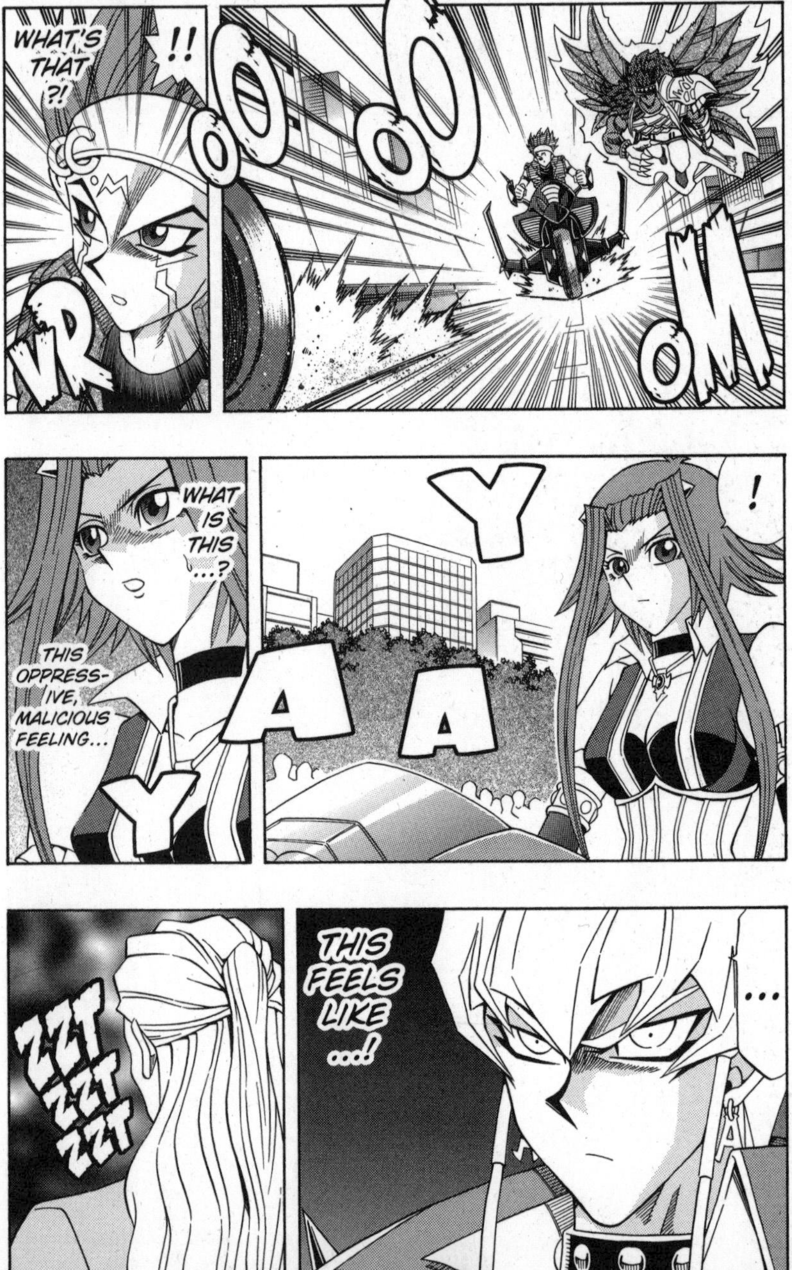
VROOOOOOM
!!
WHAT'S THAT ?!
!
YAAY
WHAT IS THIS ...?
THIS OPPRESS-IVE, MALICIOUS FEELING...
...
THIS FEELS LIKE ...!
ZZT ZZT ZZT ZZT

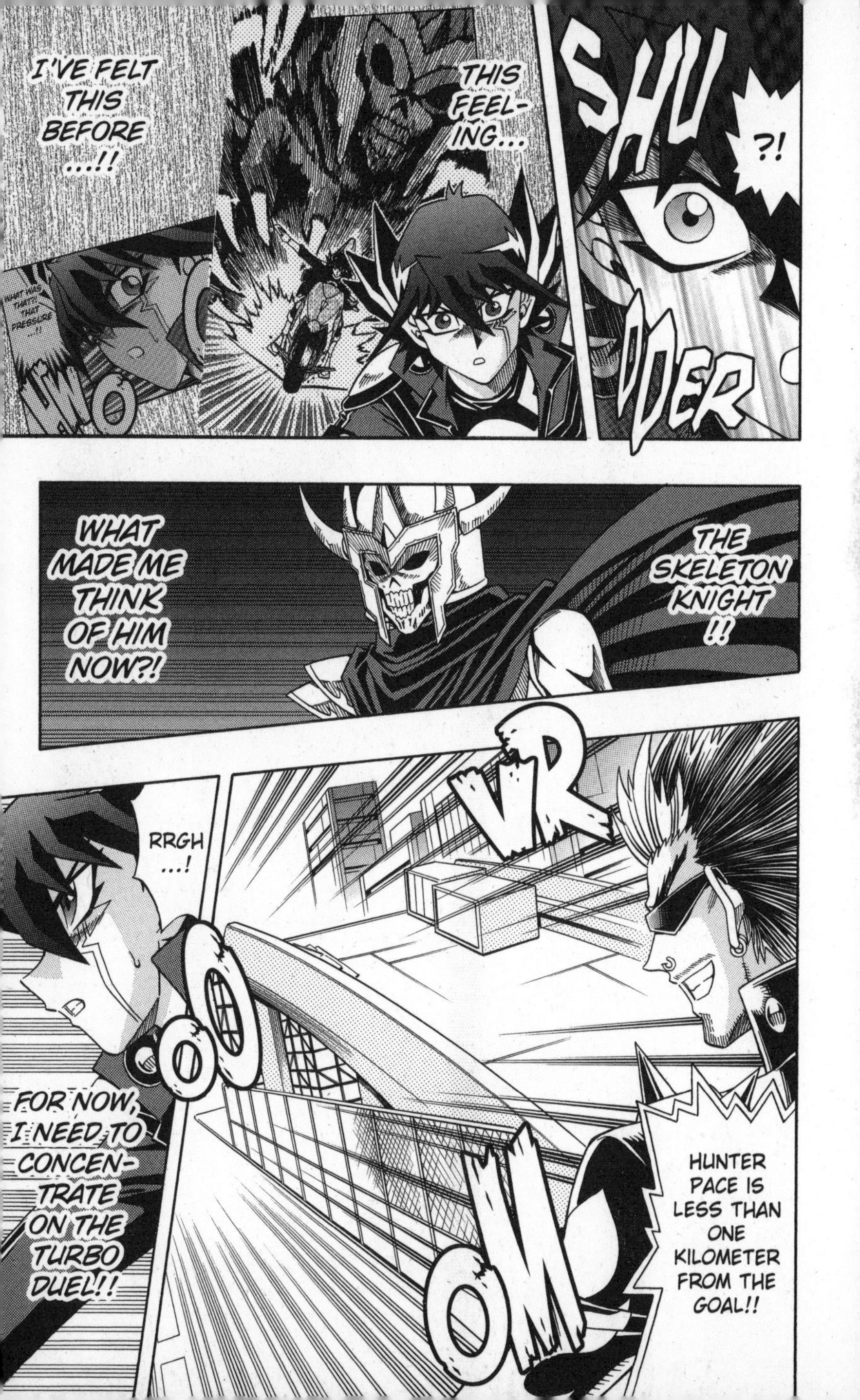
SHUDDER
?!
THIS FEELING...
I'VE FELT THIS BEFORE...!!
WHAT WAS THAT?! THAT PRESSURE...!
THE SKELETON KNIGHT!!
WHAT MADE ME THINK OF HIM NOW?!
VROOM
HUNTER PACE IS LESS THAN ONE KILOMETER FROM THE GOAL!!
RRGH...!
FOR NOW, I NEED TO CONCENTRATE ON THE TURBO DUEL!!

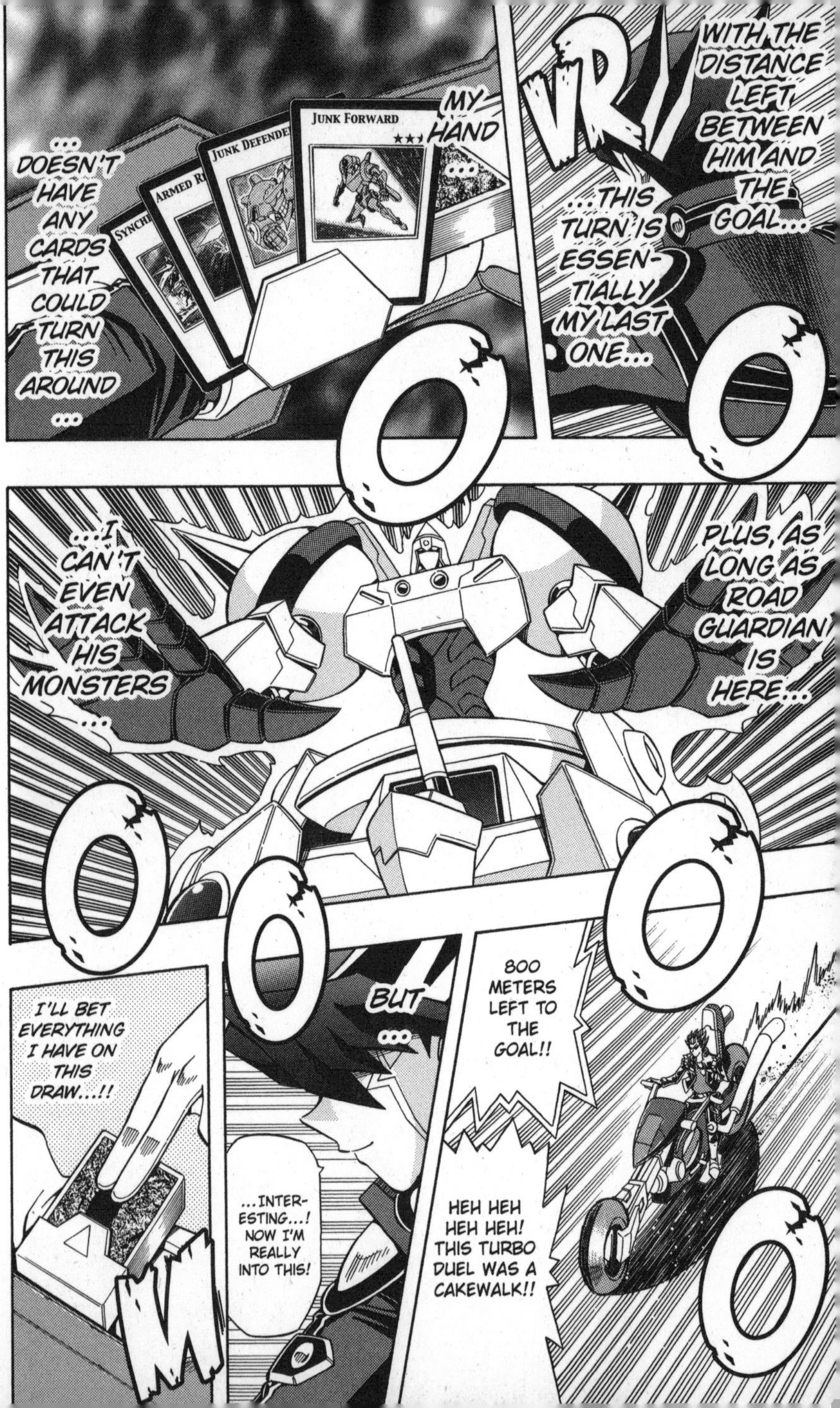
VR!!
WITH THE DISTANCE LEFT BETWEEN HIM AND THE GOAL...
...THIS TURN IS ESSENTIALLY MY LAST ONE...
MY HAND...
JUNK FORWARD
...DOESN'T HAVE ANY CARDS THAT COULD TURN THIS AROUND...
PLUS, AS LONG AS ROAD GUARDIAN IS HERE...
...I CAN'T EVEN ATTACK HIS MONSTERS...
800 METERS LEFT TO THE GOAL!!
HEH HEH HEH HEH! THIS TURBO DUEL WAS A CAKEWALK!!
BUT...
...INTERESTING...! NOW I'M REALLY INTO THIS!
I'LL BET EVERYTHING I HAVE ON THIS DRAW...!!
M

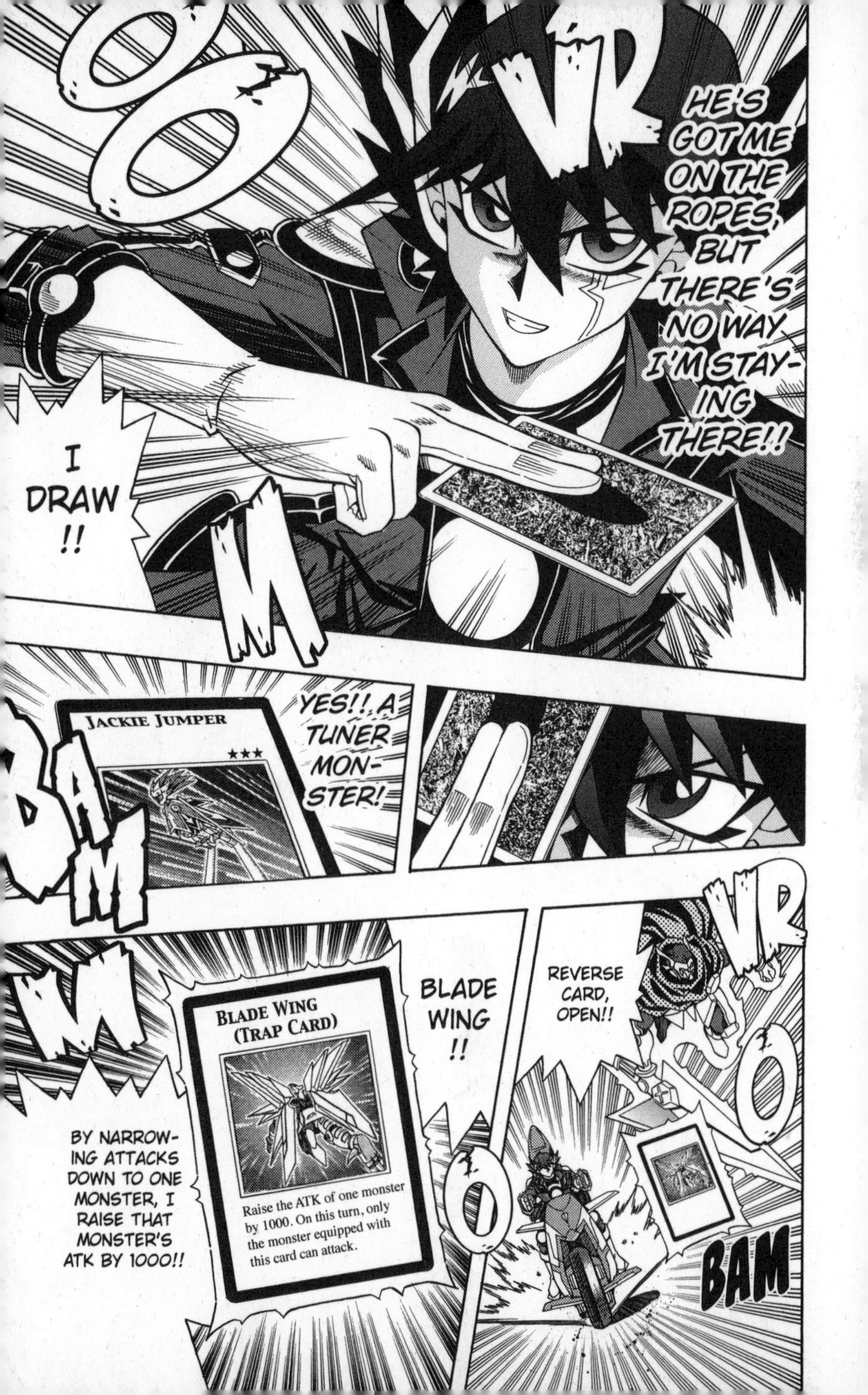
HE'S GOT ME ON THE ROPES, BUT THERE'S NO WAY I'M STAYING THERE!!
VROOM
I DRAW!!
YES!! A TUNER MONSTER!
JACKIE JUMPER
BAM
REVERSE CARD, OPEN!!
VROOM
BAM
BLADE WING!!
BLADE WING (TRAP CARD)
Raise the ATK of one monster by 1000. On this turn, only the monster equipped with this card can attack.
BY NARROWING ATTACKS DOWN TO ONE MONSTER, I RAISE THAT MONSTER'S ATK BY 1000!!
BAM

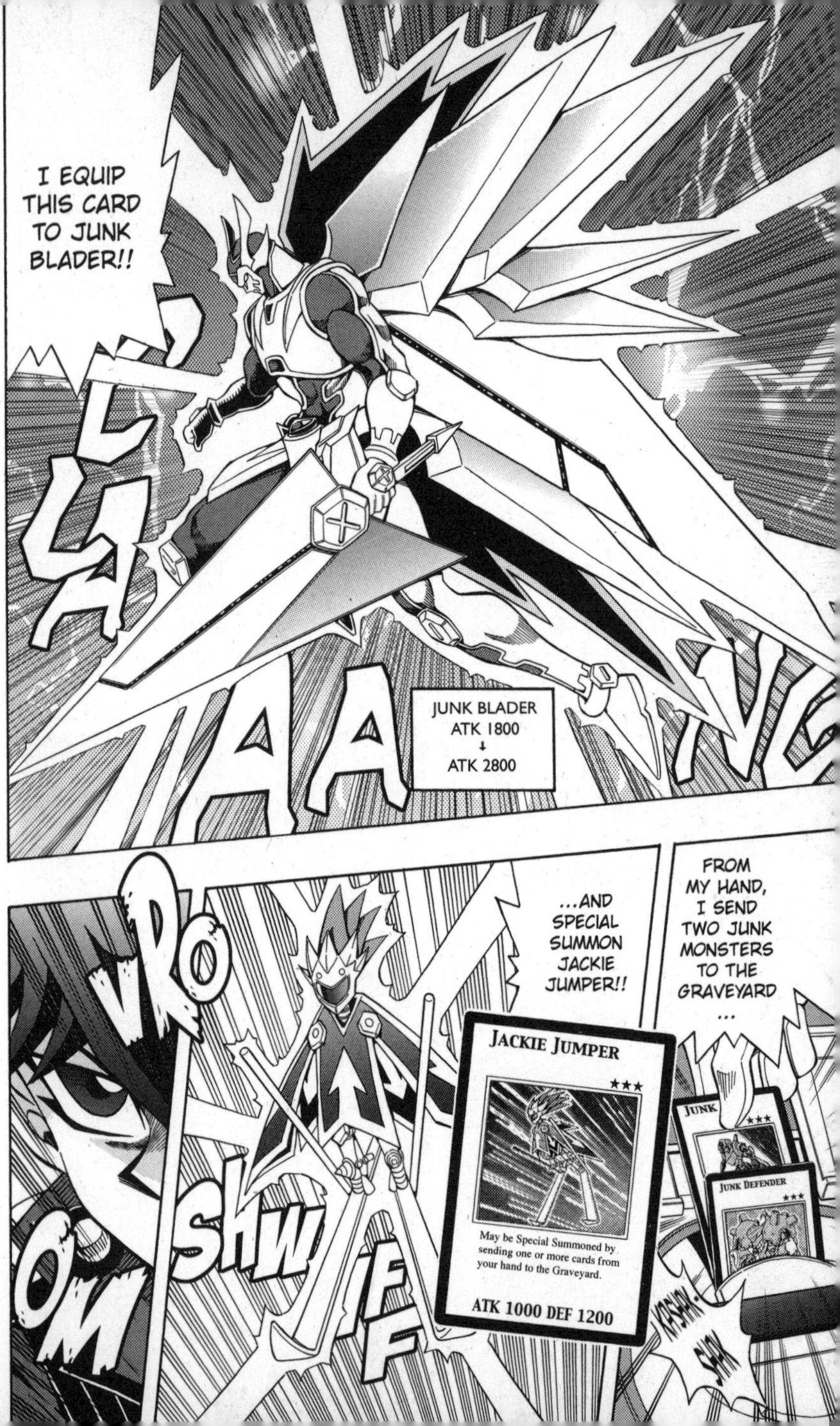
I EQUIP THIS CARD TO JUNK BLADER!!
JUNK BLADER ATK 1800 ↓ ATK 2800
FROM MY HAND, I SEND TWO JUNK MONSTERS TO THE GRAVEYARD ...
...AND SPECIAL SUMMON JACKIE JUMPER!!
JACKIE JUMPER
May be Special Summoned by sending one or more cards from your hand to the Graveyard.
ATK 1000 DEF 1200
JUNK DEFENDER

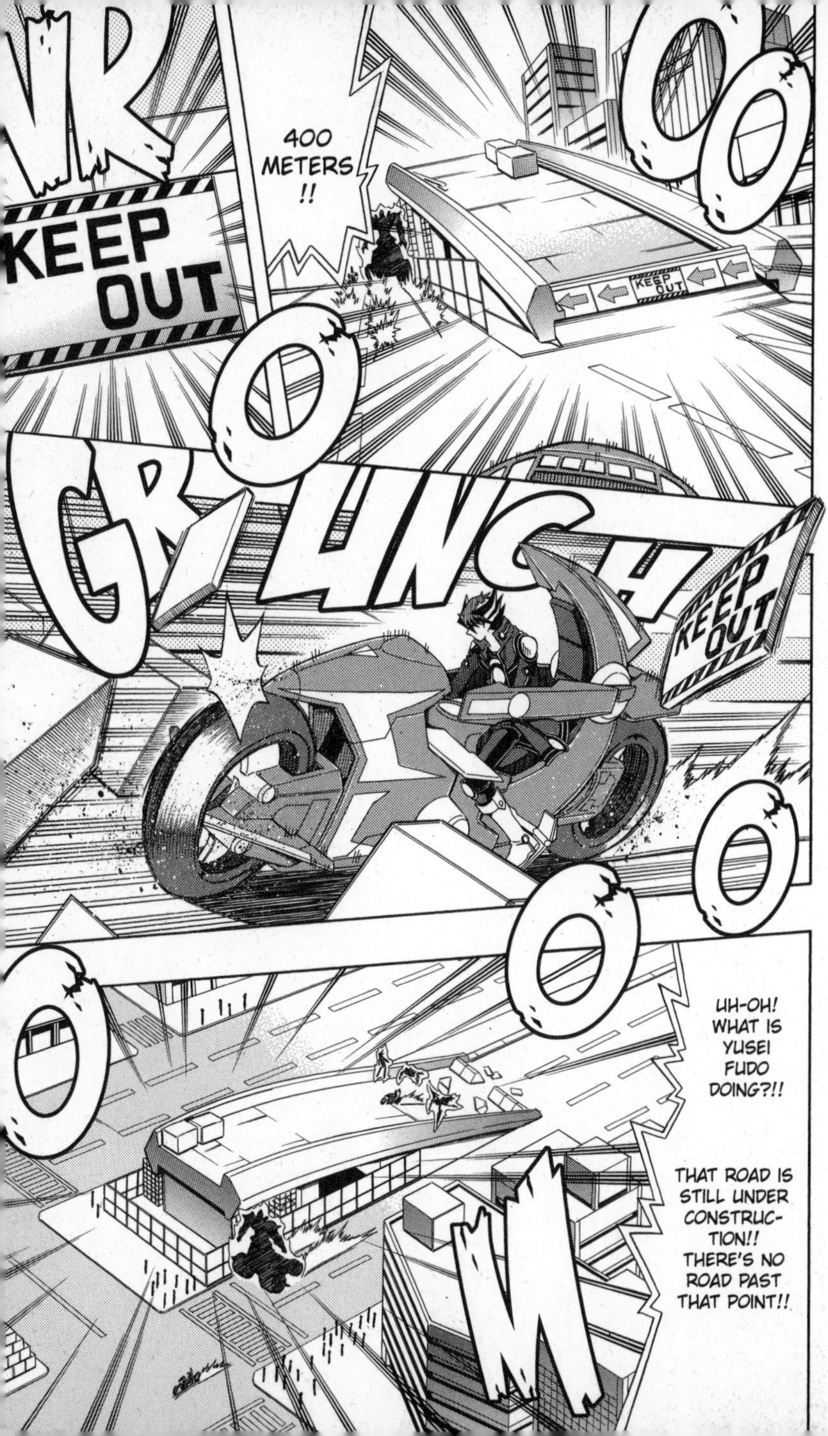
KEEP OUT
400 METERS !!
KEEP OUT
KEEP OUT
UH-OH! WHAT IS YUSEI FUDO DOING?!!
THAT ROAD IS STILL UNDER CONSTRUCTION!! THERE'S NO ROAD PAST THAT POINT!!

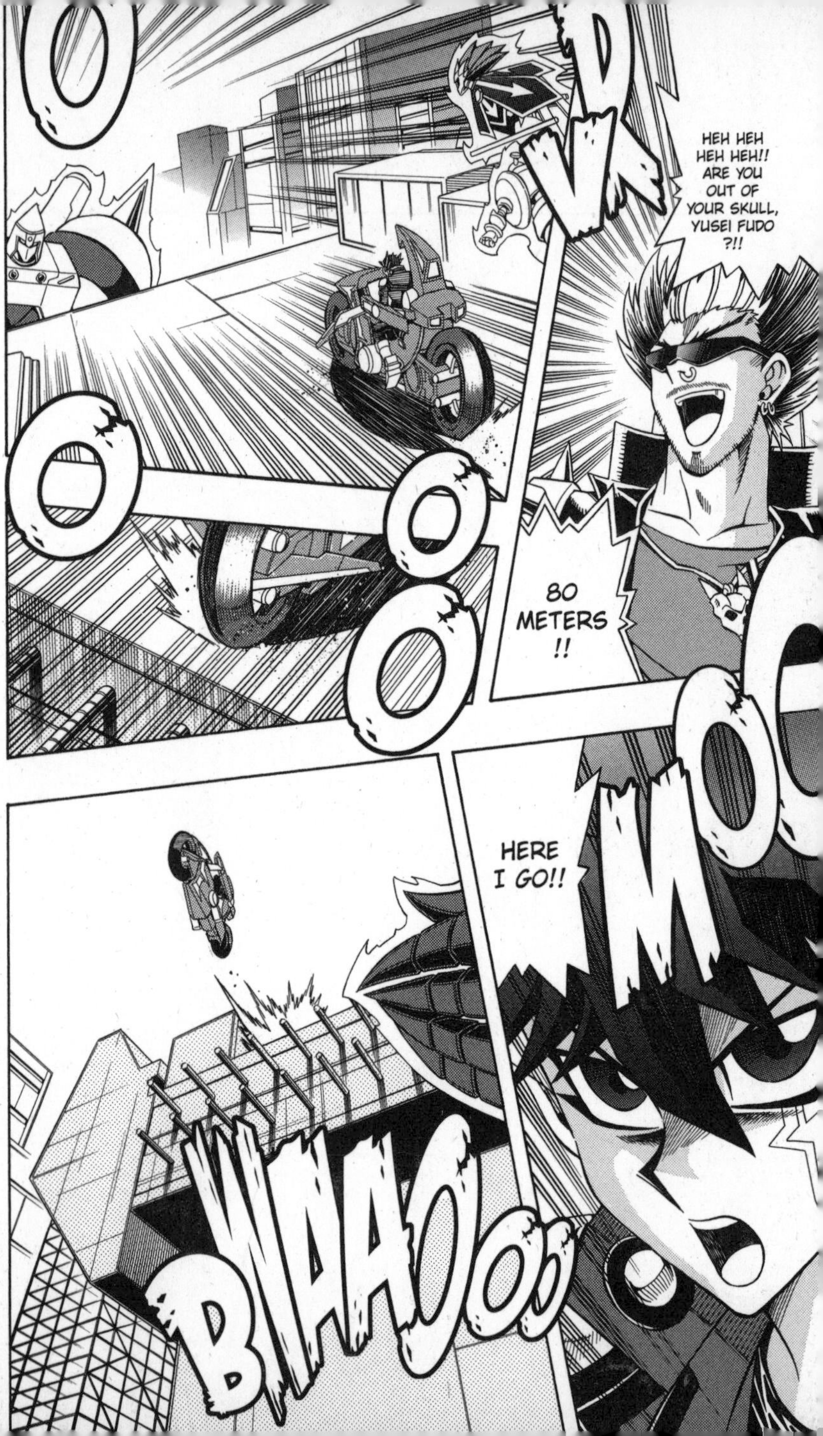
HEH HEH HEH HEH!! ARE YOU OUT OF YOUR SKULL, YUSEI FUDO ?!!
80 METERS !!
HERE I GO!!
BWAOOO

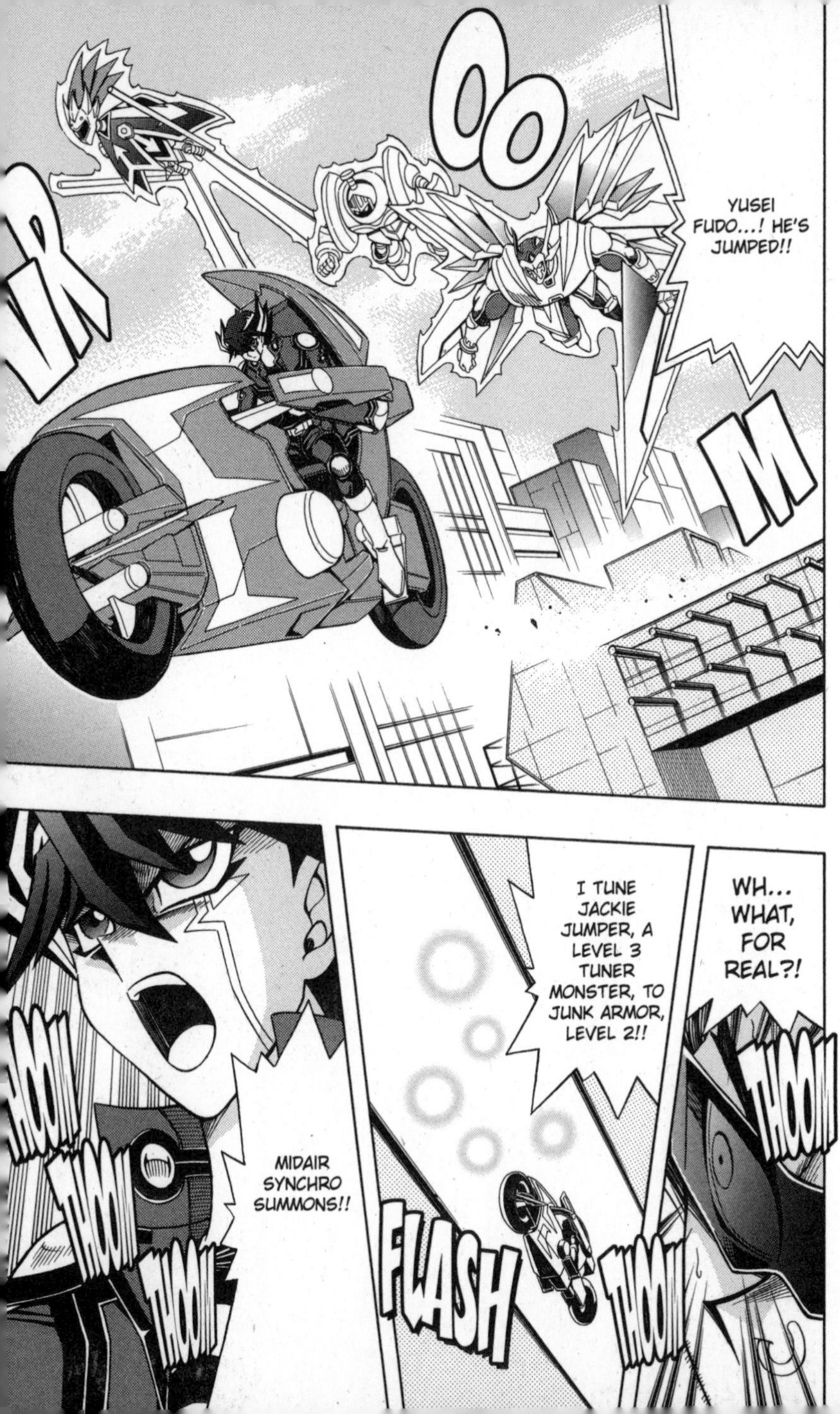
YUSEI FUDO...! HE'S JUMPED!!
WH... WHAT, FOR REAL?!
THOOM
I TUNE JACKIE JUMPER, A LEVEL 3 TUNER MONSTER, TO JUNK ARMOR, LEVEL 2!!
FLASH
THOOM
MIDAIR SYNCHRO SUMMONS!!
THOOM
THOOM

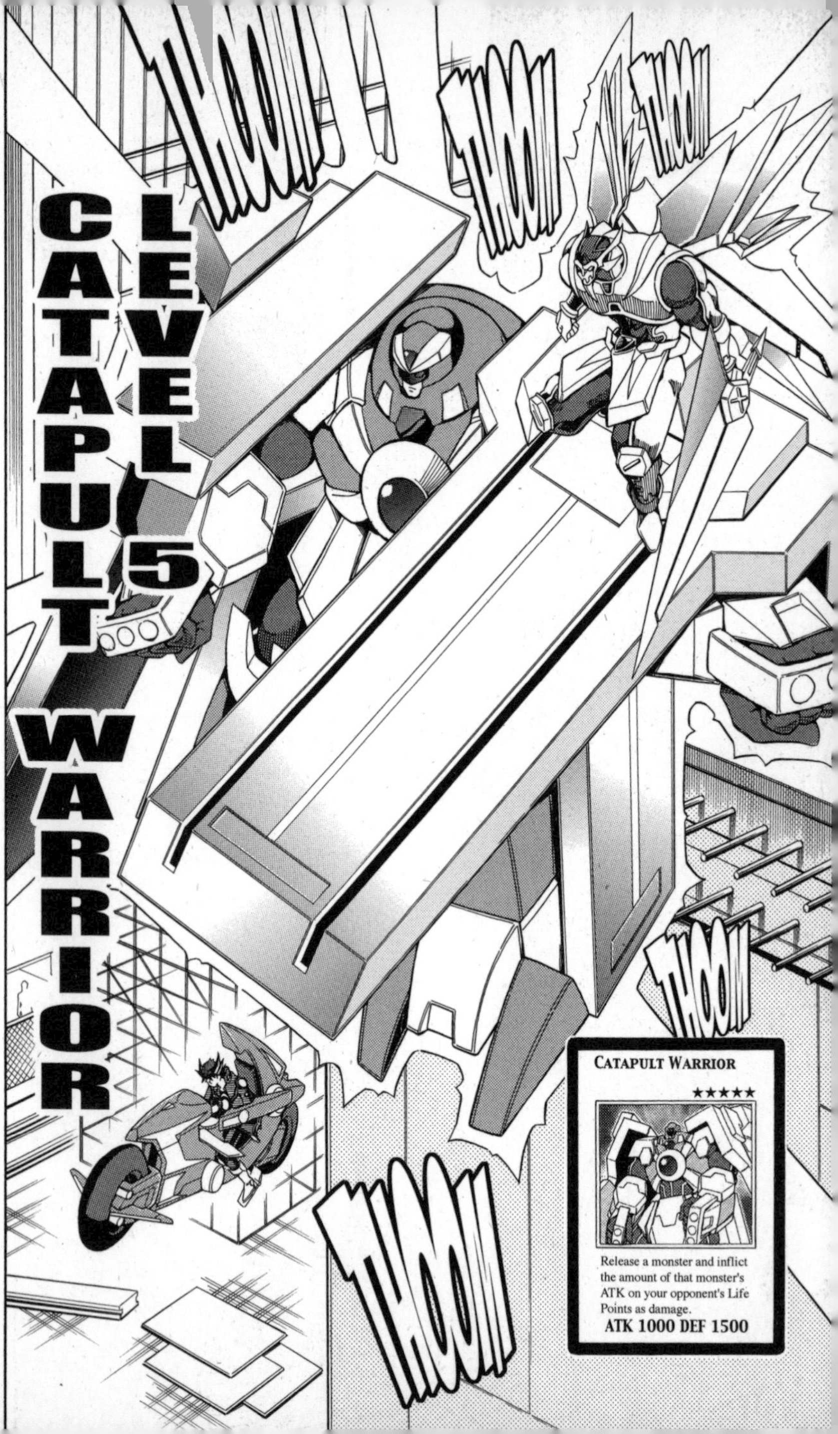
THOOM
THOOM
THOOM
LEVEL 5
CATAPULT WARRIOR
THOOM
THOOM
CATAPULT WARRIOR
★★★★★
Release a monster and inflict the amount of that monster's ATK on your opponent's Life Points as damage.
ATK 1000 DEF 1500

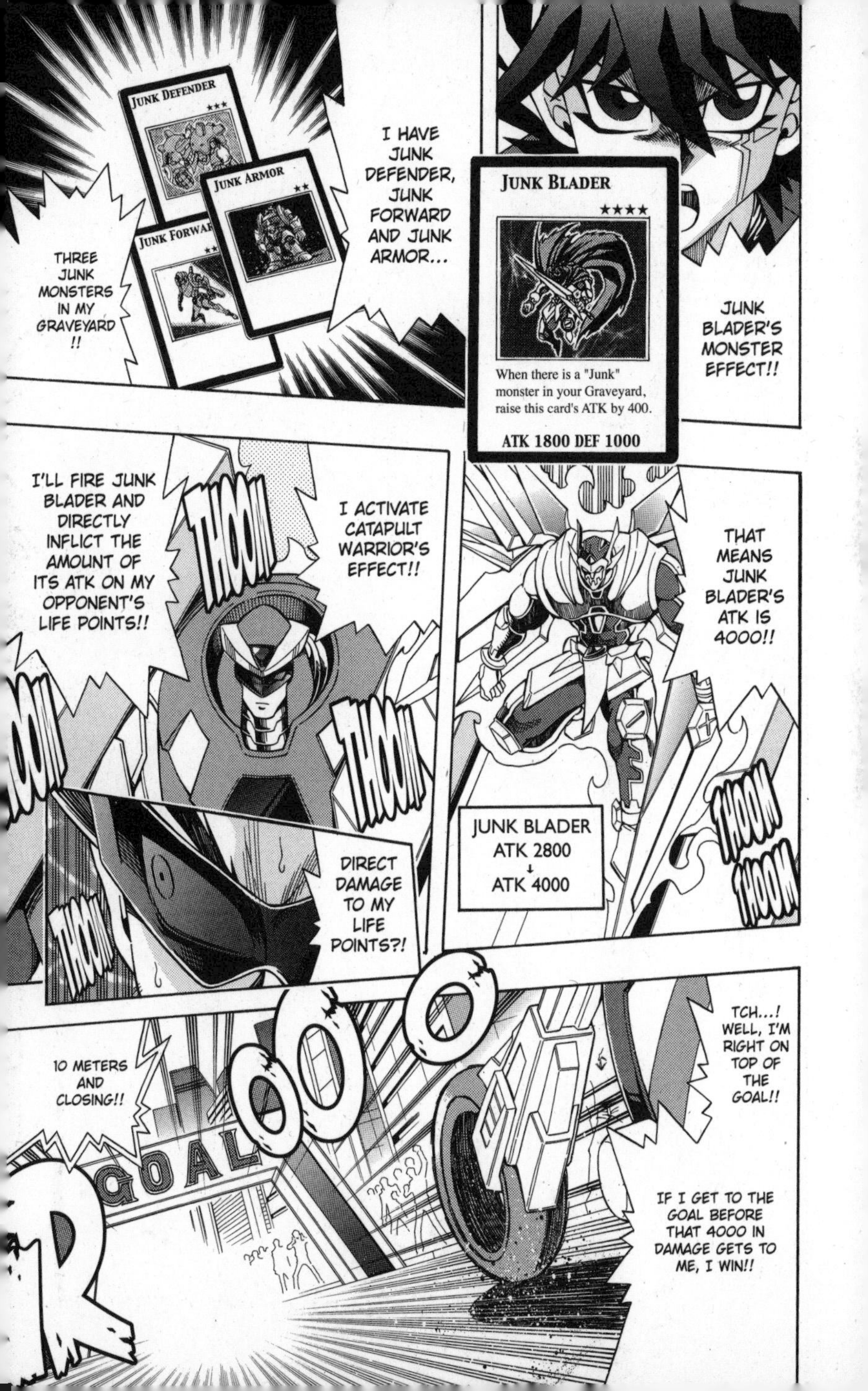
JUNK BLADER
When there is a "Junk" monster in your Graveyard, raise this card's ATK by 400.
ATK 1800 DEF 1000
JUNK BLADER'S MONSTER EFFECT!!
I HAVE JUNK DEFENDER, JUNK FORWARD AND JUNK ARMOR...
JUNK DEFENDER
JUNK ARMOR
JUNK FORWAR
THREE JUNK MONSTERS IN MY GRAVEYARD !!
THAT MEANS JUNK BLADER'S ATK IS 4000!!
JUNK BLADER ATK 2800 ↓ ATK 4000
THOOM THOOM
I ACTIVATE CATAPULT WARRIOR'S EFFECT!!
I'LL FIRE JUNK BLADER AND DIRECTLY INFLICT THE AMOUNT OF ITS ATK ON MY OPPONENT'S LIFE POINTS!!
THOOM
THOOM
THOOM
DIRECT DAMAGE TO MY LIFE POINTS?!
THOOM
TCH...! WELL, I'M RIGHT ON TOP OF THE GOAL!!
IF I GET TO THE GOAL BEFORE THAT 4000 IN DAMAGE GETS TO ME, I WIN!!
ROOOO
GOAL
10 METERS AND CLOSING!!

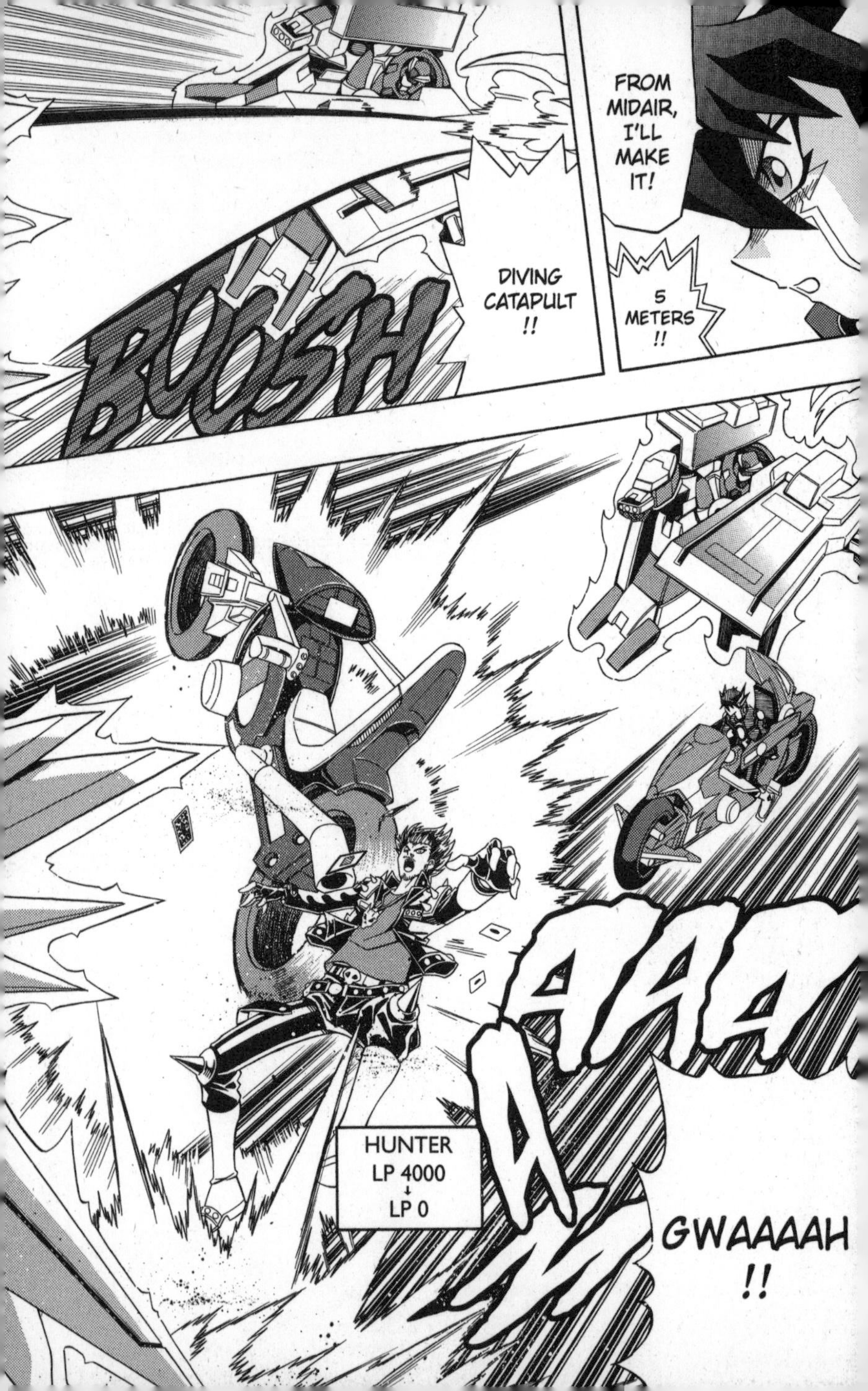
FROM MIDAIR, I'LL MAKE IT!
5 METERS!!
DIVING CATAPULT!!
BOOSH
AAAA
HUNTER LP 4000 ↓ LP 0
GWAAAAH!!

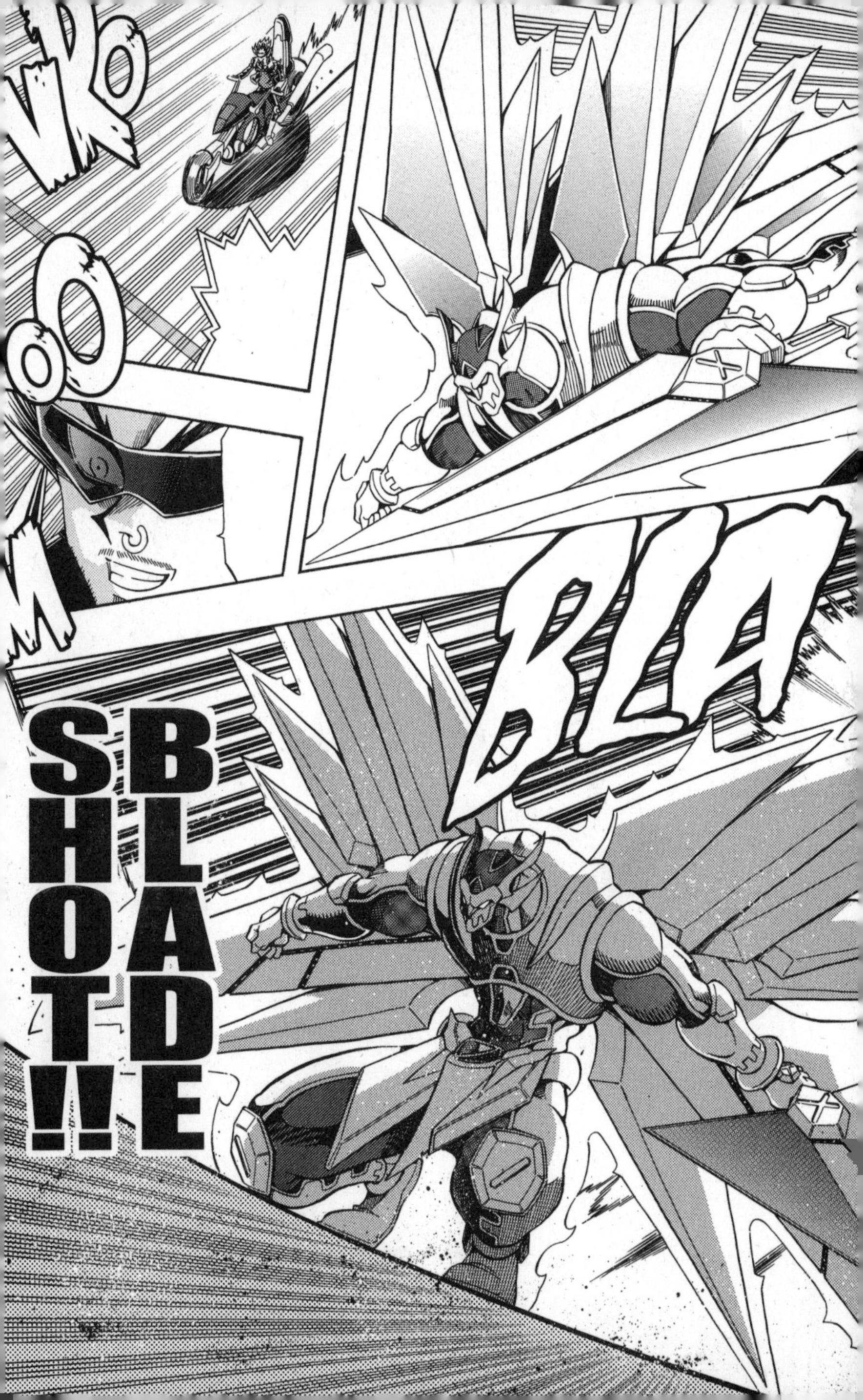
VROOOM
BLA
BLADE
SHOT!!

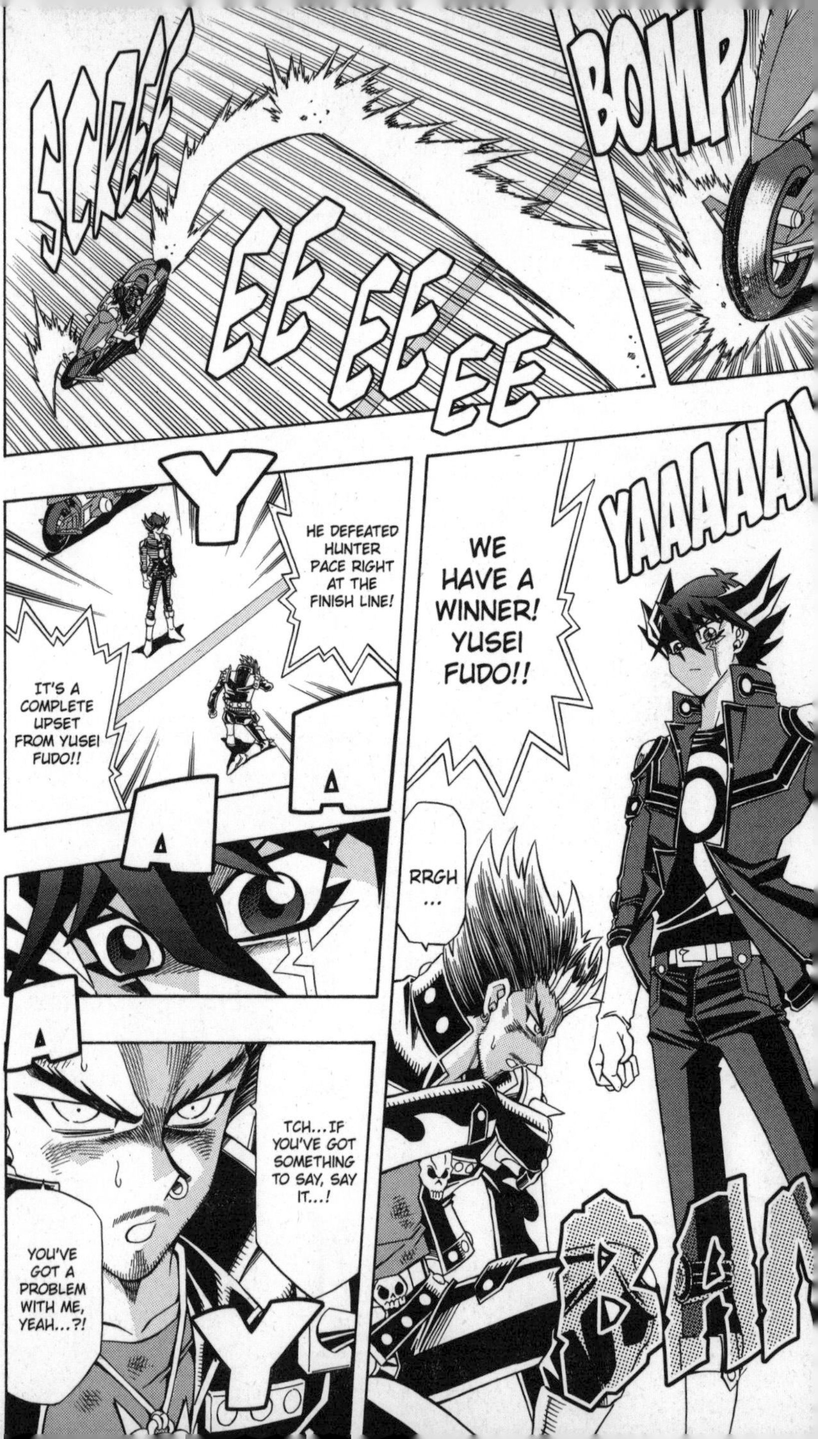

BOMP
SCREEEEEEEE
YAAAAA
WE HAVE A WINNER! YUSEI FUDO!!
RRGH ...
Y
HE DEFEATED HUNTER PACE RIGHT AT THE FINISH LINE!
IT'S A COMPLETE UPSET FROM YUSEI FUDO!!
A
A
A
TCH...IF YOU'VE GOT SOMETHING TO SAY, SAY IT...!
YOU'VE GOT A PROBLEM WITH ME, YEAH...?!
Y
BAM

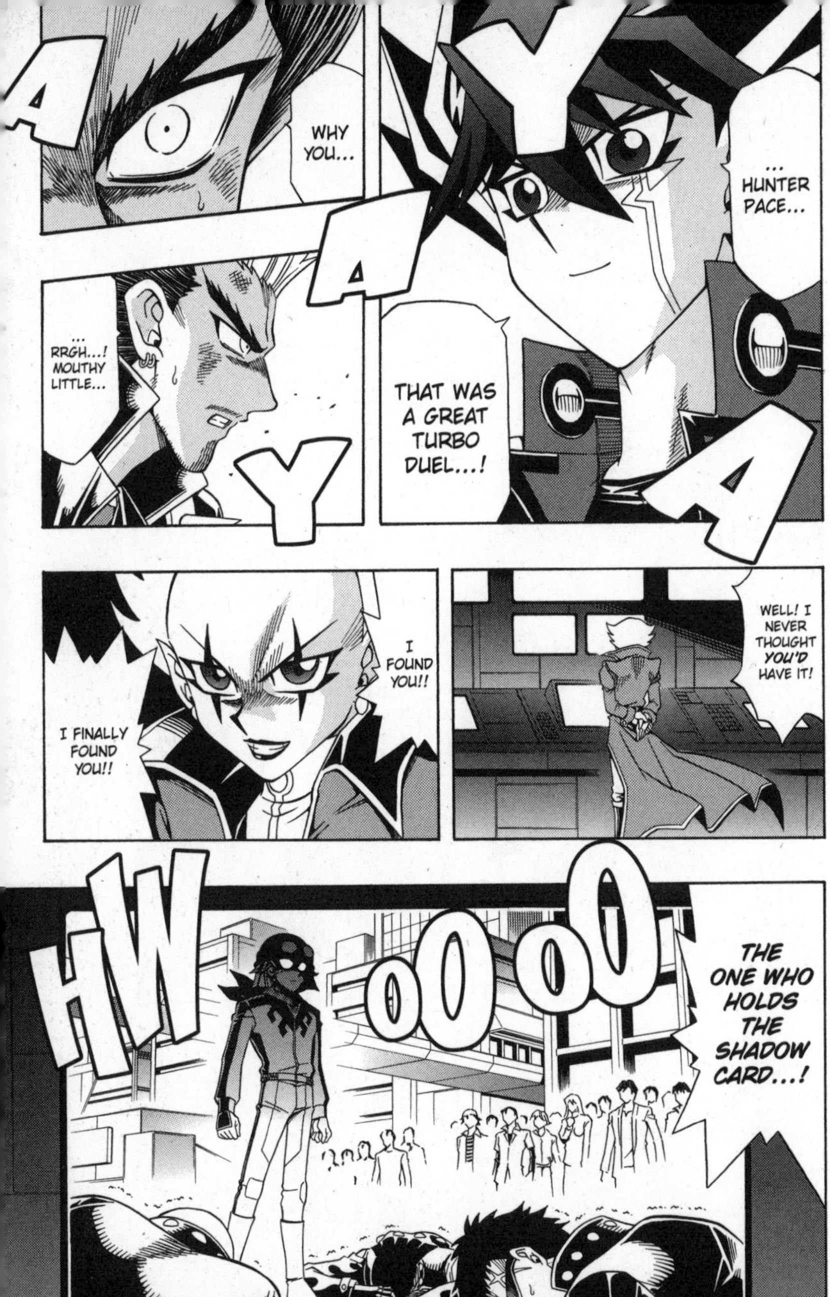
... HUNTER PACE...
WHY YOU...
THAT WAS A GREAT TURBO DUEL...!
... RRGH...! MOUTHY LITTLE...
WELL! I NEVER THOUGHT *YOU'D* HAVE IT!
I FOUND YOU!!
I FINALLY FOUND YOU!!
THE ONE WHO HOLDS THE SHADOW CARD...!

5D's TRACKS

THE 16TH

BY SATOMASA

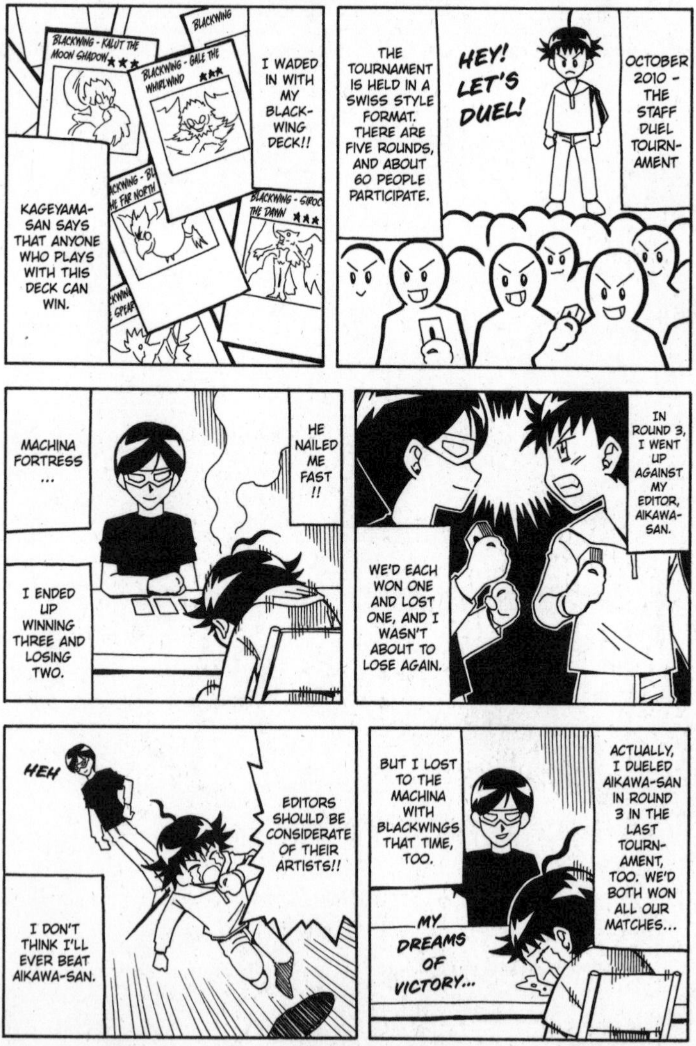
OCTOBER 2010 - THE STAFF DUEL TOURNAMENT
HEY! LET'S DUEL!
THE TOURNAMENT IS HELD IN A SWISS STYLE FORMAT. THERE ARE FIVE ROUNDS, AND ABOUT 60 PEOPLE PARTICIPATE.
I WADED IN WITH MY BLACKWING DECK!!
BLACKWING
BLACKWING - GALE THE WHIRLWIND
BLACKWING - KALUT THE MOON SHADOW
KAGEYAMA-SAN SAYS THAT ANYONE WHO PLAYS WITH THIS DECK CAN WIN.
IN ROUND 3, I WENT UP AGAINST MY EDITOR, AIKAWA-SAN.
WE'D EACH WON ONE AND LOST ONE, AND I WASN'T ABOUT TO LOSE AGAIN.
HE NAILED ME FAST!!
MACHINA FORTRESS ...
I ENDED UP WINNING THREE AND LOSING TWO.
ACTUALLY, I DUELED AIKAWA-SAN IN ROUND 3 IN THE LAST TOURNAMENT, TOO. WE'D BOTH WON ALL OUR MATCHES...
BUT I LOST TO THE MACHINA WITH BLACKWINGS THAT TIME, TOO.
MY DREAMS OF VICTORY...
EDITORS SHOULD BE CONSIDERATE OF THEIR ARTISTS!!
HEH
I DON'T THINK I'LL EVER BEAT AIKAWA-SAN.

IN THE NEXT VOLUME...

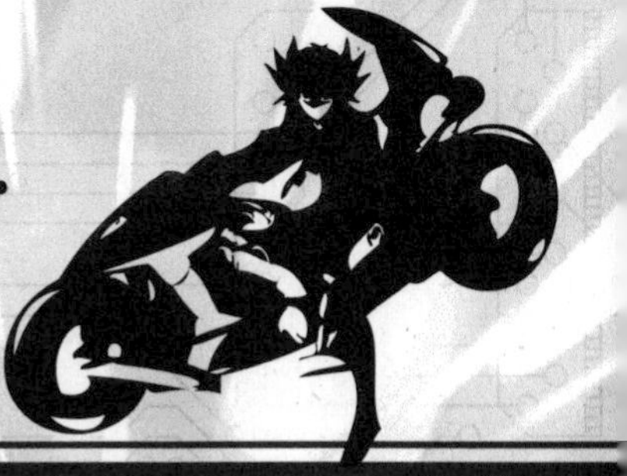

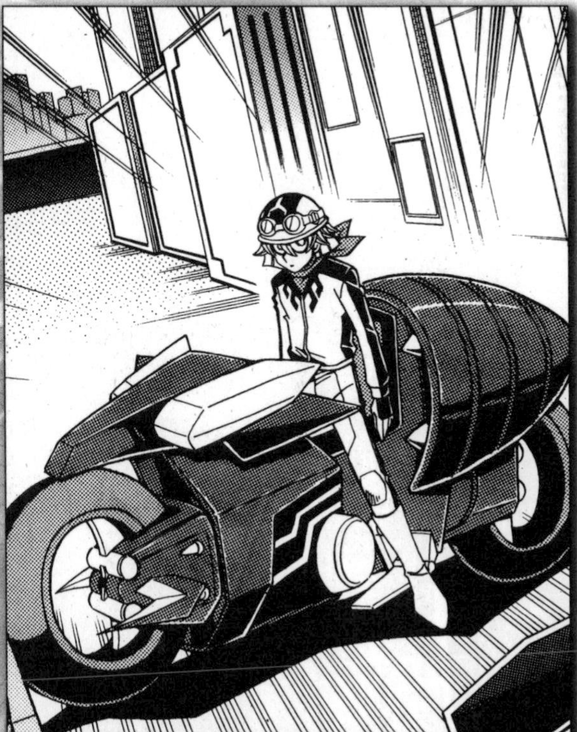

Sect gets into a Duel with Jack Atlas, and though he may have the drive he doesn't yet have the talent. Calling upon dark powers to aid him in his Duel, Sect may have to sacrifice more than he realizes in order to win!

COMING OCTOBER 2012!!

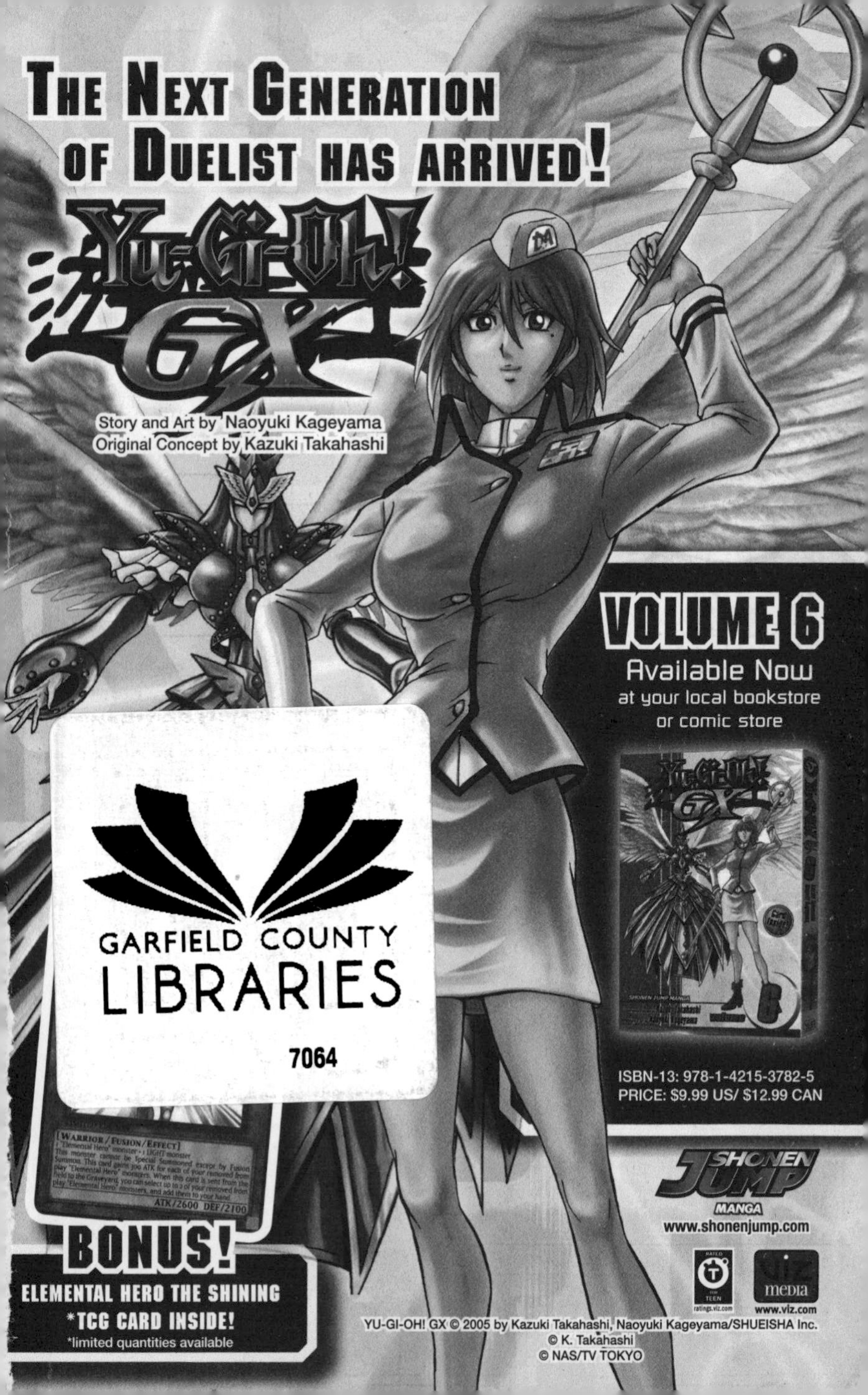
THE NEXT GENERATION
OF DUELIST HAS ARRIVED!
YU-GI-OH! GX
Story and Art by Naoyuki Kageyama
Original Concept by Kazuki Takahashi
VOLUME 6
Available Now
at your local bookstore
or comic store
ISBN-13: 978-1-4215-3782-5
PRICE: $9.99 US/ $12.99 CAN
[WARRIOR/FUSION/EFFECT]
ATK/2600 DEF/2100
BONUS!
ELEMENTAL HERO THE SHINING
*TCG CARD INSIDE!
*limited quantities available
SHONEN JUMP
MANGA
www.shonenjump.com
RATED T TEEN
ratings.viz.com
viz media
www.viz.com
YU-GI-OH! GX © 2005 by Kazuki Takahashi, Naoyuki Kageyama/SHUEISHA Inc.
© K. Takahashi
© NAS/TV TOKYO